MW01001998

Better Public Transit Systems

Better Public Transit Systems is a complete primer for performance and investment analysis of public transportation. Whether you're planning a major new public transit project, an extension or expansion of an existing system, or evaluating the needs of your current system, this book provides the tools you need to define your goals and objectives and conceive and analyze design alternatives. This completely revised Second Edition includes new material for students, whilst remaining an essential reference book.

Eric Christian Bruun currently teaches transportation engineering, planning, and modeling at Aalto University in Finland and is a guest lecturer at other universities. He has managed and participated in numerous international consulting projects. Eric has Bachelors and Master of Science degrees in Mechanical Engineering from the University of Washington and a PhD in Systems Engineering from the University of Pennsylvania.

Better Public Transit Systems

Analyzing Investments and Performance

Second Edition

Eric Christian Bruun

Routledge
Taylor & Francis Group
LONDON AND NEW YORK

from Routledge

First edition published 2007
by APA Planners Press

This edition published 2014
by Routledge
2 Park Square, Milton Park, Abingdon, Oxon, OX14 4RN

and by Routledge
711 Third Avenue, New York, NY 10017

Routledge is an imprint of the Taylor & Francis Group, an informa business

© 2014 Eric Christian Bruun

British Library Cataloguing-in-Publication Data
A catalogue record for this book is available from the British Library.

Library of Congress Cataloging-in-Publication Data
Bruun, Eric Christian, author.
Better public transit systems : analyzing investments and performance /
Eric Bruun. —Second edition.
    pages cm
  Includes bibliographical references and index.
  1. Transportation. 2. Urban transportation. 3. Local transit. I. Title.
HE305.B78 2014
388.4068'4—dc23   2013021011

ISBN: 978-0-415-70600-1 (hbk)
ISBN: 978-1-315-88291-8 (ebk)

Typeset in Galliard
by Apex CoVantage, LLC

This book's eResource can be found here:
www.routledge.com/9780415706001

Printed and bound in the United States of America by Publishers Graphics, LLC on sustainably sourced paper.

Contents

Figures

Tables

Foreword to the Second Edition

Since 2006, both the theory and practice of project alternative development, evaluation and selection has moved forward substantially. This is no doubt stemming from a combination of concerns about getting better value for money as public sector finance has come under increasing pressure, and the recognition that traditional methods don't address issues raised by sustainable development concerns adequately. This edition is intended to update and expand the material covered accordingly. Of particular importance is the additional case study presenting a state-of-the-art evaluation method from a joint project between Swedish and Danish participants.

Changes have also been made to address the many useful comments I have received from lecturers, students, and practitioners. Discussion on some topics was apparently seen to be quite detailed while on others quite terse. This reflected my views on what I thought would be most important or where other sources seemed to be lacking. In reality, it also reflected my prejudices and my comfort level with researching and writing about certain topics. Thus, based on this feedback, I have added some computational and graphical examples to clarify some concepts. In particular, I have added far more detail about demand forecasting models and about demand-responsive public transport.

I have also tried to make the book even more useful as a reference book. There are more references and additional readings on almost every topic. Practitioners and students interested in learning more about a particular subtopic in a concentrated effort should appreciate these.

Foreword to the First Edition

This book was motivated by an ongoing debate. There have been many articles in academic journals and the trade press that point to the apparent lack of imagination and failure to respond to evolving market niches by public sector transit agencies. As an example, critics can often point to the 'plain vanilla' product of 40-foot (12-meter) long buses aimed at the journey to the Central Business District for work. This remains the primary product even though populations have dispersed and trip patterns have changed. The conclusion offered by some is that public transportation should be deregulated to permit a response to unmet market. Indeed, this approach was followed in the United Kingdom in 1986. It has become an ongoing experiment.

This line of argument is countered by other analysts who strike a more defensive posture towards the industry. They point out the constraints and conflicting objectives many agencies face. Yet, if those arguing would systematically compare each other's vantage point and unspoken assumptions, they would find kernels of common truth in even seemingly contradictory arguments. The current book aims to do this systematizing.

Another motivation for this book was some recent research findings. The first part of this book tries to give a fairly sophisticated understanding of several key topics relevant to public transport project development in brief expositions. As a part of the exposition, it condenses key findings of three Ph.D. dissertations done at the University of Pennsylvania in the 1990s that explore some complex issues, while maintaining a mathematical level limited to algebra with subscripted variables. Remaining true to this restriction, it also gives a condensed presentation on mathematical modeling of transportation systems, a particularly challenging topic to make accessible using limited mathematics.

The second part of this book covers basic performance and investment analysis tools currently in use. It applies them specifically to the public transportation industry. It further discusses their strengths and limitations, particularly in light of heightened environmental awareness. The practice of investment and performance analysis is still evolving in step with the field of ecological economics and with the concern for incorporation of sustainable development principles in public policies. Thus, this author makes no claim to have definitive answers for overcoming these limitations, only some suggestions.

Differences of opinion will continue to exist, but I hope this book can be of some help to the analyst who is trying to more fully characterize transportation alternatives, to be more inclusive of costs and benefits, and to make more insightful and rigorous comparisons between project alternatives.

Preface

In an increasingly urbanized world, green growth relies on efficient urban mobility and adequate urban public transport infrastructure and services.

Cities are the powerhouses of the economy. They concentrate 80 percent of the world economic output. Efficient mobility in cities creates economic opportunities and social integration, enables trade, and facilitates access to markets and services.

Fast urban population growth – associated with urban sprawl – generates more and longer daily trips in cities, which exert significant pressure on transport infrastructure and natural resources, in particular in emerging economies.

If current mobility patterns – marked by the dominance of private motorized mobility – prevail, urban congestion will gridlock cities and energy consumption and GHG will increase by 30 percent, affecting not only the environmental performance of cities but also risking bringing their economic growth to a halt.

Shifting from private motorized modes to public transport helps reconcile economic and environmental policy priorities – which actually is the very definition of green growth.

Public Transport: Engine of Green Growth

Investing in public transport makes economic sense. And it supports the greening of the urban economy.

Moving the Economy Forward

By increasing connectivity – linking employers and their workforce or retailers and their customers – public transport generates business activity and boosts the productivity of the urban economy.

Capital investment in public transport sparks a chain reaction in business activity and generates value that far exceeds the initial investment – up to 3 to 4 times (UTP, 2003; APTA, 2009).

By using urban space more efficiently, public transport alleviates congestion and increases travel time reliability.

Mitigating GHG Emissions

Public transport emits 3.5 times less GHG per passenger per km than private cars.

If the share of urban trips made by public transport doubled by 2025, urban transport GHG emissions would be in line with commitments made under international climate negotiations.

Saving Energy Resources

Urban transport energy consumption would be decoupled from the growth in mobility if share of public transport doubled by 2025.

Such stabilization of urban transport energy consumption would be beneficial for oil importing countries, of course, but also for oil exporting countries, as the domestic oil consumption usually is heavily subsidized.

Keeping Cities Compact

Public transport supports relatively dense urban development patterns, which optimize energy and resource efficiency.

Creating Green Jobs

In addition to contributing to the competitiveness of the economy, public transport by itself is a large industry providing about 13 million jobs worldwide (operation, regulation, and supply of goods and services).

In many cities the local public transport operator is one of the largest employers (e.g. Amsterdam, Barcelona, Paris).

Research into transport investment as part of the recovery plan in the USA in 2009 provides evidence that investing in public transport produces twice as many jobs per dollar as investing in roads.

Improving Health

If the share of trips made by public transport doubled, daily mobility would provide the 30 minutes of physical activity recommended by the World Health Organization to reduce the risk of coronary heart disease and obesity by 50 percent and hypertension by 30 percent.

To deliver more and better public transport systems, supporting policies at government level could include urban public transport investment programs, including eligibility criteria and economic appraisal schemes; empowering local government by matching competences with resources and developing institutional capacity (funding, regulation, etc.); and supporting innovation in technology and policy.

This book analyzes all aspects to be taken into account to build better public transport systems.

Acknowledgements for the Second Edition

There are many people who have given me useful comments on the first edition. Many others have provided me with relevant articles, contacts and leads without any solicitation on my part. Much of what I found as a result has found its way into this edition. Special thanks must go to Prof. Steen Leleur at the Technical University of Denmark and the EcoMobility group for allowing me extensive use of their recent material as a case study.

Acknowledgements for the First Edition

I am grateful to Professor Edward Morlok for getting me started in the subject area of engineering economics, although any errors I may have committed in the course of writing this book are entirely my own. More recently, he astutely identified a missing chapter when reading the book outline. I am grateful to Professor Vukan Vuchic for guiding the students whose dissertation research I have used. Thanks also to Robert Piper, John Holtzclaw, Preston L. Schiller, Roger Boldt, David Boyce, Stenerik Ringqvist, Jienki Synn, Jeffrey Casello and Tom Matoff for reviewing various chapters within their areas of special expertise. Finally, thanks most of all to Jim Hecimovich, my editor at APA Planners Press, for both critically questioning my text and improving its clarity. Thanks also to Julie Von Bergen at APA for her invaluable assistance in proofing my final pages and getting my book to press.

Chapter 1

Premises and Content of the Second Edition

The population of the metropolitan areas of the world continues to dramatically increase as can be seen in the United Nations report *World Urbanization Prospects* (UN 2012). By 2015, more than 200 million additional people will live in cities between 1 and 5 million persons in size than did so in 2000, and approximately 200 million more will live in cities of 5 million persons or more (NRC 2003). Even some cities that would seemingly be built out due to being enclosed in a basin, such as Los Angeles, are continuing to grow rapidly, in large part because of densification. Other cities, such as Delhi, are ever expanding in geographic size, which threatens food and clean water supplies. To accommodate the population increase, public transportation investments can be expected to grow over time. In addition, nations at all economic levels are evolving with the changing nature of economic activity and with changes in resource availability and environmental restraints, hence the ever-increasing concern with *sustainable development*. Thus, the nature of services can also be expected to evolve in order to attract persons from private means of transport and to influence their daily travel patterns.

Because public transportation interacts with so many aspects of society, it is a highly interdisciplinary subject. Even to those who work in the field for a living, there will always be aspects of the subject that remain unfamiliar. Nevertheless, inclusion of these many aspects really is necessary for the sound analysis of more complex projects. Furthermore, the laws of many countries dictate the inclusion of a wide array of aspects. In the United States, the *Intermodal Surface Transportation Efficiency Act of 1991 (ISTEA)* and its successor, the *Transportation Efficiency Act for the 21st Century (TEA-21)* recognized the need for a more interdisciplinary approach than the traditional one based on analyzing each transportation mode separately and only for a narrow range of impacts. At the same time that more benefits and costs came to be formally considered in the review process, the possibility opened up to be "flex," or to transfer federal government funds from highway to transit projects. However, such projects still had to face a review process and formal analysis procedure.

Both the European Union as a whole and its member states have policies for determining costs and benefits that are to be included and in what fashion, what revenue sources can be used for which purposes, procurement regulations, and so on. It is hard for any one analyst to remain current and to understand all the legal aspects of the subject of project development and implementation, let alone the wide array of technical subjects.

There is, of course, the rest of the world as well. Nations range from having very sharply defined and enforced policies, such as Singapore, to those that are similar to the European Union nations or the United States, to those having very few policies of any kind related to urban development or transport. Moreover, limited funds can be consumed by serious corruption, even in places that ostensibly have well-defined policies. But one cannot assume that nations with weak or ineffective policies will continue on the same path and, indeed, might even have the opportunity to "leapfrog" to the state-of-the-practice if conditions are right.

Lower levels of government in the United States as well as in other nations are continually revising their planning processes to be more inclusive of costs and benefits for all transportation modes, especially when their electorates demand consideration of local concerns such as livability and mobility that reflect changing accessibility requirements and demographics. Indeed, they will often be ahead of their higher levels of government and serve as potential role models. Part of the motivation for this book is to provide some ideas and methods to these leaders, without regard to existing legal limitations and official procedures.

This book incorporates nonmonetizable and even nonquantifiable costs and benefits into investment analyses, something that is not always done satisfactorily, in large part due to lack of consensus on appropriate methods and valuations. Lack of consensus is not adequate grounds to ignore these important effects, however. This lack of consensus simply means that there will be differences of opinion over how best to include them and how best to interpret the analysis results. Perhaps a power struggle with those benefiting from the status quo might be the only way forward in some places. The increasing database of project outcomes in which rigorous and inclusive investment and performance analyses have been used should help drive convergence towards consensus.

Furthermore, public transportation is a public service usually financed with public sources. It should be influenced by public input and reflect public needs. These needs are not necessarily the same, depending upon the perspective of the various stakeholders. Therefore, analysis of proposed investments, as well as the performance of existing public transportation services, is an endeavor that should be completed as transparently and as socially inclusive as possible.

By advocating an analysis approach that considers the full array of costs and benefits viewed from both a transportation-system-wide and a societal perspective, by including costs and benefits even where there is no consensus on the appropriate evaluation technique, and by factoring public input into the analysis, and by supporting performance and outcome driven decisions, this book conforms with the *Policy Guide on Surface Transportation* of the American Planning Association (APA 2010).

In this spirit of full inclusion, the basic purpose of this book is to provide a complete primer on topics in public transportation needed for performance and investment analysis. This applies to existing public transportation systems, to extensions or expansions of existing systems, and to major new project proposals. It is intended to impart sufficient technical knowledge to the reader with some mathematical and technical education to understand important issues and the tradeoffs that are an inevitable part of most projects.

Public transportation has an often-underestimated technical complexity that can be an obstacle to proper analysis and interpretation. Knowing both the design issues and modern analysis tools is a prerequisite to development of project alternatives that are both sound and responsive to the public purpose. Books related to project investment analysis are usually generic or cover all transportation modes and therefore do not provide sufficient detail about the foundations of public transportation system design.

It is a central premise of this book that it is impossible to draw conclusions about either existing public transportation systems or proposed investments without first having some idea of which goals one is trying to meet and which are of the highest priority. Public transportation can serve a variety of goals depending upon the specific circumstances. The judgment criteria should revolve around how well these are met. Even so, different conclusions can be and are drawn by different analysts. This is due to their varying conceptions of how much weight each goal should receive. In fact, some analysts have in mind only one goal. For this reason, I stress the creation of a list of project goals as a prelude to any discussion. As will be discussed in detail in the following chapter, analysts and decision makers can then select specific design objectives likely to help meet these goals. Figure 1.1 shows a conceptual project development process.

It is another central premise of this book that a person with sufficient interest and some knowledge of mathematics can follow all key concepts and principles needed for analysis. Specifically, the mathematics required is algebra using subscripted variables. A conscious effort is made to keep this book accessible to the maximum number of persons without sacrificing essential computational concepts. An effort is also made to use nomenclature consistent with common practice and with popular textbooks on related subjects (when they exist). Unlike some disciplines, the nomenclature is not highly standardized. Even the vocabulary can be ambiguous. Italics are sometimes used to highlight the introduction of important terminology.

Most of the analysis methods presented here have sufficient sophistication to draw meaningful conclusions yet require only a calculator or spreadsheet program to use. An analyst should be able to begin by using publicly available basic data, or if one is an outsider, data shared by project teams tasked with the "official" analysis. This basic information is then used to establish a few basic design alternatives that show promise in meeting project goals and objectives, the second step shown in Figure 1.1. Further development and analysis of each alternative usually reveals that some are either not practical or effective, while others require closer investigation.

The outputs from complex mathematical planning models are treated as a source of data for furthering the investigation and for refining the analysis of various design alternatives. This part of the process is shown as the third step in Figure 1.1. Models are iterative sources of data, where the models may need to be

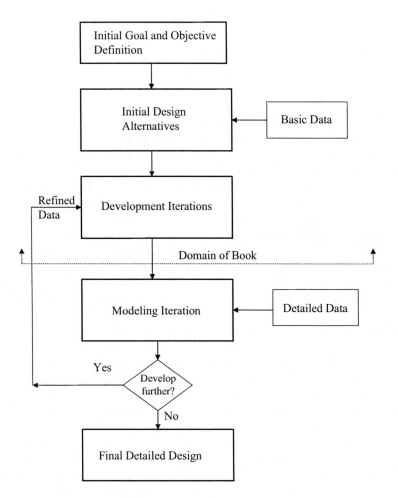

Figure 1.1 Conceptual project development process.

rerun as the assumptions used in the previous round are challenged by findings in the current round. The iterative nature of the process is shown as the fourth step in Figure 1.1. feeding back to the third step.

The domain of this book is largely limited to the first three steps of the conceptual project development process of Figure 1.1, although judging the quality and suitability of the data provided from the fourth step is a very important issue. Thus, the underlying nature and assumptions of mathematical models are important topics for a project analyst to understand, so some effort is also spent on explaining key aspects of the "modeling iteration" step.

A good case can be made that highly detailed analysis using complex modeling software and massive input data at a too-early stage only obscures important relationships, hinders insight, and excludes potential contributors who cannot fathom the obscure results and technical jargon. Models are not usually capable of making tradeoffs between all contemplated goals. Instead, each focus only on certain aspects of the project (e.g. demand forecasting or cost estimating.) Only as the project alternatives are narrowed down, and these certain aspects become more important for making critical decisions, for meeting regulatory requirements, and so on, does deep modeling expertise become helpful. At some point, the analysis of project alternatives ceases when one best alternative is selected. Only then can the final detailed design, shown as the fifth and last step in Figure 1.1, be completed.

There are certain aspects of performance and investment evaluation that current prevailing methods and models either do not address at all or address inadequately. These deficiencies are serious and cannot be ignored in any modern book on this subject. The issue of sustainable development has called into question some of the implicit assumptions of current economic tools in widespread use. Specifically, they do not properly account for depletion of nonrenewable resources or for the long-term ecological consequences of investment choices. The earth is increasingly seen to have a *carrying capacity* for human consumption. To exceed this capacity for an extended period of time brings risk of irreversible damage. A concise summary of the complex concept of carrying capacity is provided by Kenneth Arrow et al. (1995).

This book will call attention to some of the deficiencies of contemporary transportation project analyses with respect to sustainable development principles and some of the remedies that have been suggested. It does not presume to provide definitive tools and methods of *sustainable economics*, which is the revision and expansion of neoclassical economics to accommodate these issues. This discipline remains in early stages of development, although substantial progress has been made since the first edition of this book. Most of the updated material introduces and attempts to summarize some highlights. Due to length concerns, as well as the danger of misrepresenting the work of others, the reader will often be referred to more detail from other sources. This edition of the book has vastly increased the number of such references.

The book's sequence of topics was chosen to limit subject matter from later chapters that one must already know in order to absorb an earlier chapter. Material from later chapters is sometimes referenced, however, as there simply is no ideal sequence for material describing an iterative design process. The chapters may be divided into two parts.

Part 1 consists of Chapters 2 through 7. The second chapter discusses what public transportation projects try to achieve and presents some case studies based on actual project evaluations, but the reader may well be unfamiliar with some of the concepts. The third through seventh chapters explain and attempt to operationalize key concepts. These concepts are used to characterize the existing physical situation, to theorize what results can be expected from a project alternative, and to develop quantitative relationships used in designing and analyzing public transportation project alternatives.

Part 2 consists of Chapters 8 through 12. The eighth through tenth chapters focus on monetary issues. Monetary evaluation tools and cost-estimating methods are needed for comparison of project alternatives. The nature, purposes, and feasibility of projects are influenced by organizational structure. Hence, the eleventh chapter discusses the different organizational structures under which public transportation is planned, capitalized, and operated. The twelfth chapter focuses on the challenging task of combining all monetary evaluations with all other considerations in order to rate or rank overall performance of project alternatives. The content of each chapter is further summarized in the following section.

The second chapter includes a discussion of the centrality of goals and objectives to any analysis. It includes descriptions of many commonly identified goals and attempts to classify each goal as to whether it can be quantified, and if so, whether it can be expressed in monetary terms. One major source of disagreement in performance and investment analysis is over the issue of measurement of goal achievement. This chapter argues that one can measure progress towards goals only by creating measurable project objectives, designed to promote these goals. Even though many possible goals may be cited, not all are of equal importance in any given project. Even so, fuller identification and inclusion of potential goals is always better for obtaining a more complete perspective. Each goal will have different weights in the head of each analyst, and different ones again in official public policy documents and laws. Thus, another source of disagreement over performance and investment analysis outcomes stems from unstated differences of opinion as to which goals have priority, or perhaps, are relevant at all. The second half of Chapter 2 discusses case studies. These case studies will illuminate how relatively short and simple analysis can provide important insight, how goals are weighted (or not) and how objectives are measured in the real world, and the significant omissions that can occur. New to this second edition is a recent example of an actual analysis from Scandinavia that contains many of the features and qualities that this book advocates.

The third chapter deals with transit network characteristics. The relation of individual routes to a network can be important but often poorly understood. Misleading analysis results can be obtained by viewing a particular route in isolation without regard to its role in the larger network. It begins by defining some different types of network structures. It continues by discussing the way in which rights-of-way and modal technologies affect performance, and how networks need to evolve to higher performance standards as cities grow. It then develops detailed spatial and temporal characteristics of the individual transit route. Examples are the route's ridership profile and the relative importance of the different components of passenger travel time. It presents numerical performance indicators that might be helpful for the characterization of individual routes and for the identification of comparable routes. It explains how some attributes of the network are related to the mode(s) used and how others are inherent to the service area and yet others to the service design features. The role of transfers between vehicles to move within a network is emphasized, as the outcome of numerous performance and investment analyses have hinged upon either the perceived or actual role of transfers. By comparing of two different academic research approaches, the chapter attempts to provide some insight into the complex interaction between route and network, which also serves to clarify the role of transfers. Finally, the chapter discusses the demand-responsive approach, a possible service design alternative to a fixed-route network used in low-demand environments and when disabilities preclude use of fixed routes by some of the public. New material has been added, highlighting some basic service design principles and performance indicators.

Intelligent Transportation Systems (ITS), the name given to packages of information technology (IT) hardware and software applied to transportation, are discussed in the fourth chapter. ITS have implications for the types and quality of service designs. ITS are helping the traditional distinctions between scheduled fixed-route and demand-responsive services to blur, so analysts must keep up with and take new service possibilities into account. ITS are also a rich source of data both for managing existing services more effectively and for analyzing new projects. Some additional material was added about some best practices in postprocessing of archived data. Finally, ITS are discussed as candidates for investment in and of themselves.

The fifth chapter concerns the relationship of public transportation to other transportation modes. The impact of existing public transportation services as well as the contribution from nonmotorized transportation services have been often understated due to misleading data. Thus, it explains how to more fully characterize passenger travel habits by including all transport modes, motorized and nonmotorized. Some new sources of travel data are discussed that have become available since the first edition was written. The second edition has added new material on estimating total changes in energy consumption and pollution generation from various modes after a major investment has been completed, an important topic for sustainability analysis. This chapter also addresses the physical details of intermodal connections, as these can be quite important to the success or failure of a public transport project. This includes not only connections between urban public transport modes but also connections with other modes, both motorized and nonmotorized. An entirely new discussion about park-and-ride connections has been added, in response to reader comments.

The sixth chapter first discusses the space requirements of various transportation modes, both while moving and stationary. Using the results from an academic research study as a teaching tool, it also discusses the important implications of the interaction between transportation and alternative nontransportation uses for limited and valuable surface space. Since the first edition of this book, vast amounts of new material have become available on the Internet about urban densities, so this is introduced to the reader. The chapter continues with a discussion of the ecological impacts of the urban form and resultant land consumption implied by various transportation choices, as these constitute significant costs and benefits that have historically been ignored or underestimated and will only increase in importance in the future. It concludes with a brief introduction of pricing for short-term use of land (e.g. for parking) and its relationship to demand management and long-term pricing and taxation as a potential means of project financing.

The seventh chapter describes some mathematical models for performing quantitative analysis of proposed investments. In real-life projects, models are used for a variety of purposes. For example, estimates for the ridership that will result from major investments are almost always based on such models. Indeed, laws and regulation typically mandate their use for major projects. However, this doesn't mean that model results should be respected religiously. Much of the evolving state-of-the-practice in performance and investment analysis revolves around either improving models or modifying the role they play and the importance they have in the planning process.

The chapter begins with some simpler models that provide initial estimates of basic inputs. These are needed for the initial development of candidate project alternatives. An example would be rough transit ridership change estimates from rough auto travel speed changes on competing roadways. Again, additional information sources have become readily available over the Internet since the first edition. This same chapter follows with a description of the theories and methods used by larger, more complicated models requiring computer solution. Few people have the time to develop a deep enough understanding to use all the types of models currently used in modern analysis. Indeed, even modelers can suffer from fragmented expertise. Thus, this chapter continues with suggestions on how to interpret and challenge the results from complex models without being an insider to the modeling effort. In particular, it explains many of the principles and assumptions imbedded in mathematical regional transportation demand forecasting and transportation/land-use interaction models and, consequently, the strengths and limitations of their results. This second edition has added a significant amount of detail about some of the steps in response to reader comments. It continues with a list of potential errors in models, how to identify them, and what the consequences might be, once again calling attention to material that has become available that could be helpful towards rectifying errors. It concludes with a discussion of trends in model development.

The eighth chapter reviews engineering economic computational fundamentals and how these are typically applied to the comparison and evaluation of projects alternatives. It discusses the nature of the input data required. It then reviews the concepts of the discount rate and cash flow diagrams and applies them to monetary evaluation methods, primarily Net Present Value (NPV) and its close cousin, the Benefit to Cost Ratio (BCR). More advanced applications of NPV, such as lifecycle costing, are also briefly introduced. This chapter then discusses some common applications and the contexts in which these approaches are valid and when they are less valid. It also addresses opportunity costs of capital, the incidence of costs and benefits across the population, and the occasional conflicts with noneconomic values. It ends with a discussion of capital investments with very long lives and with consumption of nonrenewable resources, in particular, the proper discount rate(s) and to what costs and benefits they should apply. These raise important issues for sustainable development and sustainable economics that are not easily considered with traditional monetary cost–benefit methods. This discussion sets that stage for multicriteria analysis that comes later.

The ninth chapter develops the engineering cost model concept, a practical tool for computing input values for monetary evaluations of multiple project alternatives. It provides some detail of their development and shows their utility in analysis through examples. It extends this into *sensitivity analysis*, a method for investigating the impacts of changes in individual cost components, a topic often of great interest in performance and investment analysis. Indeed, such impacts are often the whole point of an investment. Methods of incorporating changes in the discount rate over time and changes in the inflation rate into models are also presented. Finally, this chapter also introduces methods for analyzing risk when certain cost components are not known with great certainty. New material has been added that provides an example of its use in an official analysis.

The tenth chapter develops marginal operating cost analysis. It first presents the highly useful marginal cost versus marginal revenue test. It provides marginal cost equations based on engineering cost models for both rail and road modes, as they are not the same (e.g. the rail modes can use several vehicles that are physically attached to one another). It proceeds to apply these equations together with scheduling relationships (equations and constraints) to build estimates of the annual cost of operating a route. Finally, it attempts the more difficult task of estimating marginal costs imposed on a network by passengers who transfer between routes, an important consideration when setting fares or seeking new passengers through service changes. One major change from the first edition is that the derivation of the equations has been moved to an Appendix. These derivations can be of value to those who might be interested in modifying them for their own specific application, but they are not needed to understand the basic applications.

The eleventh chapter discusses some different organizational principles for public transportation systems that exist around the world. It describes some consequences stemming from whether they are privately or publicly owned and operated. Indeed, it has implications for financing and for the motives to even consider a project. This chapter then gives a typology of common organizational principles. It continues with typologies of contracting models for operation and maintenance of public transport systems and for capital investments. This second edition now includes some updates about the United Kingdom's experience with bus deregulation and rail privatization and the official responses to public dissatisfaction. It also includes recent examples of new services that have come into existence or grown in popularity and their organizational support structure. It concludes with a discussion of professional opinion and evidence in support of various organizational types and their appropriateness in particular situations.

The twelfth and final chapter suggests some methods to combine all factors in an evaluation. It outlines some suggested steps to help assemble and organize the information. This includes scoring methods, basic data portrayal methods, and treatment of information that does not lend itself to quantification. It then proceeds towards initial ranking and possible elimination of some alternatives. The chapter continues with a discussion questioning the realism of finding one optimal alternative for a major project. In response to comments, the second edition has clarified and deepened this section to better address when mathematical optimization theory has a role to play in project alternative design and selection. It continues with some accessible, computationally tractable methods for further ranking and differentiating alternatives, without necessarily always expecting to find the "best" one. In some cases it is enough to suggest which might yield the most incremental "bang for the buck." There is a modest update about additional benchmarking groups that have come into existence and methods of increasing public participation.

When the chapter moves on to methods that are somewhat less accessible because they requiring establishing weights of importance of goals and effectiveness of techniques, it still pays particular attention to the Analytic Hierarchy Process (AHP), because this process consolidates several other methods into one exceptionally useful method that may meet the test of being understandable and transparent to decision makers and concerned citizens. New to the second edition is another multicriteria method that has proven itself by being successfully used several times in Scandinavia while also addressing some theoretical objections raised about the AHP method. Both methods are in accord with the premises set early in the book that evaluation should be as inclusive as possible of all costs and benefits, monetary and monetizable, quantitative and qualitative.

Finally, the last chapter introduces some methods of assessment that are more abstract and mathematical. These methods and others like them are unlikely to be used in an officially sanctioned evaluation process. Nevertheless, they have potential to provide insight to professional analysts and improve the state-of-the-practice of performance and investment evaluation. Some new material has been added to reflect recent research and applications of some of these methods.

References

APA (American Planning Association). 2010. *Policy Guide on Surface Transportation.* http://www.planning.org/policy/guides/pdf/surfacetransportation.pdf

Arrow, Kenneth, Bert Bolin, Robert Costanza, Partha Dasgupta, Carl Folke, C. S. Holling, Bengt-Owe Jansson, Simon Levin, Karl-Goran Maler, Charles Perrings and David Pimentel. 1995. "Economic Growth, Carry Capacity, and the Environment." *Science* 268 (29 April): 520–21.

NRC (National Resource Council). 2003. "Introduction." Chapter 1 in *Cities Transformed*, National Academy Press. Washington, DC: 9–28.

UN (United Nations). 2012. "World Urbanization Prospects: The 2009 Revision Population Database" see especially Urban Annual Growth Rate tables. http://esa.un.org/wup2009/unup/index.asp?panel=1.

Further Reading

Khanna, Parag. 2010. "Beyond City Limits." *Foreign Policy* (Sept./Oct.). http://www.foreignpolicy.com/articles/2010/08/16/beyond_city_limits?print=yes&hidecomments=yes&page=full.

Chapter 2

Establishing Goals and Objectives

To declare a project a "success" or a "failure" ignores an important fact, that a project can have several important purposes or goals, some of which may prove to have been much better served than others. Fairness would require that all stakeholders in a project be heard. Even analysts doing a disinterested assessment harbor their own biases (e.g. emphasizing particular criteria that measure performance). For these reasons, it would be wise for all parties to list goals explicitly and, if possible, to rank or weight them in order of importance.

Goals can be qualitative and broad propositions, such as "a more livable city." A thorough evaluation of project performance as it relates to each of these various goals might take many years, as the supporting evidence for some of the goals appears only over time. Compounding the complexity of analysis is the measurement of these impacts and effects. Continuing with the livability example, it could be very challenging, if not impossible, to construct an absolute scale of "livability" and then to collect the data to evaluate it. Instead, one must select proxy indicators and variables that are correlated with livability. One is likely to resort to *ordinal* rankings for some of the criteria, arguing only that one alternative is better than the other, or "the city is (or will be) more livable than it was before."

Measuring, Quantifying, and Monetizing

Compared to goals, which can be somewhat nebulous in nature, objectives are usually concrete because they are designed to enable measurement of specific outcomes. If they do not reflect measurable outcomes, they should be restated. Although objectives are usually intended to be in support of some greater goal or goals, it is quite possible to achieve an objective and fail to reach the intended goal, as the link may not always prove to be as strong as first believed. This is particularly true in modern times of rapid technological change and cultural instability, where there can be all manner of influences on a project that can't be anticipated or mitigated. Thus, if a project spans many years, it is worth revisiting objectives occasionally to see if they still support the greater goals. As an example, improved mobility for the carless could be a goal and a certain provision of trips to a central business district (CBD) a supporting objective. But if jobs have dispersed in recent years, one might want to change the objective to a certain provision of trips to each of several employment centers instead.

Financially related goals and objectives are of central importance to any investment or performance analysis, but they are not the only ones. Indeed, it is possible to justify projects that "lose" a great deal of money. Some goals and objectives that are not of a financial nature can be stated in financial terms through a conversion. Others defy all attempts. An objective such as reduced air pollution in a corridor can be measured and perhaps translated into a monetary equivalent (i.e. *monetized*.) Even when this is done, there may be a wide range of possible values to assign to a unit of pollution, for example, depending upon assumptions. In the end, some costs may still remain uncaptured. Therefore, one should explicitly state what is included in the financial analysis and how nonfinancial aspects were addressed, if at all.

Many organizations and individual researchers have made efforts to monetize an array of costs. These are usually classified into broad categories such as "social" or "environmental," although these distinctions are not fundamental. For example, air pollution is clearly an environmental issue, yet a key monetized cost arising from pollution is increased medical treatment, a social cost. Often, the values span a wide range, depending upon the assumptions and specific circumstances. Litman (2005) conveniently updates a collection of monetized estimates from numerous sources.

It can be helpful to sort goals and objectives into four categories:

1   Monetary
2   Nonmonetary but monetizable subject to assumptions
3   Nonmonetary but quantifiable
4   Not quantifiable.

Each will be defined further:

> **Monetary:** Money is the direct measure of achievement. Examples include reducing direct operating costs or increasing revenue.
>
> **Nonmonetary but monetizable subject to assumptions:** Many activities or changes to processes will not directly affect the financial performance of any formal organization. An example is to express pollution reduction as being proportional to saved medical expenses for society at large.
>
> **Nonmonetary but quantifiable:** This does not automatically imply nonquantitative, only that it is nontranslatable into monetary equivalents. For example, carbon dioxide (CO_2) emissions are quantifiable but not easily monetizable regarding their global warming contribution.
>
> **Nonquantifiable:** Some concepts are simply not amenable to quantification. As an example, improving the aesthetics of a district of a city by reallocating street space is a not only a nonmonetary goal but not quantifiable

on an "aesthetic" scale. But it is possible to ask people to give an ordinal ranking, that is, which design alternative(s) is the most aesthetically pleasing? Which is the next most pleasing? And so on.

As an example of a nonquantifiable goal, "improving aesthetics of a public transport corridor" would make a reasonable ultimate goal, but there could not be a measured objective. Instead, one might have to use proxy objectives. One such proxy would be achievement of sufficient acceptance of proposed designs through *charettes* that permit public evaluation and revision of designs. Another would be a public survey that would register public opinion after implementation.

Common Goals

What follows is a fairly comprehensive, but by no means exhaustive, list of goals of public transportation investment projects. These will be classified as to whether they are monetary, monetizable, quantifiable, or nonquantifiable. Goals can often be conflicting and will require trade-off between them. In some cases, goals are mutually exclusive. While most of these goals are straightforward, a discussion of the proper classification of costs and benefits associated with some goals may be necessary.

Common Goal 1: Reduce Operating Subsidy per Passenger

Public transportation networks can exhibit economies of density and economies of scope. As area coverage improves, service frequencies increase and connection possibilities expand; increased operating costs often can be more than offset by increasing usage and by charging higher fares (if needed). Evidence of this can be seen in older and denser cities with extensive service. Boston and Philadelphia cover more than 50 percent of their operating costs, whereas more sparse systems, such as those in Seattle and Portland, can cover less than 25 percent of their costs (FTA, 2011) despite similar fare levels. Buehler and Pucher (2011) place the US national average at about 33 percent, but this number overstates cost recovery in general as the statistics are so heavily influenced by the New York City system.

On an international basis, Jeffrey Kenworthy divided 60 world cities into those he called "strong rail" "weak rail" and "no rail" cities. A strong-rail city is defined as one where at least 50 percent of all transit passenger-kilometers and at least 40 percent of boardings are on rail modes. He found that the strong-rail cities on average covered 60 percent of operating costs, weak-rail cities 51 percent, and no-rail cities, 35 percent (Kenworthy 2008). This was based on 1995 data. When the 2005 data are analyzed, it will be informative to see how these ratios have changed in cities that have changed categories due to major investments.

There is little doubt that the fares could be raised substantially with relatively small ridership losses in most of the strong- and perhaps even weak-rail cities.

Keep in mind that monthly or seasonal passes such as the Paris *Carte d'Orange* that provide unlimited use are a great bargain to frequent travelers, given the ubiquitous network and relatively modest price. By comparison, it is doubtful that the Seattle or Portland regional systems that are of the same area coverage or speed standard could raise their fares very much to reduce subsidy, because the ridership losses from people who have access to an auto would likely offset the increased revenue from each passenger.

On the other hand, in some really large cities, such as London, where there is no monthly or season pass, it has been discovered that the Underground rail system can cover its operating costs and more, with the bus systems not far behind. In recent years, Londoners have faced high fares that generate an operating surplus that is used to partially cover the capital investment as well. This was possible because the driving alternative also was becoming increasingly unattractive, with serious congestion and high parking charges.

While the subsidy *per passenger* may be low because of a high cost recovery ratio, the absolute total subsidy may still be enormous when the scale of the public transportation network is large. It is important to recognize that while capital investment may bear fruit in lower costs on a per passenger basis, over time, the total operating subsidy required may still increase. If the total number of passengers increases enough, then connecting services also need expansion. This possibility of general system expansion might deter investments when the source(s) of any needed additional operating support cannot be established in advance.

Common Goal 2: Reduce Total Operating Subsidy

Another monetary goal, and one that should not be confused with reducing cost per passenger, is to reduce the total amount of operating subsidy required. In the aforementioned case of New York, this goal was accomplished through large fare increases made possible by the conditions auto drivers face. This, however, is possible only in a handful of cities. More typical was Mexico City. When fares were increased on the Metro after the collapse of the peso in 1994, ridership loss was dramatic, even with the superior speed of the Metro to buses. The revenue loss more than offset the operating savings.

Thus, to avoid steep ridership losses, operators in most cities or regions seek efficiencies rather than fare increases. Examples include competitive contracting of services, elimination of routes that fall below a certain cost recovery threshold, substitution of obsolescent technologies with more efficient ones, and increasing vehicle operating speeds through traffic engineering or public policy changes.

In the United Kingdom (except for London), drastic subsidy reduction was achieved by the radical and ideologically motivated step of almost total deregulation. It is characterized here as being radical, as the United Kingdom concentrated on subsidy reduction almost exclusively to the detriment of all other goals, contrary to virtually all other developed nations. All subsidy was removed except to support a small number of services deemed socially necessary. Consequently, operators abandoned large parts of their networks, concentrating services in fewer profitable corridors instead. They also forced down driver wages through intense competitive pressure on unionized operations. The United Kingdom is discussed in detail in Chapter 11.

Common Goal 3: Save Travel Time for Transportation System Users

Investments in public transportation can improve travel conditions for both its own users and users of competing modes. This will generally be true when a large amount of additional capacity is added along a congested corridor. It will be true throughout a network to the extent that it diverts persons from congested roads. One of the reasons for using complex mathematical models of transportation networks is to try to identify and quantify these time savings.

Monetized time saving can often be the single largest alleged benefit from a project. This practice of monetizing time savings for personal travel, especially for the journey to work, is criticized by me in Chapter 7. To summarize, I recommend only monetizing travel "on the clock," that is, travel done for commercial purposes, on the presumption that time saved can be productively used elsewhere. The time saved to noncommercial travelers should be left merely as "time saved" instead of the customary valuation of approximately half the hourly wage in the corridor being studied. Time saved is still quantifiable but is a nonmonetary benefit. Any information about the distribution of the time saving between users should be retained as supporting information, especially if one of the project goals was to save time for a particular portion of the population.

Furthermore, benefits to motorists from congestion reductions might recede over time. The benefit is only temporary if congestion is expected to again worsen over time. The cost of any additional delays that are generated from construction that is meant to reduce delays must also be subtracted from any benefits.

Common Goal 4: Relieve Congestion Bottlenecks and Improve Connections

A bottleneck can cause chronic delays that affect the whole network. A project may seek to relieve conditions for traffic in general, or it may only try to relieve the congestion facing transit. Examples include adding a lane, converting a lane from all-purpose or parking use to a transit lane, adding a queue bypass, installing preferential signal treatments, grade separating cross traffic, and so on.

There can be monetary benefits to transit operators from improved service reliability resulting in increased ridership. Correspondingly, there is also a time saving and travel-time reliability benefit to passengers. There are also ideally some aesthetic improvements (e.g. better streetscape conditions) for businesses and residents adjacent to former bottlenecks and possibly improved commerce. The benefits and costs to other transport system users depend upon the specifics of the project; some could face improved conditions, others, worse. There may be new costs if another bottleneck arises. Thorough analysis of upstream and downstream traffic conditions is required to ensure that the problem really is localized and not merely shifted.

At some point, traffic conditions at some activity centers become so detrimental that additional public transport service is needed to maintain vitality, but it must be attractive enough to divert some auto users. It may be that two endpoints, both being major traffic generators, are generating large volumes of traffic between each other. For example, these two generators may be on different rail lines requiring a connection and long travel time, so that far too many persons simply drive and thereby clog the shorter path between them. This, in turn, traps any public transport vehicles operating in mixed traffic as well. In such a case a laterally or grade-separated tangential rail line or bus lane between them might be the only practical solution competitive with auto travel.

Most of the costs of clearing bottlenecks are the required monetary investments, except when major disruptions to commerce and communities are involved during construction. On the other hand, benefits can be of a wide variety, revolving around time saved in traveling and renewal of the attractiveness of affected areas that have lost their luster due to chronic congestion and inaccessibility. Some of the private benefit is definitely monetizable and recapturable by the investing parties, as will be discussed in Chapter 6.

Common Goal 5: Focus Development in Selected Areas and Breach Geographic Barriers

Permanent transport facilities offering a high level of service can be coordinated with land use to create corridors of dense development and activity. However, it can't be automatically assumed that building will occur in the intended areas; the region must have demand for additional construction and there must be either land-use controls or disincentives towards building elsewhere. There can be monetary savings to the public sector from concentrating road, sewer, and other infrastructure investments (Burchell and Listokin, 1995) as well as monetary benefits to private developers from being allowed to build taller buildings, to reduce numbers of parking spaces (Shoup 2005a, 2005b), and so on.

It is often the case that one part of a city or region is not sufficiently connected to the rest. Insufficient transport capacity exists to allow further development or is preventing redevelopment. Such areas are isolated by major water crossings or hill formations. If long bridges or tunnels are required, public transport immediately becomes very competitive with automobile infrastructure, especially if there is not a sufficiently wide right-of-way to build a multilane roadway. Examples include the Lindenwold rapid transit line that uses a portion of the Ben Franklin suspension bridge to cross into central Philadelphia, the Bay Area Rapid Transit's Transbay Tube that connects both sides of San Francisco Bay, and the rapid transit tunnel linking Kowloon and the island of Hong Kong. A recent, dramatic example is the Jubilee Line extension in London that crosses under a winding Thames River four times, linking parts of London south of the Thames and the large Docklands redevelopment project to the extensive rapid transit network north of the river. Individuals benefit from better transportation options, reduced private vehicle expenditures, and so on. To the extent that this investment relieves the pressure to develop more environmentally sensitive areas but previously more accessible areas, it also supports another common goal as well. See the discussion of Common Goal 12 for more on this subject.

Common Goal 6: Transform Locale into a Different Type of Environment

Reallocation of urban space away from auto use and towards increased pedestrian and green space use is widespread in Europe. This can apply not only to main thoroughfares and shopping areas but to residential areas as well. The *woonerf* concept pioneered in the Netherlands is a hybrid, where autos still have free access to a residential street, but they must travel to a very slow speed so that children can use the street with a high degree of safety. These types of measures, however, cannot be taken without careful consideration of the effects on commerce and on any surrounding communities that might receive some diverted traffic. Public transport becomes central to achieving this goal by providing an alternative form of access when private vehicles are pushed out or their use is discouraged. For projects that convert areas solely to pedestrian use, monetary investment costs can become huge. An example was the tunnel under the main shopping street in Hannover, Germany, built to place the Light-Rail Vehicles entirely out of the way. Construction can also be highly disruptive and impose losses on commerce. Some benefits are monetary, such as any improvements (or losses) in retail sales, office rentals, land values, tourist spending, and so on. It must always be borne in mind that when viewed on a larger regional scale, some benefits are not real wealth creation but merely spending shifted from one place to another. Other benefits can be monetized, such as pollution reduction or the increase in land values. Some of the increase in value goes to land owners, but again, it can also be partially recaptured through taxation schemes.

Often, the primary intended benefits are nonquantifiable aesthetic and livability improvements. These effects can be real and can have a significant effect on the quality of life for residents. Evidence from peer cities is often available. Tourism may rise in areas redeveloped around transit, land values may rise faster along the corridor than elsewhere, or the city may begin to attract a larger share of new facilities for companies that compete for select workers. Such workers are people who can afford to discriminate against cities that are unattractive or necessitate unpleasant car commutes and will consider moving to an attractive central city, making them a good barometer of livability.

Common Goal 7: Improved Mobility for Nonauto Owners

In the United States, as of 2006, over 32.3 percent of the population did not have a driver's license. It ranged from 14.7 percent in the rural state of Vermont to 42.3 percent in the highly urban state of New York (FHWA 2007). In less auto-dependent nations, the corresponding percentages are even higher. In regions with a large concentration of retirees or children, or in very large cities, the percentage can be even higher. Furthermore, there may be persons with licenses and access to vehicles but who would prefer not to drive, as is common with the elderly living in heavily congested areas or who need to travel during hours of darkness. Mobility is a largely nonmonetary goal but is quantifiable using indicator variables such as trips per capita and average travel distance per day for target populations. It is monetary to the extent that the need and expense of chauffeuring by friends and relatives and for specialized transport services for nondrivers' school, medical, and other essential trips can be displaced or reduced by improved public transportation options.

Common Goal 8: Improve Transport System Safety

It is almost universally acknowledged by transportation planners that travel on public transportation modes is safer than travel on private modes on a per-kilometer basis. To the extent that people are diverted to public transport, there is a public benefit due to reduced medical and rescue expenses. Depending upon conditions for pedestrians, these benefits can be reduced by the corresponding increase in trips on foot. Thus, corresponding investments in pedestrian facilities need to be considered as well. In the United States, walking is relatively more hazardous than being in a motor vehicle, averaging 1.7 times the risk of fatality per hour of exposure. It is very important to note that the relative risk is about even during business hours but far higher for pedestrians during the evening and night hours—up to eight times as high. In the European Union as a whole, the relative risk is about the same, but both motorized and nonmotorized modes have substantially lower fatality rates (Chu 2003). In developing countries, by comparison, pedestrian fatality rates tend to be a far higher fraction of total transportation fatalities than in more developed countries.

There are longer-term benefits from diverting private trips to public transportation trips, as well. One is the private benefit from reduced productivity losses and insurance expenditures. Even deaths are regularly given a monetized value. Another is that regions with more use of nonmotorized modes, despite accidents, get an offsetting benefit through improved individual health. Furthermore, regions built in an urban form that revolves around heavy use of public transport and nonmotorized modes are more compact for any given population size than ones based on autos. Such regions have lower average trip length and thus lower exposure rates to opportunities for accidents. The converse is also true; suburban sprawl and increasing auto dependence will increase exposure, which is precisely what has happened in the United States since the end of World War II. Improved vehicle designs and traffic engineering improvements have reduced mortality rates in the United States, but in recent years absolute reductions in total fatalities have stopped due to increased miles of travel (U.S. Census Bureau, 2006). Other developed nations have had similar experiences.

Investments in public transportation infrastructure and vehicles investments can be targeted at improving safety while on board, in the station, or during the time spent accessing the service using nonmotorized modes. Examples of improvements include street modifications, surveillance cameras covering waiting areas and vehicles, grade or lateral separation of pedestrian paths, modification of vehicle interiors and entrances to reduce falls, rear tire guards to prevent rollovers of feet, and so on. These can translate into monetary benefits to the public transport operator in terms of reduced liability exposure, reduced system disruption due to accidents, and by stemming ridership losses from real or perceived safety problems.

Although values are routinely placed on people's lives in some conventional analyses, improving the overall safety and security conditions within a society mostly remains a higher level goal, not monetizable, but reflected instead in the reduction of pain, suffering, and grieving by loved ones after a tragedy. To the extent that pursuit of other goals succeeds in diverting persons to public transport, it also supports the safety goal.

Common Goal 9: Reduce Travel Time to Improve Scheduling Efficiency

The ability to make connections between services as well as the total cost of serving a route or line are highly dependent upon travel time. Connections depend upon practical schedules that allow repeated meeting of vehicles without excessive waiting times and delays. In some types of network scheduling, shortening travel time along selected routes could even be an overriding goal if the scheduling concept is to be viable. Another potential benefit is that the number of vehicles required to serve a route or line can be decreased without any change in frequency of service if speed can be increased sufficiently. A more complete explanation of the relationship of travel time and scheduling will be presented in the Chapters 3 and 7.

Common Goal 10: Provide Alternatives Under Road Congestion Pricing

Congestion pricing as a policy option (i.e. charging for use of roads based on demand,) is likely to increase in popularity as demand outstrips the road supply. It could do much to improve efficiency of the economy while shifting the financial burden of roads to those who benefit the most. But many institutional and political obstacles remain in most countries.

A comprehensive package that includes both congestion pricing and investment in public transportation would very likely make the concept easier to sell to politicians and the public they represent. If quality alternatives exist, a significant fraction of the public would use them, especially if these cost less (in the general sense of the word) than using the tolled road. Moreover, without adequate public transport, congestion pricing only exacerbates any existing mismatches between residences and employment. Relegating the people who can't afford the going level of road charges (no matter how compelling their need to travel by auto) to time-wasting, inadequate, public transport options, or to unemployment or employment in undesirable locations is ethically debatable.

While better public transportation as a precursor to congestion pricing seems to be implicitly understood in most of Europe and Asia, it has historically been overlooked in the United States. One can read *Urban Gridlock* (Wachs et al. 1994) and find no mention. While experts expressed much anguish over the political unacceptability of congestion pricing, and there is extended discussion over the means to bring forth viable road pricing schemes, the provision of parallel public transport services of competitive quality was not seen as playing a role. This is changing with time, and this goal will become an increasingly important one.

Many of the benefits from congestion pricing are monetary in conventional practice. It improves commercial efficiency by saving time for those users who tend to place a higher value on road space. Higher average speeds reduce commercial and public transport fleet sizes. Congestion pricing also relieves the need to financially support existing roadways from other sources by redirecting charges to the persons and firms who place the highest value on their use. The need to invest in new road capacity can also be reduced due to better temporal distribution of demand, or "peak spreading," yet another monetary benefit. To the extent that better public transport is to be considered part of a congestion-pricing program, a portion of the investment and operating costs of must be subtracted from the benefits of congestion pricing.

Permanently reducing pollution will yield further monetized benefits. (See Common Goals 11 and 12 for more details). Reduction of other negative effects (e.g. aesthetic degradation and reduced livability) that accompanies any region under severe congestion can also be expected, but these could be hard to quantify.

Common Goal 11: Reduce Energy Consumption and Greenhouse Gas Generation

There are both direct and indirect effects on energy consumption and greenhouse gas generation as a result of improving public transportation. The direct effect comes from shifting persons to a more efficient mode or by direct substitution of a more efficient technology while taking a trip between a given Origin–Destination Pair. This can occur already in the short term and continue to improve for years to come. The indirect effect stems from changes in travel patterns and behavior. This can occur in the short to medium term if the opportunity is created for significant numbers of people to replace auto trips, especially those involving *trip chaining*, where one must make multiple stops to do daily errands. It is possible to have shorter total trip lengths by going to alternative destinations where more errands can be done in one place. Over the longer term, as the urban form evolves to be more amenable to nonauto alternatives, larger numbers of persons will change their travel behavior.

There are other indirect effects as well. Sharing walls reduces energy consumption for heating and air conditioning. Denser housing reduces the distances that freight delivery vehicles must drive for distribution to stores. Indeed, there is a complex chain of impacts that might be traced.

Although public transportation is generally associated with energy efficiency, a particular project may not deliver this benefit. If ridership is low relative to the size of the vehicle and many empty repositioning movements are involved, energy consumption on a per-passenger basis may actually be higher than with an auto. As another example, if a project should make the urban fringe more accessible, it could promote sprawl. In this case, the energy reduction due to the use of transit modes for a fraction of trips could be offset by a large increase in auto trips also associated with urban fringe development. Moreover, any reduction in auto use due to a new public transport option may be only temporary until additional traffic fills the liberated road capacity. The realism of this goal depends upon corresponding efforts in auto restraint (e.g. congestion pricing), land use controls (e.g. elimination of free parking), and other factors beyond the project itself.

Energy consumption is also clearly a monetary goal to the extent that energy purchases and environmental mitigation expenditures are reduced. Although environmental damage and pollution are generally reduced whenever energy use is reduced, this is not always so. In some situations, they actually conflict to some degree. For example, a compressed natural gas engine may have cleaner exhaust than a competing diesel engine, but it also might have a lower thermal efficiency and therefore ultimately consumes more energy, albeit from a different source.

Fossil fuels extraction and consumption release CO_2, methane (CH_4), and several other compounds of lesser significance into the atmosphere as "greenhouse gases." This problem is becoming even more urgent to address on the world stage than the resource depletion itself. Reduction of CO_2 and CH_4 is quantifiable, but putting a monetary value on a particular project's contribution towards reduction is more contentious. There is more about this in the discussion of the next goal.

Common Goal 12: Reduce Pollution and Preserve Ecological Services

There are two distinct effects from investment in transit projects. First is the direct, or "end-of-pipe" effect, from a diversion of travelers from a more polluting to less polluting mode, or from a more polluting technology to a less polluting one within the same mode, for a trip between a given origin–destination. Pollution losses can generally be monetized to some extent in terms of health costs, crop losses, and so on, but with a wide range of economic values, depending upon circumstances and assumptions. The costs are statistically inferred by linking changes in levels of certain pollutants to certain trends in human and plant diseases and in output productivities. Note that some effects, such as visibility improvement, could be exceedingly difficult to monetize.

The indirect effects are longer term. These include pollution reduction due to changes in the dominant technologies in use, traveler behavior, lifestyle, and as time goes on, the urban form. But determining the spatial and temporal distribution of the benefits is problematic. Longer-term reductions of specific pollutants can be estimated and monetized, although subject to considerable uncertainty, especially as atmospheric conditions and seasons play an important role. Certain pollutants are of a localized concern while others of regional or global concern (e.g. carbon monoxide CO is a localized danger; most other exhaust products are of regional impact; the aforementioned greenhouse gases have global impact.

The relatively new discipline of *ecological economics* is based on the recognition that many natural features perform services of value to society that would be lost with their modification or conversion to other uses. There have been some economic analyses performed that attempt to monetize the value of wetlands and forests for raw material generation, wildlife reproduction, recreation, pollution cleansing, pollination, flood control, and CO_2 absorption (Costanza et al. 1996; Abramovitz 1998). Such monetized values have not yet become customary to include in financial calculations used in most officially sanctioned project evaluations but will no doubt increasingly be incorporated in the future. The goal of preserving ecological services also encompasses non-monetary but quantifiable concepts like preserving biodiversity as well as less measurable ones like preserving potential medicines that may reside in rainforests.

Objectives

Achieving objectives is the way in which progress is made towards achieving goals. These objectives must be specific and of a measurable nature if progress is to be judged. For example, an increase of X percent mode split for public transportation along corridor Y after Z months is designed to be measurable. It is difficult to provide an exhaustive list of objectives because these must be site specific if they are to be measurable.

When a community establishes multiple objectives to measure progress toward various goals, it is possible it will be working at cross-purposes or even conflicting purposes. Trade-offs will be required. As an example, improvements in transit service provision in a low-density auto-oriented community are likely to detract from system operating efficiency. As another example, an objective to steer a certain percentage of regional commercial development into a selected area in support of the goal of focusing development may conflict with preserving ecological services if it necessitates eradication of urban green areas.

It is because of the general complexity of the interrelations between objectives, including some interrelationships that may not have been foreseen, that no project can be evaluated based only on its achievements in pursuit of one goal. Its wider impact should be assessed, especially if the community has other projects underway that could interact with aspects of the transit project. The earlier that interactions and interrelations can be identified, the easier it is to make project revisions or refine project objectives. Even when identified in an after-the-fact analysis, any findings will be helpful for mitigation measures and for future projects.

There are ways to reduce the number of unforeseen results and unwanted interactions between objectives. Public involvement in the project planning stages will bring forth issues that planners trained in a limited set of disciplines might overlook. Similarly, if the project will affect how transportation labor is performed or service is provided, employee involvement can also identify issues and concerns. Projects involving advanced technologies can be particularly prone to unforeseen results, or even outright failure, if the project does not systematically involve, from planning to implementation, all parties likely to be affected. Many advanced technologies are decision-support tools that depend on appropriate data being supplied to them and on trust and acceptance by their intended users.

Mathematical models and other analyses supporting the viability of a project can be invalidated by uncoordinated actions. As an example, the initial light-rail line designed to serve Silicon Valley (San Jose, California, region) had ridership forecasts assuming no development of the parallel highway alternative. Once underway, the highway planning authorities independently began to upgrade a key adjacent highway, assumed during the light-rail ridership forecasting stage to remain a crossable, four-lane road with a median. The stations were to be accessed via at-grade pedestrian crossings, and conditions for motorists were slow. Instead, the highway was upgraded to a limited access highway. This simultaneously made access to the stations difficult (pedestrian overpasses were now required), raised the cost of the project, and reduced auto travel times in the same corridor. One result was lower than forecast ridership. Measures to mitigate some of the damage to the outcome may be possible, but there is no substitute for coordinated planning.

Any project that has a long life span is subject to extraneous events, particularly economic developments. A classic case was the Green Line in Los Angeles County, designed in the mid-1980s to terminate in El Segundo, site of numerous large aerospace factories. With the end of the Cold War came a recession in the industry. Combined with inducements to relocate to other regions entirely, these large employment generators shrunk rapidly (Wolinsky 1995). Ridership estimates were invalidated since the justification was so heavily dependent upon commuting trips to these locations. The options then became living with the reduced performance of the investment or extending the line to other large traffic generators. It was built without the extensions, but with numerous bus connections to improve its reach. As of 2002, ridership had, in fact, swelled to a respectable 34,000 riders per day as the transit-dependent population of Los Angeles continued to grow, parallel highway congestion worsened, and the El Segundo area found new uses.

This discussion points to one advantage of more *robust* projects. A robust project means one that can adapt to demographic changes and physical redevelopment of the city. It will survive unforeseen events and mistaken forecasts about ridership and operating and construction costs better. The situation is entirely analogous to betting; hedging one's bets reduces losses. Hedging also increases the chances of some unforeseen supportive actions and turns of events as well. Robustness can be explicitly considered in modern project-evaluation techniques.

Project Selection in the Real World

All major projects and most minor ones will serve a variety of objectives while creating conflict between some objectives. In the course of developing a project, more than one alternative approach is usually investigated and, in fact, external funding sources often mandate this as a condition. In the case of US federal government sources, one of the alternatives must be a "do nothing" scenario. Which alternative constitutes the best one is the crucial question. It is rarely as simple as selecting the lowest-cost method of achieving an identical set of objectives. The choice is really about selecting a package that serves some objectives better than others. The few exceptions arise for projects having a very narrow range of impacts.

Further complicating the decisions are institutional biases that favor certain outcomes. Planners will tend to investigate possibilities they best understand and where their analytic powers are strongest. Politicians will proscribe possibilities that offend their ideology or might hurt interests they represent. Jurisdictional boundaries raise issues about the willingness to cooperate for the greater good. Media may also misrepresent the possibilities to be considered, sometimes even providing a platform for demagoguery.

Especially important is external capital support. It can bias investigations towards more capital-intensive solutions and towards favored modes. A small local funding match seems like a bargain in exchange for the large economic stimulus. As an example, from its beginnings in 1956 until the passage of the Intermodal Surface Transportation Efficiency Act (ISTEA) in 1991, the Interstate Highway and Defense Act, with its 90 percent federal to 10 percent state/local match, created a huge bias for highway over public transportation investment across the entire United States. After ISTEA, the situation was equalized with both highways and transit being allowed an 80/20 split (although, in practice, only a minority of transit projects received the full 80 percent).

There can be a deeper bias inherent in the taxing and decision-making structures, however. In Western Europe, investment in public transportation competes with other public priorities, all of which are funded at least in part by high taxes related to motor vehicle use and energy consumption. This makes motoring self-financing, at least as far as direct operating, maintenance, and construction costs are concerned. Some additional user-based revenues cover all or a large part of the social and environmental costs. These costs arise from the large-scale physical accommodation within the urban form for autos and from heavy use of autos. Examples of social costs are mobility restrictions and isolation for those without autos and expenditures for traffic enforcement and traffic accidents. Examples of environmental costs were given in the discussion on common goals. How much these monetized costs will be depends upon what values one selects from what could be a wide range. A good case can be made, and indeed regularly is, that some of this revenue should be given to public transport to mitigate these costs.

By contrast, in the United States, taxes related to motor vehicle use are so low that there are no user-based revenues available for other public priorities. To the contrary, state and local governments appropriate general and property taxes to support motoring, a hidden direct subsidy (Hanson 1992; Pucher 1995; DeLucchi et al. 1996–97). Consequently, major public transport projects often require an explicit local or regional vote for financial support, usually based on unpopular sales and property tax increases. Furthermore, these taxes are unrelated to costs imposed by transport system users and therefore inequitable and open to justifiable challenges. All of this makes major public transport projects difficult to finance. It also makes long-term transportation planning, where ideally funds can be shifted around to the mode(s) where it makes the most sense in order to support of an evolving set of goals, very difficult. Instead, planning becomes episodic and biased towards the projects that can rely on the most stable funding sources. As an example, one of the reasons for the popularity of high-occupancy vehicle (HOV) lanes for so many years was because these could be financed by gasoline taxes, while a separate transit right-of-way would have required a new funding source.

The important point to be gathered from the discussion of funding sources is that real-life projects do not always start with what would seem a logical approach: selection and prioritization of goals within an available budget. Instead, the process can work backwards. Within the constraints on how existing funds can be used, and the real-life uncertainties of additional funding, which goals can realistically be addressed? Which will require strong political leadership and perhaps legislation and votes? Which goals are in practice unattainable, despite their physical feasibility?

An example of how funding sources can drive a project can be seen with the decision-making process of the U.S. Federal Transit Administration (FTA) for the recommendation of "new starts" funding. Figure 2.1 shows the set of criteria that the FTA developed based on the mandates from ISTEA for inclusion of a wider array of costs and benefits during project evaluation. There were several categories of goals towards which project designers were expected to make progress. Note that however impressed the US federal-government-appointed evaluators might otherwise be about the effectiveness or efficiency of the project in the "Project Justification" rating, local funding still plays a key role in the review, through the "Local Financial Commitment" rating. Thus, in order to have a successful review, the project composition must reflect the political conditions required for gathering local funding, conditions that may well be at odds with

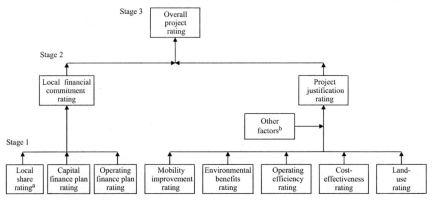

^aThe local share is the percentage of a project's capital cost to be funded form sources otherthan new starts funding
^bAccording to FTA, this optional criterion gives grantees the opportunity to provide additional information about a project that may contribute to determining the project's overall success

Figure 2.1 The FTA "new starts" evaluation and rating process.

Source: U.S. General Accounting Office, 1999.

some of the original goals of the project. It is not at all uncommon to see earlier project proponents drop out of involvement and new ones enter as the project evolves. There is guidance available to applicants that the FTA periodically issues that shares what it believes are best practices that maximize the chances for a successful proposal (FTA 2006).

Finally, there is a growing recognition, not just in the United States but across the globe, of the need for inclusion of all stakeholder, and potential stakeholders, earlier in the selection process. They must feel that their particular goals of interest and their perspectives on costs and benefits are actually taken into account and balanced fairly against the other stakeholders involved. The result will be a better final selection and a faster implementation since the aggrieved parties who might consider going to the courts, appealing to politicians to withhold funds, and so on, will be fewer. A recent example of an improved method that could be a possible role model is the subject of the last case study in this chapter.

Summary

A project analysis outcome is meaningless without stated goals. Goals should be as explicit as possible. Since goals can be of a general or even somewhat nebulous nature, specific, quantifiable objectives must be selected to measure progress towards these goals. Nonquantifiable objectives are not usable. Both goals and objectives can be categorized as to whether they are 1) monetary, 2) nonmonetary but monetizable subject to assumptions, 3) nonmonetary but quantifiable, and 4) nonquantifiable.

I produced a list of common goals. Some goals have been challenged as to their validity, particularly those involving time saving to noncommercial travelers.

I introduced historically ignored goals that involving sustainable development considerations that are likely to receive more emphasis in the future. Indeed, the type of goals as well as their relative emphasis will continually evolve over time with any society's evolution.

One must remember that objectives can conflict such that improvement of one measure can cause deterioration in another. An example would be the simultaneous objectives of maximizing ridership and maximizing revenues. Compromised levels of objective achievement should therefore be set in recognition that not all of them can reach the same optimum values as if each was the only objective.

Several alternatives are usually developed in the preliminary design stages of a project. There is a package of costs and benefits associated with each alternative, where some goals are addressed better than others. These alternatives usually can't simply be compared to see which has the lowest monetary cost. Furthermore, one can never be sure of the outcome of a complex project due to uncoordinated interactions with other projects and due to unforeseen events and unintended consequences. One lesson to be learned is that projects that can serve a variety of goals and that can readily adapt to changing demographics and physical redevelopment of the city and are still feasible even with some error in ridership and cost estimates (i.e. that are more robust) are less risky. They are also projects that are easier to justify in the first place.

Funding source restrictions and political considerations can have a profound effect on the approaches that can be used, the relative importance assigned to the various project goals, and how wide the array of alternatives can realistically be.

Case Studies

The following studies are based on real projects, but, for the purpose of illustration, the discussion extrapolates beyond what the assigned analysts may have actually done. The first case study demonstrates a typical, formal bureaucratic analysis of a new major project. (Afterwards, see LACMTA (2012) for a second analysis example.) The second demonstrates the role urgency can take in limiting the number of project alternatives. The third demonstrates a before-versus-after performance analysis based on limited data. The fourth demonstrates an analysis that was done by a private firm as well as a public agency that considered primarily monetary costs and benefits. The fifth is recent, uses some of the latest evaluation methods and can be compared to the first case study, which used an older but widespread approach.

Supporting details about what are perhaps unfamiliar concepts and computations used in these and other analyses are the subjects of the remaining chapters.

A Formal Regional Evaluation Process— Schuylkill Valley Metro

The Southeastern Pennsylvania Transportation Authority (SEPTA) operates a network centered in Philadelphia, Pennsylvania. It carries about 1.2 million passengers per day, most of whom live in the central city. SEPTA operates a City Division, a Suburban Division and a Regional Rail Division. The latter is a network with seven diametrical lines. Figure 2.2 shows the existing Regional Rail network. At the time the investment study was completed, about 110,000 passengers per day were using the Regional Rail network, whose focus is on peak-hour, peak-direction service to downtown Philadelphia. In the off-peak hours, most routes operate on one-hour headways (hourly service), and service ends before midnight. The existing lines leave large parts of the agency's service area uncovered.

The study was performed in the 1999–2000 timeframe. As proposed, the Schuylkill Valley Metro (SVM) would extend rail service from the CBD of Philadelphia to the much smaller city of Reading, 62 miles (100 kms) away. Also in its path, it would serve a portion of Philadelphia proper, currently served by buses operating in mixed traffic. It would also substantially increase service in a part of Philadelphia that now has only hourly Regional Rail service. In the suburbs, it would pass near King of Prussia, which has a large shopping mall complex and industrial and office complexes, making it one of the largest employment centers in the region. There is currently no rail service within walking distance. Even farther out in the suburbs, the rail extension would follow an existing freight corridor that parallels a major highway. This area has severe traffic congestion, no doubt due to numerous new corporate campuses and housing developments built as

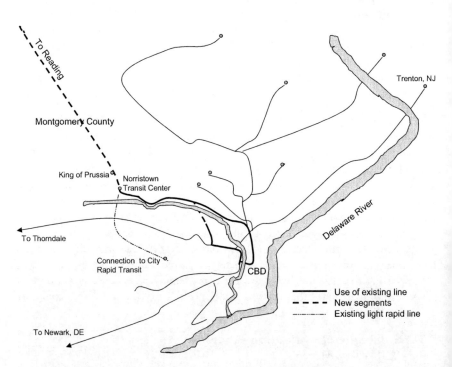

Figure 2.2 SEPTA Regional Rail network overlaid with Locally Preferred Alternative of SVM.

segregated land uses that can be reached only by automobile. The exact figures for the SVM corridor were not available, but the project analysts estimated that 120,000 acres (49,000 hectares) of farmland were lost between 1978 and 1992 in the three counties through which the SVM corridor passes (SEPTA/BARTA 2000). The losses continue. Thus, access to employment, congestion mitigation, and land conservation are all stated primary goals of this proposed project.

The planning laws of the United States require an *Environmental Impact Statement* (EIS) for all major projects that use federal government funding. To obtain federal funds, Congress also requires that the U.S. FTA rank the project relative to other projects around the nation. The criteria include a few measures of mobility improvement and environmental benefits. Operational effectiveness must be evaluated on a cost per passenger-mile basis. Cost-effectiveness is evaluated in a more abstract fashion; the incremental cost per unit of *transportation system user benefit*, which includes private passenger and freight motorists as well as transit users. In addition, there must be a financial plan that proves the long-term ability to subsidize the operation and maintenance costs as well provide the local share of the capital investment. Finally, the FTA assesses the degree of transit-supportive land use that already exists, and it evaluates the evidence supporting any claims that future patterns will be different.

Project analysts began with a long list of project goals and then distilled them into four general goals:

1   Transportation goal: safe, high-quality transit
2   Socioeconomic goal: revitalized economic and social conditions in urbanized areas
3   Environmental goal: environmental quality is preserved
4   Financial goal: resources are used efficiently and cost-effectively.

They then developed specific objectives. Almost all of the objectives used quantitative measures to facilitate evaluation of benefits and for comparison between project alternatives.

Given the complexity of the existing infrastructure, planners had a number of alternatives available to them. The existing rail lines raise the issue of sharing with freight railroads. For much of its length, the corridor is wide enough to allow new track to be laid beside the existing track. Separate track costs more to build but allows full freedom in scheduling and choice of rolling stock. Conversely, sharing track would require some investment in capacity improvements, different rolling stock that is safe to operate where heavy freight trains operate, and schedule coordination. But sharing is less expensive overall. There are also two available paths into the CBD. One is along an existing, heavily used freight corridor; the other goes along a disused Regional Rail line. Both would pass through currently poorly served sectors of Philadelphia. Both could also connect to an existing tunnel under the CBD used by all other lines. Further complicating the picture is the presence of a unique "light rapid" transit line providing yet another path into Philadelphia. This line terminates short of the aforementioned major traffic generators in King of Prussia but could reach them with a short extension.

Thus, the alternatives included variations in rolling-stock technology: light-rail, light-rail modified to run safely on freight railroads, and commuter rail technology. There was also the possibility of electrification. The modified light-rail vehicles could run on diesel, as could commuter rail, if pulled by a locomotive. Although the inner part of the proposed service is on an existing electrified Regional Rail line, a majority of it is not. It would be misleading to speak of one "line" or "route" since some of the alternatives involved two overlapping lines and use of different rolling-stock technologies on each.

The first project alternative was not really an alternative at all but a baseline for comparison. It is called the "no-build" scenario, and it seeks to estimate what would happen if the status quo trends were projected to the forecast year 2020 (20 years into the future). This includes the existing bus services and traffic conditions, plus a factor for estimated growth in population and land development extrapolating from current trends.

The second project alternative was known as *transportation systems management* (TSM). It is usually a required option to be investigated when US federal government funds are requested. The idea behind TSM is that one should identify the easy opportunities and make the best use of existing infrastructure and operational resources before assuming that more expensive solutions are required. Examples include removal of roadway bottlenecks impeding public transport, better traffic-signal coordination, and better connections between modes. See the book created by Urbitran Associates (1983) for the predecessor to the FTA for a compendium of case studies of TSM measures, which tend to be quite site specific. One can also review current individual project submittals to the FTA for additional examples of TSM measures.

The analysis was divided into stages. At Stage I, a "fatal flaw analysis" was performed on a wide array of project alternatives. This exercise identified and discarded alternatives that simply cannot meet one or more of the project goals. This still left 13 alternatives for Stage II, which was a more detailed review. At this step, analysts try to identify "dominated" alternatives, that is, alternatives that are clearly inferior to another competing alternative in almost every respect. In Stage III, six refined options were left for comparison through a formal scoring process. In the end, the highest scoring option was the Locally Preferred Alternative. Only this alternative was to be presented to the FTA for evaluation.

The capital cost estimates were computed for each of these six options based on unit costs derived from similar types of construction and from similar equipment procured elsewhere. Although cost estimating can be quite accurate for routine construction projects, given their site-specific nature, public transport projects often will have unique or unforeseen conditions (e.g. unstable soil conditions) as well as delays (e.g. a court-ordered suspension of construction). Thus, a contingency factor is usually built into these estimates.

The operation and maintenance (O&M) costs were estimated for each project alternative as well. It is not the absolute amount that counts in the analysis but the difference from the cost of providing whatever service would have been provided under the no-build scenario. Thus, this cost is labeled ΔO&M, the Greek letter delta indicating a difference. The O&M cost is not based simply on the direct cost imposed by operating and maintaining the rail line but upon the entire network of feeder buses and other related service enhancements in the same SVM corridor, less some savings from parallel bus routes that would be truncated to connect to the new line(s). The O&M cost computations were based on the local agency operating experience and cost structure to the extent possible, but variations from SEPTA's familiar existing modes introduce uncertainty into the estimates.

Ridership estimates for the 2020 forecast year was based on transportation demand models. It is not only the ridership in the early years of service that counts; the long-term ridership trend is also needed in order to assess compliance with the four major goals. This is particularly true for environmental and socioeconomic goals. It may take years for building construction, land-use patterns, and travel patterns to change as the result of a major new rail corridor. In the United States, planners have less control over factors that influence ridership than over capital investment costs and O&M costs, so the assumptions used regarding land development are important to the accuracy of this analysis. To the extent that development patterns can be controlled, the estimates become more reliable. In this case, none of the options could assume there was any legal requirement (e.g. creation of green belts parallel to the SVM corridor on both sides) to focus development along the corridor.

Three regional transportation demand models were used to estimate travel times and ridership, one from the *Metropolitan Planning Organization* (MPO) for the entire greater Philadelphia region and another from an MPO centered on Reading, Pennsylvania, the smaller city at the outer end of the corridor. In addition, an interregional model was specifically designed to correct the results for the fact that the proposed service crosses two distinct planning regions. The assumptions about the traffic volumes on the highways and arterial roads affect the resulting future travel times. This explains their central importance to estimating ridership in this, and indeed, most major rail projects. But these times, in turn, depend on the uncertain development patterns. There also remains the possibility of a major highway expansion project that could be funded separately that would invalidate all analyses and wreak havoc on ridership should the rail line be built.

Table 2.1 summarizes some key scoring information on the no-build, TSM, and the six refined options. The first is the total capital investment cost. The second is this cost converted to an equivalent annualized cost based on certain project life and discount rate assumptions. The third is the difference in O&M costs over no-build costs. The first of the two rows of passenger count represents both existing and newly attracted ridership on the existing Regional Rail line segments currently in use plus ridership on the new sections. The second row represents the current ridership plus any newly attracted riders on the connecting light rapid transit line.

The model outputs also inform behind-the-scenes professional analysis not reflected in the estimates of total ridership or other summary cost figures. Various

Table 2.1 Summary data for SVM corridor project options

	Project Monetary Costs ($M)			Passengers
	Capital Cost	Annualized Cost	O&M	
No-build				8,680 Regional Rail line(s) 9,230 Light rapid line
TSM	135	10.8	11.8	15,360 Regional Rail line(s) 9,440 Light rapid line
Option 1	1212	93.8	24.1	27,270 Regional Rail line(s) 7,340 Light rapid line
Option 2	1284	99.5	19.4	27,240 Regional Rail line(s) 17,320 Light rapid line
Option 3	1131	87.2	20.6	25,680 Regional Rail line(s) 17,390 Light rapid line
Option 4	1433	110.6	27.0	41,550 Regional Rail line(s) 9,830 Light rapid line
Option 5	1513	116.3	27.8	43,220 Regional Rail line(s) 9,730 Light rapid line
Option 6	1444	111.7	30.4	47,830 Regional Rail line(s) 9,660 Light rapid line

Source: SEPTA/BARTA 2000.

other performance indicators might have been evaluated. For instance, a *direction balance ratio* would show the extent to which travel demand is balanced in both directions. Balance has important implications for operating efficiency and as evidence of meeting the socioeconomic goal of improving Philadelphia residents' access to suburban jobs. Another example is the *space-averaged load factor*, which indicates if the outer sections of the proposed line(s) are largely devoid of riders and the extent to which service concentrates on the peak-hour, peak-direction commuter.

A table of environmental impacts and mitigations was developed for the EIS. This table is not reproduced here, but can be seen in the Executive Summary of the EIS (SEPTA/BARTA 2000). It was quite broad and would pertain to almost all of the options. It included safety and security, socioeconomic factors, and historical, archeological, and cultural resources in addition to more purely environmental considerations, such as air quality, water quality, and farmland preservation. Some of the proposed mitigations were not firm commitments but simply statements of intent to seek cooperation from local authorities.

The EIS also addressed equity of costs and benefits. These focused on the spreading of the service, financial, and environmental benefits and costs over the different income groups and between users and nonusers within the SVM corridor. It concluded the project was equitable, with substantial benefits to low-income residents of the area.

Most analyses of investments in the for-profit sector of the economy are done using *engineering economic* analysis. Using these methods, a project is *feasible* when the Net Present Value (NPV) of the stream of discounted costs and discounted benefits over the life of the project is greater than zero. The discounting is used to take into consideration the time value of money. The initial capital investment occurs in the first few years of the project and would therefore not be discounted much. Once the new service becomes operational, the stream of O&M costs that the transit agency faces each year would have to be discounted back to the present. Offsetting these costs to a lesser or greater extent would be the fares and other operating revenue collected each year as a stream of benefits, which must also be discounted. The question then becomes whether the stream of additional monetary or monetized benefits from the project is large enough to offset the remaining uncovered costs. These uncovered costs not paid by the system users or other beneficiaries represent the public subsidy required. Examples of NPV evaluation are presented in Chapter 8.

There are some difficulties doing an evaluation of the SVM project in this way. One is that some of the benefits (e.g. reduced spending on utility infrastructure if sprawl declines) can be given monetary estimates, but others cannot. Air quality is supposed to rise to a certain technical standard not expressed in monetary terms, and there can be a wide range of estimates for any particular monetized benefit where consensus cannot be reached even on intermediate compromise values. To use NPV and also honor the lack of consensus, each type of benefit for each year would have to be estimated over a range. As a result, each option would have a wide range of NPVs, perhaps spanning both negative and positive values. The comparison could well be inconclusive as a result.

Because of these issues, the "best" option was not selected as a result of a formal NPV analysis. Instead, it was selected as the best performer in a scoring process. An evaluation matrix very similar to Table 2.2 was created. Each of the four major goals has a list of objectives associated with it. Each refined option was given a grade from 1 to 5 on how well it could meet each objective. For each of these refined options, the score of all objectives associated with each goal was then averaged. Finally, for each refined option, the average scores for all of the four goals were totaled. The refined option with the highest score was deemed the Locally Preferred Alternative. Although a common technique, this averaging scheme too is open to dispute due to lack of a theoretical justification. The weight of each objective should not necessarily be the same, nor should all the goals necessarily have the same weight. But just like deciding on a monetary value, deciding on relative weights can be a contentious process in itself.

The Locally Preferred Alternative was Option 6. It is actually two lines that overlap for a portion of the service. It would use a relatively rare type of vehicle, one that looks like a Light-Rail Vehicle but is heavier and stronger so that it could operate safely on the freight tracks. It would make a loop such that both of the available paths into the CBD are served. Under Option 6, the connecting light rapid transit line would see only a minor increase in ridership and would not

Table 2.2 Stage III evaluation matrix

Objective	Option					
	1	2	3	4	5	6
GOAL 1 – Safe, High-Quality Transit						
Transit travel volume by mode	1	1	1	3	4	5
Increase in transit share	1	1	1	5	5	5
Travel time savings	1	2	2	5	5	5
Ease of availability of Intermodal Transfers	4	4	5	3	3	5
Subtotal	7	8	9	16	17	20
Average Rating for GOAL 1	1.8	2.0	2.3	4.0	4.3	5.0
GOAL 2 – Revitalize Economic and Social Conditions of Urban Areas						
Potential to affect employment in urban communities	2	2	1	3	3	4
Change in transportation volume to and from Philadelphia	1	1	1	4	5	5
Potential to affect residential and nonresidential development within walking distance of transportation nodes	3	3	3	4	4	4
Total number of low-income households within 0.5 mile of boarding point	4	4	3	4	4	3
Subtotal	10	10	8	15	16	16
Average Rating for GOAL 2	2.5	2.5	2.0	3.8	4.0	4.0
GOAL 3 – Preserve Environmental Quality of Corridor						
Ability to foster transit-oriented development	3	3	3	4	4	4
Change in greenhouse gas emissions	1	2	1	4	5	4
Change in energy consumption	2	3	1	4	5	4
Change in criteria pollutants and precursor emissions	1	3	1	5	5	5
Potential to affect weekend travel volumes	3	3	2	4	4	2
Subtotal	10	14	8	21	23	19
Average Rating for GOAL 3	2.0	2.8	1.6	4.2	4.6	3.8
GOAL 4 – Invest and Deploy Resources Efficiently and Cost Effectively						
Total annualized capital costs	4	3	5	1	1	1
Annualized capital costs per route mile	5	4	5	1	1	1
Annualized capital cost per new rider	1	1	1	4	4	5
Incremental cost per incremental passenger in 2020	1	1	1	4	4	5
Operating and maintenance cost per passenger-mile	1	3	3	5	5	5
Operating cost recovery ratio	2	3	1	5	4	5
Annual passenger-miles per route-mile	1	1	1	4	5	5
Passenger miles per total vehicle-miles	1	1	4	1	4	5
Passenger miles per total vehicle-hours	1	1	3	4	4	5
Subtotal	17	18	24	29	32	37
Average Rating for GOAL 4	1.9	2.0	2.7	3.2	3.6	4.1
Total of Averages	8.1	9.3	8.5	15.2	16.4	16.9
Rank Based on Total of Averages	**6**	**4**	**5**	**3**	**2**	**1**

Source: SEPTA/BARTA 2000.

play a major role. Option 6 is overlaid on the existing Regional Rail network in Figure 2.2.

At the time it was submitted for review, this project seemed likely to meet FTA requirements for a "recommended" project. It would be attractive to many parties. Its length means that it would pass through 51 municipalities. It would provide many suburban locations with a relief valve for their congestion while providing rejuvenation potential for the exurban end of the line. It would also provide the first new rail service for Philadelphia proper in decades. But the FTA ranked the Locally Preferred Alternative as "not recommended." Although there were other objections, the primary one was the assumption that the federal government would provide 80 percent of the capital funds, even though the relevant federal transportation law, TEA-21, actually permitted this assumption. This reaction created a lot of pressure to downscale to something simpler that costs less than Option 6, as the State of Pennsylvania was highly unlikely to be willing to pay the difference if the federal government gave only 50 percent.

At the time of the writing of the first edition in early 2006, the SVM project was under review by a SVM Task Force established by the governor of Pennsylvania. The task force was to develop a plan for a more affordable project through phasing of segments and level-of-service to be offered. It included representatives from the governor's office and the regional US congressional delegation in addition to the earlier project participants. But no resolution was ever found and the project was not resubmitted for consideration.

At this point, this author deviates from what is a fairly representative evaluation process for the United States to make some observations. Some benefits that could clearly be included were not. For example, there is evidence of significant private savings on automobile ownership and use in corridors with high-quality public transport (Newman and Kenworthy 1999) as well as reductions in water, sewer, and electric infrastructure investments due to higher development density.

A more comprehensive evaluation might have applied sustainable development principles. This could mean that some of the future costs and benefits are no longer to be discounted as much or at all on the grounds that the impacts on future generations are equally important to the current one. This observation is offered to indicate how profoundly taking sustainable development seriously might change this project outcome, or any other project outcome, where the impacts last for many decades. The last case study will present some advances in methodology, but consensus has not yet reached the point where discount rates are dramatically reduced or eliminated.

Even a fairly casual observer can notice that the existing Regional Rail lines are also in need of investment. Given that SVM is the only major expansion of service programmed for the Regional Rail system for years to come, the question has to be asked: What could be done elsewhere in the Regional Rail network with the available resources? Restated, what is the *opportunity cost* of committing all to the SVM corridor? There has been no recent official study of what could be done with an equal investment fund in other Regional Rail corridors. By developed world standards for a metro region as large as greater Philadelphia, the service is quite sparse, with headways of one hour on most routes and limited operating hours. A capital investment of the same magnitude as for the SVM corridor would have potential to increase the productivity of the whole Regional Rail network. For example, it might be sufficient to cover purchase of more efficient rolling stock, of an entirely new fare collection system and for other modernizations of what is a rather antiquated system. The savings from the resulting lowered O&M costs could then be ploughed back into supporting decreased headways of one-half hour or better on all lines and expanded operating hours. Rough estimates using simple demand elasticity calculations would predict significant ridership increases from such major headway reductions. This additional revenue too could be ploughed back into covering the cost of shorter headways. Thus, it is almost certain that, relative to the capital investment funds available, a larger number of additional riders could be attracted and more regional objectives could be achieved from investing on a system-wide basis instead of concentrating in one corridor.

Expressed in analytic terms, the incremental benefit to incremental cost ratio would likely be much higher from spreading the investment across the Regional Rail network than concentrating it in the SVM corridor. Furthermore, benefits related to the socioeconomic and transportation goals would also be spread more evenly around the region. The EIS only discussed equity within the corridor, not within the region. In principle, there is nothing wrong with concentrating investment in neglected areas, as other areas have had their turns for investment in the past. But when investment funds for a region are expected to be severely limited for the foreseeable future, concern over regional equity should be heightened. In this case, the SVM corridor was planned to receive 30-minute headways for base service with 15 minutes in the peak, while other Regional Rail lines would continue to receive only 60-minute and 30-minute headways, respectively.

There would be a way to improve the equity if the proposed project should proceed. Zoning would first have to require that development be focused upon the SVM corridor. The beneficiaries of the increase in land value close to the SVM line must then be made to contribute through tax-increment financing or other value-recapture schemes. Even without value recapture, legal commitment to build along the SVM corridor would decrease the modeling error, and consequently, the ridership performance risks of this project.

It is interesting to note that based upon Table 2.1, the TSM option would also have a high incremental benefit to incremental cost ratio. A small capital investment and increase in service would apparently generate substantial ridership. This suggests a historical lack of investment in the existing bus services within the project corridor. Even if the SVM project is ultimately cancelled, some modest investment in the bus service is indicated.

In the end, before any position is taken before or against the Locally Preferred Alternative, it must always be asked: What are the real choices? This particular project would serve the richest county in the State of Pennsylvania. It is quite possible that powerful economic interests and the politicians who represent them would withdraw support if the investment no longer supports their private goals. It does not help developers in this corridor if some other part of the region gets a new line or improved service instead. If this is the case, the only real choice might be between a rail line in the SVM corridor and a highway widening. As a result, many people who would otherwise recommend a different public transport project might support this project anyway as a defensive measure against the damage they feel an enlarged highway would cause.

This case study illustrates a few central points. One is the importance of having region-wide goals. Projects should be selected based on stated regional priorities and have substantial political support across the region. There may well be compelling arguments for concentrating limited investment capital all in this one corridor. But this should only be determined after reviewing the opportunity cost of ignoring all other regional priorities. Another point is the difficulty of using monetary evaluation methods, due both to lack of consensus on appropriate monetized values and because some goals, such as air quality attainment, are stated in nonmonetary terms. Yet another is that there are additional calculations and indicators that often provide additional insight into alternatives, not only for the official planner but for the concerned unofficial analyst/citizen. Finally, project funds may not be transferable. Political power may preclude the selection of projects with more of a chance of meeting the stated goals for the region.

Addressing Needs of Great Urgency and Severity— Delhi Metro

One of the largest cities in South Asia, and indeed the world, Delhi, also has very unhealthy air. Traffic congestion is severe, including an array of both motorized and nonmotorized modes. Since 2000, thousands of diesel and two-stroke vehicles have already been forced to either convert to compressed natural gas or be retired. But even with these improvements, the situation is still so dire that both the population's health and the ability to attract further investment to the city are at stake. Commercial investment is essential as the population continually migrates from rural areas in search of a livelihood. In this case, the primary goals of the project were quite clear and imperative.

In 1997, the Delhi Metro Rail Corporation (DMRC) was formed to construct and operate a rapid transit network. Phase I of this network is 41 miles (66 kms) long. Three miles (5 kms) are at grade, twenty-nine miles (47 kms) are elevated and eight miles (13 kms) are underground. All of it is fully segregated from all other traffic. Phase I was estimated to cost approximately $1.65 billion in 2002 US dollars. Phase II extended the lines an additional 81 miles (132.5 kms), to be built between 2005 and 2010, and was estimated to cost another $1.85 billion in US dollars (Olivier 2002). As of the writing of the first edition of this book in early 2006, 34 miles (55 kms) of the network had been completed and ridership averaged 700,000 persons per day (IRJ 2006). (As of the writing of the second edition in 2013, the first two phases are almost entirely built out and the total length ended up at 190 kms with 143 stations (DMRC 2013a).) It is currently carrying approximately 1.6 million passengers per day. For comparison, the Washington, DC regional metro is about the same length and carries approximately 800,000 passengers per day.

There was more to the project. Two hundred buses are used as feeders to the rapid transit lines. Parallel bus routes were being eliminated, but 62 miles (100 kms) of exclusive lanes were to be added elsewhere in the city. A Phase III was also in the planning stages. (As of this writing in 2013, the plan undergoing environmental assessment will extend the system another 103 kms (DMRC 2013b.) The modeling and other mathematical analysis used to assess benefits and costs was less rigorous than that used in more industrialized countries. There simply is not as much information available about the demographics or travel patterns of the population. Indeed, the size of population of the metro region is not even known with much accuracy, as it grows so quickly. Moreover, much of the development along the perimeter is haphazard and poorly documented, making a regional boundary difficult to define. Nor is it possible to use sophisticated travel demand forecasting models. These were developed primarily for roadway links used only by trucks, automobiles, and modern public transport. In this city, there are motorized rickshaws and even animals walking in the street. Pedestrians also walk in the streets because cars park on sidewalks or there are no sidewalks.

It is somewhat easier to estimate pollution emissions and fuel consumption using macrolevel models that are based on estimates of total reduction of vehicle use in the corridors where the new lines will operate. The preliminary analysis indicated that a rail rapid transit network was likely to be the only option to reduce air pollution substantially. More current estimates are for a 21 percent reduction in air pollution overall and 28 percent in the greenhouse gas CO_2, in particular, in the corridors served by Phase I. Ninety-six million fewer liters of fuel per year would also be consumed. Part of this benefit is due to a reduction of 2,600 buses in the central area of the region (DMRC 2005). Furthermore, there is potential to stem pollution increases in the future if growth is successfully concentrated along the rail corridors.

There are many critics of such rail rapid transit projects, saying they are not affordable for a developing country. Moreover, some also argue that the need for such a high-performance system is not as compelling as it is for more industrialized countries, since people at lower incomes do not have an auto alternative. Thus, they argue that a better bus network with laterally separated lanes should be created, as has been done successfully in some cities in South America.

It is true that the monetary investment cost in construction for Bus Rapid Transit (BRT) would be less due to an absence of tunnels and elevated sections. But this solution is problematic for cities of the size of Delhi. Using BRT in central district like Old Delhi would raise some other costs instead. Population densities reach about 60,000 persons per square mile (23,000 persons per square km), making the housing and business relocation requirements to widen ground-level rights-of-way formidable. The space that high-capacity BRT would require is the equivalent of a four-lane motorway. This is because passing lanes at stations would be essential for reliable operation. The passenger volumes would be so huge that a broken vehicle could not be allowed to hold up operations. In less central locations, the roads are wider, but the BRT must penetrate the core for maximum effectiveness.

After completion of an at-grade BRT (or rail) system, there would still be ongoing performance and safety issues. Enormous cross-traffic present at major intersections would also pose operational reliability problems to the BRT and possibly excessive delays to cross traffic as well. Intersections would require immediate action to clear them in case of an accident or breakdown or the BRT line would quickly back up. Keeping cows off the right-of-way might require fencing, causing a barrier effect that the rail rapid transit solution seeks to avoid.

Unless consensus could be reached in advance to implement strict traffic control measures, including any needed barriers, the risk of project failure would be high. Reaching this consensus would cause project delays. Negotiating the relocation of businesses and residents would also take time. But the need to address air pollution and traffic congestion is urgent.

The centers of many Indian cities are already very congested. In response, governments have installed regulations that limit the floor-to-ground area ratios upon further construction, while suburbs are allowed higher ratios (Pucher et al. 2004). This only causes more decentralization and aggravates the problem in the longer run through ever more dispersion of destinations. High-performance rail corridors could permit further dense development and thereby address important goals of improved accessibility, reduced pollution, and reduced fuel consumption at the urban fringes. BRT has some densification potential, as well, but if the right-of-way is too wide and time-consuming to cross, or if barrier fences are required, it many actually split districts in a manner reminiscent of limited-access highways.

Because of the city's enormous size, distances traveled are often very long. Travel times between the outskirts and more central areas can only be reasonable if speeds are high. Thus, if economic development and employment access are also to be primary goals, it again argues for the high performance of a grade-separated system. There were other economic considerations that helped mitigate the investment costs. The Delhi project received some very attractive loans, albeit with some restrictions on equipment purchases. On the other hand, there was also technology transfer from foreign suppliers to increase domestic content over time (IRJ 2006). It provided local employment and developed both project management and operations management skills that will be usable in transportation and in other sectors of the economy. Other cities in India are also developing rail projects and the rail construction, equipment and management consulting industries are growing (Olivier 2004).

Yet another justification was that without high-quality public transport systems there will also be more importation of automobiles and fuel. Thus, high-performance public transportation projects also support the goal of reducing foreign exchange loss and dependence on imported oil.

The question again needs to be asked about opportunity costs. In this case, the no-build scenario was simply unacceptable to the state and national government. But were there really any viable alternatives to the chosen one? The BRT alternative was not yet proven in its performance, especially in the central areas, or in its ability to focus development along its lines. To have any chance at success, many public policy changes would have had to occur in a short period of time. There was good reason for decision makers to be skeptical of a lower-cost alternative.

With the passing of time since the first edition of this book was written, one can now look at some preliminary results of the first BRT corridor in Delhi to see if decision makers were justified in their skepticism. The construction finally began in 2006 and it opened in 2008. But many problems arose, because in fact it did not really have the features generally thought to define a high-quality BRT system. Congestion was severe at many intersections due to lack of a preferential traffic signal control system, lane enforcement was poor due to lack of lack of staff, and the older "blue bus" services operated on the same lanes with low precision, inadequate capacity in the evenings, and other fundamental problems (Singh 2009). Despite its problems, it carried far more persons than the general lanes and was fully justified. Nevertheless, it was legally challenged by member of the privileged class who could afford private autos and criticized by a largely hostile media. It was only in 2012 that the Delhi High Court ruled on the legality in favor of the BRT (Hidalgo and Pai 2012). In retrospect, it is clear that the technical, institutional and legal issues were not addressed adequately and the line was perhaps built and operated prematurely.

This does not mean, however, that BRT is not a good idea. Now that its true capabilities and associated costs and institutional requirements have become more certain in the context of Delhi, it will probably be built in numerous corridors to form a denser mesh of high-performance lines spanning the region than could ever be afforded with just Metro alone. The commuter rail system will no doubt eventually be integrated into this mesh as well.

This case is not unique. Cities in the 10+ million population range are proliferating. Dramatic pollution reduction in the core, as well as a dramatic accessibility increase, both within the congested core and between the core and the outskirts, are urgently needed. Given the inadequacy of solutions operating on the street for longer-distance travel, solutions using modes with both very high capacity and speed are probably the only ones that can meet these key goals. Rather than selecting an at-grade mode with lower capital investment costs, perhaps containment of costs of the more expensive solution might be the best available strategy. This would maximize the size of the system that can be built with the available funds as well as bring benefits to more people sooner. In the case of Delhi, the construction (and operation) was done separately from the existing public transport institutions through a separate corporation, because the existing agencies suffered from overstaffing, inadequate revenues, inexperience in project management, and so on.

A key lesson from this case is that sometimes there are few alternatives available. The fact that rail rapid transit projects are perceived as too expensive doesn't change the physical realities facing megacities in the developing nations. In principle, much can be done in India, and elsewhere, to increase performance and efficiency of what are currently largely chaotic surface public transport operations. But it requires political reforms that take time. Furthermore, selecting the unknown commodity of BRT would have introduced risk that it would not deliver adequate performance or attract development along its corridors. In the meantime, the situation would continue to worsen.

Service Revisions in Response to Community Needs—King County, Washington

Many public transport agencies have route networks designed primarily to provide service to commuters headed towards the largest employment center, or centers, in the region. Typically, this would include the CBD of the largest city in the service area and perhaps one or two other employment centers. There are historical reasons. These were (and usually still are) the easiest markets to identify, they can be served relatively efficiently, and the lack of free parking in the CBD guarantees a certain percentage of the market. Furthermore, excessive congestion in key employment centers might cause employers to relocate and cause shoppers and tourists to go elsewhere.

In this particular case, King County Metro Transit, the publicly owned transit operator received public input, and perhaps even some political pressure, to more effectively address noncommuting trips. Specifically, services that could accommodate shorter trips of a more local nature were requested. Such trips are usually harder to attract to public transportation, as short distance trips typically take a much longer time than by automobile. To become competitive, the walking distance to a stop must be short and service must be frequent, so that waiting time at the bus stop is also short.

A service revision was tried in one sector of King County with the intent to compare the before and after performance using a few key indicators (Pratt and Evans 2004). If the results were favorable, similar redesigns of service would be done throughout the system. The key objectives included:

- service between more *Origin–Destination pairs (O–D pairs)*;
- higher percentage of travel market share on non-CBD trips; and
- increased cost-effectiveness of services by carrying more passengers at off-peak times and in off-peak directions.

The transit planning staff at King County Metro chose the city of Renton and its outlying communities. Renton lies to the southeast of the Seattle CBD. It is an older satellite city, but like the majority within this fast-growing region has many outlying lower-density communities around its periphery.

Before the revision, six bus routes extended from these outlying communities through Renton proper and into the Seattle CBD. The revised service concept involved reducing the number of such "through routes" to three "trunk routes," which requires some riders to transfer at a Transit Center in downtown Renton. This would allow consolidation of passengers heading towards Seattle in fuller and/or larger buses and the turning back of some smaller buses to provide more frequent service within surrounding communities.

The three remaining trunk routes after the revision had their peak headways reduced from 20 or 30 minutes to 15 minutes, while off-peak headways were decreased from 60 to 30 minutes. By using a timed-transfer system in which buses arrive and depart simultaneously, passengers transferring at the Transit Center would not have to wait long, despite fewer trunk routes. The shorter community-oriented routes could be timed to meet not only the through routes, but each other as well. In this way, the number of number of O–D pairs served can be further increased, albeit with quite indirect routing in some cases.

The redesigned service did, in principle, meet the first objective by virtue of connecting more O–D pairs via the Transit Center. In practice, it is pointless if passengers do not take advantage of it. The actual evidence of success would be trips made by passengers.

To measure success, planners used the change in the following indicators between 1994 and 1998:

- Passenger boarding totals
- Bus-hour totals
- Passengers/bus hour, the ratio of the previous two.

These were computed for three time periods:

- Peak period hours
- Midday hours
- All day.

Because of major employment growth during this time period, ridership gains would be expected even with a service revision. Thus, the ratio of total passengers to bus hours was used in addition to simple total passenger counts. This ratio measures productivity. If the productivity increased more in the midday period than in the peak period, this is evidence of more use of public transport for non-commuting trips. In order to further ensure that this productivity gain was not simply the result of the booming economy, a comparison was also made to a control set of routes where there were no service revisions.

No special effort was required to estimate the ridership of the "before" case, as King County Metro has long been a user of Automatic Passenger Counters (APCs). Such data are routinely collected, including boarding and alighting counts over any time period and at any particular bus stop that might be of interest; but collecting the "after" ridership data was more complicated. The set of three remaining trunk routes plus new community-oriented routes comprises all "comparable routes," defined as those covering the same service area as the routes before the service redesign. Because so many passengers who previously rode on only one bus might after the redesign ride on two, double counting was a possibility. Careful data collection could help distinguish newly attracted trips from the preexisting riders. This was done by counting passengers at two locations. One location was at a "screen line" northwest of Renton that all through-routed buses to and from the Seattle CBD must cross. The other location was adjacent to the Transit Center, and passengers were counted as buses either approached or departed. The difference between the cumulative boarding counts at the two locations estimates the additional passengers traveling only on the community-oriented routes. The results are summarized in Table 2.3.

The ridership during the peak period on the combined comparable routes did not increase with a higher percentage than the control routes. But, the trunk route productivity did increase by 62 percent during the peak periods over the previous through routes, as fewer buses carried more riders. The hours saved by using fewer buses allowed the redeployment of these hours to the community-oriented routes. The ridership during the nonpeak periods increased even more. The productivity of all comparable routes increased 45 percent during the midday period and 36 percent when totaled over the whole day. This demonstrates that the redesign succeeded in attracting more ridership growth than would be

Table 2.3 Summary of productivity analysis performed by King County Metro

Measure	"Before" 1994	Percentage change "after" 1998	
	Through routes	All comparable routes	Through routes only
Peak-Period Riders	3225	+26%	+16%
Service Hours	141	n/a	−28%
Boardings per Hour	22.9	n/a	+62%
Midday Period Riders	1594	+45%	+28%
Service Hours	54.7	n/a	+13%
Boardings per hour	29.1	n/a	+13%
All Day Ridership	5708	+36%	+24%
Total Service Hours	251.1	n/a	+14%
Boardings per Hour	22.7	n/a	+44%
Control-Routes Riders	764	+26%	
Service Hours	42	+12%	
Boardings per Hour	18.2	+12%	

Source: Pratt and Evans 1994: 10–64.

expected without the service redesign. Because these gains were much higher than the gain of 28 percent on the trunk routes alone, it strongly suggests that many persons are using the community-oriented routes for short trips, thus also providing supporting evidence of meeting the county's second objective.

The third objective of increased cost-effectiveness was clearly met on the three remaining trunk routes. In fact, before the redesign, the productivity of the through routes was actually lower in the peak periods than during midday, an untypical situation. Afterwards, it was raised from about 23 to 37 passengers per hour, versus a rise from about 29 to 33 passengers per hour on the midday services. There is not any "before" reference to compare the cost-effectiveness on the newly created community-oriented routes.

As for the first objective, it was only stated in terms of an increase in O–D pairs. Whether persons actually travel between them is a different question. This too could have been determined with some additional analysis, if alighting counts had also been investigated. This would have shed more light on how destinations changed in popularity after the service redesign. A comparison of the volumes and times of boarding and alighting at the Transit Center, in particular, would shed more light on the extent of transferring between community-oriented routes and trips simply terminating there without onward connections. Such information would have provided a quantitative measurement towards achievement of the first objective, and indeed, towards all three objectives.

King County's analysis of the Renton sector could have been used to improve estimates of various expected impacts of similar service redesigns in other sectors. First, the change in ridership with change in headway, or *headway elasticity of demand*, could give an initial estimate of ridership response to service increases in sectors having similar characteristics. More advanced, a mode-split mathematical model applied to specific routes or corridors would give even better estimates as to how many more short trips could be expected as headways decrease. For specific O–D pairs, changes in walking distances to the nearest stops, changes in time spent onboard buses and, if applicable, waiting time at the Transit Center for a connecting bus, would be inserted into this locally calibrated mode-split model.

When different O–D pairs are analyzed, one might discover that the results will not be equally positive everywhere. Substantial shifts away from public transport to auto might occur for some O–D pairs where large numbers of previous job commuters perceive unacceptable increases in travel time, excessive circuity of their trip, or other inconveniences.

In theory, a region-wide travel forecasting model, as typically maintained by a MPO in the United States (or its parallel organizations elsewhere) would provide even better estimates of the impacts. It is supposed to consider the interaction of public transport service and traffic volume changes throughout the entire regional network, not just in one corridor. These results can then be fed into an air pollution estimation model that might show a reduction when fewer short trips by autos are made. This might more than offset increases in longer trips, as short trips generate more pollution on a per-unit distance basis than long trips. But this might only be apparent using such a region-wide model.

A relevant question is whether a region-wide model is applicable in this particular context. While the "after" transit use might be substantially higher than the "before" transit use, when expressed as a percentage of the total motorized trips, it is in the single digits for all but the peak hour trips to and from the CBD. This could well render the data and hence the results statistically insignificant. This is a problem often seen where public transport is a small fraction of total trips by all modes.

The type of quantitative approach outlined in this case study does not provide definitive evidence for decision makers. The larger question is: What is more community-oriented, local transit worth to the population? There would no doubt be more trips by homemakers, the elderly, and the young with better local services. The quality of life for some persons from this improved mobility and the enhanced "livability" near Transit Centers for others because fewer autos penetrate this district than before must be weighed against the possible increases in travel time for some longer-distance commuters. Expressed in monetary terms, the total summed value of these new riders' time would very likely be less than the affected commuters' time. The latter are persons who are likely to earn above-average incomes in downtown offices in the CBD. Therefore, performance evaluation should not be based only on financially related indicators such as the monetized value of time saved by CBD commuters. It is an ongoing issue that the value of travel time can be incorporated monetarily in the formal evaluation process, but qualitative concepts reflecting the quality of life cannot be so readily included.

Technology Investment Benefiting Private Firms—Portsmouth, United Kingdom

The United Kingdom has a deregulated public transport system. Private operators of buses need to operate on a commercial basis. Thus, investments need to be justified strictly on their business merits, not their social merits. In other words, the monetary benefits must exceed the monetary costs, or the financial position of the operator will be hurt. From an analytic standpoint, this is a straightforward exercise, as non-monetary costs and benefits need not complicate the analysis.

In this particular case, the initial question is whether the private operator could have purchased a Real-Time Passenger Information (RTPI) system and been commercially successful. If not, could it still be done if a government subsidy is added? It would entail installing a communications infrastructure, video displays at 36 bus stops, and equipment on 300 buses (Crawford 2004). Although such systems are becoming ever more common, separating out any relatively minor effect on ridership due to RTPI when other factors can have an even more significant effect (such as the employment level) can be difficult. Nevertheless, there are situations where determining the effect of an RTPI on ridership might be possible. An example might be reversal of a long, steady decline in ridership one year after installation. Another might be when it is phased-in across a large region, such that a large enough database becomes available to separate this effect from others using statistical means. Such evidence from installations around the world indicates that modest increases in ridership of 1 to 2 percent can be expected as a result (Morlok, Bruun and Battle 1993; Bruun 2001).

Since the exact ridership increase cannot be known in advance but only estimated, a good way to proceed is a *breakeven analysis*, which involves computing the percentage of ridership increase needed to just cover the additional costs. If the percentage needed is below the minimum increases seen elsewhere, there might actually be an increase in annual operating profit. Should this value be within the lower range of increases seen elsewhere, the financial risk is minimal. If the investment requires a ridership gain at the high end of the range, there is a chance of monetary loss as a consequence of the investment.

The RTPI system had an initial investment cost of £3.5M (about $6.3M in 2005 US dollars) and imposes a minor increase in operating cost that can be neglected. Equipment is expected to last the life of any bus in which it is installed, the average life being 14 years. Assume that the operating firm pondering this investment must have a 15 percent *Minimum Allowable Rate of Return* (MARR). Any competing candidate investment would be expected to meet the same requirement.

The cost can be spread over the life of the investment, such that it becomes part of the annual costs seen by the operator. The multiplication factor that does this can be expressed mathematically as the *capital recovery factor* (CRF):

$$CRF = \frac{i(1+i)^n}{(1+i)^n - 1} = \frac{0.15(1+0.15)^{14}}{(1+0.15)^{14} - 1} = 0.1747$$

where:

i = MARR = 15 percent
n = average life of bus = 14 years.

The annualized cost then follows as:

Annualized Cost = RTPI System Cost × CRF = £3.5M × (0.1747)
= £611,000 per year.

Sources of revenue to cover this increased cost are increases in the number of fares collected, and possibly advertising revenue, depending on the specific technology used. Ignoring this latter possibility, a specific percentage increase in new riders will bring enough additional revenue to cover these incremental costs. The service area that would benefit from the RTPI system currently sees about 40,000 passengers on weekdays. Assuming half of that, 20,000, on Saturdays and Sundays, the approximate annual ridership would be:

Total Annual Ridership = 40,000 × (255) + 20,000 × (110) = 12.4 Million.

If the average fare paid is £1.2, the number of additional rides required is £611,000/£1.2 = 510,000. This is 4.1 percent of their current annual ridership. Based on peer experience, this is higher than could be expected. However, if the U.K. Department of Transport is willing to pay £1.5M towards the project, it lowers the private share to (3.5–1.5/3.5) * 4.1% = 2.3% increase in ridership. This is now near the upper range of what might be expected.

One justification for the government contribution is the nonmonetary benefits from diversion of previous auto users. The CBD is on an island and there are only eight lanes in and eight lanes out, used by 220,000 autos per day. It might reduce congestion and demand for parking as well as make the central area more attractive. The traffic reduction would be small enough that mathematical models would not be reliable for quantifying the travel speed and air pollution benefits. But on the other hand, it is also known that small traffic reductions at peak times can have a disproportionate benefit, due to the nonlinear nature of traffic speed with volume.

Another justification might be the growing public expectation for more information, not just in public transport but in all aspects of life. The benefit in this case might simply be the retention of existing riders: that is, ridership would have decreased without it. (This hypothesis will probably be statistically verified over time as the number of locations having RTPI increases.)

Now, assume instead that the bus-operating firm already had some Intelligent Transportation System (ITS) technologies installed. Specifically, it has a Computer Aided Dispatching/Automatic Vehicle Location (CAD/AVL) system to monitor and regulate their services. In this case, the RTPI system is a peripheral feature that can be added for a modest incremental cost. If it costs £2,000 per bus and £4,000 per sign to install the additional hardware and software, the incremental investment is then

$$Incremental\ Investment = £2000 \times (300) + £4000 \times (36) = £744,000$$

Again, annualizing the cost and using the CRF for the same MARR and equipment life assumptions:

$$Annualized\ Cost = £744,000 \times (.1747) = £130,000$$

This would require only £130,000/£1.2 = 108,000 additional rides per year, which is less than 1 percent increase in ridership. Based on peer experience, this should be easily achievable and the investment would be a sound one based on the business case alone.

This extension to this case study illustrates the concept of adding peripheral components to a core investment. If a variety of functions are desired, a phased purchase that builds on a core investment might provide a more attractive investment strategy than the procurement of separate stand-alone systems. But to make this determination, the analysis of the investment must also consider the time value of money, as not only costs are postponed. The benefits supplied by the peripheral feature are postponed as well.

For the purposes of exposition, this project was treated as if it was of interest by only one private firm. In actuality, the £2.0M balance was contributed by the local government instead, making it entirely publicly financed. The reason is that there are several private operators in the service area, such that if any one of them were to finance the project, there would be the classic "free rider" (no pun intended) problem of other operators potentially benefiting without paying. Shared infrastructure can greatly complicate the justification, financing, and execution of projects due to negotiations between parties over problematic cost-allocation issues.

A Project Evaluation Using Weighted Criteria—A Second Crossing of the Öresund

The first case study was an example of a typical multicriteria project evaluation as performed in the last few decades. This one uses some techniques that overcome some of the criticisms of the methodologies used. In particular, it addresses the use of implicitly equal or arbitrary weightings of the importance of goals and the lack of certainty about some of the key monetary and monetized cost estimates, which can call into question the robustness of a project. The infrastructure in question is not only of regional significance, but of significance to the future of northern Europe, so it was a prime candidate for an improved method.

The Öresund is the waterway between the island of Denmark (Zealand) on which Copenhagen and its satellite cities are situated, and the county of Sweden (Skåne), where the conurbation of Malmö, Lund, Helsingborg, and other, smaller satellite cities are located. Ever since the first combined rail/road, bridge/tunnel crossing opened in 2000, the region has become ever more integrated, and the capacity of the crossing is fast being consumed. Furthermore, the Fehmarn Belt will also have a new link between Denmark and Germany by approximately 2018. The situation is shown in Figure 2.3. Additional road and rail capacity between Helsingör and the Fehmarn Belt is being added (but it is a separate project). This is certain to divert much of the existing freight and passenger traffic from other existing land and ferry routes as well as generate additional travel demand for both freight and passengers from continental Europe. Thus, a second crossing somewhere near Helsingborg on the Swedish side and Helsingör on the Danish side is becoming urgent.

After much preliminary design and analysis, the decision has come down to three alternatives that are shown in Figure 2.4. The first is a two-track tunnel for passenger trains only, with a preliminary baseline cost estimate of 9.5 billion DKK; the second alternative adds a four-lane road tunnel in a second location, dramatically increasing the cost to 24.5 billion DKK; while the third more than triples the cost to 32.5 billion DKK by adding a single track for freight trains alongside the roadway tunnel.

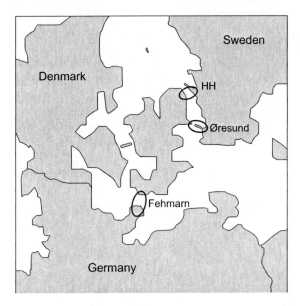

Figure 2.3 Location of new Öresund crossing and the two other crossings.

Source: Jensen et al. 2012.

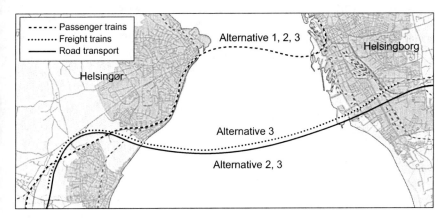

Figure 2.4 Alignments for the three alternatives.

Source: Jensen et al. 2012.

There are six basic categories of goals on which the alternatives are to be judged. The question is to what degree each of the alternatives promotes each of these goals.

1   *Socioeconomic robustness*—The monetary cost benefit analysis should still show a Benefit to Cost Ratio (BCR) greater than 1 even if the construction costs are higher and/or the time savings to transport system users is less than the baseline best-estimate computation.

2   *Improvement for passenger cars and public transport*—This is measured by the increased area of the region that can be covered in the same amount of time. Thus, improvement is defined as increased accessibility.

3   *Positive impacts on towns and land use*—This is a combined impact. First is the aesthetics and livability of Helsingborg and Helsingör with the presence of this major new infrastructure system. Second is the monetary impact on the value of housing and other facilities. Either one of these, or both, could actually turn out to be negative.

4   *Postive impacts on regional economics*—Businesses and residences should be attracted by the improved accessibility and students should have increased housing options due to improved accessiblity to universities on both sides of Öresund.

5   *Improved flexiblity in logistics*—A better network of either rail or road, or both, can reduce the supply chain costs and expand the customer base for industries, retailers, and so on.

6   *Positive contribution to the EU green corridors concept*—These are long-distance freight transport corridors that will use intermodality between rail and truck, taking advantage of the latest technologies. Shifting to intermodal reduces fuel consumption and environmental impacts. But this potential shift will not be realized if there isn't sufficient intermodal capacity available that is also of high enough quality and speed to attract this shift. The existing Öresund bridge/tunnel is near capacity.

The EcoMobility (EM) approach recently developed at the Technical University of Denmark was designed to allow a multicriteria evaluation of projects like this one that includes both the traditional economic cost-benefit analysis and some goals that are clearly incommensurable with it. It is based on holding a "decision conference" with various experts and stakeholders and a facilitator. This person uses some tools in real time to analyze and portray the intermediate results and guide further activity. The process is summarized in Figure 2.5.

The first step was to explain to all of the participants how the process is supposed to work and their role in the decision conference. The second was to go over the criteria that have already been established for evaluation. At this point, the participants can elaborate on certain ones, question the relevance of certain ones, and perhaps bring up any goals (or positive impacts) and any negative impacts that they feel have been overlooked. In this case, it would have become necessary to

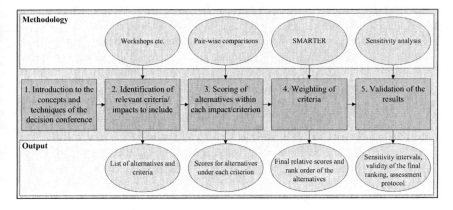

Figure 2.5 Steps of the EcoMobility model.

Source: Jensen et al. 2012.

define some additional objectives that measure progress towards these additional goals or measure these impacts that could then be used as evaluation criteria for the later steps. The next step was then to systematically compare each alternative with the others, but pair-wise, with respect to how well it meets a certain objective, how large the positive or negative impact is, and so on, until all alternatives have been compared on all of the criteria. After that comes an individual weighting of how important each criterion is, so that a relative weight can be assigned, followed by a group discussion and group weighting. The details of the pair-wise comparison and weight assigning process steps are left until Chapter 12, after some requisite background has been covered to more fully appreciate them.

In order to score the socioeconomic robustness criterion, a cost-benefit analysis was performed that included the following:

–   Construction costs
–   Operating and maintenance costs
–   Monetized travel time savings
–   Private vehicle operating costs
–   Operating costs for trains
–   Monetized environmental consequences (both local and global)
–   Fare and toll revenue from additional travelers crossing (above existing ferries).

Under the EM method, the traditional cost-benefit analysis result of either a simple NPV or benefit-cost ratio is not used. Instead the NPV or BCR is a criterion that receives special attention. Although it is a monetary value, it is based on uncertain quantities because of risks associated with construction costs and delays and on monetized estimates for other costs and benefits. Especially significant typically is the value of time saved (or lost) by the various transport system users as a result of this project. There is a significant risk that the project may not perform as intended, for example, the speed improvements are more or less, there may not be the same number and composition of people impacted as forecast, and indeed the hourly value assigned to time can itself be highly contentious and controversial. (More about this in Chapter 7.) So, the NPV or BCR is treated as a range of potential outcomes based on assigning distributions to the monetary and monetized costs that are based on historical evidence from earlier projects having similar attributes. The result is a probability curve, with the most important output being a "certainty value." This is the probability that the project will at least achieve a BCR of 1, the definition of a project being economically feasible in the traditional evaluation methods. This is discussed in more detail in Chapter 9 where cost estimating models are presented.

In this case, the resulting curves for the three projects are shown in Figure 2.6. It shows that the certainty value for the second alternative is highest at 76%, the third alternative is next at 70%, and the first alternative is lowest at only 28%. Thus, this is the order the alternatives are ranked with respect to the first criterion. The results from this criterion are then combined with the group results for all the other weighted criteria, the software is run, and results displayed to the participants of the decision conference. The third alternative had by far the highest composite score; the second, much lower; the first alternative was barely above zero, as shown in Figure 2.7.

The last step in the process is to see if the decision would change if the individuals' weights were used instead of the group weights to get the combined score.

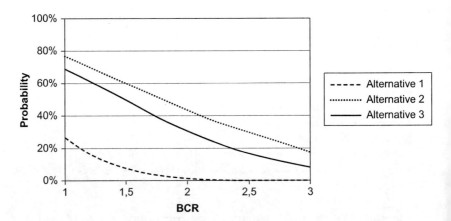

Figure 2.6 Probability curves for the risk analysis of the socioeconomic criterion.

Source: Öresund EcoMobility 2011.

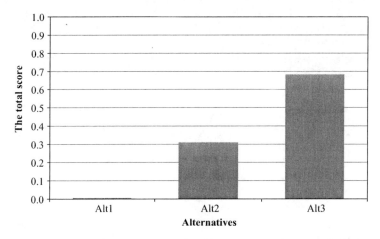

Figure 2.7 The resulting graph showing the total scores for each alternative using the combined group weighting.

Source: Jensen et al. 2012.

In fact, the individual participants' scores were similar and the result would have been unchanged. This demonstrates that the outcome is acceptable to all parties. This could have been taken one step further, where weights from parties outside the group would also be tried. If an alternative is still satisfactory for a wide range of opinions about weights, then it has achieved concordance. This concept is the basis for a class of other multicriteria methods called Concordance Analysis, which will be discussed briefly in Chapter 12.

References

Abramovitz, Janet R. 1998. "Putting a Value on Natures 'Free' Services." *Worldwatch* 11 (1): 10–19.

Bruun, Eric. 2001. "Justifying ITS from a Business Standpoint." *Public Transport International* 50 (1/6) (November): 26–30.

Buehler, Ralph, and Pucher, John. 2011. "Making public transport financially sustainable," *Transport Policy* 18 (1):126–38.

Burchell, Robert W., and David Listokin. 1995. *Land, Infrastructure, Housing Costs, and Fiscal Impacts Associated with Growth: The Literature on the Impacts of Traditional versus Managed Growth.* Paper prepared for Alternatives to Sprawl conference, March 1995, Brookings Institution, Washington, DC.

Chu, Xuehao. 2003. *The Fatality Risk of Walking in America: A Time-Based Approach.* Proceedings of the Walk21 Conference on Health, Equity and the Environment, Portland, OR. http://www.walk21.com/papers/Chu.pdf

Costanza, Robert, Olman Segura and Juan Martinez Alier, eds. 1996. *Getting Down to Earth: Practical Applications of Ecological Economics.* Washington, DC: Island Press.

Crawford, David. 2004. "Port City's Bus PORTAL." *ITS International* 10 (November/December): 30–40.

Delucchi, Mark et al. 1996–97. *The Annualized Social Cost of Motor Vehicle Use in the United States.* Vols. 1–23, Report UCD–ITS–RR–96–3. Davis: Institute of Transportation Studies, University of California at Davis.

DMRC (Delhi Metro Rail Corporation). 2005. *Route Map.* http://www.delhimetrorail.com/commuters/route_map.html. Accessed 2005.

———. 2013a. *Project Updates.* http://www.delhimetrorail.com/project_updates.aspx. Accessed 16 July 2013.

———. 2013b. *EIA for Phase II Corridors of Delhi Metro*: page 39. http://www.delhimetrorail.com/projectsupdate/DelhiMassEIA.pdf

FHWA (U.S. Federal Highway Administration). 2007. *Licensed Drivers by Sex and Ratio to Population-2006 1/. Table DL-1C.*

FTA (U.S. Federal Transit Administration). 2006. *Guidance on New Starts Policies and Procedures.* Washington, DC: FTA Office of Planning and Environment.

———. 2011. *National Transit Database.* Washington, DC: U.S. Department of Transportation. http://www.ntdprogram.gov. Accessed March 13, 2013.

Hanson, Mark. 1992. "Automobile Subsidies and Land Use: Estimates and Policy Response." *Journal of the American Planning Association* 58 (1) (Winter): 60–71.

Hidalgo, Dario, and Madhav Pai. 2012. "A Developed Country Is One in Which Rich People Use Public Transport." *New York Times Blog*, 26 October. http://india.blogs.nytimes.com/2012/10/26/a-developed-country-is-one-in-which-rich-people-use-public-transport/

IRJ (International Railway Journal). 2006. "Delhi Metro Expands to Tackle City's Growing Pains." *International Railway Journal* (February). http://www.railjournal.com

Jensen, Anders Vestergaard, Inga Ambrasaite, Kim Bang Salling, Michael Bruhn Barfod and Steen Leleur. 2012. "The EcoMobility Modelling Framework for Sustainable Transport Planning." In *Rethinking Transport in the Øresund Region: Policies, Strategies and Behaviours*, edited by Carl-Magnus Carlsson, Tareq Emtairah, Britta Gammelgaard, Anders Vestergaard Jensen and Åke Thidell. Lund, Sweden: Lund University, 149–164.

Kenworthy, Jeffrey. 2008. "An International Review of the Significance of Rail in Developing More Sustainable Urban Transport Systems in Higher Income Cities." *World Transport Policy & Practice* 14 (2): 21–37.

LACMTA (Los Angeles County Metropolitan Transportation Authority). 2012. "Evaluation of Alternatives." Chapter 7 in *Final Environmental Impact Statement/Environmental Impact Report*, March: 7–1 to 7–32. http://media.metro.net/projects_studies/westside/images/final_eir-eis/Chapter%207%20Comparative%20Benefits%20and%20Costs.pdf

Litman, Todd. 2005. "Social Benefits of Public Transit." In *Online TDM Encyclopedia*, Victoria Transport Policy Institute. http://www.vtpi.org/tdm/tdm54.htm

Morlok, Edward, Eric C. Bruun and Kimberly Battle. 1993. *Advanced Vehicle Monitoring and Communication Systems for Bus Transit: Benefits and Economic Feasibility.* Report UMTA-PA-11-0035-91-1. Washington, DC: U.S. Federal Transit Administration.

Newman, Peter, and Jeff Kenworthy. 1999. *Sustainability and Cities.* Washington, DC: Island Press.

Olivier, Mike. 2004. "Metro Rail Being Introduced in Seven States." *Urban Transport International* 55 (October): 26–29.

———. 2002. "Delhi moves into the 21st Century." *Urban Transport International* 43 (September/October): 18–20.

Öresund EcoMobility. 2011. *Demo of the EcoMobility Decision Conference.* Presentation on October 2011. http://www.oresundmobility.org

Pratt, Richard, and John E. Evans IV. 2004. "Bus Routing and Coverage." In *Traveler Response to Transportation System Changes.* Report 95. Washington DC: National Academy Press, Transit Cooperative Research Program, 62–66. http:// www.tcrponline.org

Pucher, John. 1995. "Urban Passenger Transport in the United States and Europe: A Comparative Analysis of Public Policies." *Transport Reviews* 15 (2): 99–117.

Pucher, John, Nisha Korattyswaroopam and Neenu Ittyerah. 2004. "The Crisis of Public Transport in India: Overwhelming Needs but Limited Resources." *Journal of Public Transportation* 7 (4): 1–20.

SEPTA/BARTA (Southeastern Pennsylvania Transportation Authority/Berks Area Regional Transit Authority). 2000. *Schuylkill Valley Metro Major Investment Study/Draft Environmental Impact Statement.* Philadelphia, PA: SEPTA.

Shoup, Donald. 2005a. *The High Cost of Free Parking.* Chicago, IL: American Planning Association.

———. 2005b. *Parking Cash Out.* Planning Advisory Service Report 532. Chicago, IL: American Planning Association.

Singh, Jaspal. 2009. *Delhi BRT System—Lessons Learnt.* http://ebookbrowse.com/delhi-brt-system-lessons-learnt-pdf-d178839615.

Urbitran Associates. 1983 *Transportation Systems Management: Implementation and Impacts: Case Studies.* Washington, DC: U.S. Urban Mass Transit Administration.

U.S. Census Bureau. 2006. "Fatal Motor Vehicle Accidents—National Summary: 1990–2003." *Statistical Abstract of the United States.* http://www.census.gov http://www.fhwa.dot.gov/policy/ohim/hs06/pdf/dl1c.pdf

U.S. General Accounting Office. 1999. *FTA's Progress in Developing and Implementing a New Starts Evaluation Process.* Report RCED–99–113. Washington, DC: U.S. Government Printing Office.

Wachs, Martin et al. 1994. *Curbing Gridlock: Peak Period Fees to Relieve Traffic Congestion.* Special Report 242. Washington, DC: Transportation Research Board, National Academy Press.

Wolinsky, Julian. 1995. "The L. A. Green Line: A Cautionary Tale." *Transit Connections* (June): 31–35.

Further Reading

Arora, Anvita and Geetam Tiwari 2007. A *Handbook for Socio-economic Impact Assessment (SEIA) of Future Urban Transport (FUT) Projects.* Transportation Research and Injury Prevention Program (TRIPP). New Delhi: Indian Institute of Technology.

Bullard, Robert D., Glen S. Johnson and Angel O Torres. 2004 *Highway Robbery: Transportation Racism and New Routes to Equity.* Cambridge, MA: South End Press.

Chatman, Daniel, Robert Cervero et al. 2013. *Predicting Fixed Guideway Transit Success. HANDBOOK.* Project H-42, Transit Cooperative Research Program. Washington, DC: National Academy Press. http://www.tcrponline.org

Chatman, Daniel G., and Robert B. Noland. 2013. "Transit Service, Physical Agglomeration and Productivity in US Metropolitan Areas." *Urban Studies* 50: 1–21.

Deen, Thomas B., and Richard H. Pratt. 1992. "Evaluating Rapid Transit." Chapter 11 in *Public Transportation: Planning, Operations, and Management*, 2nd ed., edited by George E. Gray and Lester A. Hoel. Englewood Cliffs, NJ: Prentice Hall. http://ntl .bts.gov/data/letter_am/chapter_11.pdf

Duthie, Jen, Ken Cervenka, and S. Travis Waller. 2013. "Environmental Justice Analysis: Challenges for MetropolitanTransportation Planning." *Transportation Research Record* 2013: 8–12.

ECO Northwest, and Parsons Brinckerhoff Quade & Douglas. 2002. *Estimating the Benefits and Costs of Public Transit Projects: A Guidebook for Practitioners*. Report 78. Washington, DC: National Academy Press, Transit Cooperative Research Program. http:// www.tcrponline.org

Himanen, Veli, Martin Lee-Gosselin and Adriaan Perrels. 2005. "Sustainability and the Interactions between External Effects of Transport." *Journal of Transport Geography* 13: 23–28.

Jeon, Christy Mihyeon, and Adjo Amekudzi. 2005. "Addressing Sustainability in Transportation Systems: Definitions, Indicators, and Metrics." *Journal of Infrastructure Systems 111* (1) March: 31–50.

Jones, Peter, and Karen Lucas. 2012. "Social consequences of transport decision-making: clarifying concepts, synthesising knowledge and assessing implications." *Journal of Transport Geography* 21: 4–16.

Nelson, Arthur C. 1997. "Social Benefits of Transit: Case Study of Metropolitan Atlanta Rapid Transit Authority." *Transportation Research Record* 1576: 125–31.

Owen, Ben, Aileen Carrigan and Dario Hidalgo. 2012. *Evaluate, Enable, Engage: Principles to Support Effective Decision Making in Mass Transit Investment Programs Principles to Support Effective Decision Making in Mass Transit Investment Programs*. Washington, DC: EMBARQ Global. http://www.embarq.org

Sustainable Development Commission. 2011. *Fairness in a Car Dependent Society*. http:// www.sd-commission.org.uk

Chapter 3

Route and Network Analysis

Public transportation routes are the ultimate output of public transportation agencies. However, routes cannot be understood in isolation from the network in which they operate. The network configuration is often central to performance and investment analysis, even of a single route. This configuration is the product not only of conscious choice by current managers but also of the inherited urban form: its road patterns, development densities, geographical features, previous infrastructure investment decisions, demographics, and public expectations. Thus, the existing network facilitates or hinders how well investment and performance goals can be met.

This chapter addresses several interrelated topics. The organization of it is shown in Figure 3.1. It corresponds with an evaluation process that can be followed for an individual route. The first two sections provide background. One presents numerous types of networks seen in actual practice. The next discusses how different levels of rights-of-way and public transport modes with different levels of performance might fit into a network as well as how a network can be expected to evolve as it increases in size. The third section examines the fundamental relationships needed both to design routes and to plan their operations. The discussion is extended from these basic relations into speedup and efficiency improving techniques. The fourth section uses some recent research as a teaching tool to explain the trade-offs of various network design and operating principles.

Performance indicators are introduced throughout the chapter, as these are the means for making comparisons to other services and for informing decision making. Much of the mathematical exposition of performance indicators as well as speedup and efficiency-increasing techniques is shown in Appendix 3.A.

The analyst might sometimes conclude that no combination of modes and services will give the desired performance at reasonable cost on a particular route, or even in an entire section of the network. Thus, the last topic in this chapter is *demand-responsive* service, also often referred to as *paratransit*. This is an alternative to fixed-route transit when fixed routes are deemed nonviable due to low performance measures or because passengers have special requirements. Modern transit planning requires knowledge of such alternatives when fixed route services seem infeasible, so a brief introduction to demand-responsive service planning is also provided.

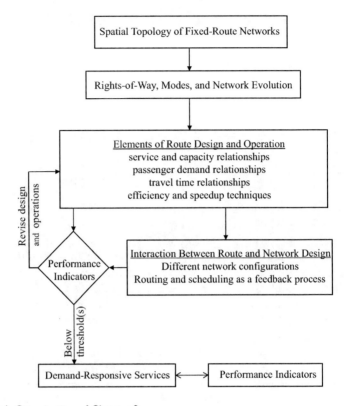

Figure 3.1 Organization of Chapter 3.

Spatial Topology of Fixed-Route Networks

There is a variety of basic network configurations. Some of the most common will be shown schematically. Figure 3.2a shows some directly connected points, without interchange to other routes. The semicircle indicates that the routes cross over one another but that there is no interchange (no connection between services). If there are no intermediate stops on a route, only endpoints, it is a *shuttle* operation. The remaining examples of network types all have interchanges. Figure 3.2b shows a grid network. Each of the remaining network types in Figure 3.2 is oriented relative to a center, which could be the center of the largest city in a region but could also be a subregional center, such that there is a hierarchy of networks. (It is quite possible that subregions will have different basic configurations, especially if the topographical features are different or if they were developed in different eras.) The radial network of Figure 3.2c is distinguished from the diametrical network in Figure 3.2d by the termination at the center instead of continuation through to the opposite side. Tangential additions as shown in Figure 3.2e provide routes that do not pass through a center but instead connect the arms. The composite grid-diametrical network tends to concentrate services towards the center as in Figure 3.2f, yet also has a degree of parallel grid-like coverage as well.

The next figure shows some common service connection concepts. The *trunk-and-feeder* network of Figure 3.3a is like a radial network in that feeder routes converge and terminate on a point, but then passengers must transfer to another route (the trunk) that consolidates the traffic. The *trunk-and-branch* network of Figure 3.3b again converges on a point, but now the routes share the same path along the trunk section. The routes schedule vehicles from different branches to arrive at the trunk section on an alternating basis. Figure 3.3c shows an elbow network, which has the property that each route crosses at least three other routes,

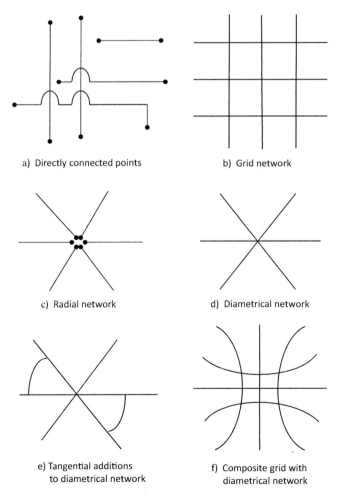

a) Directly connected points

b) Grid network

c) Radial network

d) Diametrical network

e) Tangential additions
to diametrical network

f) Composite grid with
diametrical network

Figure 3.2 Some basic network design concepts.

which greatly increases the number of direct connections between lines without concentrating transfers at a center. Figure 3.3d shows a situation where some services on a line require transfer and others provide through service as a branch.

Another network type not shown is the *ubiquitous* network. It essentially means one that has not developed according to a dominant pattern but has evolved by expanding to connect points that have large travel demand between each other with direct links. The eventual result is excellent coverage of the city. Paris and Tokyo are two examples.

It is possible to deeply analyze many aspects of a network using *graph theory* and other disciplines. Analysts can prepare descriptive indicators that describe network size, form, and topology. As examples one can examine.

- the number of Origin–Destination pairs (O–D pairs) requiring no connection;
- O–D pairs requiring X connections;
- the number of closed loops generated by the network;
- the amount of overlap of routes;
- number of paths between an O–D pair; and
- other descriptors.

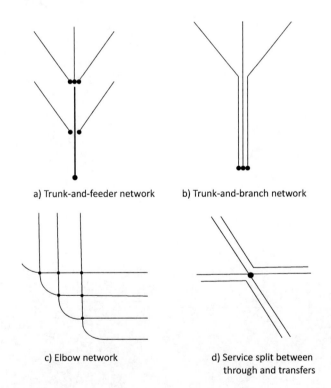

a) Trunk-and-feeder network   b) Trunk-and-branch network

c) Elbow network   d) Service split between through and transfers

Figure 3.3 Some through versus connecting concepts.

These can provide some insights into the coverage by and quality of service offered. Summary indicators at the network level will also work. These become of serious interest when comparing prospective major changes to physical connections and to the operating plan of already highly complex networks. The interested reader is referred to Musso and Vuchic (1988) and Synn (2005), but it is not necessary to know such descriptors and indicators for a basic understanding of networks.

It is important to keep in mind that "networks" need not be comprised of only one vehicle technology. It is sometimes useful to divide networks into hierarchies, where each level is based on services that have similar speed or capacity characteristics and play similar roles. Indeed, large public transport systems typically develop several different network maps showing only one level of the network on each. As an example, a pocket map may show all rapid transit lines and some express bus routes, but not local buses and streetcars. Different maps would have these.

Rights-of-Way, Modal Technologies, and System Evolution

The spatial relation a route has to a network is only a partial description. It also requires that the qualities of the right-of-way be considered. Table 3.1 defines different standards of rights-of-way, with examples of real-life systems provided for clarity. The scheme is consistent with that proposed by Vuchic in his textbook, *Urban Transit: Systems and Technology* (2007a). Right-of-way A (ROW A) is total grade separation to allow for a high-speed, highly reliable, and safe operation. Right-of-way C (ROW C) is operation in mixed traffic, with no special provision for public transportation vehicles. Right-of-way B (ROW B) is in between; it uses lateral separation, typically separate lanes or a median. However, it is not full separation because of intersections. It gives speed, safety, and reliability performance somewhere in between Rights-of-way A and C. As to be expected, investment costs tend to increase with the higher right-of-way standard.

Table 3.1 Different standards of rights-of-way

Definition	Examples
A Grade separation	Paris Metro, Vancouver SkyTrain
B Lateral separation	Gothenburg LRT, Oslo bus/taxi lanes
C Mixed traffic	Most bus and streetcar (tram) systems
Combinations are also possible:	
A/B	Karlsruhe LRT—railroad and lateral street sections
A/C	San Francisco streetcars—tunnel and mixed street section

Three points need to be stressed about the vehicle technologies operated. First, some vehicle designs are committed to only one standard of right-of-way, while others can be used on more than one. As examples, rapid transit vehicles can be used only on a dedicated facility, while Light-Rail Vehicles (LRVs) can operate in the street or on a dedicated right-of-way. There are also locales where two modes share the right-of-way, even though they may have different performance characteristics that might impede one another. An example would be buses and LRVs both operating on a shared right-of-way B.

The second point about vehicle technologies is that some designs currently restricted to one standard of right-of-way can be modified to operate on a higher or lower standard of right-of-way, while for other designs it may be impractical or impossible. As examples, LRVs can be equipped to operate on railroads but commuter railroad trains can never operate on streets due to their length and turn radius. Indeed, the LRV has become popular precisely because it is opportunistic in its use of rights-of-way. The trade-off is that the multicapable vehicle must be more complex and might not operate equally successfully on each category of right-of-way.

The third point is that operational constraints continually evolve with vehicle technology. As an example, there are now road vehicles with electronic guidance of lateral positioning, that is, the vehicle is guided along a path automatically instead through the steering wheel (but without the positive guidance that tracks or concrete beams provide). As another example, some fuels restrict vehicles to a shorter range, which affects the ability to schedule vehicles. As yet another example, electric vehicles are increasingly equipped with auxiliary power sources allowing occasional off-route operation.

The history of transit development is one of continual replacement of vehicles, wayside, and control center components such as traffic signal controls, fare collection machines, passenger information systems, and so on, with continually more capable vehicles and systems. This, in turn, allows changes in the way that routes and networks are structured and operated. Replacement may occur as equipment begins to become unreliable and/or expensive to maintain, but may also occur midlife in order to benefit from an upgrade as soon as possible.

Investment decisions should always consider whether the proposed project should be amenable to future upgrades, to mixing with operations on other standards of right-of-way, and, in general, to operational advantages or restrictions that may be implied by technological changes. Investment in nonstandard equipment, and especially modes using proprietary technology must be done with caution. Future costs can be raised beyond the point of viability. Examples of proprietary technologies that may have no alternative components suppliers include monorails, airport people movers, and bus guidance systems.

The history of transit development is also one of geographic expansion. As cities get larger, they tend to get denser in the center, of which skyscrapers are dramatic evidence. At the same time, distances to outlying districts would become longer. Thus, both the level of demand and the lengths of routes would increase. Congestion on roads would increase together with the increased activity. With increases in congestion and route length come increases in travel time. At some point, increase in demand is no longer addressed simply by adding more vehicles but by the use of larger vehicles. At some point, travel time is also addressed through increases in right-of-way standard.

Thus, there is a general evolution towards more and larger vehicles, then towards modes with higher capacity and faster speeds. The smallest town may never evolve past a minibus or taxi operating on demand. As cities get larger, buses operating on right-of-way C may grow into articulated buses and some corridors may be upgraded to right-of-way B. LRVs may be joined to become trains, the right-of-way B corridor upgraded to right-of-way A in highly congested areas, and routes might be lengthened. In the largest cities, rapid transit lines may get larger trains and increasing frequency of service and the network many continue to expand indefinitely.

Some cities have developed differently primarily they have focused on accommodating the automobile, presenting new and more difficult evolutionary challenges. An urban region may increase in developed area much faster than it increases in population. Thus, density of built-up areas may actually decrease. Metropolitan Chicago is an excellent example: it still has huge demand for travel to the central business district (CBD), but has depopulated in many of the surrounding districts. Over the decades since World War II, much of the population, and many of the newer employment locations, have steadily migrated outwards (Sen et al. 1998). The consequently lower demand for transit through these reduced-density corridors makes the investment in higher standards of rights-of-way hard to justify. On the other hand, this improvement is needed to shorten travel times over the increasingly long distances from the CBD to where the population is shifting. In the United States and elsewhere, the problem is exacerbated in many post–World War II communities. As will be discussed further in later chapters, street layouts that focus and collect traffic on a few arterial roads hinder both transit access to residential areas and pedestrian access to transit.

Research, experimentation, and dissemination of partial solutions to service design challenges continue. The analyst needs to stay abreast of trends.

Elements of Route Design and Operation

It is possible that the analyst might conclude that no current combination of modes and services will give the desired performance at reasonable cost on some routes or in entire sections of the network. One choice might then be to alter the route network anyway, accepting whatever cost consequences that brings. Another choice could be to abandon uneconomic service in some sections. Yet another could be to entirely restructure the network to better suit community goals. Regardless, understanding the network relations between routes will help to make informed and defensible decisions. Thus, there is an extended discussion of both individual routes and the network.

Important Route and Network Attributes

The distance traveled through a spatial network and the routing particulars of the travel path are important, but incomplete, information. The time consumed by the user to travel the complete path from origin to destination further paints the picture. Additional attributes or features of a given route and of its connecting services within the network are needed to help complete the picture. Some that are usually important are listed in Table 3.2. Together these attributes describe *connectivity* to the remainder of the network. Connectivity is defined as the possibilities for, and convenience of, travel between points in a network. Of these listed attributes, the route patterns that form a network have already been discussed. Most of the others will be defined more rigorously in the course of this chapter.

The number type and physical design details of transfer facilities for connections to and from nontransit means is also important and is discussed in detail in Chapter 5.

Some Fundamental Level-of-Service and Capacity Relationships

Some fundamental concepts must be defined before proceeding further. The *Level-of-Service* is the quantity of service available as seen from the perspective of the user. One of the key measures of this is the *headway*, h. It is defined as the time separation between vehicles measured at a particular point, usually expressed in minutes, but sometimes in seconds. The *frequency* of service, f, is its inverse, $1/h$. It has the units of vehicles per unit time past a particular point, usually

Table 3.2 Some important route and network attributes

Route pattern (radial, grid, composite, etc.)

Temporal demand profile on each route (peaking factors by time of day)

Spatial demand profile (distribution along routes)

Operating speeds along routes

Frequency along routes

Frequency of connections

Stop or station spacing along routes

Area coverage

Transfer facilities—between public transport services

Transfer facilities—between public and other modes

---

expressed in units per hour. A conversion factor of 60 minutes per hour is used when headway is expressed in minutes, making frequency $60/h$ instead.

Frequency, or equivalently, headway, is, in and of itself, an important performance indicator for a route from the user perspective. Ceteris paribus (i.e. all else being equal), the higher the frequency, or equivalently, the shorter the headway, the more convenient is the service.

A distinction needs to be made between vehicles per hour and *Transit Units* (TUs) per hour. Transit Unit accommodates the fact that vehicles may actually be coupled together and move as one unit. The terminology m-car long TU or m-car long train, will be used when it is necessary to specify length. (The terms *consist* or *rake* to signify a train of variable length, are also used by many rail professionals). Therefore, the number of vehicles passing a point may be *m* times as high as the frequency. The resulting *line capacity* is computed by multiplying vehicle capacities with frequency or inverse of headway:

$$Line\ Capacity = mC_v f = mC_v\ (60/h)\ [spaces/hour],\qquad (3\text{-}1)$$

where C_v is the sum of both seated and standee capacity for the particular vehicle design. Inserting the multiplication factor m allows for an m-car long TU. The factor *m* is always 1 for buses (except for the rare case where they pull trailers). Except when capacity is strictly limited to the number of seats present (no standees), the line capacity value is not truly fixed, but based on assumptions about the level of crowding that will be tolerated by standees. What is considered merely crowded in Japan or China, for example, would be socially unacceptable in most of North America or Europe. This can be seen by comparison of vehicle specifications. Crowding of about 4.0 persons per square meter is the upper limit in North America and Europe when calculating available spaces. For Asian and South American vehicles, crowding of up to 6.0 persons per square meter is often assumed.

The maximum frequency of service, f_{max}, is set by one of two safety considerations. The first is the *way capacity*, which is based on the safe stopping distance the following TU must maintain when the leading TU begins to stop. This is a function of the kinetic energy that must be dissipated by both TUs. This takes a certain amount of time given the relative deceleration rates of the two TUs when braking in an emergency. This time is the minimum safe headway, h_{min}, which is also the inverse of f_{max}.

There are different stopping regimes one can assume, which are defined by the relative braking rates of the leading TU and following TU in case of an emergency stop. The most stringent is that the following TU could still brake normally if the leading TU hit a brick wall stopping instantaneously. This is reasonable for fully automated but possible overdesign for other systems, so less stringent ones that do not assume instantaneous stopping are often used. No safe stopping regime ever assumes that the following TU must have an emergency braking rate higher than the leading TU. Way capacity only applies to running on open sections without stopping, analogous to driving on a motorway or the wide-open road. It is not usually the defining factor for the maximum safe frequency.

The defining factor is usually the *station capacity*, which is a function of the fact that a TU must decelerate, dwell (stand) at a station or stop, and accelerate back to cruising speed. Generally, the station with the longest dwell time dictates the capacity of the entire line, although sometimes it can be a station that requires slow approach or departure speeds. The time it takes for this cyclic process gives h_{min} based on station capacity. See Vuchic (2007b) for the derivations formulas for both way and station capacity and for some realistic values for different modes.

There are two other important properties of station capacity for design purposes. One is that for any given TU with a given acceleration and deceleration rates and total length, there is an optimal cruising speed between stations that maximizes the capacity. The reason is that there is a tradeoff between the proportional increase in length of right-of-way consumed by a TU as the number of spaces inside increases and the safe standoff distance, which increases with the square of cruising speed. Another property is that for a given accelerating and braking rates, the larger (longer) a TU gets, the higher the optimal speed. Conversely, very small (short) TUs can only reach their maximum potential capacity at slow speeds. (Very small vehicles consume too much of the length of the right-of-way as unproductive standoff distance when speeds get too high.) The relationship between line capacity, size and speed is shown conceptually in Figure 3.4. Again, see Vuchic (2007b) for some realistic values for various modes and TU sizes.

Spatial and Temporal Relationships of Passenger Demand

Demand for travel varies by time of day, and offered services must change as well. Thus, the temporal demand profile needs to be known. This demand profile is

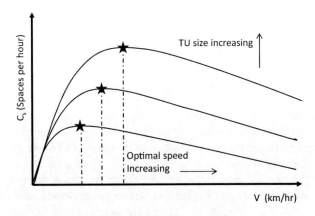

Figure 3.4 Station capacity as a function of speed and TU size.

an aggregation of the various functions that individuals perform throughout the 24-hour day. Typically, the fraction of trips related to commuting rises substantially near major shift changes at industrial facilities and near the beginning and end of business hours for offices and other commercial facilities. Such large spikes in ridership are of great concern to transit planners. However, how much and at what times of day the demand rises and falls on a given route depends on the both the particular characteristics of the area it serves and the role the route plays within the network. As examples, a route serving major factories or a CBD is likely to have high peaks of demand at commuting times, while one serving a shopping district and a hospital might have peaks, albeit less pronounced, in the midday and evening. A tangential connector between major radial corridors could have steady demand throughout the day from persons merely passing through to reach other lines, independent of any origins or destinations along the route.

Understanding the nature of demand throughout the day is critical for selecting types of services, types of modes, indeed for basic network design. Services, even the network configuration to some extent, can be varied throughout the day. The complexity of responding to changes in demand with continual service changes, however, places practical limits on such adjustments that can be made. Apparent savings in operating costs and improvements in responsiveness to demand may well be offset by other costs and difficulties incurred in attempting to reliably manage many service changes throughout the day.

Ridership can be visualized simultaneously as a function of position along a route and by time of day through a three-axis diagram of ridership, hour, and location of the route segment. An example is shown in Figure 3.5. Only five, one-hour sections are shown for clarity. Each direction should have its own diagram. A one-hour section parallel to the position axis shows the number of passengers per hour on each route segment for this one-hour block of the day. A cross-section parallel to the time axis shows the number of passengers per hour on one route segment for each one-hour block of the day instead. Thus, section X-X in Figure 3.5 shows the number of passengers at a particular route segment for these same five one-hour periods. In this case, it is cross-sectioned at the location where the highest maximum of the day is seen. This value is labeled P_{max} on the figure. P_{max} need not be at the same location at different times of the day. The route segment at which this occurs is often referred to as the *Maximum Load Section*, or *MLS*.

The spatial demand profile will tend to vary depending on the type of route. This will place limits on how efficiently the capacity of vehicles can be used as well as the resulting economic performance. The most common type of route is one that heads radially towards the center. It tends to accumulate riders towards the center inbound and to lose riders outbound. Crosstown and tangential routes tend to have more even ridership and to have a higher turnover of passengers. They may build or decrease ridership towards the middle depending upon

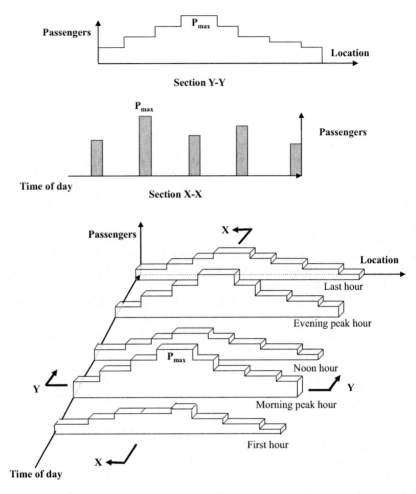

Figure 3.5 Hourly ridership as a function of location and time (only five hours are shown for clarity).

whether they are serving more of a feeder role to radial or major trunk routes or more of a local service role. An express route will be like a radial route in the zone where stops are made and then have nonchanging ridership on the express sections. A route that has large centers at both ends will be much better balanced. In theory, if the centers had equal demand with identical profiles, ridership would be even. Thus, extending routes to reach a second center is highly desirable. See Figure 3.6.

A useful summary indicator to help characterize temporal distribution of ridership is the *peak-hour factor*, α, defined as the ratio of the highest maximum

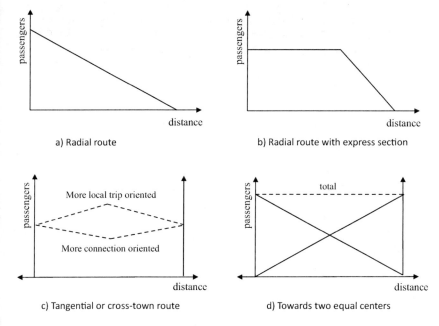

Figure 3.6 Some spatial demand profiles.

demand, P_{max}, to the total ridership for the day on this same segment and in the same direction:

$$\alpha = \frac{P_{\text{max}}}{P_{\text{total}}} \quad 0 < \alpha < 1.0 \quad [\text{ - }].$$ (3-2)

An alternative definition sums both directions, but this obscures when one direction has far more ridership than the other does, and is not recommended. The choice of one hour is arbitrary, so a "peak of the peak" 15-minute time period, or an entire peak period of several hours is sometimes used instead. Obtaining the data contained in a three-axis ridership plot is discussed next.

Passenger Counts

Passenger count information is central to all route and network analysis. Even if it is a hypothetical design, little can be done without at least assumptions about passenger demand and its distribution along a route. In this section some definitions are provided and applied to enable continued development of further route and network performance indicators.

In general, it is highly desirable to get alighting counts in addition to boarding counts. Let $a_{j\,j}$ be alightings at stop j and b_j be boardings at stop j. Let there be n route segments. Therefore, there are $n + 1$ stops, but there can be no alighting at the originating terminal of the route, so that a_1 equals zero. Note that b_{n+1} must also be zero since there can be no boarding at the end terminal. For any run, the difference between the accumulated boardings and accumulated alightings after any stop j gives the current passenger count on route segment j:

$$P_j = B_j - A_j = \sum_{i=1}^{j} b_i - \sum_{i=1}^{j} a_i \quad \text{[passengers]}, \tag{3-3}$$

where P_j is accumulated passengers onboard after stop j, B_j and A_j are accumulated boardings and alightings after stop j, summed from the stop 1 to stop j. The relevant definitions of the boarding and alighting variables are shown in Figure 3.7a. Figure 3.7b shows the passenger count, which is the difference of the cumulative boarding and alighting curves. Note that the accumulated number on board on the last segment before arriving at the end terminal, B_n, must equal the total alighting there, A_{n+1}.

The difference between the current passenger count and the TU's capacity gives the current level of occupancy. When expressed as a ratio, it is defined as a *point load factor*, δ_j, on route segment j:

$$\delta_j = \frac{P_j}{mC_v} \quad 0 < \delta_j < 1.0 \quad [\,\text{-}\,], \tag{3-4}$$

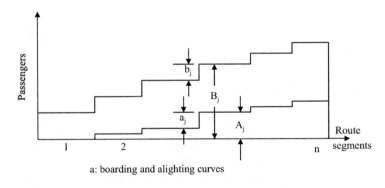

a: boarding and alighting curves

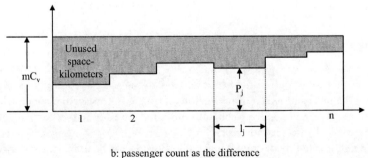

b: passenger count as the difference

Figure 3.7 Definitions related to passenger boarding and alighting (of a single run).

where, as before, m is the number of vehicles in the Transit Unit and C_v is the passenger capacity of the vehicle type. The point load factor indicates the degree of crowding on any one segment of a route. To assess the use of capacity over the whole route, the length of each route segment, l_j, is also needed. The total passenger-distance consumed is compared to the total space-distance offered, defined as a *space-averaged load factor* or *utility ratio*. Mathematically, this is the weighted passenger-distance used divided by the total space-distance offered:

$$\xi = \frac{\sum_{j=1}^{n} P_j l_j}{m C_v L} \quad 0 < \xi < 1.0 \quad [\,\text{-}\,]. \tag{3-5}$$

In graphical terms, the numerator is the area under the P_j curve in Figure 3.7b and the denominator is the entire rectangular area of height $m C_v$ and length L. It is possible to have a value greater than 1.0, in both the point load factor and space-averaged load factor. Physically, it means that crowding exists beyond the standard used to compute the nominal vehicle capacity. This indicator can also be done based on an hourly average, which is the situation that Figure 3.5 portrays. This is then the weighted passenger-distance for all TUs over the course of an hour, divided by the total space-distance offered per hour (line capacity):

$$\xi = \frac{\sum_{i=1}^{f} \sum_{j=1}^{n} P_j l_j}{m C_v f L} \quad 0 < \xi < 1.0 \quad [\,\text{-}\,]. \tag{3-6}$$

An alternative definition gives the *two-way* space averaged load factor, where passenger distance is summed in both directions and $2L$ is used instead of L. See Appendix 3.A for a numerical example. Also, see the same appendix for the concept of *short turning*, a technique to increase the utility ratio.

Boarding and alighting counts are straightforward to measure, but they do not provide information on the particular O–D pairs between which individuals are traveling. In order to obtain this information, a means of linking a boarding by one individual to an alighting by the same individual must be established. Rail systems with entry and exit gates reading a fare card can retain this information readily. "Smartcards" and other advanced stored-value media can add this capability to rail and bus systems not having fare gates, if the media also are read on exit as well as entrance. Least reliable, but often the only way to get trip O–D pair data, is to survey passengers periodically. A complete set of information about travel between all O–D pairs is referred to an *O–D matrix*. Appendix 3.A presents another performance indicator that can be used for estimation when less complete information is available.

Example 3.1

A) The following pairs of boarding and alighting data were collected on a single run of a route with eight stops: (0,15) (2,8) (3,6) (0,5) (2,6) (4,12) (8,7) (40,0). Compute the number or persons on board on each for each route segment and the highest point load factor if the route is served with a bus having a capacity of 60 persons.

Use Equation 3-3. It is helpful to set up a table to simplify the computations, as shown below:

	a_i	b_i	A_i	B_i	P_i
Segment					
1	0	15	0	15	15
2	2	8	2	23	21
3	3	6	5	29	24
4	0	5	5	34	29
5	2	6	7	40	33
6	4	12	11	52	41
7	8	7	19	59	40
8	40	0	–	–	–

Using Equation 3-4, the highest point load factor occurs on segment 6: $\delta_6 = 41/60 = 0.68$ passengers/space.

B) Next, assume that the actual O–D matrix is available as given below for the peak direction and that the length of each segment is 0.5 mile. Compute the one-way space averaged load factor.

from/to:	2	3	4	5	6	7	8
1	–	2	1	0	1	1	3	7
2		–	2	0	0	1	0	5
3			–	0	1	2	2	1
4				–	0	0	1	4
5					–	0	1	5
6						–	1	11
7							–	7

Using Equation 3-5 the computation of one-way passenger-miles is straightforward:

$$\Sigma P_i L_i = 2(0.5)+1(1.0)+0(1.5)+1(2.0)+1(2.5)+3(3.0)+7(3.5)$$
$$+2(0.5)+0(1.0)+0(1.5)+1(2.0)+0(2.5)+5(3.0)$$
$$+0(0.5)+1(1.0)+2(1.5)+2(2.0)+1(2.5)$$
$$+0(0.5)+0(1.0)+1(1.5)+4(2.0)$$
$$+0(0.5)+1(1.0)+5(1.5)$$
$$+1(0.5)+11(1.0)$$
$$+7(0.5) = 101.5 \text{ passenger-miles}$$

The one-way result is:

$$\xi = \frac{\sum P_j l_j}{C_v L} = \frac{101.5}{(60)(3.5)} = 0.48 \text{ passenger-miles/space-mile}.$$

Almost half of all available space is used.

The Components of Travel Time

Travel on scheduled public transportation can be viewed as a series of movements and waits, where the relative importance of each trip segment varies with the length of the trip and the nature of the waits. Although travel time and its components can be understood to an extent without the aid of mathematical expressions, travel time is ultimately a quantitative concept. The relative size of each term in the series of waits and movements, as well as their relative sizes for alternative transportation choices, is central. The viability of projects cannot be studied without this knowledge.

The quality of the travel experience matters as well as the quantity of time. As will be discussed in detail in the Chapter 7, numerous studies show that people perceive waiting time as more onerous than in-vehicle travel time. Therefore, waiting time is equivalent to a longer in-vehicle travel time. The usual method of trying to account for quality is to add a multiplication or weighting factor to waiting times. In-vehicle travel time is rarely weighted for perceived service quality, although this too undoubtedly affects ridership in practice. In this immediate discussion, weighting factors are not included as the focus is on actual trip time, not perceived travel time.

Total user travel time using only one link of public transportation can be expressed by the sum of several terms:

$$T_{O-D} = t_a + t_{wa} + T_1 + t_e, \tag{3-7}$$

where T_{O-D} is the time for a user to get from Origin to Destination (O–D), t_a is *access time*, the time elapsed traveling from the passenger's origin to the boarding point of public transportation, t_{wa} is *waiting time* until departure, T_l is the in-vehicle travel time, and t_e is *egress time*, the elapsed time traveling from the alighting point to the final destination.

The access and egress times, t_a and t_e, are not always straightforward computations. Walking speed may not be constant if there are grades, staircases, or intersections with long crossing delays. Furthermore, although access time is walking distance divided by walking speed, walking distance is not "as the crow flies." A walker must follow a rectangular grid in most cases. This decreases the number of addresses reachable from a transit stop within a given access time. The equal time contour is not really a circle as commonly drawn, but a rectangle with its corners in the 0, 90, 180, and 270 degree positions. See Piper (1977) for a detailed graphical explanation of access times within a grid street system. An extreme case of access restriction, perhaps even dysfunctionality, is a modern street network without pedestrian shortcuts that uses *cul de sacs* (i.e. dead-end roads having houses laid out in a circle.) Despite the physical proximity of an address to a transit stop as the crow flies, the walking distance becomes three sides of a rectangular grid, creating an onerously long access distance. Another example of a serious access restriction, which, if not recognized, would cause a major miscalculation in access time, is a contiguous wall separating residences from the arterial road on which the transit stops.

The travel time, T_l, is equal to the travel distance on public transportation, L_l, divided by the *average operating speed*, v_o. The speed is the result of repeating cycles of an acceleration phase, a cruising phase, a deceleration phase, and a standing phase. Average operating speed over a whole line or route is computed very easily by dividing the route or line length by end-to-end travel time between terminals. Operating speed is, in and of itself, a valuable performance indicator. It corresponds with the speed experienced by customers.

Two situations will be analyzed with the help of mathematical expressions. The first is when T_{O-D} is "short," the second when T_{O-D} is "long." This dialectic provides insight on which components of the total travel time are important as a function of travel distance.

Short Trips

An auto user typically can depart without delay, spending little time in the vehicle before arriving at a nearby destination. Since the travel time by auto is short, in order for transit to be a competitive choice, T_{O-D} must be short. All time components must be short if the total, T_{O-D}, is to be short. But since transit can have other advantages (such as not needing to park), it need not be as short. However, the shorter it is, the more trips that will be diverted from auto. One way to reduce the waiting time, t_{wa}, of course, is for the passenger to arrive just before a scheduled vehicle. However, travelers going a short distance want to be able to depart their origins at random times. If the headway becomes so long that a traveler must consult a schedule, it will be far quicker to use an auto or perhaps even to walk the entire distance.

The general equation for T_{O-D} can be modified for departure from an origin at random times. Traveling without regard to a schedule, the average waiting time will be equal to one-half of the headway. Thus, the average total travel time for short trips can be written as:

$$T_{O-D avg} = t_a + t_{wa\ avg} + T_1 + t_e = t_a + \frac{h}{2} + \frac{L_1}{v_o} + t_e. \tag{3-8}$$

By studying the terms, it is apparent that headway, h, is a variable the planner can influence directly as a scheduling decision. The operating speed, v_o, can be influenced by traffic engineering, by right-of-way standard, by distances between stops and by vehicle acceleration and braking rates. However, since L_1 is short by definition for short trips, an increase in the operating speed will have little effect on total travel time since the term it affects is already small. In order for the access and egress times, t_a and t_e, to be short, the boarding and alighting stops must be nearby. This can be addressed by shortening access and egress paths, by relocating a route, or by creating additional routes. In summary, for competitive short distance travel times, operating speed is relatively unimportant, but headways must be short and walking distances limited.

Example 3.2

A) Compute the total travel time for a trip using three different modes, with the bus having three headways of 5, 10, and 15 minutes.

The total access and egress distance to transit is 0.25 miles (0.4 kms). The distance on transit is 1.9 miles (3 kms). The other modes follow the same route for the same total distance. Assume the following average operating speeds: walk 3.1 mph (5 km/h), bike 9.9 mph (16 km/h), bus 12.4 mph (20 km/h), and auto 18.6 mph (30 km/h). A table is constructed for each travel-time component of Equation 3-8:

Time Component	$t_a + t_e$	T_1	$h/2$	T_{O-D}	Ratio to Auto
Service Condition					
auto	0.8	6.0	0	6.8	1
bike	1.5	11.3	0	12.8	1.9
bus h = 5	4.8	9.0	2.5	16.3	2.4
bus h = 10	4.8	9.0	5.0	18.8	2.8
bus h = 15	4.8	9.0	7.5	21.3	3.1

Note that the bicycle's slower average speed than the bus is more than offset by not needing to walk or wait for the bus. Note also how a longer headway significantly increases the ratio of bus travel time to auto.

B) Compute the total travel time for the three modes (bus for h = 5 only) for a range of distances. Start with 0.6 miles (1 km) through 3.1 miles (5 kms) in even increments.

Distance T_1	T_{O-D} (minutes)				
	0.6 mi (1 km)	1.2 mi (2 kms)	1.9 mi (3 kms)	2.5 mi (4 kms)	3.1 mi (5 kms)
Service Condition					
auto	2.8	4.8	6.8	8.8	10.8
bike	5.3	9.0	12.8	16.5	20.3
bus h = 5	10.3	13.3	16.3	19.3	22.3
Ratio of bus to auto	3.7	2.8	2.4	2.2	2.1

Note that ratio quickly becomes more unfavorable to buses as the distance becomes very short. As distances become shorter, persons with an auto may still choose the bus. But there must be adverse offset to the time difference, such as parking being highly inconvenient or expensive.

Long Trips

At the opposite end of the spectrum of urban travel are the long-distance trips. In contrast to short-distance travel, the operating speed, v_o, becomes very important to total travel times as L_1 gets long. Within limits, travelers are more willing to consult a schedule for long trips so that t_{wa} can be minimized by shifting of departure times to arrive at the boarding point for minimal wait. They are also willing to walk longer distances or, in terms of the travel time equation, consume more access and egress times, t_a and t_e, since these are small fractions of overall travel time. This is the basis for the common North American rule of thumb that people are willing to walk one-quarter mile (0.40 km) to a bus stop and one-half mile (0.80 km) to a rail station. The difference arises from the generalization that rail trips tend to be longer. The actual distance varies from one individual to the next, of course. In general, this distance depends on local walking conditions and is influenced by prevailing cultural attitudes. In developing countries, the distances persons will walk also tend to be substantially longer, due to lack of an auto option and to avoid additional fares.

Example 3.3

A) Compute the total travel time for a peak-period trip using three different modes, where the regional train has a headway of 30 minutes and passenger arrives either randomly or just timed to meet the schedule.

The total access and egress distance to transit is 0.5 miles (0.8 kms). The distance traveled on the train is 12.4 miles (20 kms). The other modes follow the same route for the same total distance. Assume the following peak-period average operating speeds: walk 3.1 mph (5 km/h), bike 9.9 mph (16 km/h), train 24.8 mph (40 km/h), and auto 18.6 mph (30 km/h).

Again, a table is constructed for the travel time components:

Service Condition	Travel Time Component (minutes)				
	$t_a + t_e$	T_1	t_{wa}	T_{O-D}	Ratio to auto
auto	1.6	40	–	42	1
bike	3.0	75	–	78	1.9
train h = 30, random arrival	9.6	30	15	55	1.3
train h = 10, timed arrival	9.6	30	0	40	0.95

Note that the bicycle is by far the slowest option. (The trip would be physically demanding as well.) The train is reasonably close to the auto even with a random arrival time at the station. The train is actually faster than the auto if one arrives just before departure. In practice, the schedule may or may not be so convenient for an individual, as it could imply wasted time at one or both ends of the trip.

B) Compute the total travel time for the three modes for distances ranging from 6.2 miles (10 kms) through 18.6 miles (30 kms).

Service Condition	T_{O-D} (minutes)		
	6.2 miles (10 kms)	12.4 miles (20 kms)	18.6 miles (30 kms)
auto	22	42	62
bike	41	78	112
train h = 30, random arrival	40	55	70
train h = 30, timed arrival	25	40	55
Ratio of timed train to auto	1.1	0.95	0.89

Note that as the distance becomes longer, the higher average speed of the train more than offsets the access time and travel time becomes steadily better than the auto.

> **C) How will the ratio change with traffic conditions?**
>
> The train mode with right-of-way A will not be affected by congestion, while the auto mode on right-of-way C will slow down. Thus, during peak hours, the travel time advantage shifts in the favor of the rail mode. The impact on bicycles depends upon the degree to which they are separated from the auto traffic stream.

In summary, the travel time on the vehicle becomes the dominant component of travel time as L_l increases. Therefore, v_o must increase as well in order to be competitive. Wait time can often be self-minimized by the user, as persons are willing to accept longer access and egress times for long trips.

Timed-Transfer Concept

When services are frequent, waiting times tend to be short, on average only one-half the already short headway of the route for which one is waiting, so that coordination is not necessary. Such is the case with grid systems in large cities, which typically run with uncoordinated services on crossing routes. When services cannot be frequent, wait time between alighting from TU 1 and the boarding of TU 2 can be reduced by using the *timed-transfer* concept. It requires that the various routes arrive and depart at the center of radial and diametrical lines at approximately the same time. In addition to cutting the wait time, it provides connections from origins on one route to destinations on every other route sharing a timed-transfer meet.

If there are n radial routes operating out of a center (a diametrical route is treated simply as two radial routes connected at the hub), the total number of possible connections from an origin on a particular route to a destination on another is $n-1$. Since there are n routes, the total number of connections is $n(n-1)$. Thus, a transfer center with four lines has twelve pairs of permutations of one-way connections. The number of route connections, without regard to direction of travel, is $n(n-1)/2$. Thus, there are six different route combinations that can be paired to perform round trips.

This method also builds demand on individual routes. By collecting passengers with destinations on several different routes this method permits a higher frequency of service on each. This is the same principle most major airlines and package delivery firms use, although they tend to use the terminology *hub-and-spoke system* to describe the concept; but using the highest frequency of service on a particular route can be justified only where demand is sufficient. The timed-transfer technique still allows even the less popular routes to still meet higher frequency routes. The lower demand routes will operate at a submultiple of the higher frequency routes. Only a fraction of the higher frequency runs will connect to them.

Timed-Transfer Network

As a region becomes larger in size but services remain infrequent, one of the few viable methods to connect Origin–Destination Pairs that are not served by routes operating out of the same center, is to establish multiple centers. If there are n_1 routes at the first hub and n_2 routes at the second, counting the interconnecting route only once, there is a total of $n_1 + n_2 - 1$ routes. The number of connection possibilities for each such route is $n_1 + n_2 - 2$. The total number of combinations of route pairs then follows as $(n_1 + n_2 - 1)(n_1 + n_2 - 2)/2$.

If each center is connected by at least one direct route to all other hubs, a maximum of only one more wait time is introduced to any destination on any route radiating from a timed-transfer center. This second wait time can also be minimized if, once again, the TUs meet for a timed transfer. However, having a TU operating from one center meet those from another center is a more difficult proposition than meeting only those at a single center because it requires that both the arrival and departure times from each center be synchronized. Further, the travel time between hubs must be slightly less than a multiple of the headway between timed transfer connections in order to provide time for passengers to alight, walk, and board another vehicle. Such a system is a *timed-transfer network*, or TTN.

As an example, a two-center TTN would have a total of 21 route connection pairs. Connecting vehicles all have travel times of slightly less than 30, 60, or 90 minutes and arrive at both centers at approximately the same time, say 3 to 5 minutes before the scheduled departure time. At the scheduled time, they all depart simultaneously. The concept is shown in Figure 3.8 for a two-center example where all routes have the same number of vehicles assigned, and all except for one route have the same *cycle time, T*, defined as the time that it takes to do a complete cycle of the route back to a starting point. The one that takes double the time to eventually connect between the two centers can only arrive and depart half as often as the others do. Only if the fleet assigned to this route were doubled, it could then arrive and depart from both centers simultaneously like the others.

Operation of TTNs can create an overriding investment goal of shortening travel time of selected routes in order to reduce them sufficiently to make timed-transfer meets. See Maxwell (1999) for a more detailed description of timed-transfer networks and Maxwell (2003) for a hypothetical TTN developed for the San Francisco Bay Area.

Timed transfers have certain operational advantages. Routes are shorter when feeding into centers than with through routing, so TUs return to the center more often. As a result, it can be both practical and efficient to shift vehicles of different sizes between routes during the course of the day to reflect changes in demand between them. If a rail mode is used, capacity can be adjusted simply by changing the length of the TU. This is an important operational advantage that can be traded off against the higher investment cost in rail infrastructure and vehicles. There will be cost analysis examples showing this advantage in later chapters.

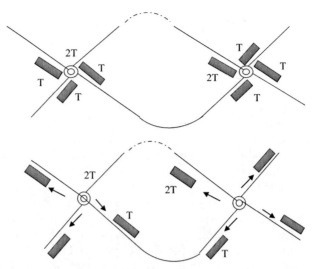

a) First pulse: bus on connecting route with double cycle time at right center

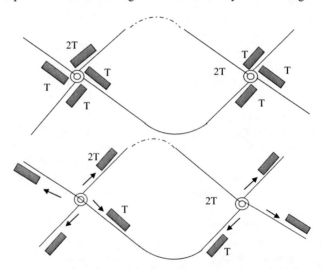

b) Second pulse: bus on connecting route with double cycle time at left center

Figure 3.8 Two center timed-transfer example with equal number of buses on all routes.

Performance Indicators and Service Improvement

Temporal aspects, such as the need for cyclic operations, form network constraints. The fact that timed-transfer services need to meet at approximately the
same time in order to maintain network connections introduces constraints on
scheduling. Spatial aspects, such as topographical features and travel distances

Table 3.3 Some route performance indicators

	Range	Boundary Conditions	Comments
Frequency (or headway = $1/f$) U	$f_{min} < f < f_{max}$	f_{max} is function of vehicle, control system, right-of way f_{min} is set by policy	increases with demand diminishing returns from increase to already high f operation near f_{max} is unreliable
Operating speed U,O	$0 < v_0 < = v_{max}$	$v_o = v_{max}$ express operation	increases with higher standard of right-of-way, with signal priority, and longer station spacings
Line capacity U, O	$C > = 0$	$C = C_{max}$ when $f = f_{max}$	operation at C_{max} can not be maintained due to impossibility of capacity recovery after any delay
Point load factor U,O	$0 < \delta_j < = 1.0$	$\delta_j = 1.0$ full space utilization on route segment j	$\delta_j > 1.0$ means overcrowding beyond standards on route segment j increases towards center on radial and diametrical lines
Peak-hour factor O	$0 < \alpha < = 1.0$	$\alpha = 1.0$ all demand only in this one hour	commuter-oriented services tend to be higher
Space-averaged load factor O	$0 < \xi < = 1.0$	$\xi = 1.0$ full space utilization $\xi > 1.0$ crowded beyond standard	radial tends to be lower, tangential and grid tend to be higher $\xi > 1$ only possible with overcrowding beyond standard on many segments
Deadhead factor O	$\beta > = 0$	$\beta = 0$ route terminus at depot	base services tend to have lower factor, supplemental peak services higher, temporary storage near route terminus can reduce ratio
Schedule efficiency ratio O	$\gamma < = 1.0$	$\gamma = 1.0$ using minimum terminal times	ratio tends to decrease with increasing headway ratio tends to increase with im-proved travel time reliability
Direction balance ratio O	$\eta > = 0$	$\eta = 1.0$ balanced demand $\eta > 1.0$ off-peak is actually higher	commuter-oriented and radial services tend to be lower
Turnover ratio O	$\tau > = 1.0$	$\tau = 1.0$ no turnover	radial tends to be lower, tangential and grid to be higher radial can be increased by short-distance fares on outer segments

U = of interest to user, O = of interest to operator.

along routes as well as distances to and from depots, form additional network constraints. Performance indicators that quantify some of these effects are in Appendix 3.A.

Since routes and the schedules under which they operate are central elements of the product delivered to the public, service must be designed primarily to meet the public's needs. The requirement to both work within the network constraints and yet also provide an effective service (i.e. one responsive to the public needs) can limit the efficiency of the use of resources. Thus, a public transport system could have a dedicated work force with efficient work rules, use modern equipment that is inexpensive to operate, and still have relatively low efficiency. The converse could also be true. Nevertheless, in the interest of making the best use of resources, there are almost always measures available that can be taken to speed up service and improve efficiency. Some of these are also presented in Appendix 3.A.

The performance indicators presented in this chapter are summarized in Table 3.3. They are only suggestive. Analysts should always consider creating additional indicators that fit the peculiarities of their particular project. Only four of the indicators are of interest to the system user, while all of them are of interest to the agency planning the service. The two load indicators, operating speed, schedule efficiency, and turnover ratio all focus on an individual route and are computed for individual runs. A time-averaged indicator can easily be created for each by summing the individual results for each run and dividing by the number of runs.

Interaction Between Route and Network Design

The effect on the network from the existence of a route must also be considered. The complex interaction between variables, however, makes estimation of the effects from changes to a given route upon the network a tricky business. This holds true even with the assistance of mathematical models available to some analysts. These may overcome large computational burdens but do not overcome the often limited understanding of these interactions. Therefore, one must try to anticipate relevant interactions and consider them even without the aid of models.

Different Network Configurations Having an Equal Operating Budget

A route's performance before and after a change will be evaluated differently if it is viewed as an independent entity instead of as an element in a more complex mechanism. Nowhere does this difference between individual route performance and network performance come into sharper relief than in the issue of introducing transfers. The differences will be analyzed with the aid of two recent studies. The first study analyzes an isolated route as through service and the same service involving an intermediate transfer. The second study analyzes the different factors that influence route design and transfers between routes.

Liu, Pendyala, and Polzin (1998) provide an analysis of the effects of transfers on ridership on a single route using a mathematical simulation model from a New Jersey Transit study of the New York–New Jersey commuting corridor. It thus builds its analysis upon aggregated statistics that include potential passengers from high-income, exclusive neighborhoods of lower-density as well as urban poor living in much denser, traditional communities. Not surprisingly, ridership decreases when routes are broken into shorter sections and transfers are introduced. They find this result "discouraging," because even though steps can be taken to decrease the transfer wait time, the transfer itself is not eliminated. This is too pessimistic, since their underlying assumption is one of constant frequency of service. If more than one route can be altered at the same time to allow transfers between them at a common location, as is usually the case in real networks, a more relevant assumption is one of equal operating budgets for several alternative bundles of services within the same area.

As an example, Figure 3.9 shows a commonplace situation where there are three basic types of service configuration that might serve a subregion distant from the center of a network. Assuming a similar operating budget for each one, a listing of some key attributes or features is provided for comparison. The first is direct service to the center on each route, another merges them at a common trunk section, and the third breaks the routes into segments terminating between outer and trunk sections, mandating a transfer to continue towards the center.

The left-most or "direct radial" configuration in Figure 3.9 provides direct routing towards the center. It provides the shortest travel time and direct service to the center, but it requires travelers going to destinations on other routes to transfer in the center. Thus, except for destinations on the same route, routing is circuitous and travel time is long.

The middle or "radial branches sharing common trunk section" configuration reroutes travelers to and from the outer branches to a common trunk section. It improves connectivity because it opens up the possibility of transfers between outer points on the branches without going all of the way to the center first. Focusing on only one route highlights the negatives of a more circuitous trip for those going to the center and the need to transfer for those going between outer points, while neglecting the positive features. One of these positive points is the very existence of connections between outer origins and destinations without going all of the way to the center. In reality, there may never be a more direct route between them when there is low demand. If there is, it will likely be of low frequency.

There is another potential positive for the network as well from the "radial branches sharing trunk section" configuration. It increases the frequency of service and capacity along the corridor into which all of the routes have been funneled. Thus, this reconfiguration would be very attractive in situations where one corridor needs more service and the inner areas through which the other routes would no longer operate still have sufficient coverage from other routes.

So far, the middle configuration in Figure 3.9 has not enabled increased frequency on the branches. For a route operating with a given vehicle size, replacement with smaller vehicles is always a possibility in order to increase frequency along the entire route, but this is often impractical. Operating costs do not go down in direct proportion with vehicle size, so total capacity would be reduced. Moreover, if the trunk route is already congested, more vehicles only aggravate the situation.

Now the logic of the right-most configuration in Figure 3.9, the "radial feeders with separate trunk section," becomes clear. If connectivity between outer points is important, traffic needs to meet at a common point closer to the outer ends. If this has to be done in any case, a cooperative use of modes can improve frequency on the branches as well as the trunk. By operating fewer but higher capacity TUs on the trunk section, the saved Vehicle-Hours from the smaller vehicles that otherwise would have operated on this section can be reinvested into increasing the frequency along the branches. Thus, even better connectivity can be offered to all points. The Liu et al. (1998) model did not consider this possibility but did recognize the negative attribute of the separate trunk section configuration; the fact that transfers are now mandatory for all travelers between the trunk and branches. Nevertheless, on balance, this is often a good trade-off when viewed from a network perspective.

There is empirical evidence to support this contention. Thompson and Matoff (2003) compared nine US transit systems. They were categorized as:

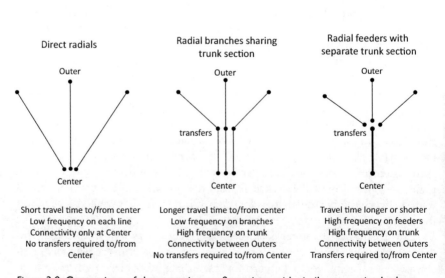

Figure 3.9 Comparison of three service configurations with similar operating budgets.

1   traditional all-bus radial systems serving the downtown;
2   mixed bus and rail radial systems serving the downtown;
3   express bus services superimposed on the radial services; and,
4   what they refer to as "postmodern" systems, which are essentially trunk-feeder systems.

They found that the postmodern systems had lower costs per passenger and that they had more off-peak trips. This is as expected because they had a larger number of destinations available throughout the day. Furthermore, the traditional radial systems had declined in ridership while the express bus services showed modest ridership gains, but the postmodern systems showed the largest ridership gains. These results have been further corroborated by studies of additional US cities by Brown and Thompson (2008, 2009).

An interesting extension to their research is the idea of still trying to serve multiple destinations across the region with similar service levels, instead of focusing on the CBD, even when there is no rail mode. They found large differences in performance between two regions that have many features in common (the counties surrounding Ft. Lauderdale and Ft. Worth), including similar funding support levels. The former, that uses a grid design, gets substantially higher ridership than the Ft. Worth network that is focused more radially on the CBD (Brown and Thompson, 2012).

The need to accommodate a large accumulation of passengers also can be an argument for the use of a separate trunk configuration. At some point, an upgrade of the trunk to the ROW B for its entire length or even to ROW A standard becomes justified. Many large public transport networks with very high ridership use the radial feeders with separate trunk configuration and witness a large volume of transfers. When rail technology is used, another advantage of this configuration is that peak demands on the trunk can be accommodated at low marginal cost, through the simple lengthening of TUs. Some examples will be given in the chapters on cost estimation.

However, any cost savings from this accumulation of passengers is very much dependent upon the local prevailing labor costs. Del Mistro and Bruun (2012) found that the relative operating cost for the buses on the recently installed Bus Rapid Transit system in Cape Town, South Africa provide no real cost advantage given the low costs of the existing minibus services, even with the advantage of high speeds on a substantial section of ROW A. This would continue to hold true even with for a range of higher costs associated with strict safety and crowding standards and moderate increases in hourly wages. There may still be service advantages, but only if headways are so short that transfer times are minimal from the minibus feeder lines. Otherwise, if headways are long for the larger vehicles on the trunk route, in theory, minibuses should also be allowed to merge onto the ROW A section, thus avoiding transfers, if this provides a faster and more reliable overall travel time than using the previous routes. Similar results would no doubt hold true in many other locations where labor costs are low.

Routing and Scheduling as a Feedback Process

The traditional method of analyzing networks is to separate the routing phase from the scheduling phase. Routes are first created that reflect the designers' knowledge about travel patterns and existing available infrastructure. Scheduling then follows as a procedure to match supply with demand but, ideally, there should be feedback. The total user trip time of passengers should be considered and fed back to the route generation stage. In actuality, access and egress times usually treated as constants can instead be treated as variables to be influenced by the location of routes. The waiting times are also influenced by frequency of service, which again depends upon route network design. The in-vehicle travel time, too, is influenced by the *circuity* of routing, defined as the ratio of actual path traveled to the shortest path. Once again, this is a function of network design. Figure 3.10 shows scheduling that incorporates all of these aspects in the routing analysis in an iterative process.

In practice, routing and scheduling have rarely been done simultaneously except in the most theoretical manner to gain general insights. The problem is too complex mathematically; the complete form is an optimizing mathematical program of astronomical computational size and fearsome complexity, which includes integer variables and nonlinear constraints. Approaches have been used historically that reduce the problem size by discarding unlikely routing possibilities early in the process and through mathematical simplifications that exclude a few of the variables affecting total user travel times. Optimization is then aimed at one of three objectives:

1   minimization of the sum of all user travel times (not including access and egress times);
2   minimization of operating costs as approximated by the total number of vehicle operating hours and kilometers; or
3   minimization of total social cost, which is, in effect, some combination of low user travel times and low operating costs.

In the third optimization objective, the one most applicable to real network designs, the results are typically candidate route network designs that provide a paired set of a good service solution to the public with a low-cost solution to the operator. This requires a sophisticated analyst who understands the model limitations, can pre-reject poor candidate solutions, and can then select among results that require multiobjective trade-off. These stringent requirements have resulted in its limited applicability in the real world to date.

Research by Lee (1998) fully incorporates user total travel time. It avoids the massive optimization problem and resulting implications for advanced analyst ability as well as undesirable simplifications that partially defeat the purpose of the analysis. Instead, starting with a given set of origins and destinations (an O–D matrix), it initially provides direct connections where passenger flows are high,

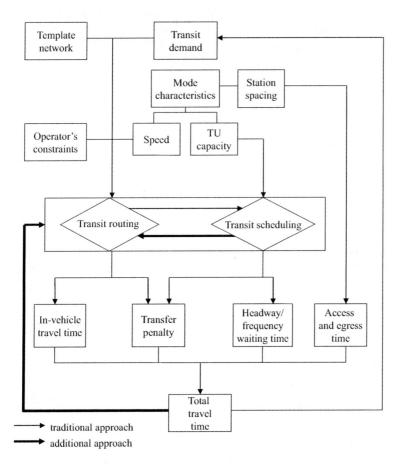

Figure 3.10 Relationship between routing and scheduling.

Source: Lee, 1998.

and frequent connecting routes from areas where passenger flows are lower. It then iteratively adjusts routes and frequency of service on routes (scheduling) until the minimum sum total of all user travel time is achieved. This is not a true optimization procedure but provides a "near optimum." Its results are insightful and the approach can even be implemented for real-life project analyses.

In Lee's model, there are three critical input variables the analyst can adjust: level of passenger demand, travel time on links, and the transfer penalty. This penalty takes the form of weighting factor applied to waiting times. The first two types of inputs are clearly grounded in physical reality, whereas the transfer penalty represents an average that could change with time, change with the types of passengers, and change with quality of transfer facilities. It must be seen for its relative rather than absolute influence on results.

Lee describes three distinctly different types of networks generated according to the relative values of the input variables: demand level, travel speed, and the transfer penalty. Figure 3.11 is an aid to help to explain the differences. It has a matrix of nine points, each of which must be served as both an origin and destination. The demand between the various O–D pairs and the operating budget are both fixed. Each different route connecting some of these points uses a different line type to distinguish it.

The *transfer-oriented* network is shown in Figure 3.11a. It consists of relatively few, short routes with relatively high frequencies, and tends to provide moderate in-vehicle travel times. Two of the routes are short, connecting only three points, the third extending between five points. Transfers take place at the middle of the network between three diametrical routes. Despite transfers, the waiting times are relatively short, due to the relatively high frequencies.

The *transfer-avoidance* network is shown in Figure 3.11b. There are still only three routes, but they meander. Two of them connect six points, the third connecting seven. It has somewhat lower frequencies because longer routes spread the limited number of vehicles the operating budget can support farther apart. It also has longer in-vehicle travel times on average for its passengers because of longer, more circuitous routing. There may still be attractive transfer points, but the average waiting times will be somewhat longer since frequencies are somewhat lower.

The *directly connected* network is shown in Figure 3.11c. There are now 10 routes, none of which connects more than three points. Although the routes are short, because they are so numerous, average frequency must be substantially lowered. It has the shortest travel times underway and relatively few transfers because of direct connections for the majority of popular O–D pairs. However, because frequency is lowered, there is likely to be a longer wait for a vehicle. Furthermore, for those trips that do require a transfer, a long wait time is again likely.

Lee also studied a much larger hypothetical simultaneous routing and scheduling problem. He found solutions that could be characterized as each the three aforementioned types of networks. Lee then subjected each type of network to "high" or "low" input values for demand, travel speed and transfer penalty, in various combinations. Some interesting relationships between network type and the levels of these inputs were identified.

Each network type is evaluated as being incompatible/inferior performance, adequate performance, or good performance after being subjected to these different combinations of input values. The transfer-oriented network can give good or adequate performance at any level of demand. High travel speeds actually favor it because speed can compensate for the long waiting times for connections riders might expect under low demand conditions. Not surprisingly, and indeed by definition, a high transfer penalty discourages use of a transfer-oriented network. The transfer-avoided network, also as to be expected, has good performance with a high transfer penalty, but only in combination with a high travel speed. This is

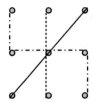

a. transfer-oriented transit network

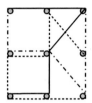

b. transfer-avoidance transit network

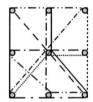

c. directly connected transit network

Note: different line styles are used to indicate individual routes

Figure 3.11 Three types of transit networks.

Source: Lee, 1998.

because circuitous routing combines with low travel speed to cause excessively long user travel times. Nor does the transfer-avoidance network perform well when demand is high. If demand is high, frequent service can be justified; the circuitous routing causes more delay than would be caused by transfer wait times. Lastly, the directly connected network seems to work adequately with most input values, except for the important and common case of low demand levels. This is not surprising because frequencies must then also be low and, consequently, wait times must be long. These results are summarized in Liu et al.'s (1998) conclusion that not properly including the transfer effect will overestimate ridership can be elaborated upon and somewhat disputed with these additional insights. Looking at the parameters they used, it represents a composite of potential users, so it is not known what the specific transfer penalty would be for subclasses of potential users. The penalty would be lower for captive riders having few alternatives, the young and fit, leisure travelers, and others with trips of a nonwork nature. It would be higher when and where the network caters to auto owners, higher income persons, and so on. Since the transfer penalty will vary from high to low given this wide range of user types, it would be more accurate to use a prediction model where the high transfer penalty is applied to only part of the population. Moreover, the effect on ridership might be offset, perhaps even more than offset, by the increased number of destinations and frequency enabled by the existence of a transfer point.

Many small networks in the developed countries would likely be classified according to Lee's scheme as having low demand and low travel speed inputs, with transfer penalty ranging on the low side. This follows from the type of ridership that can be expected. Most persons with a high penalty would use autos almost exclusively. Under these circumstances, referring again to Table 3.4, the direct-connected network and transfer-avoided network would both be ill advised. The former because the service frequency would be very low, the latter because the trip times underway would be very long. This leaves the transfer-oriented network, as it is the only one that can give overall adequate service under these circumstances. This probably explains the widespread use of timed-transfer centers in small networks.

Network Economies

The current discussion, even though it refers to research using mathematical models, really does not express controversial conclusions. It is well known that there are *economies of density*, meaning that high density of demand makes route and networks more efficient. It is also well known that there are *economies of scale*, meaning that large systems can collect passengers from more routes who are interested in connecting to any other particular route, again raising efficiency. The small systems, minimally funded systems, and low-density systems that evolved towards transfers did so because it is the best option they have to the challenge of operating in far-from-ideal circumstances.

Table 3.4 Conceptual relationship among network types and critical inputs

	Demand		Travel Speed		Transfer Penalty	
	High	Low	High	Low	High	Low
Transfer-oriented network	O	O	O	--	X	O
Transfer-avoidance network	X	O	--	X	O	--
Directly connected network	O	X	O	O	O	O

O = good or adequate, X = inferior or incompatible, -- = no strong relationship.
Source: Lee, 1998.

Network operations research models raise another interesting issue. Depending upon the objectives set for them, a different right-of-way in the same corridor could have been selected for a high-capacity, high-frequency operation with parallel routes receiving much less service or finding themselves redesigned to feed the higher capacity route. Conversely, several parallel routes of similar capacity and frequency might have been created. This throws into question the concept of *cross-subsidizing* routes. Economists arguing for deregulation of buses in the United Kingdom argued that better performing routes should not have to subsidize inferior ones, but when viewed from a network perspective, individual routes do not exist only to serve particular communities but to serve larger objectives, such as the need to concentrate passenger flows for the sake of high-frequency service. Allowing higher fares to be charged or service to be removed because a route is not "profitable" might disrupt system design and arbitrarily penalize those using the inferior route. The empirical evidence from the early years following the UK deregulation did indeed show network performance degradation through large ridership losses after reduction of service on some unprofitable routes (Pickup et al. 1991; Fawkner 1995). More recent trends and government responses to them are discussed in Chapter 11.

Demand-Responsive Services

When performance indicators reveal that a service is below an acceptable threshold, an alternative to fixed routes can be considered. There are several typical types of applications for demand-responsive services. They can serve low-demand areas, perhaps in the productivity range of 1 to 10 persons per Vehicle-Hour. Of increasing importance is the accommodation of persons with disabilities that prevent or deter them from using fixed routes. Since they usually use smaller vehicles, they can go where these larger vehicles cannot fit or are not welcome. They can also serve infrequently made trips between O–D pairs that fixed routes cannot serve effectively. In sum, they can extend the network into fringe areas and to people who otherwise could not be accommodated.

The key characteristic of all demand-responsive services is that they depend upon the specific requests they receive. In addition, such services may have no preset route and offer nonexclusive rides, such that pickups and drop-offs overlap. The cost of providing service and the quality of the service are highly dependent upon the rules used to assign trips. Taxis provide the best service by having no schedule, by responding immediately, by having no route of any kind, and, in most cases, by carrying only one party. Accordingly, they usually cost the most to provide. To control costs, publicly funded services usually offer a less exclusive service. Selecting a demand-responsive service design and its operating rules is a large topic all by itself. There is also a lot of controversy over what the best solution is given the specifics of the operating environment and the potential ridership. It can be very hard to estimate what the costs and revenues of an alternative service would be in order to make a comparison and it can be quite impractical to disrupt user expectations with continual experimentation. Furthermore, services are often regulated as to the objectives that they must meet in order to prioritize use of a tight budget, further constraining experimentation. As a result, planners rely heavily on peer examples. They also depend upon software assistance to design and analyze services, even if the underlying assumptions imbedded in this software and the implications for this proposed service design may not be fully understood.

The design principle for basic taxi service is quite simple. First, distribute taxis to areas where experience has shown that demand is likely to be present. Some demand is then matched simply by hailing from the street. The remaining trip requests are accepted by telecommunications and assigned to vehicles nearby. In some applications, each vehicle's location and status is continually reported to the dispatcher to improve the assignment process. In smaller towns, the vehicles may just be waiting at a stand since the response time is short under all circumstances.

East 2nd Street? The "on-demand" fixed-route service design is also quite simple. The vehicle operates on a fixed route, but it is only dispatched if at least one service request is made, thereby saving resources when no one will be riding it.

Other service possibilities quickly become more complicated. There are design principles that are typically used, however, whether through manual effort or computer algorithms. The first step is to build "skeleton routes," or "quasiroutes" around *subscribers* (i.e. persons who make recurring requests to be picked up and dropped off at the same times and same locations). The next step is to insert other trip requests into the closest quasiroute having enough available time to make the pickup and drop-off. After all trips have been initially accommodated, then revisit all routes to see if some trips could be swapped between routes or could be reinserted into other routes, given the changes that have occurred since the initial insertion.

The same quantitative productivity and efficiency indicators used for fixed routes, such as trips per hour, cost per passenger, and cost per unit passenger-distance, can still be used to assess whether proposed changes are improvements. Table 3.5 gives further performance indicators. In some operations, it is permissible to use taxis and other occasional providers to accommodate trips that do not fit well into the quasiroutes. Although it raises coordination issues, this can be less expensive than using a larger vehicle carrying only one person or one that must deviate far from all other pickups and drop-offs. Coordination can also be difficult when trips are administered by one municipality, but numerous trips cross from it into others, and vice versa. When there are major imbalances in trip flows, one provider may want compensation from another. It is generally easier to have a regional provider, or at least a regional broker.

There are further complications to developing schedules. Callers making requests must either be assigned a trip immediately in a *real-time* scheduling process or be called back after many are scheduled simultaneously in a *batch* scheduling process. If one assigns a trip immediately to obviate the need for a callback, opportunities for swapping and reinserting trips are diminished. On the other hand, there are costs of having to call back. This increases the time and complexity of making reservations for the call taker, while also forcing the trip requestor to give longer advance notice.

Another complication is that there are pickup and drop-off time windows. A requestor can often not be given the exact time they requested but given a range of time when the pickup and drop-off can be expected. The wider the window, the easier it is to develop efficient schedules. On the other hand, this detracts from the quality of the service the requestor receives.

Yet another complication is the total time any rider spends on board. It is not reasonable to hold someone captive as the vehicles meanders around until, eventually, the vehicle comes to the vicinity of their drop-off point. Thus, there is typically a constraint of maximum time on board. In the United States, this is typically set at about twice the amount of travel time it would take to go from the origin (pickup point) to the destination (drop-off point) using the fixed-route network.

The complexity of developing schedules and returning calls to trip requestors is such that, at some point, a scheduler cannot manage all of the constraints effectively. Even if they can be met, the solution is not likely to be very efficient. Thus, computer scheduling/dispatching packages are used in all larger operations. Based on a survey of the industry, some researchers set a threshold for fleet

Table 3.5 Design and analysis considerations for demand-responsive operations

Some Performance Indicators	Factors Determining Basic Service Structure
Efficiency	
Operating cost per passenger trip	Eligible ridership
Operating cost per vehicle-hour	Routing and scheduling algorithms
Operating cost per vehicle-kilometer	Advance request vs. immediate response
Operating cost per passenger-kilometer	Use of Intelligent Transportation Systems (ITS)
Passenger revenue over operating cost	Door-to-door vs. curb-to-curb service
Average trip length per passenger	Regional versus municipal service area
Productivity	**Factors Influencing Vehicle and Quasiroute Assignment**
Passenger trips per vehicle-hour	
Passenger trips per vehicle-kilometer	Subscription trip (forms part of route skeleton)
No-shows over scheduled trips	Whether origin and destination are in same zone
Trip denials over total trips requested	
Service quality	Slack time available
Average system speed	Sharing common origin or destination
Average time onboard	Mobility device capacity constraint
Circuity (shortest over actual distances)	Person already been declined once
On-time pickups over total pickups	Maximum time onboard limit
On-time drop-offs over total drop-offs	Congestion delay risk
Response time (immediate and return trips)	Service disruption to other vehicle(s)
Complaints	Marginal cost of accepting trip

size where computer assistance becomes necessary at about 30 vehicles (Lave, Teal and Piras 1996). On the other hand, such software also takes time and skill to set up properly. It requires adequate and current information about travel times along streets and map coordinates that link to street addresses. The results are also very sensitive to the parameters that reflect the time windows allowed, the time on board allowed, and to rules about connecting passengers with other services. However, as discussed in the next chapter, technological advances are steadily improving the ability to estimate parameters as well as assisting in the daily operations.

There may also be eligibility requirements for the persons requesting trips. If eligibility is strict, at first glance it seems that demand can be reduced and costs contained. On the other hand, it may actually lower productivity and waste resources as vehicles travel through neighborhoods where latent trips by non-eligible persons are denied. Technological improvements are continually influencing such trade-offs in favor of more complicated service designs that might combine previously separate passenger-market niches. These can blur traditional boundaries between operating domains of public transport agency fixed and demand-responsive services, human service agencies, and private transportation. This will be discussed in more detail in the next chapter.

The complexity of setting up and managing a demand responsive service can be seen from the list of considerations in Table 3.5. Many decisions about the basic service structure have to be made, and revisited, in order to maintain a cost-effective service. On a daily basis, decisions have to be made about how particular vehicles will operate, unlike fixed route systems. It is quite common to outsource demand-responsive services to firms that specialize in it, but there is no escaping the need to provide some basic guidance about the service structure and about the expected service quality.

Summary

This chapter began with a description of spatial network types. There are advantages and disadvantages to each. There may be subnetworks within a region that reflect road-building patterns of different eras, different topographies, and different modes. Networks tend to evolve as cities and demand grow and as travel distances become longer to include higher-capacity TUs and faster modes.

Three primary right-of-way standards for individual routes were introduced. ROW A is total separation from all other traffic, and usually requires tunnels, elevated sections, and other measures requiring substantial investment. ROW C is simply operating in mixed traffic, with little distinction from general traffic. ROW B provides lateral separation from other traffic, but not full separation because of intersections. This gives performance in terms of speed and reliability somewhere in between A and C.

Temporal and spatial distributions of demand are needed to form a picture of the needs to be satisfied. Passenger demand varies by time of day and location. The three-axis diagram was presented as an insightful method for displaying this information. Indicators were introduced to characterize passenger demand and usage of available capacity.

The methods that can be used for data collection and the completeness of the information depend upon the installed technologies, because manual methods are tedious and expensive. One of the most important is the method of fare collection, but there are also devices made specifically for automatic passenger counting.

The various components of travel time (access time, waiting time, in-vehicle travel time, transfer waiting time, and egress time) were analyzed as to their relative importance as a function of travel distance. Key points are that service frequency must increase for shorter-distance trips and speed must increase with longer-distance trips in order to be competitive with the automobile. Further, the timed-transfer concept is often used to reduce transfer wait times and to connect O–D pairs on different routes.

The need to run cyclic schedules and the inherent properties of infrastructure alignments introduce constraints that limit efficiency of time usage. Some suggested route performance indicators were defined that help to characterize its efficiency both in comparison to other routes in the same network and against peer routes elsewhere.

Methods to speed up operations and increase efficiency were described. The least expensive is usually just to increase transit stop or station spacing. Vehicle acceleration and braking rates can be increased. Public policy can also be changed such that merging transit vehicles have the right-of-way. Traffic Signal Priority that favors transit is becoming easier to implement as it becomes localized at only one intersection at a time, although queue bypasses are sometimes necessary if it is to be effective. Reducing dwell times at stops can be accomplished through faster fare collection techniques, public education, and the use of vehicles with more door channels. Short-turn versions of routes can sometimes be created on long routes. Extending routes can sometime be done as layover time permits.

Route interaction with the network, especially the issue of transfer time being weighted more heavily by users than in-vehicle travel time, was analyzed with the aid of two research studies. The study by Liu, Pendyala and Polzin looked at a route mostly in isolation. It studied the effect of a break in journey versus a single ride from origin to destination. It found that ridership loss could be significant but did not include the possibility of an offsetting effect from the additional destinations available at the transfer point. The study by Lee (1998) was done in a network context. Briefly stated, Lee's network analysis classified three network types: transfer-oriented, transfer-avoidance, and directly connected. They were described as to how well they performed as a function of "high" and "low" levels of demand, travel speeds, and transfer penalties. The results were summarized in Table 3.4. Similar to the isolated route study, Lee found that when demand is low and speeds are low (the most difficult operating environment), a high transfer penalty argues against a transfer-oriented network, but the additional insight from Lee's model is that the other types of networks are even worse in this same situation. In smaller networks, high transfer penalty travelers probably use autos and cannot be attracted anyway. Most potential riders are those who have a low transfer penalty. Thus, transfer-oriented networks are commonly used in smaller cities.

There are economies-of-scale and economies-of-density in transit networks, but the concept of cross-subsidization of routes used by some economists was challenged on the grounds that there is some latitude in network design. Which route is chosen to become a high-capacity trunk line can be somewhat arbitrary. Furthermore, routes often serve a network purpose beyond serving origins and destinations only along its own length.

Fixed routes are supplemented by demand-responsive services. These are characterized by a lack of a preset route, a preset schedule, or both. These services are applied to very low-demand areas or to accommodate riders with special needs or disabilities that prevent them from using fixed routes. The service design principle usually involves building ad-hoc, daily quasiroutes that build around subscription users. As demand-responsive operations get larger in scale, efficiency and productivity can be greatly enhanced by scheduling software and by use of advanced technologies. There are many policy and setup decisions and complicating factors involved in demand-responsive operations such that it is common that they are outsourced to specialist firms.

Appendix 3.A

More Indicators Related to Efficiency and Speedup

Indicators of Efficient Use of Resources

In order to quantify the effects of scheduling constraints, the basis scheduling equations need to be analyzed. The fundamental relationship for a simple cyclic route is:

$$T = N\,h, \tag{3-9}$$

where T is the *cycle time*, or time for a vehicle to return to its initial position, and N is the number of Transit Units required to maintain a constant headway, h. N must be integer, while h is usually divisible into 60 minutes (e.g. 2,2.5,3,4,5, 6,7.5,10,12,15,20,30) so that the schedule can repeat hourly in *cyclic operations*. As a consequence, T can take on only discrete values.

If a route is of length L having an operating speed v_0 in both directions, then T is composed of the two travel times underway plus two terminal times, one for each route end:

$$T = 2\frac{L}{v_o} + tt_1 + tt_2 \qquad tt_{\min} \le tt_1,\, tt_2. \tag{3-10}$$

The value tt_{min} is the minimum time that a vehicle can be scheduled between arriving at a terminal and then departing in the opposite direction again. This minimum is set by the minimum time specified or contractually required for vehicle operator breaks and by the need to reposition TUs when the passenger alighting and boarding locations are not the same. In practice, there often is a need to add extra time, or *slack*, to schedules to allow for delays from congestion, heavy passenger loads, and other randomly recurring events. Also, in practice, in order to meet the constraints on the cycle time that arise from the integer restriction on N and clock headway restriction on h, either or both of the terminal times must usually be extended anyway. Thus, a TU may have to stand at terminals for periods longer than tt_{min}. In so doing, it stands at a terminal instead of doing productive work. In this way, scheduling inefficiency stems from the requirements to not run behind schedule repeatedly and/or to maintain cyclic operations. It can be useful to define a ratio of the minimum possible cycle time to the schedule-constrained cycle time, or *schedule efficiency ratio*:

$$\gamma = \frac{T_{\min}}{T} = \frac{2\dfrac{L}{v_o} + tt_{1\min} + tt_{2\min}}{2\dfrac{L}{v_o} + tt_1 + tt_2} \qquad \gamma \le 1.0 \quad [\,\text{-}\,]. \tag{3-11}$$

Scheduling relationships will be developed and used further in connection with the estimation of the cost of operating routes in a later chapter.

Example 3.4

A) A route has the following properties: operating speed of 11.2 mph (18 km/h), a one-way length of 6.8 miles (11 kms), and a headway of 15 minutes. The union agreement states that total terminal time for each round trip should be at least 15 percent of the total travel time. Find the number of vehicles required, the minimum cycle time, the actual total terminal time, and the schedule efficiency ratio.

Using Equation 3-10:

$$2L/v_o = 2(6.8\ miles)(11.2\ mph/60) = 73.3\ minutes$$
$$tt_{min1} + tt_{min2} = 0.15(73.3\ min) = 11\ minutes$$
$$T_{min} = 2L/v_o + tt_{min1} + tt_{min2} = 84.3\ minutes$$

From Equation 3-9, $T = N(15)$ is also a requirement, where N is integer. To not violate the union constraint, T_{min} must be rounded up, not down, to find the minimum cycle time. The fleet size must be 6, as it is the first integer value giving a rounded value higher than 84.3 minutes:

$$T = 6\ (15) = 90\ minutes$$

The actual total terminal time must then be:

$$tt_1 + tt_2 = 90 - 73.3 = 16.7\ minutes$$

The schedule efficiency ratio follows directly from Equation 3-11:

$$\gamma = \frac{T_{min}}{T} = \frac{84.3}{90} = 0.94$$

Another source of unproductive time is *deadheading*, the repositioning move-ments of vehicles when they are not in scheduled revenue service. These stem from travel between the depot and the starting and ending terminals for a day's work, and from any repositioning between routes during the day. It can be useful to define a ratio of total Vehicle-Hours to Revenue-Vehicle-Hours, or *deadhead factor*:

$$\beta = \frac{Total\ vehicle\text{-}hours - Revenue\ vehicle\text{-}hours}{Revenue\ vehicle\text{-}hours} \qquad \beta \geq 0 \quad [\text{-}]. \qquad (3\text{-}12)$$

Some care is needed when comparing routes, especially routes from peer sys-tems. What constitutes revenue Vehicle-Hours can be somewhat arbitrary to define, particularly when demand is unbalanced in opposite directions of a route. It is in fact very common during certain hours for demand to be much higher in one direction. Even when accepting passengers in the off direction, a TU's primary task may be to reposition to the peak direction. In some cases, it may use an express path such as a parallel highway to return to the peak direction more quickly.

Example 3.1 (continued)

C) Compute the two-way space-averaged load factor, if the same vehicle deadheads on the return trip.

The two-way factor is found by doubling the length and adding zero passengers for the second direction:

$$\xi = \frac{\sum P_j l_j + 0}{C_v 2L} = \frac{101.5 + 0}{(60)2(3.5)} = 0.24 \; passenger - miles/space - mile.$$

Note the dramatic 50 percent reduction in space efficiency.

In the interest of a better comparison, one can create a threshold of ridership in the off direction, below which the movement is declared a deadhead. The total boarding counts for the peak and off-peak directions during the peak period are compared as a *direction balance ratio*:

$$\eta = \frac{total\ boardings\ in\ off\text{-}peak\ direction}{total\ boardings\ in\ peak\ direction} \quad \eta \geq 0 \quad [\text{-}]. \tag{3-13}$$

For example, if an agency chose a threshold of $\eta = 0.10$ and the calculated value was less, most off-peak direction runs would be considered deadhead runs as would those at its prospective peers. Their associated service hours would be subtracted from the Revenue-Vehicle-Hours total. The exceptions would be the few runs made to meet any minimum frequency standard, as some base service is always offered regardless of demand. In this way, comparisons can be made using a common definition.

Absent the complete picture that O–D pair information provides, there is another indicator to characterize demand that can be of practical value. Even without knowing the lengths of segments between stops, the ratio of total boardings to accumulated passengers arriving at the end terminal, P_n, or *turnover ratio*, can be computed. It roughly implies the length of trips. Mathematically, this ratio is:

$$\tau = \frac{\sum_{j-1}^{n} b_j}{P_n} \quad \tau \geq 1.0 \quad [\text{-}]. \tag{3-14}$$

The word *turnover* alludes to the concept of space being occupied by more than one passenger over the course of a run. A ratio of exactly 1.0 would mean that no passengers alighted before the terminal. This is approximately the case with many radial commuter services, particularly in the peak period. Other types of alignments, particularly tangential or cross-town grid routes, or perhaps even the same radial route at a different time of day, would have a higher ratio. Since turnover is proportional to fare revenue collected, this is a particularly important indicator of financial performance when a complete O–D matrix is not available. In general, services that accumulate passengers have a lower turnover ratio and collect less revenue per unit passenger distance than those with higher turnover ratios. If the fare structure is flat (i.e. if fare is the same regardless of distance) this is strictly true.

Example 3.1 (continued)

D) Compute the turnover ratio for this example. Use Equation 3-14:

$$\tau = \frac{\sum_{i-1}^{7} b_i}{P_7} = 59/40 = 1.48 \; persons/space$$

Speedup and Efficiency Increasing Techniques

Beyond its use for determining which operations are to be declared deadheading, the direction balance ratio is important for characterizing the efficiency with which demand can be served. The closer to 1.0, the more equal the demand in opposite directions. Generally, a route with a large traffic generator at only one end will have a lower direction balance ratio than one with more distributed origins and destinations. Extending a route that begins at one major traffic generator to reach a second major traffic generator would greatly improve the balance ratio. An example would be an extension of a route that has a CBD at one end to a major airport at the other end.

Up until this point it has been assumed that the number of TUs, N, is fixed for any given headway, h. However, N is not truly fixed; rather it is just treated as fixed since partial vehicles cannot be removed from service while in operation. In reality, as cycle time is reduced, at some point, N can be reduced by 1 to $N-1$. The difference in cycle time from T to the reduced cycle time, T', that is required is exactly h, as can be shown by the following derivation based upon Equation 3-9:

$$T' = (N-1)\,h = N\,h - h = T - h. \tag{3-15}$$

Each of the variables in Equation 3-10 is a candidate for change. Changing v_0 might require some investment or route modification. Increasing v_0 is the most advantageous way to reduce T to T'. It not only reduces operating costs by requiring one fewer TU while providing the same headway, it can also reduce the capital cost since a smaller fleet need be supplied for this service. Furthermore, noticeably higher operating speed increases ridership on long trips and, consequently, the fares collected, which in turn lowers the operating subsidy required

The least expensive way to increase average operating speed is to increase stop or station spacing for new designs and removing existing stops for existing routes. Often, stops are very close together, ostensibly for the convenience of the passengers, but it can be easily shown that increased access and egress distances are usually more than offset by decreases in time onboard the vehicle. If operating speeds are slow because there are consistently heavy passenger loads or gradients along a route, a vehicle design with a higher output propulsion plant and better brakes may be needed. These will restore acceleration rates and braking rates to the normal range.

In some cases, operating speed is inconsistent. Success at reducing inconsistency can often permit the reduction of terminal times, tt_1 and tt_2, when these were originally set long to accommodate a wide variation in travel times. Public policy changes will sometimes alleviate random delays and thereby reduce variability of travel times. For example, in some regions, there are laws requiring merging buses to receive the right-of-way in conjunction with clearly marked bus pullout locations. This saves them the random time loss associated with the wait for a gap to open in traffic.

Transit can be favored and thereby be both sped up and reduced in inconsistency through signal retiming and by altering signal phases when a bus is detected. Traditional methods of providing *Transit Signal Priority* (TSP) involved expensive equipment both wayside and onboard the vehicle, and perhaps revision to a centralized, computerized traffic signal control network. As control technologies have improved over time, decentralized control of signals one intersection at a time requires less time and effort to implement. Queue bypasses at busy intersections in conjunction with TSP can be used when auto traffic otherwise would trap transit vehicles in the queue. There is more about this in Chapter 4. Another measure is the "bus bulb," where the sidewalk is extended to the traffic lane, allowing bus passengers to board and alight without pulling to the side. Efforts can also be made to cut the *dwell time* at stops, defined as the time actually spent with the doors open. Vehicles can be selected which have more door channels so that boarding and alighting queues are shorter. Fare collection procedures can be sped up. For example, prepayment and contact-less fare media (which can be read from a distance) both reduce the time each individual spends in doorways. In addition, the public can be educated in proper boarding and alighting procedures. Fare collection can also be moved off of the vehicle. Indeed, moving fare control away from the boarding and alighting areas around doors is one of the defining characteristics of Bus Rapid Transit (BRT) and Rail Rapid Transit (RRT) modes.

Shortening the route length, *L*, is also a possibility. One strategy is to redesign a meandering route to follow a shorter course in order to reduce length sufficiently to save one TU. As another strategy, if passenger demand is significantly higher on one portion of a route, some of the vehicles can operate over a shorter length in a *short-turn* operation. In this case, there can actually be savings of more than one vehicle. This can be easily modeled by dividing the basic route into two subroutes, a short one plus a long one. This strategy can be applied only to the extent that the lower frequency of service on the nonoverlapping section of the longer route remains high enough to meet any minimum frequency standards.

Use of time can sometimes be improved by extending route length, L, instead, to put to use time otherwise spent standing in the terminal. The extra distance, ΔL, that it might be possible to extend a route with existing total terminal time, $tt_1 + tt_2$, is given by:

$$2\Delta L = v_o(tt_1 + tt_2 - tt_{\min 1} - tt_{\min 2}). \qquad (3\text{-}16)$$

In practice, whether the route should be extended would also depend on the potential ridership and the availability of a new terminus. Moving a terminal for an extension that carries little ridership would introduce a new form of inefficiency in the form of poor use of vehicle capacity.

Example 3.4 (continued)

B) How much would the route have to be shortened to save one TU?

The revised cycle time must meet the fleet integer constraint of Equation 3-15:

$T' = (N - 1) h = (6 - 1) 15 = 75 \ minutes$

But the revised cycle time must also meet the travel time requirement of Equation 3-10:

$T = 2L'/(v_o'/60) + tt_{min1} + tt_{min2} = 2L'/(v_o/60) + 0.15(2L'/(v_o/60))$

Inserting values gives:

$75 = 2L'/(11.2/60) + 0.15(2L'/(11.2/60))$

Solving the expression for L' gives 6.1 miles (9.8 kms). Thus, the route must be 0.7 miles (1.2 kms) shorter.

C) How much could the route be extended without requiring an additional vehicle? Use Equation 3-16:

$\Delta L = v_o \ (tt_1 + tt_2 - tt_{min1} - tt_{min2})/2$
$\quad = (11.2/60)(16.7 - 11)/2$
$\quad = 0.53 \ miles \ (0.86 \ kms)$

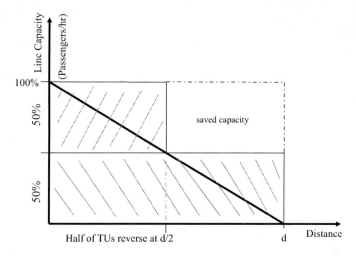

Figure 3.12 Short turning to better match capacity with demand.

Another major category of efficiency increases stem from better matching of space supply to demand. It is inherent that a radial route will need less capacity as it gets farther away from the center. The capacity can be reduced by short turning a fraction of the vehicles. This number is limited not just by capacity needed but by the headway on the outer section. The reduced service must still meet with minimum headway set by policy and not be so long as to reduce demand.

As an example of the possible efficiency gain, Figure 3.12 shows a simple situation of a radial route where half the TUs are reversed at half the distance to the end of the route. Using the utility ratio, Equation 3-5, would give a result of 0.5 if all TUs operate all the way to d. This can be seen by inspection without calculation since the denominator, the space-kilometers available per hour, is a full rectangle of 100% line capacity $\times d$, while the numerator, the space-kilometers used, is a triangle half this size. If, on the other hand, half the TUs reverse at $d/2$, then the total space-kilometers available is two rectangles, each with the same TU size as before but half the frequency and thus line capacity. The combined space-kilometers offered is the sum of the two reduced line capacities multiplied by their line distances. The result is 50% capacity $\times d/2$ plus 50% capacity $\times d$ for a total of 75% of offered capacity compared to without short turning. Since the ridership is unchanged, the utility ratio has improved to 50/75 from 50/100.

References

Brown, Jeffrey R. and Gregory L. Thompson. 2008. "Service Orientation, Bus–Rail Service Integration, and Transit Performance Examination of 45 U.S. Metropolitan Areas," *Transportation Research Record* 2042: 82–89.

Brown, Jeffrey R., and Gregory L. Thompson. 2009. "Express Bus Versus Rail Transit: How a Marriage of Mode and Mission Affects Transit Performance." *Transportation Research Record* 2110: 45–54.

Brown, Jeffrey R., and Gregory L. Thompson. 2012. "Should Transit Serve the CBD or a Diverse Array of Destinations? A Case Study Comparison of Two Transit Systems." *Journal of Public Transportation* 15 (1): 1–18.

Del Mistro, Romano, and Eric C. Bruun. 2012. "Appropriate Operating Environments for Feeder-Trunk-Distributor Public Transport Services." In *Proceedings of the South African Transport Conference*, Johannesburg, July.

Fawkner, J. 1995. "Bus Deregulation in Britain: Profit or Loss?" *Public Transport International* 95 (6): 18–23.

Lave, Roy E., Roger Teal and Patricia Piras. 1996. A *Handbook for Acquiring Demand Responsive Transit Software*. Report 18. Washington, DC: National Academy Press, Transit Cooperative Research Program. http://www.tcrponline.org

Lee, Young-Jae. 1998. Chapters 2 and 4 in *Analysis and Optimization of Transit Network Design with Integrated Routing and Scheduling*, Ph.D. Dissertation, University of Pennsylvania, Department of Systems Engineering, Philadelphia, PA.

Liu, Rongfang, Ram M. Pendyala and Stephen Polzin. 1998. "Simulation of the Effects of Intermodal Transfer Penalties on Transit Use." *Transportation Research Record* 1623: 88–95.

Maxwell, Ross R. 2003. "Converting a Large Region to a Multimodal Pulsed-Hub Public Transport Network. *Transportation Research Record* 1835: 128–36.

_____. 1999. "Intercity Rail Fixed-Interval Timed-Transfer System: Applicability of the Integrated *Takhtfahrplan* Strategy to North America." *Transportation Research Record* 1691: 1–11.

Musso, A. and V. R. Vuchic. 1988. "Characteristics of Metro Networks and Methodology for their Evaluation." *Transportation Research Record* 1162: 22–33.

Pickup, Laurie et al. 1991. *Bus Deregulation in the Metropolitan Areas*, Aldershot, UK: Avebury/Gower.

Piper, Robert R. 1977. "Transit Strategies for Suburban Communities." *AIP Journal* (December): 380–85.

Sen, Ashish, Siim Soot, Vonu Thakuriah, Paul Metaxatos, Vidya Prasad, George Yanos, Duck-Hye Yang, Victor Rivas, Lise Dirks, Kathleen Stauffer, Pamela Freese and Trisha Sternberg. 1998. *Highways and Decentralization*. Final Report. Chicago: Urban Transportation Center, University of Illinois at Chicago. http://www.uic.edu/cuppa/utc/publications/f30.pdf

Synn, Jienki. 2005. *Systems Approach to Metro Network Design*. Ph.D. dissertation, University of Pennsylvania, Department of City and Regional Planning, Philadelphia, PA.

Thompson, Gregory L. and Thomas G. Matoff. 2003. "Keeping Up with the Joneses: Planning for Transit in Decentralizing Regions." *Journal of the American Planning Association* 69/3 (Summer): 296–312.

Vuchic, Vukan R. 2007a. "Urban Passenger Transport Modes." Chapter 2 in *Urban Transit: Systems and Technology*, 45–90. Hoboken, NJ: Wiley.

Vuchic, Vukan R. 2007b. "Transit System Performance: Capacity, Productivity, Efficiency and Utilization." Chapter 4 in *Urban Transit: Systems and Technology*, 149–201. Hoboken, NJ: Wiley.

Further Reading

Bunker, Jonathan. 2012. "Passenger Transmission and Productiveness of Transit Lines with High Loads." *Transportation Research Record* 2274:144–53.

Ceder, Avishai. 2007. *Public Transit Systems Planning and Operations*. Oxford, UK: Elsevier.

Derrible, Sybil, and Christopher Kennedy. 2011. "Applications of Graph Theory and Network Science to Transit Network Design." *Transport Reviews* 31 (4): 495–519.

Grava, Sigurd. 2003. *Urban Transportation Systems: Choices for Communities*. New York: McGraw-Hill.

Gupta, Diwakar, Hao-Wei Chen, Lisa Miller and Fajarrani Surya. 2008. *Improving Capacity Planning for Demand-Responsive Paratransit Services*. St. Paul: Minnesota Department of Transportation. http://www.lrrb.org/PDF/200809.pdf

KFH Group, Inc., Urbitran Associates, Inc., McCollom Management Consulting, Inc. and Cambridge Systematics, Inc. 2008. *Guidebook for Measuring, Assessing, and Improving Performance of Demand-Response Transportation*. Report 124. Washington, DC: Transit Cooperative Research Program, National Academy Press. http://www.tcrponline.org

Lee, Young-Jae, and Vukan R. Vuchic. 2005. "Transit Network Design with Variable Demand." *Journal of Transportation Engineering* 131 (1): 1–10.

McLary, James L., Agneta Stahl and Sharon Persich. 1993. "Implementation of Service Routes in the United States." *Transportation Research Record* 1378: 21–27.

Shioda, Romy, Marcus Shea and Liping Fu. 2008. "Performance Metrics and Data Mining for Assessing Schedule Qualities in Paratransit." *Transportation Research Record* 2072: 139–47.

Simon, Jesse, and Peter Furth. 1995. "Generating Bus On/Off Matrix From Demand Data." *Journal of Transportation Engineering* 111 (6): 583–93.

Thompson, Gregory L. 1997. "Achieving Suburban Transit Potential: Sacramento Revisited." *Transportation Research Record* 1571: 151–60.

Tiwari, Geetam, and Deepty Jain. 2012. "Accessibility and Safety Indicators for all Road Users: Case Study Delhi BRT." *Journal of Transport Geography* 22: 87–95.

Tomazinis, Anthony R. 1975. *Productivity, Efficiency, and Quality in Urban Transportation Systems*, Lexington, MA: Lexington Books.

Vuchic, Vukan. 2005. "Planning and Selection of Medium and High Performance Transit Modes." Chapter 12 in *Urban Transit: Operations, Planning and Economics*, Hoboken, NJ: Wiley, 553–612.

Wirasinge, S. C. 2003. "Initial Planning for Urban Transit Systems." Chapter 1 in *Advanced Modeling for Transport Operations and Service Planning*, edited by William H. K. Lam and Michael G. H. Bell. Oxford, UK: Pergamon, Elsevier Science.

Zhang, Ming. 2007. "Bus versus Rail: Meta-Analysis of Cost Characteristics, Carrying Capacities, and Land Use Impacts." *Transportation Research Record* 2110: 87–95.

Chapter 4

The Impact of Intelligent Transportation Systems

The availability of more information can only help performance and investment analysis. Fortunately, information technology (IT) designed specifically for application to transportation, referred to as *Intelligent Transportation Systems* (ITS), are continually improving. Many are already mature, and their benefits have been established for some, but not all, potential applications. As a common example, Automatic Vehicle Location (AVL) systems based on Global Positioning System (GPS) technology is a practical feature fast becoming "core functionality" at transit operations across the globe. This technology, in turn, supports improved operational control, enhances the information available to keep passengers informed, and provides valuable data for management oversight and planning. ITS inform operational performance and investment analysis with a higher quality and quantity of data than has historically been available.

ITS enable new service opportunities that will only make them increase in importance over time. Furthermore, the investment in ITS is largely a capital expenditure that is intended to reduce operating expenditures. If it fulfills its promise, the same amount of work can be done with fewer vehicles, additional ridership will be attracted, and other monetary benefits will accrue. Rolling stock and physical plant maintenance and investment strategies should also improve. There will also be benefits to other agencies and to the public at large.

Because of their importance as information sources, an enabler of new services, elements of investment packages, and a tool to be used to simplify benefit- versus-cost analysis, the analyst needs to be familiar with ITS.

Barriers to Integration and Hybrid Services

Within the public transport sector in the developed nations, fixed-route and demand-responsive services have traditionally been planned and operated separately. The latter were used to supplement the fixed-route network in special niche markets. Some examples include: accommodating people with disabilities; serving areas with impediments to using fixed-routes (e.g. lack of sidewalks); serving low-density communities that have insufficient demand to support fixed routes; and serving *many-to-one* trips (i.e. trips for workers who live near each other and all work the same shift at a large factory). This last application is often done through privately managed carpools and vanpools, but they can be coordinated or even operated by public agencies.

The distinction between fixed-route and demand-responsive services is blurring with time. There is increasing economic and social pressure to find a way to integrate the two. Demand-responsive trips have very high average costs per passenger compared to fixed-route trips, creating an economic incentive to bring passengers into the fixed-route system. There are also many unmet social needs, particularly in low-density communities. Yet, demand-responsive services often pass through poorly served communities without being either authorized or organizationally capable of picking up passengers who are not part of their predetermined niche market.

Some of the obstacles to integration are institutional. Dispatchers for fixed-route and demand-responsive operations may be in far-removed locations and not in the habit of communicating well. In developing nations, private firms will often be in direct competition and are loathe to cooperate with one another. In many cases, the funding sources forbid commingling resources or passengers, even if might be to the benefit of all. Particularly in the United States, paratransit employees will often work for a different union than employees of the fixed-route agency, if they work for a union at all. Any wage or work-rule discrepancy might then create an obstacle to integrating operations. Private operators under a standing contract with a public agency to provide supplementary capacity might take a more lucrative assignment at the moment they are summoned. Thus, major reorganization and new contractual relationships may be required.

The remaining obstacles are technological and are being removed. Communication with vehicle operators historically was via voice radio of limited availability and was time-consuming for dispatchers. Once underway, the driver had limited communication capability, making requests on short notice hard to accommodate and removing the impetus for faster scheduling and reservation methods. Thus, software that would plan pickups and drop-offs in demand-responsive service was mostly used in the *batch-processing* mode; in other words, the operating plan was generated the evening before. Trip requests also had to be made well in advance, from one to several days. More recently, an increasing array of digital radio options has boosted communications capacity. Modern Mobile Data Terminals (MDTs) mounted onboard vehicles adjacent to the operator have enabled easy and automated manifest changes to be transmitted while also relieving the vehicle operator from responsibilities for documentation previously logged on paper.

ITS facilitate services that previously were impractical and difficult to manage. They are permitting the reduction of reservation time for demand-responsive services and a switch from batch processing to near real-time scheduling. An example is the "Prontobus" used in suburban Bologna, Italy. It will run on a fixed timetable, but unlike less sophisticated operations, only if at least one passenger notifies the dispatch center of their intention to ride between 35 to 60 minutes (depending upon the route length) before the scheduled departure time from the terminal stop (Claroni 2003).

Other applications ITS facilitate are *hybrid services*. These will be increasingly common over time. Two important examples are presented here. They are shown side by side in Figure 4.1 for comparison. On the left is the replacement of a long demand-responsive trip across town with a short *demand-responsive feeder* that makes a timed-transfer connection with a fully accessible fixed-route service. If necessary, the procedure is reversed at another timed-transfer point to carry this person to the final destination. ITS will help to ensure that the connections are kept, particularly important for those with disabilities who may not be able to wait long periods of time without shelter. On the right is *route-deviation* service. The vehicle deviates for anyone, or only for eligible persons—it works because a few minutes of slack time are built into the schedule. The driver must learn to slow down if no deviations are requested.

The ITS also help to automate the request and scheduling process. Persons with disabilities will get far shorter reservation times (perhaps only a few minutes) until vehicle arrival. Through hybrid services, more people with disabilities will be able to use the fixed-route system. *Mainstreaming*, the ability of persons with disabilities to join the remainder of society, is an important societal goal in many nations. The operating agency also benefits by finding a more cost-effective

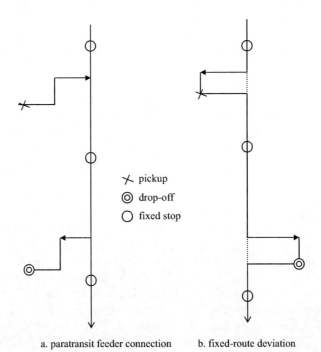

✗ pickup
◉ drop-off
○ fixed stop

a. paratransit feeder connection   b. fixed-route deviation

Figure 4.1 Two examples of hybrid services.

solution to low-productivity services. See Bruun and Marx (2006) for a detailed explanation and evaluation of a successful service. For more examples of hybrid services and some suggested market niches, see, for example, Morlok, Bruun, and Vanek (1997), Koffman (2004), and Brake et al. (2007).

Even able-bodied passengers can benefit from the creation of hybrid services that address previously unmet travel needs. Such services can be used as a replacement for fixed routes. The idea is to deviate even for able-bodied passengers late in the evening, very early in the morning, or whenever demand is low. Since different niches are prevalent at different times of day, it is also possible the same vehicle can operate in more than one type of service over the course of the day. With the ability to change the stops that are fixed as demand reveals itself, route-deviation services also can play a role as a demand-probing tool. All of these possibilities require sophisticated fleet management that ITS can provide.

In order to take advantage of these possibilities, ITS investment plans should build in the capacity for network solutions that can readily integrate all types of service under one operational control package and one scheduling package. Route indicators and performance measures will also need to be adjusted to reflect the incorporation of lower-productivity services into higher-productivity services. Otherwise, an institutional obstacle may present itself when managers who are evaluated on these indicators raise objections. At the time of this writing, there is not an industry-wide consensus on how this should be done.

The analyst should stay abreast of trends. New types of IT-related services could alter travel decisions by individuals. ITS successes may well influence the selection of investment alternatives.

Real-Time Operational Control

The ITS that have the most potential for monitoring and controlling operations is a complex package known as Computer Aided Dispatching/Automatic Vehicle Location (CAD/AVL). The AVL portion tracks an entire fleet of vehicles with continual updates. This information is displayed as vehicle icons on a map with zooming features that permit dispatchers to view selected areas in closer detail. The CAD portion provides features specifically of value to a dispatcher. It keeps track of the runs to which particular vehicles and operators are assigned. There may also be color coding of vehicle icons to call attention to vehicles that are running too early or too late. A dispatcher who is well trained in recovery tactics can use this information to take corrective action to help overcome service irregularities. When timed transfers are used, the dispatcher can make decisions whether to dispatch the waiting vehicles or to hold the connecting vehicle at a stop. This is an especially valuable feature for networks on long headways and for the last connection of the day to any route. The dispatcher and operator communicate mostly with preset messages displayed on an MDT, but they can use a voice radio when required.

With fleets that are small, the system is largely using existing PC and cellphone technology and it can be managed by one person. For larger fleets, the costs for the various CAD components can easily double the price per vehicle. In particular, it may be necessary to have a dedicated digital radio system. It must have the range to reach a far-flung fleet and the capacity to poll a large number of vehicles frequently. It must also be able to quickly establish communications, not just to selected individual vehicles but to groups of vehicles in particular regions, on particular routes, and so on. Furthermore, some advanced applications have Automatic Passenger Counting (APC) components that allow for the monitoring and recording of boarding and alighting, linked to precise locations. Cumulative passenger counts can be used to indicate when overcrowding reaches a certain threshold so that additional vehicles can be added. A few applications even measure the weight of passengers, which is actually a better indication of crowding than counts because it takes into consideration the size of the passengers.

It is also possible to monitor fare collection in real time when using contactless smartcards. This can then be compared to real-time APC data. The knowledge that boardings far exceed passengers counted is helpful for fare enforcement. This last one is an example of the many applications that are still limited in their use, at the time of this writing, but can be expected to grow in popularity.

When engine sensors and other vital-sign sensors are connected to the ITS communications system, it is possible to transmit sensor outputs outside of the normal range to the dispatcher and maintenance department in order for immediate decisions to be made whether the vehicle should remain in service. If the incipient problem does not require withdrawal from service, the maintenance staff can already be prepared to do the required work when the vehicle returns to the depot.

Transit Signal Priority (TSP) technologies are becoming increasingly sophisticated as individual signals incorporate their own computational ability. Measures to increase the reliability of monitoring travel times both decreases the need for active intervention and make intervention more effective when it does become necessary. There are two basic categories of priority, *passive* and *active*. Passive refers to measures that do not require any vehicle detection or communication with the public transport vehicle. These include signal timings, physical features like queue bypasses, and traffic regulations specifically designed to favor public transport movement over private vehicle movement. Active measures react to individual vehicles and involve either detection, communication, or both. The measures may be relatively minor, such as extending a green signal phase for a few seconds. At the other end, they may be fairly sophisticated, such that the signal reaction depends upon how early or late the approaching vehicle is, upon requests for priority made by public transport vehicles approaching the same intersection on cross streets, and where the signal currently is in its cycle of phases.

The time savings from TSP depends upon the aggressiveness with which it is used. If a schedule is written for a route without even passive TSP, and active TSP is then added, such that it is granted only if vehicles are running significantly late, the only likely impact is a decrease in the variability of travel time along the route from one run to the next. At the opposite extreme of active TSP is *preemption*, which means signals switch to favor transit at all times without regard to other traffic, analogous to what fire trucks receive. In between is a range of measures. Depending upon the congestion levels and physical design features installed in the specific corridor to aid public transport, travel-time reductions of 10 to 25 percent are possible. Generally, even active TSP does not require any actions by the dispatcher but is done either automatically or upon a manual request by the vehicle operator.

One example of a TSP treatment is shown in Figure 4.2. It is relatively low cost and fairly easy to implement because it does not require a full lane dedicated to buses., nor does it require synchronization and the attendant timing and communication complexities. It is simply controlled by local communication through a low-cost weak radio. Still in its infancy at the time of this writing is "center-to-center" communication. This obviates the need for additional communication devices, as the CAD/AVL system reports the transit vehicle location and other needed information to the traffic signal control center. The center then sends a message to the appropriate traffic signal instead of through its existing communications infrastructure. This has an additional advantage, namely that upstream and downstream traffic-signal control requests could also be taken into consideration in the priority-granting decisions.

Real-Time Passenger Information (RTPI) is a logical extension from real-time operational control. This is not only for the convenience of the public. The passengers can actually help the recovery from operational irregularities if they are informed of events that disrupt service and are given specific advisories relevant to

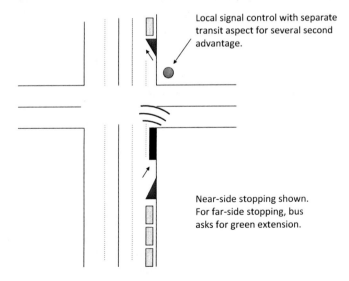

Local signal control with separate transit aspect for several second advantage.

Near-side stopping shown. For far-side stopping, bus asks for green extension.

Figure 4.2 Transit Signal Priority using queue bypass.

their particular location. As an example, when some passengers take an alternative routing, it relieves the backlog of persons and subsequent crowding and boarding delays on the service that may have been delayed.

Planning Information

It is very difficult to know how well one's existing services are performing if one does not have information about ridership, running times, revenues as a function of route, transfer volumes, and so on. Yet, getting detailed information was traditionally so expensive and time-consuming that it was done infrequently. Persons had to be paid to stand at street corners to check schedule adherence or to ride vehicles to count passengers. In the end, the reliability of such data was also often in question. Data from road departments about traffic conditions vital to planning analyses and mathematical modeling could also be awkward to obtain and require clumsy conversion efforts. Now, modern ITS can make data collection more frequent, reliable, and affordable. This is especially true if one is sharing the costs of the same investments with other agencies with a stake in that data.

Outputs Generated by Intelligent Transportation Systems

Here are some of types of ITS outputs highly useful to analysts:

- *Time and Location:* Valuable by itself, AVL is also key data for other ITS because time and location identifies and links all other data tied to the same event.
- *Summary Management Reports:* Totals of vehicle-distances and vehicle-hours operated, revenue collected, fuel consumed, major breakdowns, missed trips, and other information that provide an overview of operations can be automatically collected and distributed on a daily or as-needed basis. This is especially valuable in connection with the monitoring of contract operators to ensure that they deliver the service promised.
- *Schedule Adherence and Travel-Time Distribution Statistics:* Comparison of where a fixed-route schedule intends vehicles to be versus where they actually are from one run to the next and one day to the next allows operators to develop a statistical distribution. Operators can also analyze closely related data, such as travel time between selected fixed stops and between the starting point and finishing point of a route. For demand-responsive services, it is also possible to compare estimated arrival times on manifests created by software versus actual performance times.
- *Traffic Probe Information:* When road-based public transport vehicles are deadheading or operating in express service, their AVL transmissions provides a good indication of current travel times and the state of congestion. When analysts assemble and combine these records with other road-sensor information about traffic volumes, the result can be statistical distributions of speed versus traffic volumes and speed by time of day. This information is

particularly needed for efficient demand-responsive scheduling because these vehicles move at the speed of general traffic. It is also needed for analysis of the conditions faced by the competition (i.e. automobile users).

- *Passenger Count Statistics:* Through detectors at the doors, it is possible to get the boarding and alighting counts as a function of time and location along a route. It may also be possible to construct an Origin–Destination matrix. These are already obtained at distance-based rapid transit fare-gate systems (e.g. as in Washington, DC). Instead of passenger counters at the doors, operators employ card readers at both entrance and exit gates. Systems without gates that use contactless smartcard readers can also be used if passengers are required to present their card during both boarding and alighting.
- *Maintenance Statistics:* Sensors measuring vital signs of the engine, transmission, and other major components, and other important readings can routinely send data to maintenance management system (MMS) software packages, where it is stored and analyzed to monitor trends.
- *Revenue Collection:* It is possible to identify how much was collected from each individual at each stop, what discounts were used, and which type of fare medium was used. If smartcards are read at both boarding and alighting, it is even possible to know exactly how far each passenger traveled on each link of a connecting trip. This has the potential of making fare apportionment automatic and precise between agencies that have all agreed to use the same fare-collection media.

Examples of Analysis Applications

There are numerous benefits to having the high quality and quantity of data that ITS can make available. Some of the most important ones are listed here.

Route performance indicators. The examples listed in Table 3.3 can actually be computed regularly and with some confidence in their accuracy and timeliness by developing computer algorithms that process the relevant outputs. Consider the following:

- *Better matching of supply to demand:* Historically, infrequent travel-time measurements and passenger counts meant the amount of service offered did not always get adjusted in pace with changes in ridership. It could well be possible that some routes were overcrowded while others had excess capacity. With more information, operators not only can adjust service with each schedule change, they can identify cyclical variations by season and long-term trends. Resources will be more efficiently used, and compliance with any performance standards improved.
- *Generation of more efficient schedules:* Operators can use statistics from the databases to update schedule adherence, travel times, and passenger counts for each route. This facilitates regular detection of changes. Adjustments can be made accordingly. For example, long a user of APC data, Tri County Metropolitan Transportation District (Tri-Met) serves Portland, Oregon, and

its suburbs. A researcher at Portland State University performed a schedule study for Tri-Met in 2002. He found that 81 of the 104 routes had excessive running, layover, and recovery times, while 23 had inadequate time. His estimate was that new schedules could generate about $7 million annual savings for a peak operation of about 600 buses without any adverse impact on passengers (Strathman 2002).

- *Troubleshooting of route performance:* Planners can quickly identify where service has deteriorated below standards. They might also be able to isolate precisely what causes recurring problems or chronically inadequate performance. They can distinguish locations where congestion occurs, where there are boarding and alighting delays, and where planned connections tend to be missed. They can perhaps also identify intersections, whole streets, or selected stops that would benefit from physical changes or alterations in the timing of traffic signals.

Post-processing packages with such tools are available from some of the CAD/ AVL vendors, but they have also been developed by university researchers and can be obtained for a modest price. See, for example, the short summary by Muller and Knoppers (2013) of a package referred to as TRITAPT, developed at the Technical University of Delft. Extensive examples of its use in analyzing route performance are given in Furth et al. (2003).

Continual optimization. There is synergistic benefit from ITS when both the real-time performance of the transit network and the historical planning information reinforce each other. Together, they make what Professor Theo Muller refers to as "quality feedback loops" (shown in Figure 4.3). It shows two loops that lead towards service improvement as a result of gathering data. The left loop leads to better real-time operational control and RTPI. Operational procedures, such as dispatcher tactics to recover from delays, are regularly modified to improve performance. The right loop leads to regular revision of the service plan based on the performance and demand information available for each route from the analysis of archived data. The basic idea is to optimize schedules given the existing physical street layout and traffic signal control. This same archived database, in a more advanced application, can also be used to study how changes in TSP, street layouts, and other elements could be made to further improve performance. The process is repeated regularly. Results are fed back to improve schedules and operations again, in a process of continual optimization. This is, in fact, done extensively in the Netherlands (Muller and Furth 2000).

The aforementioned rescheduling of Tri-Met was an example of using the right loop. It was done by manual analysis of the archives, which raises the costs and skill level required. As ITS continue to mature, it will become a common practice to automate much of the analysis to permit more direct feedback between the operational-control software, the scheduling software, and other analysis tools.

Better performance estimates for new services of existing design. Geographic Information Systems (GIS) can provide demographic information about communities making it possible to link this information to route performance statistics. Such

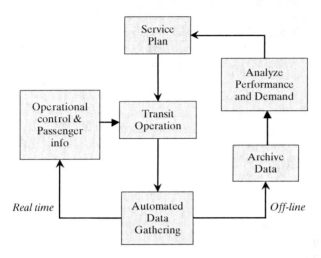

Figure 4.3 Two quality feedback loops: Real-time and planning
Source: Theo Muller and Peter Furth, 2003.

linking allows for closer analysis of why existing services are or are not effective. By finding routes that can serve peer communities with similar characteristics and similar performance indicators, such as those presented in Chapter 3, the clever planner can better select the appropriate type of service(s) and estimate the results.

Better selection of new types of services. The better the statistical database of passenger travel patterns and the operating performance of each mode in each part of the region, the easier it is to identify the strong and weak points of each type of proposed service. The data may indicate the need for something derivative or a totally new approach. In-depth analysis of this data should lower the risk of failure (not meeting expectations) of innovative services. For example, analysis of this data should allow the operator to:

- select appropriate areas for route-deviation services;
- choose which stops to make fixed and which to make optional;
- identify how much slack time should be added to the schedule to permit deviations; and
- determine demand thresholds for demand-responsive feeders versus fixed-route feeders.

Finally, such data can allow operators to determine where *service routes* would be most effective (defined as the most effective routes for connecting major destinations of the car-less elderly and disabled). These are special routes that tend to meander around because they put a premium on accessibility instead of speed. To plan them requires detailed information about passenger origins and destinations.

Better maintenance and asset management. As the database of various vehicle subsystems and components grows within an MMS, it is possible to identify chronic equipment problems as well as to document when and where these problems develop. This, in turn, allows the gradual conversion to *predictive maintenance*, which is a better alternative than traditional time-based and distance-based maintenance that wastes resources and is punctuated by disruptive and costly repairs. Predictive maintenance revolves around determination of optimum component servicing and replacement intervals, optimization of inventories, and a reduction in the incidence of breakdowns. Such maintenance can also be extended to many stationary systems and components (e.g. power distribution systems for electrically powered vehicles).

Transportation mathematical model inputs. Mathematical models play an important role in formal project analysis. ITS supply both more current and statistically accurate inputs than historically were possible. As will be discussed further in the chapter on mathematical models, speed versus traffic volume curves for key roads across the network are model inputs of central importance. Similarly, public transport travel-time distributions and passenger-demand distributions across the network are both important for models as well as for individual route analysis.

Targeting of investments. All information is potentially usable towards investment analysis. It needs to be stressed that improved information removes the need for much speculation about causes of poor operating performance of various routes or parts of the network. When operators understand the nature of deficiencies better, they can devise better solutions and decide which investments are necessary. In a broader sphere, general asset management can be improved by prioritizing capital towards the most urgent physical-plant maintenance and repair needs, towards those upgrades with the highest productivity-increasing potential, highest safety-enhancement benefits, and other such targeted purposes as identified by analysis of the data.

Security Benefits

ITS technology that helps to monitor and guard public transportation users, employees, and facilities has received increased attention in the first half decade of the twenty-first century. Attacks on airliners, the bombing of commuter trains in Madrid in 2004, and the bombing of a bus and rapid transit in London in 2005 have brought security to the forefront. But security concerns are not new. Potential passengers have often cited fear for their personal security as one of main reasons for not using public transportation. Both passengers and employees have been afraid of assaults onboard vehicles and at waiting points. Vandalism has also been an ongoing concern. What is new is the expansion of security to permit monitoring of entire tunnel and bridge systems, and huge stations and terminals. Moreover, the information must be collected and disseminated such that emergency management and response are quick and effective.

There are a variety of generic audio and video surveillance systems that can be used in buildings and large facilities that already have substantial electrical and communications infrastructure. Closed-circuit television has been a mainstay for years. With the advent of miniaturized microphones and cameras connected through the Internet, the cost of comprehensive coverage has been decreasing. Security staff can simultaneously watch numerous monitors, but storing all incoming video and audio data records indefinitely requires massive storage capacity. Instead, many sites only store records for a limited time, in case they should be needed for an investigation.

Locations in the field, such as bus stops, can be more problematic because power and communication lines may not be readily available. In such cases, installing lines can be expensive. Alternatively, security systems can use radio communications instead of landlines, and batteries can be used for power, but with implications for additional field maintenance and staffing. Storage capacity may be even more limited. Transmission of information in real time may also be limited only to situations where an alarm is activated.

Security devices onboard vehicles are the most challenging element in such systems due to the need to transmit data through communication devices that may already have heavy demands due to other ITS. Similarly, electrical power may also be at a premium. The amount of the electrical load on a public-transit vehicle increases as the number of electronic devices on the vehicle increases. This is likely to be an issue particularly when air-conditioning is needed because it competes for the electric power generated onboard. Thus, to minimize duplication, security features are often integrated into CAD/AVL and other ITS features.

A covert alarm has become a standard feature of CAD/AVL systems. Activated through a hidden switch and with no visible indication of its activation, it can be used during robberies and assaults. The location and an emergency signal are sent to the dispatcher. If a vehicle is normally monitored by being polled every minute or two, position reports may well be sent every few seconds instead. In some applications, operators use a covert microphone so that the nature of the emergency can be ascertained. It is also possible that video surveillance systems that normally record only for possible later review could begin to send images in real time. On systems with limited radio capacity, operators can enable real-time transmissions by preempting routine transmissions.

The vehicle operator need not be the one to activate the alarm. This feature can also be triggered automatically. A vehicle that has gone substantially off route can cause an alarm. An attempt to move a vehicle by an unauthorized person can be detected since an ID code is required to log in to a CAD/AVL system. If a valid ID is not entered before the vehicle moves, it will cause an alarm. A few places have even installed a feature that requires the operator to blow into an alcohol-measuring tube before the vehicle can be started.

Fire and exhaust-fume detection has long been installed in stations and tunnels. This is being expanded to include poison gas and bomb detection, although, as of this writing, large-scale implementation is rare. Cost is likely to decrease over time but will still be proportional to the size of terminals and length of tunnels, such that large systems will undoubtedly incur significant costs. A complementary strategy is to have passengers pass through explosive and gas detectors similar to those used to screen airport passengers. Their widespread application will depend upon the speed at which queues can be processed. Public transportation passenger facilities depend far more upon rapid ingress and egress for their efficient functioning than do airports. Thus, any sensing must be done quickly.

As of this writing, bomb detection equipment portable enough and quick enough to install in a bus doorway has already been developed in Israel. The repeated targeting of public transportation in Israel has accelerated the decline of public transportation use, reducing it towards only those persons who have no other alternative (Garb 2003; Maryon 2004). Should the fear of attack spread to other nations, it could have serious consequences. It would undermine other ongoing efforts to make public transportation more attractive. Thus, the cost of security measures must be weighed against not only the real security they provide but also against the perceived security to the public. Estimating the value of human life can be highly controversial, as can deciding when enough steps have been taken. On the hand, special funding sources may be available, and there may be offsets such as reduced insurance costs.

Other Benefits to Passengers and to the Public at Large

There are several real benefits from ITS to the passenger and to the public at large, plus, as of this writing, some benefits waiting to be realized. In general, passengers get better service. AVL means that real-time information can be provided to waiting passengers, based on actual location, not scheduled location. This information is made available at major terminals, at stops, over the internet, and through mobile phones, especially smartphones.

A potent force for improved RTPI is the increasing availability of third-party applications for smartphones, some of which have no official affiliation with service providers. The information request does not even need to be linked to a static origin or destination location. A query can be made from a random location, perhaps not even at a stop. As open-source data become the norm, these applications will continue to proliferate.

Transit agencies are already using social media in a variety of ways. For example, these can be very effective for increasing community outreach, to keep the public informed of current events, and to strengthen a brand and public image (UITP 2012). Their use can also be expected to increase dramatically in the future. No doubt many of their uses and consequences will be different than we imagine today.

Plus, services can be more reliable and attractive. Vehicles can be held at transfer points to guarantee connections. It is important to note that these improvements alter the perceived waiting time—people do not mind waiting as much when they have information. If aggressive operational control is used, there will be less *bunching* on routes with short headways. Bunching is the annoying phenomenon of two or more vehicles showing up together after a long service gap, the first of which is overcrowded. Thus, there will be fewer long waits. TSP and quickly processed smartcards will also help to speed passenger journeys.

The better planning data collection enabled by ITS means adjustments can be made to schedules more often to reflect changing conditions across the route network. Passengers will be more satisfied when adjustments are made to schedules when needed to maintain comfort and service standards. The passenger also benefits from new hybrid services that address previously unmet travel needs.

Measures that increase the security of public transportation system assets usually simultaneously increase public security. But the public is not necessarily aware of these security features. Since the perception of security also counts, operators need to inform the public about them. The contribution to security from other measures, such as route-deviation at night, will be readily apparent.

The public at large can also benefit from ITS. When AVL information is available, it is possible to inform even nonriders about the status of each travel option. This can be done through roadside signs, smartphones with specialized applications, phones using social media, kiosks, and the Internet. Because this same information allows for wiser and quicker incident management for road and public transport agencies, the disruptions from accidents, road closures, special events, and even routine congestion need not be as severe. More indirectly, better public transport services can reduce auto use and its adverse consequences to the community. Better service and more efficient operations increase fare revenue while also reducing costs, thus reducing public subsidy requirements for the same amount of service.

There are also ITS developments that may or may not be viewed as beneficial. As examples, smartcards that can track an individual's progress across town and video surveillance onboard vehicles may be viewed as violations of privacy by many. Smartcards that charge by distance may seem equitable to some, but others may face much more expensive travel. Passenger reaction needs to be anticipated and public consensus may be required prior to investment.

Summary

Intelligent Transportation Systems provide far more usable information for both operational control and for performance analysis than has historically been available. ITS are also a common candidate for investment analysis in and of themselves.

ITS also permit hybrid services that previously would have been difficult to manage. Although fixed-route and demand-responsive services have traditionally usually been treated separately, the higher cost per passenger of demand-responsive services and the currently unmet travel needs of the general population are both creating pressure for integration. Hybrid services can reduce costs of serving the disabled while giving them better service and addressing some of these unmet needs.

The agency can have better control of operations in real time, perhaps cutting the fleet requirement on some routes and the number of reserve vehicles.

Well-trained dispatchers will be able to use recovery tactics effectively in the case of service disruptions. TSP technology that increases the operating speed of transit can improve efficiency and generate increased ridership. ITS also make the use of timed-transfer networks more reliable and attractive.

When using ITS, planning data are collected and archived far more frequently and with more reliability, and perhaps even at less total cost, than with manual methods. This facilitates computation of accurate and timely route and network operational performance indicators, better matching of supply to demand, and better matching of area characteristics to appropriate services.

A synergistic benefit is achieved when the results from changes in real-time operational control measures and changes in service plans both generate new data. These data can then be fed back in two quality feedback loops to continually improve both operations and service plans in a process of continual optimization. It is also easier to share data with highway agencies to identify problem areas, to jointly adjust signal timings and intersection designs, and to address other items of mutual interest.

Analysts can also use the archived data as inputs to mathematical models. They can obtain and load accurate information about travel-time statistical distributions, origin and destination patterns, and nonpublic transport speeds into such models.

Security is of increasing importance. Large facilities can use generic video and audio surveillance. Gas and bomb detection is becoming increasingly common in stations and tunnels. Smaller locations in the field must either have power and landlines installed for communication or install radio communications and batteries that have implications for maintenance staffing. To minimize the need for duplication, vehicle security devices are usually integrated with CAD/AVL and other ITS. Covert alarms are a standard feature. Video surveillance on moving vehicles is usually done with records for later review due to communication capacity constraints, but immediate transmission is also possible. Perception of security is also important, so features need to be made known to the public.

Improved RTPI reduces perceived waiting time by passengers. It has proven very popular. It is widely available at stations and stops, on the Internet, and on mobile phones. Many highly capable applications have been developed for smartphones. Open-source data policies mean that an increasing number of third-party applications can be expected.

Transit agencies are already using social media in a variety of ways. For example, these can be very effective for increasing community outreach, to keep the public informed of current events, and to strengthen a brand and public image. Their use can also be expected to increase dramatically in the future.

The public at large can also get better information about possible itineraries and about travel conditions on all possible travel choices, not just transit. They can also expect better incident management and better advisory information. Less directly, better services can also reduce car use and improve the urban environment. Higher ridership and more efficient operations can reduce the public subsidy requirement.

Finally, ITS can produce an array of information and influences upon a public transportation system. As an example, Figure 4.4 traces possible consequences

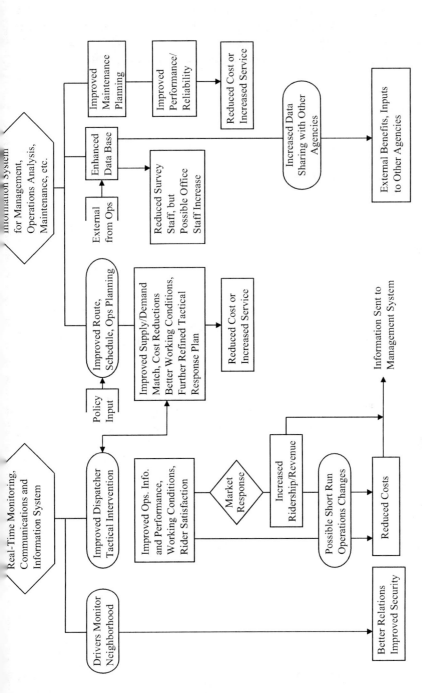

Figure 4.4 Use and importance of AVMC systems.

Source: Morlok, Bruun, and Battle, 1993.

of a CAD/AVL system (referred to as an AVMC system in this figure). Similarly, tracing the potential influences and the resulting costs and benefits for any proposed ITS is wise. Through this process, it could become apparent that seemingly high short-term investments are outweighed by long-term benefits.

References

Brake, Jenny, Corinne Mulley, John D. Nelson and Steve Wright. 2007. "Key Lessons Learned from Recent Experience with Flexible Transport Services." *Transport Policy* 14: 458–66.

Bruun, Eric, and Eric Marx. 2006. "Omnilink: A Case Study of a Successful Flex-Route-Capable Intelligent Transportation System Implementation." *Transportation Research Record* 1971: 91–98.

Claroni, Claudio. 2003. "Prontobus: A Demand Responsive Transport System," *Proceedings of the 55th Union International des Transport Publics World Congress*, Madrid, 4–9 May, Brussels, Belgium.

Furth, Peter G., Theo H. J. Muller, James G. Strathman and Brendon Hemily. 2003. *Uses of Archived AVL-APC Data to Improve Transit Management and Performance: Review and Potential*. TCRP Web Document 23 (Project H-28). Washington, DC: Transit Cooperative Research Program, National Academy Press. http://www.tcrponline.org

Garb, Yaakov. 2003. "Transit Terror: The View from Jerusalem." *Sustainable Transport* (Fall): 12–17.

Koffman, David. 2004. *Operational Experience with Flexible Transit Services. Synthesis* 53, Washington, DC: Transit Cooperative Research Program, National Academy Press. http://www.tcrponline.org

Maryon, John. 2004. "Bomber-Proof Buses." *Urban Transport International* 53: 27.

Morlok, Edward, Eric C. Bruun, and Francis Vanek. 1997. Chapter 2 in *The Advanced Minibus Concept: A New ITS-Based Service for Low Density Markets*. Report PA-26–700D. Washington, DC: U.S. Federal Transit Administration.

Morlok, Edward, Eric C. Bruun and Kimberly Battle. 1993. *Advanced Vehicle Monitoring and Communication Systems for Bus Transit: Benefits and Economic Feasibility*. Report UMTA-PA-11-0035-91-1. Washington, DC: U.S. Federal Transit Administration.

Muller, Theo H. J., and Peter Knoppers. 2013. *TRITAPT—TRIp Time Analysis in Public Transport*. http://tritapt.nl/

Muller, Theo H. J., and Peter Furth. 2003. "AVL and APC: Useful by Design." Presentation at the Massachusetts Institute of Technology, August.

———. 2000. "Integrating Service Planning with Analysis, Operational Control, and Performance Monitoring." *Proceedings of the 2000 ITS America Annual Meeting*, Boston, MA.

Strathman, James G. 2002. "Tri-Met's Experience with Automatic Passenger Counter and Automatic Vehicle Location Systems." Appendix A in *Uses of Archived AVL/APC Data to Improve Transit System Performance and Management*. Interim Report (Project H-28). Washington, DC: Transit Cooperative Research Program, National Academy Press. http://www.tcrponline.org

UITP (Union Internationale des Transport Publics). 2012. Special Edition on "Social Media and Public Transport." *Public Transport International* 61 (6/6) (November/December).

Further Reading

Ambrosino, Giorgio, J. D. Nelson and M. Romanazzo, eds. 2004. *Demand Responsive Transport Services: Towards the Flexible Mobility Agency*, Rome, Italy: Italian National Agency for New Technologies, Energy and the Environment (ENEA).

Bertini, Robert L., and Ahmed El-Geneidy. 2003. "Generating Transit Performance Measures with Archived Data." *Transportation Research Record* 184: 109–19.

Bihn, Friedhelm, ed. 1994. *Differenzierte Bedienungsweisen: Nahverkers-Bedienung Zwischen Grossen Verhersaufkommen und geringer Nachfrage.* Cologne, Germany: Verbund Deutscher Verhkersunternehman. http://www.vdv.de (in German).

Boyle, Daniel. 2008. *Passenger Counting Systems, Synthesis* 77. Washington, DC: Transit Cooperative Research Program, National Academy Press. http://www.tcrponline.org

Bruun, Eric C. 2001. "Justifying ITS from a Business Standpoint." *Public Transport International* 50 (1/6) (November): 26–30.

Chandra, Shailesh, and Luca Quadrifoglio. 2013. "A Model for Estimating the Optimal Cycle Length of Demand Responsive Feeder Transit Services." *Transportation Research B* 51: 1–16.

Maccubbin, Robert P., Barbara L. Staples, Firoz Kabir, Cheryl F. Lowrance, Michael R. Mercer, Brian H. Philips and Stephen R. Gordon. 2008. *Intelligent Transportation Systems Benefits, Costs, Deployment, and Lessons Learned: 2008 Update*. Report No. FHWA-JPO-08-032. Washington, DC: U.S. Federal Highway Administration.

McManus, Sean. 1997. "Flexible in Flanders." *Intelligent Fleet Management* (November/December): 106–07.

Nickel, Bernard E. 1993. "Citybus, Quartierbus, Ortbus." *Der Nahverkeher* 111 (6): 21–37 (in German).

Parker, Doug J. 2008. *AVL Systems for Bus Transit: Update. Synthesis* 73, Washington, DC: Transit Cooperative Research Program, National Academy Press. http://www.tcrponline.org

Potts, John F., Maxine A. Marshall, Emmett C. Crockett and Joel Washington. 2010. A *Guide for Planning and Operating Flexible Public Transportation Services. Report* 140, Washington, DC: Transit Cooperative Research Program, National Academy Press. http://www.tcrponline.org

Stough, Roger, Mark E. Maggio and Dinjian Jin. 2001. "Methodological and Technological Challenges in Regional Evaluation of ITS: Induced and Direct Effects." Chapter 2 in *Intelligent Transport Systems*, 13–46, edited by Roger R. Stough. Cheltenham, UK: Edward Elgar.

TCRP (Transit Cooperative Research Program). 2005. *Innovations in Bus, Rail and Specialized Transit. Research Results Digest* 70, Washington, DC: Transit Cooperative Research Program, National Academy Press. http://www.tcrponline.org

Velaga, Nagendra R., John D. Nelson, Steve D. Wright and John H. Farrington. 2012. "The Potential Role of Flexible Transport Services in Enhancing Rural Public Transport Provision." *Journal of Public Transportation* 15 (1): 111–131.

Westerlund, Yngve. 2005. *Future Vehicle Requirements for Flexible Transport Services.* Presentation at Third Coordination of CONcepts for NEw Collective Transport (CONNECT) Workshop. Manchester, 9 November. http://projectapps.vtt.fi/Connect/_Rainbow/Documents/connect/Yngve.pdf

Chapter 5

Characterizing and Influencing Modal Relationships

The demand for urban public transportation is very much affected by the qualities of the environment in which it operates as well as the availability and qualities of any connecting transportation. Some of the relevant attributes of these connections can be captured in planning models that generate demand estimations and other design and performance requirements. Others cannot, but nevertheless will bear on the future success of a project. Any identifiable projects and recent policy changes that might affect connecting services must be considered. Evolutionary trends must also be studied, with the intent of determining their long-term impact. Investments must be viewed as interacting with a continually evolving physical environment and public policy regime. This chapter focuses on the various ways in which passenger travel habit data can be used to help characterize situations as well as how conditions external to a project can influence performance and investment outcomes.

Characterization of Mode Split and Usage

Relationships must be established between the motorized and nonmotorized modes, primarily walking and bicycling, before analysts can truly assess whether a system or project can achieve goals, objectives, and performance outcomes related to travel behavior modification. It is all too common to ignore nonmotorized modes in mode-split calculations and measurements. In serious investment planning that could result in significant use of nonmotorized modes, they must be taken into account. In cases where pedestrian and bicycle trips are a very small fraction of total trips, such as in extremely auto-oriented and rural areas, it may not be technically feasible to include them. These fractions are less than the confidence interval of the model outputs; that is, they are below the "noise level." However, this should not simply be assumed without investigation.

Much misunderstanding, as well as occasional, intentional, disinguous representation, can occur when analysts do not include nonmotorized modes in mode-split tabulations. When this happens, mode-split differences between even the most public-transport-oriented city and auto-oriented city can appear to be minimal. It is a fact that better public transportation networks will almost always manifest themselves, not only with higher use, but also with more pedestrian trips. The features of a city and transport system that promote public transport use support walking as well. To ensure that analysts properly represent and measure the mode split and related travel behavior indicators they must be aware of several issues in preparing the data.

Using passenger distance traveled (passenger-distance) can confuse the issue of characterizing urban travel when long-distance trips and intraregional trips are aggregated to provide state, provincial, or national figures. Aggregation makes such values useless for urban investment analysis and, more insidiously, masks potentially huge differences in travel behavior between subregions within the larger aggregation.

One crucial distinction that analysts cannot overlook is between the mode split based on number of trips and the mode split based on passenger-distance. Using passenger-distance as the measure can virtually eliminate the contribution of pedestrian trips, as they are short by nature, at least in the more prosperous nations. The apparent contribution of bicycle trips will also be diminished; although they are longer than trips on foot, they are still shorter on average than motorized trips. But the relative shortness of trips does not mean they are unimportant. On the contrary, much of the value of certain urban development patterns is that they obviate the need for some motorized trips. Indeed, replacing long motorized trips with short nonmotorized ones could be a medium- to long-term goal of a major project that involves densification of land use along a public transport corridor.

While mode-split figures would show little error in a severely sprawled area by excluding nonmotorized modes, they would be far off the mark in its associated inner city. Such figures can be misused to deny the effect of public transport systems and urban development patterns. Thus, analysts must define relevant service areas so that the baseline situation is known and intended desired changes can be detected and measured if they occur.

Urban trip pattern changes have many possibilities that can influence not only segment length but also total trip length and length of travel over the whole day. For example, a *trip chain* with an auto from the office to the dry cleaners to the day care facility to home might be replaced with a transit trip to a station where laundry and child can be picked up in the immediate vicinity, followed by a walk home. Thus, the modes, number of trip segments, and trip length all change in such a scenario.

Longer-distance trips can be influenced in fewer ways than urban trips. As trip length increases, the distance between cities becomes dominant, and the actual destination and particular routing within either city becomes insignificant. While modal occupancy can be changed, or the mode itself can be changed, there is relatively little change in total trip length.

An example of data presented in a fashion that hides meaningful differences in travel patterns is shown in Figure 5.1. This figure is very similar to a figure from *Future Drive* (Sperling 1995, 7). But rather than using the derived source

(Schipper and Myers 1993), a more complete dataset from the original research is used (Schipper et al. 1992). Furthermore, for clarity of comparison, only the data for the two years 1970 and 1987 are shown, excluding all intermediate years.

The book by Sperling made erroneous arguments, enabled by a poor presentation format. The dependent variable is total annual person-kilometers of travel by automobile for each of eight nations as a whole, expressed as a percentage of total travel by all modes. In this presentation format, all nations except Japan would appear to be very similar and, indeed, this was a point made by the book's author: "In most affluent countries, automobiles already meet 75 to 85 percent of domestic travel requirements" (Sperling 1995, 7). This quote calls attention to the first aspect of this presentation format that appears to support the author's point: passenger-kilometers are plotted as a percentage rather than an absolute value. Percentages have little meaning in a context where transport policy recommendations are to be given. Energy consumption, pollution generation, and all other costs and benefits to society likely to be of interest to an urban transportation policy analyst or transit planner are all proportional to absolute values of motorized travel, not to percentages. When the data for the same two years of 1970 and 1987 are re-plotted in absolute values, as in Figure 5.2, the United States has double the automobile passenger-kilometers of the next nearest of the eight countries.

The second misleading aspect is that this presentation format aggregates rural and intercity travel with urban motorized travel, while ignoring nonmotorized modes. These are the most energy efficient modes. Ignoring them is an ironic

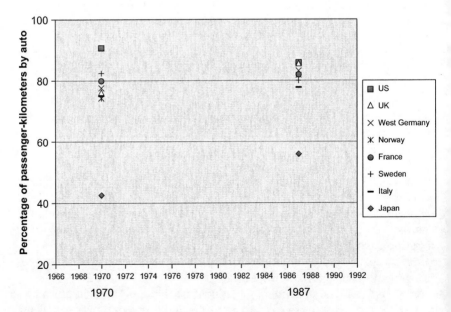

Figure 5.1 Passenger travel statistics presented in misleading fashion.

Source: Sperling 1995, 7.

omission considering that energy consumption reduction is one of the primary themes of the aforementioned book.

Should analysts add nonmotorized modes, the apparent contribution to urban mobility would still seem insignificant due to the massive contribution to total passenger-kilometers from rural and intercity trips. If analysts subtract the rural/intercity component, nonmotorized modes would become somewhat more significant on a per-passenger-kilometer basis. But the statistics still would understate their role in urban trip-making because the shorter nonmotorized trips obviate the need for some of the longer motorized trips. An example is walking to the corner store to get a pack of cigarettes or carton of milk versus driving to the nearest strip mall. Thus, it is very helpful if both the average number of urban trips and average total distance traveled per day are documented.

A dramatically different picture can emerge when data are only for urban trips, non-motorized modes are included, and the number of trips is the dependent variable instead of passenger-kilometers. John Pucher (1995) presented average mode-split percentages on a trip basis for several countries, shown here as Table 5.1. One city's mode split within a nation can vary substantially from the next, as can its average trip length, so this data would not be usable for analysis of a specific project. But since Sperling's quote referred to national percentage data, the comparison is valid. On average, only Canada had an urban mode split close to the United States. The rest of the nations are not at all similar. It is not argued

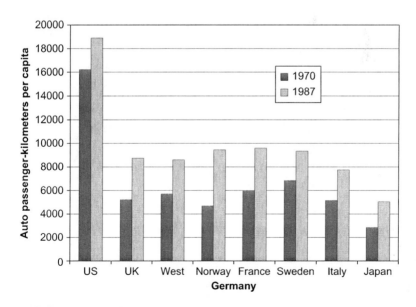

Figure 5.2 Statistics from Figure 5.1 replotted in absolute values.

Data Source: Schipper et al. 1992.

here that only the number of trips is important; indeed, it was already argued that passenger-distance is also of interest. Rather, it is argued that passenger-distance must also be used judiciously if the purpose is to characterize a situation and to monitor any changes that occur over time.

Since the first edition of this book, Buehler and Pucher (2012) have updated Pucher's statistics for most of these countries. One new summary statistical indicator that should lay to rest the claim that all of the richer and more developed countries are similar, (except possibly Japan), is Number of Public Transport Trips per Capita (statistics vary between 2005 and 2010 depending upon availability). Switzerland is in a class by itself at 237; Sweden and Germany are tied at 139. At the lower end, Canada is at 55 and the Netherlands is only 51, but these are still double the US average of 24. More detailed statistics are provided for Germany and the United States in particular, with different breakdowns of ridership by income class, gender, trip purpose, and so on. Controlling for gender, age, employment, car ownership, population density, metropolitan area size, and day of the week, Buehler and Pucher found that Germans were five times as likely to ride transit as were residents of the United States and that German rides per capita continues to grow while they have stagnated in the United States, although absolute ridership is steadily increasing. More recent statistics for the last few years, as they become available, may well reveal that the United States is now increasing in trips per capita as well, as many transit systems are carrying record ridership and face capacity problems.

Table 5.1 Urban modal split as a percentage of total trips by nation

| Country | Mode of Transportation | | | | |
	Car	Transit	Bicycle	Walking	Other(s)
USA	84	3	1	9	3
Canada	74	14	1	10	1
W. Germany	53	11	10	26	0
France	47	12	5	30	6
UK	62	14	8	12	4
Switzerland	38	20	10	29	3
Sweden	36	11	10	39	4
Netherlands	45	5	30	18	2
Italy	42	16	5	28	9
Austria	39	13	9	31	8
Denmark	42	14	20	21	3

Source: Pucher 1995.

Not all data is from the same year, but all are from the early 1990s.

One sound approach to travel-habit characterization for a particular city or region is used by the German firm *Socialdata* in its tracking of mode split of German cities over time. It tracks mode split on a percentage basis but also tracks an average daily per-capita trip length, found by adding the total for all modes and dividing by the total population. These two types of indicator can together reveal changes in trip patterns and travel behavior over time, although they do not reveal how much the trip length has changed for each mode. This, too, could be generated from the available data. When applied to Munich, as shown in Table 5.2, it was found that the combined mode-split for public transportation, bicycling, and pedestrians increased from 56 to 59 percent over 21 years, with virtually no increase in per-capita daily trip length. Together these indicators suggest that the large investments in public transport and nonmotorized mode facilities that began with preparation for the 1972 Olympics and reached fruition over this time span prevented the incessant growth in annual vehicle-kilometers traveled (VKT) that was seen in so many other cities.

For preliminary analysis and when budgets do not permit a survey to obtain new data, existing data must be used that may be out of date. However, as with other performance indicators, assistance in setting targets for mode-split changes after an investment or service expansion can be obtained by studying peers. Such peers would have similar characteristics about size, density and demographics, but would have more public transport lines of a specific nature or a higher service level on a similar network. Of particular importance for identifying peers would be finding suitable estimates for average trip lengths by mode. The European Platform on Mobility Management (EPOMM 2013) has collected mode split data on a trip basis for 268 cities in Europe with over 100,000 in population, 54 with less than 100,000, and 12 non-European cities. The number is steadily increasing. There are also often links to the source studies and additional details for each city.

To restate succinctly, travel statistics should be disaggregated into urban and intercity/rural travel components. Modal split in terms of trips is essential if one has goals or objectives that include changes in travel patterns. Mode split in terms

Table 5.2 Mode-split percentage by trip and daily travel indicators for Munich

	1976	1982	1989	1992	1995	1997
Walking	31	29	24	24	23	22
Bicycling	6	10	12	15	14	13
Motorbike	2	1	0	0	0	1
Car as driver	29	30	31	29	30	31
Car as passenger	13	8	9	7	8	9
Public transport	19	22	24	25	25	24
Travel time (min)	69	70	69	69	67	66
Distance (km)	21	21	22	22	22	22

Source: Socialdata GmbH 1999.

of passenger-distance is also essential for resource consumption, pollution generation, and cost-benefit calculations.

Characterization of Resource Consumption and Pollution Generation

National versus Regional Statistics

One common problem with available data is that it is aggregated for a nation, state or province as a whole. This is not useful for urban or metropolitan area analysis. In mathematical terms, trips, passenger-distance, and energy consumption can be disaggregated by similar methods. If each mode is identified by a first subscript, k, and urban versus intercity/rural by a second, then in mathematical terms trips are expressed as:

$$x_k = x_{kU} + x_{kI,} \tag{5-1}$$

where x_k is the total number of trips or passenger-distance by mode k, x_{kU} is the number of urban trips or passenger-distance on mode k, and x_{kI} is the number of intercity/rural trips on mode k.

The formulation for modal energy consumption involves a *modal energy intensity* coefficient, I_k, for each mode k. I_k is expressed in energy per unit passenger-distance, which incorporates average vehicle occupancy. In mathematical terms, it is expressed as:

$$I_k x_k = I_{kU} x_{kU} + I_{kI} x_{kI.} \tag{5-2}$$

Thus, when tracking energy consumption as related to trip making, the modal energy intensity coefficients are also subject to change. The urban auto intensity, I_{aU}, which includes driver and passengers, will increase as auto passengers are diverted to other modes and thereby reduce average occupancy. This will somewhat offset the reduction in x_{aU}, auto passenger-distance.

An example of how opportunistic data can sometimes be disaggregated follows.

Example 5.1

Listed are some available national statistics for a hypothetical nation.

- An estimate based on reported annual odometer readings, auto ownership, and population:

    $X_A = (50 \ million \ persons)(7,400 \ miles/person/year) = 370 \times 10^9 \ miles$
    per year

- An estimate based on travel-habit surveys and diaries of a sample of the population. It is for all private travel where both the origin and destination are not within the same metropolitan area:

$X_{AI} = (50 \text{ million persons}) (2{,}000 \text{ miles/person/year})$
$= 100 \times 10^9 \text{ miles per year}$

- An estimate based on travel-habit surveys and diaries of a sample of the population. It is for all travel not taken by private transportation:

$X_P = (50 \text{ million persons}) (1{,}200 \text{ miles/person/year})$
$= 60 \times 10^9 \text{ miles per year}$

- An estimate based on the itineraries of all tickets sold by the intercity bus and rail industries:

$X_{PI} = 30 \times 10^9 \text{ miles per year}$

- An estimate based on the itineraries of all domestic tickets sold by the airline industry:

$X_F = X_{FI} = 50 \times 10^9 \text{ miles per year (no metropolitan plane travel)}$

A) Estimate the national average urban mode split on a per unit-distance basis for the auto and public transportation modes.

The urban components follow as:

$X_{AU} = X_A - X_{AI} = (370 - 100) \times 10^9 = 270 \times 10^9 \text{ urban miles per year}$
$X_{PU} = X_P - X_{PI} = (60 - 30) \times 10^9 = 30 \times 10^9 \text{ urban miles per year}$
$X_{FU} = X_F - X_{FI} = (50 - 50) \times 10^9 = 0 \text{ urban miles per year}$

The national average urban mode split then follows as:

Auto: $270/(270 + 30) = 90\%$
Public: $30/(270 + 30) = 10\%$
Flying: 0%

The mode split per unit-distance estimate based on total statistics instead would have been:

Auto: $370/(370 + 60 + 50) = 77\%$
Public: $60/(370 + 60 + 50) = 12.5\%$
Flying: $50/(370 + 60 + 50) = 10.5\%$

B) Estimate the energy intensity of urban auto use.

The best way might be to find it indirectly using the difference between national total consumption statistics and intercity statistics. These latter two are likely to have more accurate estimates:

The national total energy consumption by private autos is known fairly accurately from fuel sales:

$$I_A X_A = 14.77 \times 10^9 \text{ gallons per year}$$

The estimated national average Intensity, I_A, can be found by dividing by the estimate of total person-miles by auto. The result is 14.77/370 or 0.040 gallons/person-mile.

Estimates for average intensity for intercity driving are probably more accurate than for urban driving for two reasons. First, fuel consumption estimates are more accurate for constant speeds. Second, vehicles can be sampled for occupancy along highways fairly easily. In this case, average intercity fuel consumption is estimated at 22 miles per gallon while average intercity vehicle occupancy is estimated at two persons per vehicle. Using the basic definition of intensity:

$$I_{AI} = (1/22 \text{ gallons per mile})/(2 \text{ persons}) = 0.02727 \text{ gallons/person-mile}$$

The unknown intensity is found using this equation:

$$I_A X_A = I_{AU} X_{AU} + I_{AI} X_{AI}$$

Insert the given estimates to solve for the unknown value:

$$14.77 = I_{AU} (270) + (0.02727) (100)$$

This gives an average urban intensity of $I_{AU} = 0.0450$ gallons/person-mile, which is substantially worse than the intercity value. Average urban occupancies are also usually far lower. If the urban average occupancy is roughly estimated at only 1.2, then the fuel consumption rate would be 0.045/1.2 gallons per mile, or 18.5 miles per gallon. This lower value would also be expected with more stop-and-go driving.

Totals versus per Unit Statistics

Another common difficulty is that fuel efficiency and emissions information is available only on a per-unit-distance basis, perhaps corrected to a per-person-distance basis with a division by an average occupancy (load factor). There are an increasing number of sources available for such data. See, for example, James Strickland's (2013) website. the report by Condon and Dow (2009), or the statistics available from the FTA (2010). In the popular view, this is often synonymous with what efficiency means, but this is a naïve interpretation. This type of comparison is fine for trips that are "at the margin," that is, trips that can be directly substituted for one another. However, when a project is expected to potentially create significant changes in energy consumption or emissions across a city or region, it is the totals that count instead. To appreciate the range of differences between cities, see Figure 5.3, which shows energy consumption per capita by private passenger transport for 58 higher-income cities.

Differences in specific mode shares and average trip lengths cause differences in GHG emissions and regional energy consumption on the same order of magnitude as the more often studied changes in vehicle fuel efficiency and the corresponding volume and cleanliness of exhaust. (There will be more discussion in the next chapter about interaction with land use and urban form.) Indeed, the single largest goal of many transit investments is to dramatically change the mode split and trip lengths in certain corridors and thereby to also significantly change the regional totals. Furthermore, there can be a *rebound effect* where a more efficient vehicle that lowers operating costs stimulates some additional travel that offsets some of the gains. Thus, one-to-one comparison for a trip of the same distance by various modes can be highly misleading.

Figure 5.4 shows the additional information and multiplications involved to get totals for carbon emissions. The formula would be similar for other pollutants, using the specific pollutant content in a fuel, or mix of fuels, instead. For fuel consumption, the last term would represent the energy content of the fuel, or mix of fuels. These mixes can be complicated, varying seasonally. Mixes will be changing over the years as new power sources become available and others are retired, and as more pure electric and hybrid-electric vehicles come into service. Thus, it may be necessary to do computations of totals on a year-by-year basis in some cases. See the book by Vanek, Albright and Angenent (2012) for further

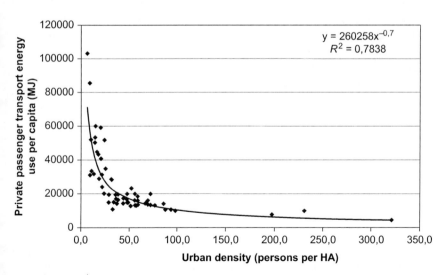

Figure 5.3 Urban Density versus per capital private passenger transport energy use in 58 higher income cities. Approximately 1995 data. (MJ = Megajoules; HA = Hectares)

Source: Jeffrey Kenworthy 2001. Millennium Cities Database.

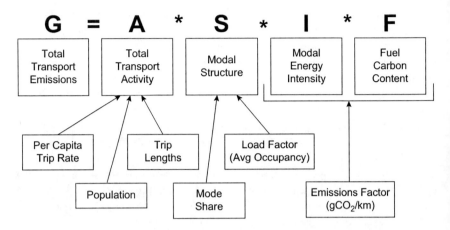

Figure 5.4 Information needed to compute total carbon emissions for a mode.

Source: Ashwin Prabhu and Madhav Pai 2012. Figure 2, p. 19. Copyright, National Academy of Sciences. Reproduced with permission of the Transportation Research Board.

discussion. In particular, see the chapters entitled Transportation Energy Technologies and Systems Perspective on Transportation Energy.

Finally, it is also important to note that transit vehicles can vary greatly in their fuel consumption rates depending upon their *duty cycle*. Thus, average values from manufacturers and testing laboratories should be avoided if results from similar operating environments are available. For example, Clark et al. (2006) found very large differences in fuel efficiency between bus operations on the Mexico City schedule and the standardized European Transient Cycle. Furthermore, the diesel-electric hybrid showed much less difference in performance, thereby demonstrating that the type of propulsion plant also plays a role in whether site-specific duty cycles are needed.

Influencing Modal Relationships

Connectivity to other modes, including to and from the final destination as a pedestrian, is of vital importance to an individual's travel decisions and the resulting mode split. The term is used here as an all-inclusive one for an entire range of attributes or characteristics that influence the availability and convenience of public transportation between given origins and destinations. Many of these were described in Chapter 3, including the route or line patterns, frequency of service, frequency of connecting services, frequency of connections, area coverage, comfort and reliability standards, and so on. Similar attributes can be used to describe the connectivity to intercity or long-distance modes. The remainder of this chapter is concerned with those parts of trips not already discussed; the nonmotorized portions and potential transfers to intercity and line-haul portions of trips.

Physical connectivity is defined here as the availability and convenience of the physical movement for individuals from one mode to the next, from the origin to the first motorized mode, and from the last motorized mode to the final destination. Close proximity is no guarantee that connectivity will be satisfactory to encourage transfers. Conversely, longer walking distances can be acceptable if there is an aesthetically pleasing or suitably sheltered route, or if there are aids such as moving walkways that are found in major airports and major rail stations.

Intracity Trips

The conditions that pedestrians and bicyclists are subjected to can have a large impact on public transport use. Although this might seem obvious, it is the details that count, and these must be reflected in the inputs to planning tools used for estimating ridership. In reality, a model may simply assume that certain persons are willing to walk to public transport if they are located with a fixed distance, regardless of actual local conditions. However, even if public transport service were frequent and reliable, it would still not attract as much ridership as one might compute using demand forecasting models. If the access provisions are poor, the walking time can be much longer than implied by map distances.

There are numerous situations where poor physical conditions for access by non-motorized modes can be a deterrent. Table 5.3 lists many attributes that can affect connectivity and deter transfers. Busy roads without sidewalks can be dangerous. Wide intersections, divided highways, and wide streets with medians can also deter choice users, especially children and the frail elderly, as the need to cross such roads can be a source of anxiety. Even if they are safe, walking on the shoulder or waiting along one can be unpleasant, even in good weather, and outright unacceptable to all but the hardiest choice riders under rainy or muddy conditions. Setbacks of buildings from streets on long driveways can also expose persons to the weather in the course of walking to a public transport stop. Even destinations that have negligible walking distances can have built-in deterrents. In sprawling commercial and office developments common to the United States, adjacent buildings may have a fence or embankment separating them while residential buildings may be on cul de sacs without pedestrian shortcuts. These can make even a short walk difficult or almost impossible. Marshall and Garrick (2010) found a statistically significant correlation between cities in the United States that have grid street patterns and shorter block distances with an increased use of nonmotorized modes and transit.

Even if the first walk can be negotiated, additional walking trips, such as for lunch or to the dry cleaners, may not be as easy. The needs of the individual to visit scattered destinations or ones with impeded paths between them may militate in favor of private auto use. Such trip chains are very difficult to serve either with nonmotorized modes or with public transportation. Thus, it is also important that numerous services be close together and that they have nonmotorized friendly connections. (Many of us who insist on walking despite conditions have blazed trails through hedges, down embankments, and around fences.)

Table 5.3 Physical connectivity attributes that deter transfers to and from public transportation

From/To Nonmotorized Modes	From/To Motorized Modes
lack of sidewalks	exposure to elements
no pedestrian shortcuts	steep or long staircases
long setbacks of buildings	crowding
wide intersections	long walks
divided highways	bulky or heavy luggage
dangerous or fast traffic conditions	lack of escalators or elevators
inadequate bicycle paths	
insufficient bicycle storage capacity	
inadequate bicycle security	

The situation with bicycling is similar. Bicycles are an increasingly popular access mode in many northern European cities, in large part because bicycle paths and adequate storage facilities have been provided. In Japan, the paths are often less than perfect, but efforts are made to provide massive storage, in some places including guarded storage houses using conveyor systems similar to those used by dry-cleaning stores. Bicycles serve to greatly enlarge the area that can be reached from a station without providing motorized connections, such as park-and-ride facilities or feeder buses. When the bicycle can be carried on the motorized mode, it becomes a feeder at both ends. Newer trains in some urban areas now have ample space in each car for bicycles (and luggage). Other trains, which were not designed for them, will permit them during off-peak periods. Buses also carry racks, which, because they are externally mounted, have a capacity of two bicycles at any time of day.

Geography and weather are beyond the ability of the planner to influence. Hilly terrain can limit the potential ridership; referring back to Table 5.2, it is no coincidence that the flat Netherlands and Denmark have exceptionally high bicycle use on average. Unpredictable weather patterns with sudden rain or ice conditions can deter bicycle ridership as well. In some locales, bicycle use would be highly seasonal, which would translate into significant changes in public transport demand at different times of the year. The bike riders in Copenhagen, for example, are a hardy lot, so this does not pertain to everyone. In general, however, bicycle riding depends on seasons and weather, and transit demand fluctuates accordingly.

There are measures that can be taken to influence bicycle ridership. Provision for carrying bicycles on transit vehicles can increase transit use when crowding conditions permit. Employers and transit agencies can both be asked to help by providing adequately large, secure storage facilities. Some additional encouragement to bicycle use can be given by employers by adding showers and lockers at the workplace. Perhaps most important of all, bicyclists must feel safe in their interaction with motorized traffic. There are two schools of thought about how safety should be achieved. One is that bicyclists should be separated as much as possible. The second is that bicycles should be incorporated into the same traffic stream. The latter requires public education and enforcement. It important to note, and perhaps to inform the public, that a comprehensive review of the health and safety literature on bicycling by Pucher, Dill, and Handy (2010) reveals that the health benefits from riding a bicycle far exceed the safety dangers in all but the most hazardous locations.

In general, bicycle facilities are potentially an inexpensive way to improve connectivity and influence travel habits, but the actual degree of use one could expect will vary on a case-by-case basis. The analyst must confirm that bicycle storage facilities are at least large enough for the lowest estimated volume of connecting persons; supply must always at least meet expected demand or it will be impossible for this demand to be satisfied. People will stop trying to use their bicycles almost as fast as the experiment begins if it is too difficult to find a place to secure their bikes. See the aforementioned study by Pucher et al. for a longer list of suggestions.

It can be insightful to read the survey results of persons who were using the automobile for short trips. In a major study from the United Kingdom, persons taking trips of eight kilometers or less were asked what alternatives they perceived and which they might actually be induced to try. About 31 percent said they might walk, another 31 percent might actually use a bus if service were more frequent, and 7 percent might bicycle. It was also clear from the survey that people generally needed more education about the benefits from using alternatives (Mackett and Ahern 2000). Another report generated by the same study also provides a useful review of data from other locations (Mackett and Robertson 2000).

To the extent that demand forecasting models capture any details of local access conditions and connectivity, they are usually focused on the work trip. There is much less information collected about the influence of local details of the urban form on nonwork trips. But what influences the choice of mode for these trips is actually more important to understand if one is trying to influence the lifestyle of the work-trip-riding-only public and the entire nonriding public. Portland, Oregon, is one city that has developed some modeling adjustments that may be roughly transferable to other US cities (Rajamani et al. 2003). Similarly, an analyst might be able to find some model adjustments from peer cities that could give close estimates for their own city of interest.

Connections between motorized modes can have similar deterrents to those for access via nonmotorized modes since, once again, access ultimately depends upon walking. Adjacent stops for different modes may not be effortlessly and directly connected. As an example, Philadelphia actually has two 30th Street Stations, one for long-distance trains and for Regional Rail, the other an underground station for streetcars and rapid transit. Connecting between them requires going into the weather and across a very busy intersection where one can be severely splashed. During precipitation, the crosswalk actually floods to form a lake. Despite the proximity, this utter lack of amenity must surely reduce the use of this transfer point and perhaps public transportation use in general. As will be discussed further in the Chapter 7, demand forecasting methods need to reflect the reduced ridership that no doubt results from poorer-than-average access conditions.

Intercity Trips and Trips Involving Luggage

The deterrent effect becomes more pronounced when a journey involves luggage or bulky or heavy items. The presence of toll barriers and the lack of elevators, escalators, or baggage trolleys causes discomfort at best and an insurmountable obstacle at worst for smaller or slightly built persons. However, the attribute that can severely limit the practical use of transit for access to longer journeys is a physical separation requiring leaving the environs of the transit facility altogether.

An example offered in the first edition was Washington, DC, where few people would walk from Union Station (either from the Metro station underground or the intercity trains on the ground level) to the intercity bus terminal that was several blocks away along a narrow sidewalk, and one that was usually deserted at night. Instead, virtually all travelers who could afford to do so would either take a taxi to access an intercity bus (not all were at the same terminal) or simply drive their own auto the entire way to their final destination. This is especially true if similar conditions can be expected at the other end of the line-haul segment of their trip.

This can be contrasted with most northern European cities where the intercity train station is immediately adjacent to the bus or the tram station serving both intracity and suburban destinations. Level changes are avoided, but when necessary, gentle ramps and escalators are provided. At an increasing number of airports, a train station is immediately underneath the terminal; a few are offering baggage trolleys that can even be used on escalators or permit luggage check-in to occur at a hotel or downtown terminal. Again, the connectivity attributes may not necessarily be captured in demand estimating models.

As an update: It seems that I was not the only one to recognize the poor connectivity conditions near Union Station. Indeed, since 2006 there has been a huge increase in competitors to both Amtrak and the incumbents of the old bus station. They were simply boarding on street corners using no terminals, or even ticket offices. The city government must have tired of the chaos and from complaints from businesses on the streets, from residents, from persons making connections, and from those needing to find "stops" in an unfamiliar city. One floor of the parking garage in Union Station has been converted into an intercity bus terminal. With intercity trains and city buses one level down, and the Metro in the basement, it is now more reminiscent of a European terminal and more in keeping with the expectations for a large capital city.

There can be other reasons for low use of transit to access longer-distance modes, of course, such as high fares and unreliable or inconvenient services on the intercity mode. Potential changes to these services must be considered as well. The ridership changes in particular need to be anticipated as best as possible. In some cases, one might want to expand the scope of a project, possibly involving financial contributions from the connecting modal organizations to the mutual benefit of all.

The insignificant role of intercity bus and intercity rail in all but a few markets in the United States can in part be explained by the lack of convenient transit terminals or stops, often combined with inconvenient schedules necessitating long waits at connecting points. Poor connections create a self-reinforcing stasis, as the lack of transit suppresses use of public intercity modes, while the lack of public intercity modes necessitates the ownership of an auto if one regularly makes such trips. As the rate of auto ownership increases, more efforts must be taken to attract people out of their autos, but fewer resources are available to do so. The alternatives then become reduction or elimination of service or the provision of subsidy.

After intercity buses were deregulated in the United States in the 1980s, wholesale abandonment of service occurred as unprofitable routes were abandoned. In some cases, rural transit systems were expanded or even created in response, often based on sharing vehicles used for medical trips or other specialized services. Where service remains exceedingly sparse, there is insufficient frequency and regularity of connection possibilities to form the basis of an intermodal center where local, rural, and intercity services can meet to exchange passengers. This holds true in almost all of the rural towns and smaller cities in the United States and Canada. By contrast, far more towns in Europe still have a functioning intermodal terminal, however simple or elaborate it might be. If there is no rail station, it may be not much more than a centrally located bus stop or small bus terminal conveniently adjacent to a taxi stand.

There are some positive examples from North America where connectivity is better. The Northeast Corridor from Washington, DC, to New York is the region best linked by frequent and competitively fast train service. It therefore captures many choice riders who own cars or could afford to fly on one of the air-shuttles instead. In a synergistic relationship, each of the major cities along the line has ubiquitous taxi service. Most have large parking facilities, in a similar manner to airports. Most have frequent public transport connections, although, like Philadelphia, the physical connection may not be equally convenient to all transit modes.

The ultimate improvement in physical connectivity was perhaps pioneered in Karlsruhe, Germany, in 1992, when light-rail vehicles started operating on the regional railway network, entering and exiting the city tram network near the train station. The lower cost of operation enabled increased service frequency and simultaneously eliminated the need for a transfer for many individuals. Thus, viewing an inbound trip, there is more frequent service at the boarding point and more frequent service to destinations in the city center, but without the typical offsetting requirement of a transfer between modes. The increase in ridership was so dramatic (four times the number previously using the affected regional railway route) that it started a whole raft of similar projects (Drechsler 1994).

Park and Ride

The question of whether connections to and from the auto mode should be encouraged or discouraged has been a subject of controversy for many years. There are different schools of thought. Some say that it is unrealistic to try to reach everyone with a walking distance connection, so therefore it is better to get auto drivers to go most of the way on transit than none of the way. Others say that the money spent and space expended on park-and-ride facilities would be better spent on improving local transit feeder/distributor connections and perhaps using any land next to a major transit station or terminal for a *Transit Oriented Development* site instead.

For a major activity center where parking is tight or congestion is daunting, such as a central business district or hospital complex, it is clear that successful diversion of drivers to park and ride, rather than lose them to another, more auto-friendly destination, could allow this center to keep growing. On the other hand, there is also evidence that regions that depend more on park and ride perform worse on the per-capita-transit-use indicator. Indeed, there seems to be a strong inverse correlation, as shown in Figure 5.5. Overdependence on park-and-ride lots, if used as a ridership-building strategy, would not appear to be too effective. However, this type of graph does not say anything about how far away the park-and-ride facilities are located, nor for what purposes the trips are taken. As always, there are also problems with defining a "region," so this type of aggregated analysis should not be used to draw conclusions about a particular situation in a particular region.

Research results have been quite limited that would give transit planners guidance about when a park and ride is effective in keeping people from driving to other destinations instead of the one that the park-and-ride serves. It only makes sense to try if there are sufficient environmental and major activity-center strengthening benefits that justify this investment. The opportunity cost would be using an equal amount of available funding to serve nonmotorized travelers by improved facilities and/or adding local feeder transit instead. A recent study by Mingardo (2013) surveyed 738 park-and-ride users at nine train stations in the Rotterdam and The Hague region. In the Hague, he found that in the absence of a park-and-ride facility, 39 percent of the users would have taken transit all the way, 22 percent would have ridden their bicycle part or all of the way to their destination, and 20 percent would have left their car somewhere else in the vicinity of the station. In Rotterdam, 30 percent of users would have used transit and 4 percent would have bicycled. (However, 39 percent said they would not have made the trip because their park and ride has been in existence so long they have never used any other alternative, so no conclusion was drawn that they were diverted from transit.) A similar result that a significant portion of travelers were diverted from transit was obtained from a survey of bus-based park and ride in the Cambridge, England, area (Meek, Ison, and Enoch 2011).

When taking into account the extra auto driving distances and resulting emissions due to those people who otherwise would not have driven in the absence of park and ride, Mingardo computes that "peripheral" stations near the activity centers have

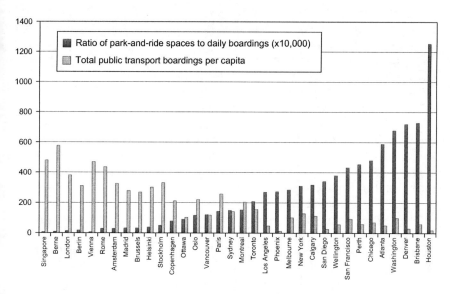

Figure 5.5 Inverse relationship of per capital transit ridership to park-and-ride provision.

Source: Schiller and Kenworthy 2011 (condensed version reduced from 100 cities).

a net negative environmental effect while "remote" stations that intercept people farther away have a net positive environmental effect, at least in the context of the Randstad region. One conclusion from this study might be that the distance where benefits cross over from negative to positive for any particular region should be the subject of study for any major new project where park and ride is contemplated. On the other hand, Meek et al. did not find remote park-and-ride sites too promising in the context of the Cambridge region, but did find that a hub and spoke (timed-transfer) system could provide a genuine reduction in vehicle-kilometers traveled.

One final observation is that new projects that involve expanding a rail line into a previously unserved "remote" territory should be distinguished from efforts to attract users to existing lines. If it is the former, the extension may create a huge environmental cost through emissions and consumption of agricultural lands or forests. In such a case, the provision of "remote" park and ride would probably play an important role in the selling of remote development by enabling an otherwise auto-based lifestyle but with the possibility of commuting in comfort.

Summary

The relationships of urban public transport modes to each other, to intercity modes, and to the community through nonmotorized modes all play a role in the performance of public transportation systems. Indicators such as mode-split percentages must be carefully designed so that they can detect differences that may arise from investment projects or operational changes. Breakdown of travel by number of trips is important to capture the contribution of nonmotorized modes, while breakdown by passenger-distance is necessary for estimation of social costs such as pollution generation and energy consumption. Ideally, both number of trips and trip distances should be tracked.

There are an increasing number of data sources available on the Internet for fuel efficiency and emissions, but comparisons on a one-to-one basis for a trip of the same length can be highly misleading. From an energy consumption and emissions standpoint, it is the totals that count. The purpose of many transit investments is, in fact, to dramatically change the mode split and trip lengths in certain corridors and thereby also significantly change the regional totals. These totals will also be influenced by changes in vehicle technologies and fuel mixes for each mode, both of which can be expected to change over time.

Planning models used to estimate demand do not necessarily capture important details of physical design or traveler willingness to perform multimodal trips. Indeed, some models do not even include nonmotorized modes. Demand forecasting models for public transport may assume access travel times based on map distance without regard to actual walking conditions or physical barriers. These models also tend to focus on the work trip, with fewer quantitative tools available to predict mode choices for nonwork trips. Model inputs and outputs should be scrutinized accordingly. Adjusted models used by peer cities can sometimes be used to estimate the errors created by established models used by planning authorities.

Pedestrian and bicycle access can be improved through physical changes to streets, through separate shortcut paths, through proper accommodation for bicycles on public transport modes such that they can be carried onboard, and through accommodation for bicyclists at the workplace. Perhaps most important is that that pedestrians and bicyclists feel safe in their interactions with motorized vehicles. Otherwise, any other improvements are not likely to receive much usage.

Intermodal connections where rural, local, and intercity services meet can facilitate more public transport use as well as make travel conditions easier for existing users. In larger cities, these various travel niches can be connected with convenient terminal designs that limit walking and exposure to the elements. In many smaller cities, however, there is insufficient frequency and regularity of the various services to establish good connectivity between them. But they can still colocate a taxi stand with local and long-distance bus stops.

Quantum improvements in connectivity between modes is possible, as proved by the example of the pioneering merger of urban light-rail with suburban rail services in Karlsruhe, Germany. Rather than easing the transfer, the system eliminated transfers and increased frequency by using vehicles that can operate on both rights-of-way. Such dramatic improvements can also cause dramatic changes in travel behavior.

Provision of park-and-ride lots tend to have an inverse correlation with percapita transit ridership, so reliance upon them as a ridership-building strategy is in general not warranted. Recent research from the Randstad area of the

Netherlands indicates that a significant number of persons would use transit or bicycles if there were no park and ride nearby. So the net environmental benefit can be negative if the location is close to activity center, but becomes positive as the location becomes more remote. On the other hand, researchers of the Cambridge, England, area questioned whether even "remote" lots are worthwhile.

References

Buehler, Ralph, and John Pucher. 2012. "Demand for Public Transport in Germany and the USA: An Analysis of Rider Characteristics." *Transport Reviews* 32 (5): 541–67.

Clark, Nigel N., Enrique Rivero Borrell, David L. McKain, Victor Hugo Paramo, W. Scott Wayne, Walter Vergara, Ryan A. Barnett, Mridul Gautam, Gregory Thompson, Donald W. Lyons, and Lee Schipper. 2006. "Evaluation of Emissions from New and In-Use Transit Buses in Mexico City, Mexico." *Transportation Research Record 1987*: 42–53.

Condon, Patrick M., and Kari Dow. 2009. "A Cost Comparison of Transportation Modes." Sustainability by Design No. 7. *Foundation Research Bulletin*. Vancouver: Design Centre for Sustainability, School of Architecture and Landscape Architecture, University of British Columbia.

Drechsler, Goerg. 1994. "Karlsruhe Trams Cross More City Boundaries." *Railway Gazette International* (November): 719–21.

EPOMM (European Platform on Mobility Management). 2013. *TEMS—The EPOMM Modal Split Tool*. http://www.epomm.eu/tems/index.phtml. Accessed April 2013.

FTA (U.S. Federal Transit Administration). 2010. *Public Transportation's Role in Responding to Climate Change*. Washington, DC: U.S. Department of Transportation. www.fta.dot.gov/documents/PublicTransportationsRoleInRespondingToClimate Change2010.pdf

Kenworthy, Jeffrey. 2001. "Millennium Cities Database and Mobility in Cities Database." Brussels, Belgium: UITP. http://www.uitp.org/knowledge/Statistics.cfm

Mackett, Roger, and A. A. Ahern. 2000. *Potential for Mode Transfer of Short Trips: Report on the Analysis of the Survey Results*. London, UK: Department of the Environment Transport and the Regions. http://www.ucl.ac.uk/transport-studies/shtrp.htm

Mackett, Roger, and S. A. Robertson. 2000. *Potential for Mode Transfer of Short Trips: Review of the Existing Data and Literature Sources*. London, UK: Department of the Environment Transport and the Regions. http://www.ucl.ac.uk/transport-studies/shtrp.htm

Marshall, Wesley E., and Norman W. Garrick. 2010. "Effect of Street Network Design on Walking and Biking." *Transportation Research Record* 2198: 103–15.

Meek, S., S. Ison and M. Enoch. 2011. "Evaluating Alternative Concepts of Bus-Based Park and Ride." *Transport Policy* 18 (2): 456–67.

Mingardo, Giuliano. 2013. "Transport and Environmental Effects of Rail-Based Park and Ride: Evidence from the Netherlands." *Journal of Transport Geography* 30: 7–16.

Prabhu, Ashwin, and Madhav Pai. 2012. "Buses as Low-Carbon Mobility Solutions for Urban India: Evidence from Two Cities." *Transportation Research Record* 2317: 15–23.

Pucher, John. 1995. "Urban Passenger Transport in the United States and Europe: A Comparative Analysis of Public Policies." *Transport Reviews* 15 (2): 99–117.

Pucher, John, Jennifer Dill and Susan Handy. 2010. "Infrastructure, Programs, and Policies to Increase Bicycling: An International Review." *Preventive Medicine* 50: S106–S125.

Rajamani, Jayanthi, Chandra R. Bhat, Susan Handy, Gerrit Knaap and Yan Song. 2003. "Assessing the Impact of Urban Form Measures on Nonwork Trip Mode Choice After Controlling for Demographic and Level-of-Service Effects." *Transportation Research Record* 1835: 158–74.

Schiller, Preston, and Jeffrey Kenworthy. 2011. "Walk-to Transit or Drive-to Transit?" *Proceedings (Charter Papers) Walk21, Vancouver, BC, October.* http://walk21.com/paper_search/results_detail.asp?Paper=803

Schipper, Lee, and Steve Myers. 1993. *Energy Efficiency and Human Activity.* Cambridge, UK: Cambridge University Press.

Schipper, Lee, Ruth Steiner, Peter Duerr, Feng An and Steiner Stroem. 1992. "Energy Use in Passenger Transport in OECD Countries: Changes since 1970." *Transportation* 19: 25–42.

Socialdata GmbH. 1999. Data provided to author upon request. Munich, Germany. http://www.socialdata.de

Sperling, Daniel. 1995. *Future Drive: Electric Vehicles and Sustainable Transportation.* Washington, DC: Island Press.

Strickland, James. 2013. "Energy Efficiency of Different Modes of Transportation." http://www.builditsolar.com/References/EfficiencyTransport/strickland.htm

Vanek, Francis, Louis Albright and Largus Angenent. 2012. *Energy Systems Engineering* 2nd ed. Chapter 15 on Transportation Energy Technologies: 477–522 and Chapter 16 on Systems Perspective on Transportation Energy: 523–72. New York: McGraw-Hill Professional.

Further Reading

Buehler, Ralph, and John Pucher. 2012. "Walking and Cycling in Western Europe and the United States: Trends, Policies, and Lessons." *TR News* 280 (May–June): 34–42.

Carré, J. R. 2000. "Présentation d'une méthode d'analyse de séquences piétonnières au cours des déplacements quotidiens des citadins et mesure de l'exposition au risque des piétons." *Rapport INRETS* no. 221 (Mai).

Doolittle, John T., Jr., and Ellen Kret Porter. 1994. *Integration of Bicycles and Transit.* Synthesis of Transit Practice 4. Washington, DC: Transit Cooperative Research Program, National Academy Press. http://www.tcrponline.org

Evill, B. 1995. "Population, Urban Density, and Fuel Use: Eliminating Spurious Correlation." *Urban Policy and Research* 13 (1): 29–36.

Guo, Jessica Y., Chandra R. Bhat and Rachel B. Copperman. 2007. "Effect of the Built Environment on Motorized and Non-motorized Trip Making." *Transportation Research Record* 2010: 1–11.

Litman, Todd. 2003. "Measuring Transportation: Traffic, Mobility and Accessibility." *ITE Journal* 73 (10): 28–32.

Morency, Catherine, Martin Trépanier and Marie Demers. 2011. "Walking to Transit: An Unexpected Source of Physical Activity." *Transport Policy* 18: 800–06.

Tolley, Rodney, ed. 2003. *Non-Motorized Transportation Demand Management, Sustainable Transport: Planning for Walking and Cycling in Urban Environments.* Cambridge, UK: Woodhead Publishing.

Virkler, M. R. 1998. "Prediction and Measurement of Travel Time Along Pedestrian Routes." *Transportation Research Record* 1636: 37–42.

Willson, Richard, and Val Menotti. 2007. "Commuter Parking versus Transit-Oriented Development: Evaluation Methodology." *Transportation Research Record* 2021: 118–25.

Chapter 6

Space Requirements and Impacts from Land Use

Transportation modes vary greatly in both the space they require and the impacts they impose at various levels, from local neighborhoods, through the region as a whole, up to the entire ecosystem. No evaluation of a major project would be complete that did not consider the relative space consumption and array of potential impacts of various project alternatives. In many countries and regions, elaborate processes are in place to ensure these are not neglected. Because of increasing financial and environmental pressures, jurisdictions that currently have poorly developed or poorly regulated public transport systems and/or weak land-use regulations can be expected to also begin requiring assessments of space impacts from transportation projects.

Literature about recommended design details and dimensions of public transportation infrastructure and about the details and recommended dimensions for various types of neighborhood designs is now widely available. The purpose of this chapter is not to reiterate such information. Rather, it is to present basic principles and insights about how transport and nontransport land uses coexist and the impact of changes in their balance. One other purpose of this chapter is to raise awareness of some factors that have not always been included in evaluation but will be more frequently in the future. The chapter concludes with a discussion of the relation of pricing to land use.

Development Density and Transportation Activity

It seems intuitive that higher densities of development would be associated with higher levels of transportation activity. But the relationship is more complex than the number of trips simply being proportional to density. The physical details of development greatly influence both the type and volume of activity possible, even if the density is nominally said to be the same. A description of how some of these details affect transportation follows.

The concept of density can be ambiguous when the included area is not fully described. The included area might be such that buildings and infrastructure are concentrated on some portions of the parcel of land in question, while other portions might be parks, left undeveloped, or be entirely undevelopable, such as streams, rivers, ponds, or steep embankments. Some cities even include bays or large, totally undisturbed fringe areas. Thus, some care must be taken when making comparisons. Corrections are often required.

Analysts have developed some terms to reduce ambiguity. *Net density* refers to only the developed or constructed-upon land, while *gross density* refers to an average across an entire tract of land. Different design forms can ultimately end up with the same number of total inhabitants on the same-size tract of land. The gross population density is the same, yet the net population densities are different. Merlin (2001) offers an example that will help make this clear. He compares three different forms seen in the Paris region. Each tract has a gross area of 26,600 square feet (2,520 square meters), half of which is developable. The total number of inhabitants in each is 79. The first form uses 10 percent of the gross land to provide 36 dwellings of 740 square feet (70 square meters) each, the second uses 17 percent of the gross land to again provide 36 dwellings of the same size, and the third uses 33 percent of the available land to provide 24 dwellings of 1,100 square feet (105 square meters). The smaller dwellings have an average occupancy of 2.2 persons, while the large dwellings have an average occupancy of 2.8. This results in a *net* population density of 64 persons/acre (157 persons/hectare) for the tracts having smaller dwellings and 54 persons/acre (133 persons/hectare) for the tract having larger dwellings.

To generalize from this comparison, there are at least three useful commonly seen methods of describing development intensity: 1) *The Floor Area Ratio (FAR)* describes how many floor equivalents are built on top of a base footprint where not all floors need to span the full base area, 2) Dwelling Units/Area gives the average area per household, and 3) Population/Area describes the average amount of space each person occupies. The FAR is inherently a net density, but the other two can be either a net or gross density, depending upon the area used. Lee et al. (2011) have compiled a database called the "Density Atlas" using these three definitions for a wide variety of cities. It is quite informative and worth spending some time perusing.

A higher net population density will mean, all else being equal, that a single given public transport stop can serve more people within a given walking distance; however, even this is not necessarily true if the stop is located within the portion of the gross area without dwellings. Further complicating the picture is the fact that a longer walk through the area without dwellings may be more attractive if the area is a park or nature preserve than would a shorter walk to a stop in close proximity to the dwellings. This stop may be in a noisy location, one that requires crossing a major road to reach, or be otherwise unappealing. Furthermore, the path "as the crow flies" may not be a good indicator of actual walking distances. A grid road network with long block lengths or an urban form using cul de sacs can both greatly increase walking distances if no pedestrian shortcuts are installed. Furthermore, lack of suitable sidewalks or wide roads with heavy traffic may also necessitate a roundabout path. As a result, a smaller fraction of total transportation activity will be nonmotorized. To reiterate from the earlier chapter discussing the relationship of public transport to other modes, the local details matter.

It may also seem intuitive that similar net population densities (or commercial development densities) will create a similar number of motorized trips and, thus, create similar congestion levels. But neither the number of activities nor congestion levels need be proportional to net density. If land uses such as residential areas and stores are physically separated, or if nonmotorized options are lacking, more motorized travel activity will be generated. Large cities with older urban forms can have up to 25 percent nonmotorized trips; some districts will have a higher percentage, others will have a lower one. By contrast, in many post–World War II suburban and rural tracts, this number can be close to zero. Compounding this, the same newer type of urban form that evidently deters nonmotorized trips also tends to concentrate motorized trips on a few arterial roads. Figure 6.1a shows a *neotraditional* urban form (a resurrection of pre–World War II forms) where a grid of relatively narrow streets disperses auto traffic onto numerous

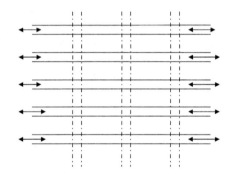

a: neotraditional street layout with narrower, parallel paths

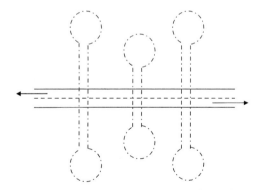

b: post–World War II design concentrating traffic on one path

Figure 6.1 Traffic volume dispersal and concentration.

parallel paths. Nonmotorized and transit trips have numerous routing possibilities as well. Contrast this with Figure 6.1b, typical of many post–World War II tracts, where all trips are focused on a central road, including transit, which has only one option of serving this corridor. This can eventually overload this road and necessitate numerous traffic signals and eventual road widening. This growth in motorized trips causes both deterioration in transit speed and further impediments to accessing transit. The end result of final tract build-out is often an unpleasant environment for pedestrians, a barrier effect to reaching transit stops, and transit service subject to delays.

If a new area is built using a neotraditional urban form instead, the ultimate capacity of the road network is actually higher, as measured in the Vehicle Miles Traveled (VMT) it can support. At the same time, this form allows traffic engineers more latitude in setting turning rules and signal phases that are more conducive to nonmotorized travel, perhaps no traffic signals at all. Clearance times where all directions receive a red signal for safety can also be reduced or eliminated because of the smaller intersection sizes. In case of road blockages, the neotraditional form also provides alternative paths. A comparison of the two forms is shown in Figure 6.2.

Relaxation of zoning that separates land uses and acquisition of narrow rights-of-way across private land to create a grid-like network of shortcut paths for nonmotorized trips can reduce the congestion in some existing layouts. This is already standard design practice in northern Europe. The increasing number of advanced elderly who can no longer drive and the congestion caused by large numbers of children who must be chauffeured to school during the morning rush hour suggest that shortcut retrofits are likely to become more common in the United States in the future.

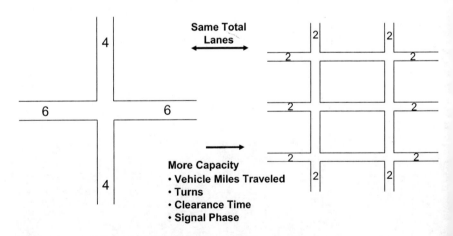

Figure 6.2 Comparison of neotraditional to major arterial networks.

Source: Kulash 2006.

So far the discussion has primarily revolved around residential land use. In such case one can divide the dwelling floor area by the number of residents to reach a unit-floor-area consumption factor, f. But for other uses, such as industrial or retail, the value of f will depend upon the precise nature of the use. A single lathe workstation in a machine shop will take more space than a secretarial work station; a car dealer will need more space per employee than a convenience store, and so on. Even vehicle storage areas can be viewed as a retail use, with trucks requiring more space than cars and off-street parking taking more space than on-street parking. The specific type of use is of importance for estimating not only the level of transportation activities that will result from a given land use, but the timing of the use. As examples, a retail shopping center will generate activity throughout the day, but an office building might generate only travel activity at the beginning and end of the working day.

The unit-floor-area consumption concept is used because of its relation to the available space at ground level. In any healthy urban area, ground space is highly valuable. Thus, buildings have additional floors to multiply the amount of floor area available to be consumed over a given amount of ground space thereby increasing the FAR. In this chapter a similar quantity to the FAR, the development intensity factor, I, will be used to increase the amount of economic and residential activity proportional to the number of added floors.

Land Consumption by Public Transportation Modes

Land requirements for rights-of-way are a vital consideration for many public transport projects. Not only do such requirements have implications for the physical appearance and functioning of the city, the availability, or lack thereof, has serious implications for the cost of any project. Indeed, the project viability often hinges on the various rights-of-way options and their relative costs. While costs are ultimately site specific, some generalizations still can be made.

1   *Grade-separated alignments will cost more than at-grade alignments.* The separation is achieved by the use of elevated structures or tunnels. In some situations, modest lengths and favorable construction conditions for grade-separated alignments can minimize costs. At the opposite extreme, special construction techniques and difficult work locations entail high elements of cost risk. Historical examples included the Transbay Tube crossing San Francisco Bay using a special earthquake-resistant design, and the danger of natural gas leaks into the Red Line tunnel under central Los Angeles that delayed construction. Lower-cost alternatives that analysts can consider are overpasses and underpasses.

2   *Modes using positive guidance will cost more than modes requiring an operator for steering.* Tracks, switching, signals, and other rail infrastructure that provide positive guidance are far more complex and expensive than simple

paved surfaces that instead depend upon an operator to guide the vehicle. Tracks need not only be for steel wheel on steel rail. There can be rubber-tired trains, sometimes seen on rapid transit (examples include Mexico City and Paris) but often seen on *people movers* used in airports and for local circulators.

There are other forms of less-prevalent guidance systems as well. Buses have used lateral wheels that follow low vertical walls; these systems are referred to as *O-bahn*. Elevated monobeam structures supporting vehicles that use both vertical and lateral tires to straddle it are known as *monorails*. But monorails are proprietary designs that, unlike the more standardized rail technology, can only be extended using designs from the same vendor. They are also not simple to use in networks requiring switching between lines, so they are seen much less frequently than conventional rail designs. More recently, there are rail-vehicle-like *Bus Rapid Transit* (BRT) buses that contact single beams under the center of the bus or use optical guidance. As of this writing, it is not clear which, if any, of several competing designs will become widespread in their usage.

3   *Grade separation allows higher performance and higher levels of safety.* The separation from other traffic removes vehicles from congestion and unanticipated behavior by other motorists. Analogous to a freeway, it also removes conflicts from cross traffic. The ability to maintain speed regardless of ground-level traffic conditions and the reliability of travel time made possible by exclusive use offset the higher costs of such separation and are often key justifications for the expenditure.

4   *Guided vehicles need narrower rights-of-way than unguided vehicles and have higher levels of safety.* The positive guidance of steel rails removes the need to allow the vehicle operator latitude to maneuver—a driver could never manually safely maintain a narrow path at higher speeds. The aforementioned O-Bahn guideway allowed buses to run at speed in narrow tunnels designed for rail vehicles as in Essen, Germany. On the surface, the middle of this guideway can remain unpaved, minimizing the busway intrusion into sensitive green areas while totally excluding autos (Tebb 1993). Examples include Adelaide, Australia, or Leeds, England.

Positive lateral guidance does not remove the possibility of fore/aft collisions between vehicles in the system but does remove the possibility of weaving and sideswipe collisions. The fore/aft collision danger can also be removed through the use of signal systems with automatic braking when signals are violated.

5   *Grade-separated alignments use far less surface area than at-grade alignments.* A tunnel uses no surface space, although surface space may periodically be required for stations to access the tunnel. Elevated sections for rapid transit and regional rail lines covering an entire four-lane road using columns along the outside edge (e.g. the "L" in Chicago) block light and require a high degree of maintenance because they are made of steel (e.g. painting). Modern reinforced-concrete designs are built with a center column such that it can

be located in the median of a road, although additional surface space is still needed at stopping locations. The resulting quality of the adjacent surface area can still be an issue—the elevated section can block light, generate noise, and be perceived as visually unattractive. This can offset the savings from reduced right-of-way consumption. It may not be acceptable to some districts with intense nonmotorized activity or concern about aesthetic values. As an example, the city of Berkeley, California, paid extra to place the BART line in a tunnel, not only under its CBD, but under the length of the city. Cities to north and south have elevated sections.

6 *Opportunistic alignments reduce investment costs but usually provide fewer benefits.* One example of an opportunistic alignment is a median along a freeway. It will minimize right-of-way acquisition. On the other hand, it requires public transport riders to walk long distances over or under lanes and subjects then to significant noise and localized air pollution. It is also an expensive site for intensive development due to the many physical constraints of building alongside and perhaps even over a wide highway, but could still be of interest when there is great pressure from an expanding population. Another example of a common opportunistic alignment is an abandoned freight railroad right-of-way. These rarely pass through the sections of the city with highest ridership potential. Walking distances are longer and ridership is reduced accordingly.

Much of the controversy surrounding major public transport projects hinges on whether the additional costs from separated rights-of-way are justified. This question is not properly answered by looking only at passenger-related and operations-related performance indicators of the various project alternatives. A major project interacts with all other land uses in the area as well. All project alternatives should be compared for their relative land-use impacts, not only to each other but also against the continued viability of present land-use trends. A major project could well change the composition of land use and the mix between transport and nontransport purposes. The goal of altering the balance and composition of land use may, in fact, be a key justification of a project. In some cases, such as the Jubilee Line extension completed in London in 2000, such a change in balance was the whole point. The Canary Wharf Docklands area was not sufficiently accessible, and development was stalled without the addition of a high-capacity, high-speed rail service.

At this point, I will describe the *time-area* concept because it is a valuable tool to help quantify how transportation consumes urban space. It unifies the analysis of both moving and stationary (parked) vehicles. The general case is shown in Figure 6.3, where a vehicle (or in the case of a train, the cars of the train) moves along a right-of-way of width, W. As it moves, it occupies both an area due to its own size, plus a *shadow* that is used to maintain a reaction and safe braking distance. The length of the shadow increases with speed. Thus, the shadow length, $S(t)$, varies with time as the vehicle accelerates, cruises, and decelerates through its driving cycle. The product W x $S(t)$ is the *Instantaneously Occupied Area*. As the vehicle proceeds over time, the size of the area it sweeps across changes. Mathematically speaking, the total time-area consumed is the integral of the Instantaneously Occupied Area with respect to time over a chosen analysis time period, T. But the solution of the time-area formula for the general case of a random travel profile will not be presented here.

The simple case of a vehicle moving at constant speed and maintaining just enough shadow for safe operation is sufficient for a conceptual understanding. This corresponds to automobiles moving as a platoon along arterials with synchronized traffic signals or along freeways during congested peak periods. The resulting equation for average time-area consumed per auto is then:

$$\overline{TA} = \frac{WL}{q} = \frac{WL}{kv}, \qquad \left[\frac{\text{distance}^2 - \sec}{\text{vehicle}} \right] \qquad (6\text{-}1)$$

where q is the flow rate of vehicles in one lane, expressed in vehicles per hour. The flow q can also be expressed as the product of density of vehicles, k, defined as the spacing of vehicles per unit distance, with speed, v, defined as distance traveled per unit time. The latter formulation calls attention to the fact that there is a speed and density combination that maximizes q and thus minimizes time-area consumption per vehicle. The relationship between flow, speed, and density is discussed further in the Chapter 7.

The solution for the case that represents a typical urban bus travel profile is somewhat more complicated. Instead of a constant speed with perhaps an occasional stop at a traffic signal, the bus travel profile involves repeating a cycle of standing, accelerating, cruising, and decelerating. The equation is not shown, but it is easily derived. The insertion of reasonable values for standing times, acceleration and deceleration rates, and speed then enables completion of the computation. The interested reader is referred to Bruun and Vuchic (1995) for computational examples or Shin (1997) for rigorous derivations.

The average time-area consumed can be converted from a per-vehicle basis to a per-person basis by dividing by the average vehicle occupancy, α_{avg}:

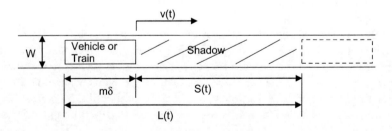

Figure 6.3 The components of Instantaneous Area Occupancy.

$$TA_p = \frac{WL}{\alpha_{avg}q} = \frac{WL}{\alpha_{avg}kv} \cdot \left[\frac{distance^2 - sec}{person}\right] \qquad (6\text{-}2)$$

Comparing the relative time-area consumption between using a bus for the journey to work versus an auto reveals the space implications of relying upon automobiles as the primary means of urban transportation instead of public transportation. Rather than simply evaluating the time-area equations and comparing the numerical results, it is more insightful to graphically portray the situation. When traffic flow is constant, the total time-area consumed per person is simply the area within the rectangle formed by Instantaneously Occupied Area, on the vertical axis, and journey travel time, on the horizontal axis. An example that is approximately to scale is shown for a journey to work on Figure 6.4. There are two comparisons: bus versus auto during the peak period and bus versus auto during the off-peak period. When they both operate in mixed traffic (ROW C), both modes will typically have slower speeds than during the off-peak. Furthermore, the auto is faster than the bus in both cases. But the price is paid by the much higher Instantaneously Occupied Area requirement for the auto. It is also typical that auto occupancies are lower during the peak periods, precisely when space is at a premium. The bus, on the other hand, is typically just the opposite: it has the highest occupancies during peak period.

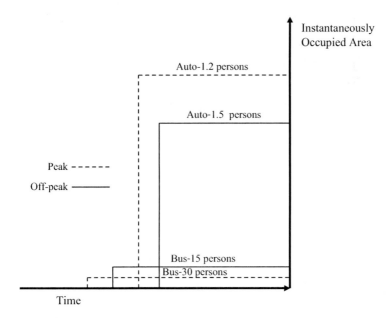

Figure 6.4 Time-area consumption comparison between modes for journey to work on right-of-way C.

At least two observations can be made. One is that the marginal space benefit of diversion of an automobile user to transit during the peak period is very high. Another is that dedicating space for transit might be justified by the more efficient use of space. An upgrade to ROW B (where an entire lane is laterally separated) will increase the speed of the bus during the peak period. It will help to cause the highly space-efficient diversion of some automobile users to the bus. If the upgrade goes to ROW A (full grade separation), the surface-level time-area consumption for the bus goes to almost zero. The speed not only increases further, it would remain the same regardless of congestion at street level. It would thus cause even more diversions to transit by auto users. With enough diversion, street-level space could be liberated for nonmotorized or even nontransportation uses. Such a benefit might sometimes justify much higher investment costs.

The story of space consumption for the journey-to-work is not complete if it does not also include the time-area consumed by vehicles that must be stored over the course of the workday. It is computed similar to a moving vehicle, but without a shadow. This further impact on urban space requirements can also be shown conceptually using the time-area concept. Figure 6.5 shows an automobile and bus similar to the previous figure arriving to work during the peak period. An equal amount of time-area is consumed on the journey home from work. But now parking the auto is also seen to occupy substantial time-area, in fact, more than while driving. When a multistory parking garage is used, the parking area requirement must be adjusted higher than for on-street parking, as the ramps and maneuvering areas must also be prorated across all of the parking stalls (roughly 30 percent higher). Note that no storage time-area consumption is attributed for

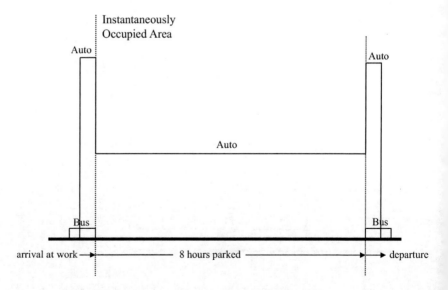

Figure 6.5 Time-area consumption for peak hour commuting.

a bus occupant on Figure 6.5, as the bus can be stored outside of the central area containing the most valuable land.

Thus, another observation can be made using the time-area concept. Transit investments can sometimes be justified by reduced storage space requirements. This can translate into a monetary benefit of land that can be put to more valuable nontransport uses. Furthermore, removal of large parking garages tends to improve the local pedestrian environment, which although not directly monetizeable, is an important goal of some transit projects.

Balancing Land Consumption between Transport and Nontransport Uses

While the previous discussion indicates that public transport uses space more efficiently than automobiles on a per-person basis, it does not explain how much transportation activity can occur before the urban transportation system reaches capacity. How much and what type of economic and residential activity can occur before capacity is reached for a given amount of transportation infrastructure is an important question. An answer is also needed in order to estimate the reduced costs if existing infrastructure is used more intensely in lieu of new infrastructure. There is evidence of significant potential savings from intensification of land use rather than expansion and sprawl, not only for both freight and passenger transport but also for water, sewer, and electric infrastructure (Burchell and Galley 2003; Burchell 1998; Burchell 1997). There should also be a reduction in social costs (Freilich and Peshoff 1997). Furthermore, there is evidence that there can be substantial savings in personal expenditures on transportation (Kenworthy et al. 1997). All of these could serve to offset investment and operating support for public transportation.

What constitutes a sustainable transportation development path for cities is also a question of increasing importance. Pressure is mounting to preserve surrounding watersheds, agricultural lands, forests, and wetlands near cities. Because there is evidence of a dramatic reduction in fuel consumption, and consequently greenhouse gas generation, as the density of cities increases (Newman and Kenworthy 1989, 1999; Kenworthy 2008), an intensification strategy for existing cities might also be considered. As the number of large and even megacities in the world increases and their populations continue to grow, finding answers to the question of how to develop sustainably is becoming more urgent. A large part of the solution is likely to be closer-to-optimal use of urban land. "Optimal" use is narrowly defined here such that the city still functions within the transportation capacity of the network, without leaving urban land underused in locations that have the transport infrastructure to support more economic and/or residential activity. A city where this condition is met can be said to have achieved *balance* between its transport and nontransport land uses.

Studying how the balance of transportation and nontransportation land uses would be achieved requires the use of a fairly complicated mathematical model. Shin (1997) developed a useful one for conceptually understanding the interaction between these two major categories of land uses. Its starting point is a concentric city with residential and employment activities distributed in a pattern such that residential-related activity moderately increases in intensity as it approaches the center, while employment-related activity increases much more steeply. These activities require a certain amount of space in and of themselves; workers occupy buildings that average 10 stories in height (FAR of 10) and that increase in number steeply as one approaches the center. Residents occupy buildings that average three stories in height on the remainder of the land used for nontransport purposes. In turn, these employment and residential activities generate transportation activities that consume land for transport purposes. Figure 6.6 shows the process. The left side of this figure traces the steps used to sum all nontransport land use; the right side traces all transport land use. The bottom middle shows the total of the two land-use categories. The sum of the land used for transport and nontransport use must not exceed the developable land. Further details about some of these steps will be provided in Chapter 7.

In this hypothetical model, a central city is assumed to end at a radius of 5 kilometers (3.1 miles) from the center, with the remainder of the city along with its residential and economic development intensity tapering off to zero at infinity. Only 60 percent of the central city is developable, the rest being public parks, rivers, wetlands, embankments, and other natural barriers to development. Thus, there is a total developable area of 47.1 square kilometers (18.2 square miles). The parking capacity is sufficient to permit an accumulation of auto arrivals within the central city over a two-hour peak period, with some space still reserved for midday transportation activities. Only 10 percent of autos can park on the street, the remainder in three-story garages. Table 6.1 lists more key assumptions and values.

The defining feature of the central city versus the remainder of the city is that there is no storage space allocated for public transport use within it, even though transport activity becomes denser as it approaches the center. The central city has rapid transit that consumes no surface space and which carries 40 percent of all motorized trips during a two-hour peak period. The central city initially has bus service that carries 35 percent of all motorized trips during this same period, the remaining motorized 25 percent carried by private automobile. All public transport rights-of-way initially have spare capacity. Vehicles are not crowded beyond Level of Service (LOS) standards, and additional vehicles could be added to the existing rights-of-way. Trips generated as a result of residential and economic activity are distributed in a realistic fashion, but wholly symmetric in nature due to the concentric shape of the city. As would be expected, the number of trips increases towards the center as the number of origins and destinations increase (see Figure 6.8). See Shin (1997) for a more complete explanation of all assumptions and parameters used.

Table 6.1 Initial assumptions and values for Shin's model

Total regional personal activities during the peak period		

10 million

    7 million are residential based

    3 million are employment based

Activity distribution

22.5% of peak hour residential trips involve central city travel

75.1% of peak hour employment trips involve central city travel

(See Shin [1997] for computational methodology)

Unit area consumption factors

residence related	$f_h = 45$ m^2/person	(475 ft^2/person)
employment related	$f_w = 30$ m^2/person	(320 ft^2/person)
parking, off-street (90%)	$f_h = 30$ m^2/person	(320 ft^2/person)
parking, on-street (10%)	$f_h = 23$ m^2/person	(243 ft^2/person)

Sufficient reserve parking for midday parkers averaging 1 hour stays

Development intensity factors

residence related, initial average	$l_h = 3$	—
employment related, initial average	$l_w = 10$	—

distributed with respect to radius using exponential (Sheratt's) function

Land usage

total central area	78.5 km^2	(30.2 mile^2)
unusable	31.4 km^2	(12.1 mile^2)
total usable	47.1 km^2	(18.1 mile^2)
nontransport	30.4 km^2	(11.7 mile^2)
residence related	23.6 km^2	(9.1 mile^2)
employment related	6.8 km^2	(2.6 mile^2)
transport	16.7 km^2	(6.4 mile^2)

Vehicle occupancies

auto, peak period	1.2 persons/vehicle
bus, peak period	30 persons/vehicle

Duration of activities

2-hour peak-period, symmetric at each end of the day

To summarize, they were inspired by a city the size of New York, with Manhattan similar to the central city, and the outer boroughs the remainder of the region. (The additional commuting from outside the city proper is neglected.) These assumptions would also be reasonable for a somewhat smaller European or Japanese metropolitan area. It might roughly approximate metropolitan Munich, Germany, for example. Munich has a dense core of at least 10 kilometers (6.2 miles) in diameter with a multitude of rapid transit, as well as commuter and LRT lines. The metropolitan region for Munich, Southern Bavaria, has only 4.9 million people as opposed to New York City's city population of about 8 million and much larger regional population, so some adjustment would be needed to rerun this model. But most of the assumptions used by the model would still be appropriate, and the results would be similar, only reduced proportionately.

The first exploration using this model is to move towards increased auto use (and probably away from sustainable development). The total developable land is still fixed at the same amount. But the mode split will change from 25 percent auto use to 40 percent of motorized trips, with bus decreasing from 35 to 20 percent. Rapid transit use is unchanged at 40 percent. The amount of travel activity is to be unchanged such that no motorized trips have to be eliminated.

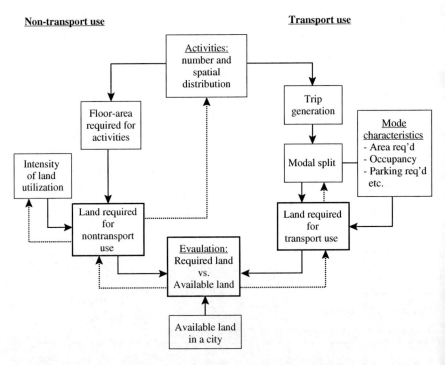

Figure 6.6 Conceptual diagram of the split between transport and nontransport use.

Source: Shin 1997.

The situation is shown in Figure 6.7 with the initial condition being labeled A, and the final condition being labeled B. The land required for transport, G_T, would have to increase from about 24 square kilometers (9.3 square miles) to about 32 square kilometers (12.4 square miles). In order for the number of employment-plus-residential activities to really remain constant, the reduced area available for nontransport modes would have to be used much more intensely, with many more floors added to the remaining buildings to compensate for the loss of land to automobile driving and storage.

The second exploration is to question how much can development intensity increase before the ability of the transport infrastructure to support it within a given LOS standard is exceeded. This scenario would make optimum use of existing transport infrastructure. As previously defined, this occurs when land use intensity is sufficient that the transport and nontransport land uses are exactly balanced. Both this intensity, and the ratio of land uses that brings balance, will change with the distance from the center, r. This intensity can be found by using the fundamental relationship that development intensity is the ratio of total area used for employment-related plus residential-related activity at this radius, r, divided by the land available for nontransport use at this same radius. The total area that can support this economic and residential activity can be computed by multiplying the unit floor-area consumption factor, $\overline{f}(r)$, an average for the mix of activities for this radius r, with the amount of trips generated by this activity,

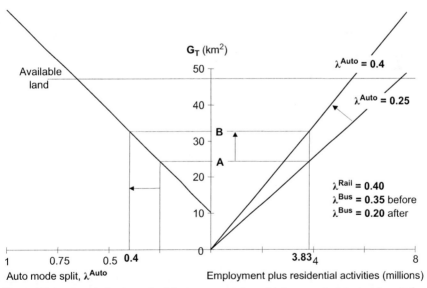

Figure 6.7 Increase in land required for transportation with increase in auto mode split for a theoretical central city of 5 km radius (3.1 miles) and 60 percent usable land.

Source: Shin 1997.

$p(r)$, at this same radius. The total land available for nontransport use is the total land available, $\bar{g}$, minus the land required for transport use within LOS standards, $g_T(r)$, again, based on this same radius. The result is an equation for average development intensity:

$$\bar{I}(r) = \frac{p(r)\bar{f}(r)}{\bar{g} - g_T(r)}$$

(6-3)

Shin solved this equation for a range of values for r. The results are shown in Figure 6.8. The initial development intensity curve shows the average intensity factor prevailing with the initial assumptions. The optimum development intensity curve is much higher in the center at 14 floors, but drops off steeply to only three near the city border, as the density of both employment activity and of the public transport network decrease.

An important observation can be made from even this cursory review of Shin's elaborate research. Development intensification of the remaining nontransport land in conjunction with a higher auto-mode split that would fully offset the reduction in nontransport land is quite unlikely. A much more realistic accommodation to an increase in the number of people attempting to drive to the central area would be shifting activity outwards because land farther out costs less and becomes more accessible when more people use autos. For a highly readable narrative of further details about how this "negative feedback" process works, see the famous book *Death and Life of Great American Cities* by Jane Jacobs (1961).

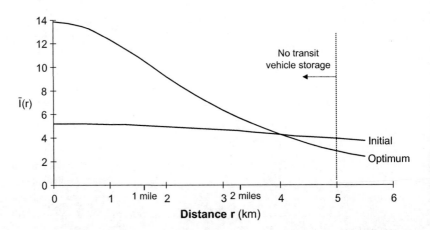

Figure 6.8 Optimum average development intensity as a function of distance from the center for a theoretical central city of 5 km radius (3.1 miles) and 60 percent usable land.

Source: Shin 1997.

Another possible accommodation to the automobile might be encroachment on previously "undevelopable" land. Examples include the widespread construction of freeways along riverfronts and bays during the 1950s and 1960s across the United States. Accommodation through outward expansion or through encroachment on undevelopable land would both work against sustainable development. In the opposite direction, the optimum development intensity curve suggests how much more intensely the central area of existing cities might be developed without an increase in land needed for transport use.

The results from Shin's model might seem intuitively obvious to some whose careers involve urban planning or urban transportation. But when public policies are being developed and specific projects are being evaluated, it is still worthwhile to inform the discussion with this type of analysis for the benefit of those to whom it might not be so obvious. If possible, one should seek similar quantitative answers more closely applicable to the particular situation. These will help to define both the urban development intensity objectives and the additions to the transportation network, if any, that would be required to achieve these objectives. From these follow the types of transit project alternatives that decision makers need to consider.

Ecological Impacts of Land Consumption Due to Transport Choices

The amount of land used for transportation can be a significant fraction of the total land in an urban area, but it is not always clear what land should be included in determining this ratio. For instance, roads to access houses in a tract have to exist even when automobiles are not the dominant means of transportation. Nonmotorized modes and emergency vehicles would still require roadways to some extent, while autos and trucks would still need access on occasion for loading and unloading. Should retail uses dedicated to autos such as dealerships, auto parts stores, and gasoline stations be included? What about streets that also serve as pedestrian malls for part of the day? It is not only paved land that is of concern. What about medians and buffer areas alongside major arterials and freeways? Thus, there is an ongoing debate about the size of this fraction.

Fortunately, it is not necessary to settle this debate. The more relevant question is how much additional land will be consumed or, conversely, be released for other nontransport uses by each project alternative? If additional land is required, how much less new land will have been developed than if current trends had continued? The change in balance between transport and nontransport uses means that the ecological impact from nontransport use cannot really be separated from that for transport use.

While there is an array of possible environmental impacts from various choices in urban form and the resulting types and quantities of land uses, some are typically already identified and quantified in separate analyses. For example, air pollution and greenhouse gas generation of a region are already predicted with separate models that take into account the amount of auto driving, truck driving, and transit use to be expected given proposed changes or additions to an existing urban form. Of concern here are the ecological impacts not traditionally directly included in project analyses, which have been neglected outside environmentalist circles. Recently, more attention has been turned towards both water and land ecology as damage has become apparent and as sustainable development has become a goal.

Impervious surfaces are increasingly recognized as a major determinant of ecological health (Arnold and Gibbons 1996; Environmental Resources Center 1997; Frazer 2005). Pavement for streets, sidewalks, and parking are impervious surfaces, but not the only ones. Roofs also are impervious, but they too are indirectly related to transportation, since auto-dependent urban forms with lower-density housing will also have more roof area per inhabitant than forms with higher density multistory buildings.

Table 6.2 shows the results from a study from Olympia, Washington, a city of 44,000 persons. It measured the percentage of impervious surfaces as function of three different land-use types—high-density residential, multifamily, and commercial. The total impervious surface ranged from 40 percent for high-density residential to 86 percent for commercial. The portion of impervious surface directly related to transportation was dominant in each case, ranging from 63 percent to 70 percent. While the residential values are likely to be good estimates for other cities with similar residential densities, the commercial value is probably too high for larger cities. Because of higher land values, the parking lots would likely be smaller and development intensity higher. Ferguson (2005) provides some typical values for combined roof plus pavement ranging from only 12 percent for a two-acre (0.8 hectare) residential lot to 65 percent for a one-eighth acre (0.05 hectare) residential lot, up to 95 percent for shopping centers (strip malls).

Runoff of water is both increased and redirected by replacement of natural surfaces with impervious surfaces. Runoff can cause hydrological system disruption, including flooding and erosion, with permanent topsoil loss. It also delivers pollutants (e.g. pathogens, phosphorous, heavy metals) into groundwater and streams. In at least one experiment, streets were identified as having the highest quantities of such pollutants of all impervious surfaces (Arnold and Gibbons 1996).

There are other ecological impacts as well, particularly from road building and widening in previously undeveloped areas. These include aquatic wildlife disturbances, fragmentation of terrestrial species habitat and migration paths, wetland destruction, biodiversity reduction, erosion of hillsides, and propagation of exotic species. For the interested reader, Hourdequin (2000) has edited a *Conservation Biology* volume that provides an overview of the full range of ecological impacts. (Relevant articles from this volume are listed in Further Reading.) A range of monetary estimates for some of these impacts are provided by ecological economists, including Robert Costanza et al. (1996, 1997) and Ierland et al. (2001).

Another ecological impact stems from the demise of agricultural lands and sources for wood products in the vicinity of cities. Agricultural lands in particular are at risk since one of the historical reasons for the location of cities was the

Table 6.2 Impervious surface coverage for three land uses in Olympia, Washington

Surface Coverage Type	High-Density Residential 3–7 units/acre (7.4–17.3 units/hectare)	Multifamily 7–30 units/acre (17.3–74.1 units/hectare)	Commercial
1 Streets	16	11	03
2 Sidewalks	03	05	04
3 Parking/driveways	06	15	53
4 Roofs	15	17	26
5 Lawns/landscaping	54	19	13
6 Open space	n/a	34	n/a
Total impervious surface (1–4)	40	48	86
Road-related impervious (1–3)	25	31	60
Road-related as percentage of total impervious surface	63%	65%	70%

Source: Arnold and Gibbons 1996

proximity to prime quality farmland. As these disappear, supply chains lengthen. This, in turn, decreases local self-reliance and increases energy consumption for freight movements. Research suggests that energy consumption growth and its attendant adverse ecological consequences could be abated with more localized production of textiles, wood and paper products, and especially agricultural products (Vanek and Morlok 2000).

Two hypothetical designs are mentioned here as worth study. One is by Vanek and Vanek (1999) that discusses the effect of decentralizing to smaller regions using local sourcing instead of dependence upon large distribution centers. If demand is uniformly distributed, each halving of region size reduces transport distance not by half but by the inverse of the square root, or about 71 percent. These smaller cities could then be linked with one another by frequent transit service. Another is the circular "carfree reference city," originally developed by Joel Crawford, which is then compared by Matthews (2005) to Wallingford, in Seattle, a pre–World War II district with mostly modestly sized single-family houses. He equalized the gross area for each resident at 3,000 square feet (279 square meters) and developed a range of performance indicators. One of the main points is that all residents can be close to parkland and close to utilitarian destinations with lots of land left for potential use for agriculture or forests by using the carfree reference district combined with an extended green area adjacent to the district. Space would be saved by autos not penetrating this district, but there would be little need for one, either. Motorized transport would only be needed to connect to the farther away districts.

Ideally, analysis results specific to a particular city and its surrounding suburbs and watersheds should be obtained, rather than using estimates based on limited findings from elsewhere. When pondering changes or expansions to an existing urban form, each alternative form having varying degrees of transit and auto dependence could then be ranked with respect to the percentages and types of impervious surfaces, loss of agricultural land, and other ecological impacts they are likely to generate. These should inform the types of transit-project alternatives to be developed and to be used in the evaluation of these alternatives.

Pricing of Land Use for Demand Management and Project Financing

Urban economics shows that land use can be affected by pricing in the same way as electric power or telephone use. This is particularly true of parking. Changing the pricing structure can sometimes make a large difference in promoting the efficient use of space. It could provide the incentives for many auto users to either switch modes or to travel at different times. One particularly egregious practice will prove the point.

"Early Bird" pricing gives a steep discount to persons who arrive early and stay the entire workday. In central areas where space is very valuable for nontransportation uses, the "right" amount of storage space can be a contentious issue. Too little space and then commerce that depends upon access by personal vehicles and by freight vehicles will suffer. Too much space dedicated to storage and the character of the central area will transform into an auto-oriented one, and its attractiveness to workers and nonworkers alike will suffer. Early Bird pricing causes too much parking to be used by persons who do not need their autos during the day and too little parking to be available for short-term parkers who may actually need their autos. It furthermore creates pressure to allow more parking garages to be built since the high prices created by the shortage undermines retail businesses, clinics, and other such destinations that depend upon short-term visitors with automobiles.

Pricing flaws are not always as obvious as in the previous example. Incentives for travel choices are not always visible through out-of-pocket expenditures, but they may be through the details of the taxation system or other indirect means. For example, in the United States until fairly recently, providing "free" parking facilities for employees was a business expense while transit fares were an after-tax private expense to the employee. One way used to help remedy this double standard was to provide a "cash out" incentive for employees who do not use their free parking benefit. This is not only fairer to the public transport user, but it also promotes the aforementioned highly desirable diversion from auto to transit at peak hours.

By capping parking for newly constructed buildings through ordinances (as opposed to mandating minimum parking requirements, the status quo in many places), and by unbundling it from housing rents, prices can be driven up for auto owners and down for nonowners. For a comprehensive discussion of the

numerous ways in which parking is financed and priced, and the positive consequences of careful reforms, see Donald Shoup's books. One is on the previously
underresearched topic of the "theory of parking" (2005a) and the other provides
practical suggestions how to unbundle parking prices (2005b). Although written
primarily using some US examples, similar policies and practices and similar issues
arise in other countries as well.

Historically, road tolling was indifferent to the time of day. Tolling that varies
with congestion levels to control peak-period demand along freeways was politically unacceptable in many nations for years but is becoming more accepted as
pressure builds from demand rising much faster than capacity. By raising prices
during the peak period, automobile users can be encouraged travel at different
times or to shift to transit modes, again promoting the highly space-efficient diversion from auto to transit at peak hours. Tolling to cross a cordon that encloses
an entire area will control the volume of demand to use a particular road and
limit the number of vehicles accumulating in the central area. Thus, it is a way to
indirectly regulate demand for parking at the same time. This technique has been
used for over a decade to fully enclose several moderate-size cities in Norway and
to control access to the core of the large cities of Singapore. With its successful
introduction in central London, accomplished without tollbooths, a precedent
has no doubt been set.

Much of the history of public transportation describes it as a tool for opening
up land for development and for increasing its value. With the advent of reliable
solutions to the electric traction design problem (specifically, the third-rail and
the trolley pole) in the 1890s came a rush of "streetcar suburbs." This important breakthrough lowered the cost of operating streetcars dramatically versus
horse-drawn omnibuses and rapid-transit versus steam-driven trains. Landowners
quickly realized it would be worthwhile to provide a transport system to access
their lands. When the land became built out, the developers often lost interest
in maintaining the transport system unless fares could be high enough to cover
the operation and maintenance of the system with a profit. This, combined with
often misguided public policies that prevented fare increases, spelled the neglect
or demise of many transit lines and set the stage for public takeovers across the
United States and some other countries.

When economic development officials realized that land developers in modern
times still benefit from the increased value of land along public transport corridors but no longer pay for their construction, operation, or maintenance, they
created *Tax-Increment Financing* (TIF). The idea was simply that anyone who
profited from the increased land values resulting from public investment should
help pay for it through tax surcharges. These are usually applied only to a limited
strip of land adjacent to where a new transit corridor will be constructed. Furthermore, the improved access must be seen as substantial and permanent if TIF
is to be politically acceptable. See Smith and Gihring (2012) for a bibliography
of reports on the added value that has been seen along transit corridors. For an
exceptional case that provides compelling evidence that it sometimes is a public

scandal NOT to recapture some value, see *Taken for a Ride* by Don Riley (2002). The author recounts the case of the aforementioned Jubilee Line. Since it had to cross under the River Thames four times, at £3 billion, it was exceptionally expensive to construct. On the other hand, it increased land values by approximately £13 billion; however, none of the land-holding beneficiaries paid anything towards its construction.

The same increase in value due to the development of a transit corridor can have the perverse effect of making living along it less affordable. Indeed, lower-income persons who cannot afford an auto and therefore depend on transit might be the least able to afford any increased property taxes, higher monthly mortgage, or TIF assessments. There is a way to counteract such a decrease in affordability. Conventional mortgage eligibility computations make assumptions about the number of autos in a household that may not pertain to dwellings located near transit corridors, especially so within regions that have a network of relatively frequent transit services and good area coverage. Holtzclaw et al. (2002) found that each doubling of residential density in Chicago reduces auto ownership by 33 percent and annual distance traveled per auto by 32 percent. The reductions for Los Angeles and San Francisco were even higher. Fourchier (2001) divided residents of the Paris region into two types of zones, "lower" and "higher" net human density. He found that residents in the higher-density zones traveled 63 percent less per day, on average. The Location Efficient Mortgage® takes into account these reduced expenses in determination of mortgage eligibility. As of this writing, it was only available on an experimental basis in a handful of cities.

One taxation scheme is of special interest because it addresses so many issues, not only in public transportation investment but also in urban development in general. It is based on the theories and public policies recommended by Henry George (1839–1897). The concept is that economic rent accrues to landowners through no input of their own. Much of the value accrues from the infrastructure in place. Land is much more valuable when there is reliable electricity, water, sewers, and so on. This, of course, goes for being located along transit corridors as well. The landowner is simply capturing the rent that comes from a finite amount of land with the proper attributes needed for a particular use, but the owner did not pay to install these attributes. Accordingly, a *Land Value Taxation* (LVT) scheme replaces the existing property taxes and TIF assessments using a different formulation. It puts the emphasis on the location of the property rather than on the value added by construction of buildings and other facilities.

The LVT would not only raise funds towards repaying capital investments in transit, it would create incentives to concentrate urban development along transit corridors. First, the higher tax on location creates an incentive to sell abandoned and low-value use properties in these corridors (e.g. surface-level parking lots). Second, the much lower tax on property improvement removes the disincentive to build more expensive structures and upgrade existing ones out of fear of higher assessments. Some proponents of LVT believe that the unearned economic rents are so high that LVT could actually replace most other taxes with a single tax and perhaps obviate the need to collect transit fares. See Foldvary (2006) for a primer on LVT. See Daly and Cobb (1989) for a brief introduction to the broader benefits of LVT towards promoting sustainable development. See Batt (2002) for a more detailed explanation of the connections between land economic rents and transportation.

Summary

There are three basic types of development density; Floor Area Ratio, Dwelling Units/Area and Population/Area. Gross area is defined as total land and net area as the actually built-upon land, so it is important to be sure what area definition is used. Lee et al. (2011) have compiled a "density atlas" of many cities around the world that could serve as peers.

No evaluation of a major project would be complete that did not consider the relative space consumption and array of potential impacts of the various project alternatives, but the relationship of travel activity is not simply one of being proportional to density. The physical details of development influence both the type and volume of activity possible. A higher net population density will mean, all things being equal, that one given public transport stop can serve more people within a given walking distance; however, the local details matter because longer distances can sometimes still be attractive to walkers.

If different types of land uses are physically separated, or if nonmotorized options are lacking, more motorized travel activity will be generated. Large cities with older urban forms can average 25 percent nonmotorized trips, while many post–World War II suburban tracts can have close to zero. Concentrating traffic on select arterial roads instead of dispersing it over a grid of roads also contributes to congestion. New construction using neotraditional urban forms can have higher capacity than arterial designs yet be more conducive to use of nonmotorized modes.

Project viability often hinges on the various rights-of-way options and their relative costs. While costs are ultimately site specific, some generalizations still can be made.

- Grade-separated alignments will cost more than at-grade alignments.
- Modes with positive guidance will cost more than modes that require steering by a vehicle operator.
- Grade separation allows higher performance and higher levels of safety.
- Guided vehicles need narrower rights-of-way than unguided vehicles and have higher levels of safety. Positive lateral guidance does not remove the possibility of fore/aft collisions; separate signals are required.
- Grade-separated alignments use far less surface area than at-grade alignments, but the resulting qualities of the adjacent surface area can be an issue.
- Opportunistic alignments reduce investment costs but usually provide fewer benefits.

Much of the controversy surrounding major public transport projects hinges on whether the additional costs from separated rights-of-way are justified. A major project could well change the balance of land uses and the composition of land use, both for transport and nontransport purposes. Therefore, the relative impacts of various project alternatives should be compared to each other as well as to the continuation of present trends.

The time-area concept was used to show that the marginal space benefit of diversion of an automobile user to transit during the peak period is very high. Thus, dedicating road space for transit might be justified by its more efficient use of space. An upgrade to ROW B will increase the speed of the bus and will help to cause the highly space-efficient diversion of some automobile users to the bus. Parking the auto for an entire workday was also seen to occupy even more time-area than the journey to work and back. Reduced road and storage space requirements can translate into a monetary benefit of land that can be put to more valuable nontransport uses.

What constitutes a sustainable transportation development path for cities is a question of increasing importance. This was investigated using a complicated mathematical model of a large city, designed for understanding the interaction between the transport and nontransport land uses. The first exploration was to move away from sustainable development and towards increased auto use instead. The total developable land was fixed, but the mode split increases from 25 percent auto use to 40 percent of motorized trips. The result was that about 33 percent more land in the central area would have to be dedicated to transportation use. But development intensification of the remaining nontransport land to fully offset it would be quite unlikely. The second exploration asked the question: How much can intensity of development increase before the ability of the transport infrastructure to support it is exceeded? For this particular set of assumptions used by Shin, the analysis showed that development intensity could be increased from an initial average of about 5 floors to 14 floors near the center without an increase in transport land.

Furthermore, there is evidence of significant potential savings from intensification of land use rather than expansion, not only for transport but also for water, sewer, and electric infrastructure. There is also a reduction in social costs and substantial savings in personal expenditures on transportation with reduced sprawl. These savings could serve to offset investment and operating support for public transportation.

Recently, more attention has been turned towards ecology as damage has become apparent and as sustainable development has become a goal. Impervious surfaces, in particular, are increasingly recognized as a major determinant of ecological health. Runoff from surface can cause hydrological disruptions, including flooding with permanent topsoil loss. It also delivers pollutants into groundwater and streams. There are other ecological impacts as well, including aquatic wildlife disturbances, fragmentation of terrestrial species habitat and migration paths, wetland destruction, biodiversity reduction, erosion of hillsides, and propagation of exotic species.

Yet another ecological impact stems from the demise of agricultural and forest lands. Energy consumption growth, lengthening of supply chains, and increase of impervious surfaces, with all of their attendant adverse ecological consequences, could be abated with more localized production. This would be enabled by higher development intensity in lieu of expansion.

Through changes in pricing structure, land use can be affected in the same way as electric power or telephone use. This is particularly true of parking, where it can provide incentives for auto users to either switch modes or to travel at different times. By raising tolls during the peak period in accordance with congestion levels, automobile users can, again, be encouraged to shift to transit modes or to travel at other times. Both promote the highly space-efficient diversion from auto to transit. Tolling to cross a cordon line will control not only demand to use a particular road but also it can limit the number of vehicles accumulating in the central area.

Much of the history of public transportation was as a tool for opening up land for development and for increasing its value. It was the realization that land developers in modern times still benefit from the increased value of land that prompted TIF. The same increase in value due to the development of a transit corridor can make living along it less affordable. Researchers found that each doubling of residential density in Chicago reduces auto ownership by 33 percent and annual distance traveled per auto by 32 percent, with even larger reductions elsewhere. The Location Efficient Mortgage® takes into account these reduced expenses.

Land is much more valuable when there is reliable electricity, water, sewers, and so on. In other word, location is most important. Furthermore, economic rent accrues to landowners through no input of their own. Accordingly, a Land Value Taxation (LVT) scheme would put emphasis on the location of the property rather than on the value added by construction. It would not only raise investment funds, it would also create incentives to concentrate urban development along transit corridors and to sell abandoned or underused properties along these same corridors.

References

Arnold, Chester L., and C. James Gibbons. 1996. "Impervious Surface Coverage: The Emergence of a Key Environmental Indictor." *Journal of the American Planning Association* 62 (2): 243–58.

Batt, William H. 2002. "Modeling Land Rent and Transportation Costs." Paper presented at the Third Annual Global Conference on Environmental Taxation, April 12–13, Woodstock, VT, Center for the Study of Economics.

Bruun, Eric, and Vukan R. Vuchic. 1995. "Time-Area Concept: Development, Meaning and Application." *Transportation Research Record* 1499: 95–104.

Burchell, Robert. 1998. *The Costs of Sprawl Revisited. Report* 39. Washington, DC: Transit Cooperative Research Program, National Academy Press. http://www.tcrponline.org

——————. 1997. "Economic and Fiscal Costs (and Benefits) of Sprawl." *The Urban Lawyer* 29 (2): 159–81.

Burchell, Robert W., and Catherine C. Galley. 2003. "Projecting Incidence and Costs of Sprawl in the United States." *Transportation Research Record* 1831: 150–57.

Costanza, Robert, Olman Segura and Juan Martinez Alier, eds. 1996. *Getting Down to Earth: Practical Applications of Ecological Economics.* Washington, DC: Island Press.

Costanza, Robert et al. 1997. "The Value of the World's Ecosystem Services and Natural Capital." *Nature* 387.

Daly, Herman E., and John B. Cobb, Jr. 1989. *For the Common Good.* Chapter 13 on Land Use: 252–67 and Chapter 17 on Income Policies and Taxes: 315–31. Boston, MA: Beacon Press.

Environmental Resources Center. 1997. *Polluted Urban Runoff: A Source of Concern.* Madison: Cooperative Extension of the University of Wisconsin. http://cleanwater .uwex.edu/pubs/pdf/urban.pdf

Ferguson, Bruce K. 2005. *Porous Pavements.* Boca Raton, FL: CRC Press.

Foldvary, Fred E. 2006. *The Ultimate Tax Reform: Public Revenue from Land Rent.* Civil Society Institute Santa Clara, CA: Santa Clara University. http://www.foldvary.net/ works/policystudy.pdf

Fourchier, V. 2001. "The Case of the Paris Region, and Its Urban Density and Mobility: What Do We Know? What Can We Do?" Chapter 19 in *Compact Cities and Sustainable Urban Development,* edited by Gert De Roo and Donald Miller. Aldershot, UK: Ashgate, 241–50.

Frazer, Lance. 2005. "Paving Paradise." *Environmental Health Perspective* 113 (7) (July): A456–A462. http://www.ncbi.nlm.nih.gov/pmc/articles/PMC1257665/pdf/ ehp0113-a00456.pdf

Freilich, Robert H., and Bruce Peshoff. 1997. "The Social Costs of Sprawl." *The Urban Lawyer* 29 (2): 183–98.

Holtzclaw, John, Robert Clear, Hank Dittmar, David Goldstein and Peter Haas. 2002. "Location Efficiency: Neighborhood and Socio-Economic Characteristics Determine Auto Ownership and Use—Studies in Chicago, Los Angeles and San Francisco." *Transportation Planning and Technology* 25 (1) (March): 1–27. http://www.tandf.co.uk/ journals/online/0308-1060.html

Hourdequin, Marion, ed. 2000. "Special Section on Ecological Effects of Roads: Introduction." *Conservation Biology* 14 (1): 16.

Ierland, Ekko C., Jan van der Straaten and Herman R. J. Vollebergh. 2001. *Economic Growth Valuation of the Environment: A Debate.* Northampton, MA: Edward Elgar.

Jacobs, Jane. 1961. "Erosion of Cities or Attrition of Automobiles." Chapter 18 in *The Death and Life of Great American Cities.* New York: Random House, 338–71.

Kenworthy, Jeffrey. 2008. "An International Review of The Significance of Rail in Developing More Sustainable Urban Transport Systems in Higher Income Cities," *World Transport Policy & Practice* 14 (2): 21–37.

Kenworthy, Jeffrey, Felix Laube, Peter Newman and Paul Barter. 1997. *Indicators of Transport Efficiency in 37 Global Cities: A Report for the World Bank.* Perth, Australia: Institute for Science and Technology Policy, Murdoch University.

Kulash, Walter. 2006. "The Car in the City." Presentation to the Union League of Philadelphia, 31 May. Available from Glatting Jackson Kercher Anglin Lopez and Rinehart, Orlando, FL.

Lee, Tunney, Randall Imai, Catherine Duffy, Victor Eskinazi, Justin Fay, Patricia Molina, Sze Ngai Ting, Jue Wang and Jenni Won. 2011. Density Atlas. Cambridge: Massachusetts Institute of Technology. http://densityatlas.org

Matthews, Robert S. 2005. *The Production of Sustainable Urban Space: A Comparative Analysis of Wallingford and the Carfree Reference District.* Master's Thesis, University of Washington, Department of Urban Design and Planning, Seattle.

Merlin, Pierre. 2001. "Urban Density, Transport and the Quality of Life." *Public Transport International* 50 (1/6): 40–44.

Newman, Peter, and Jeffrey Kenworthy. 1999. *Sustainability and Cities*. Washington, DC: Island Press.

_____. 1989. *Cities and Automobile Dependence: An International Sourcebook*. Brookfield, VT: Gower Technical.

Riley, Don. 2002. *Taken for a Ride: Trains, Taxpayers and the Treasury*. London, UK: Centre for Land Policy Studies.

Shin, Yong-Eun. 1997. *Analysis of City/Transportation System Relationship to Land Consumption*. Ph.D. Dissertation, University of Pennsylvania, Department of City and Regional Planning, Philadelphia, PA.

Shoup, Donald. 2005a. *The High Cost of Free Parking*. Chicago, IL: American Planning Association.

_____. 2005b. *Parking Cash Out*. Planning Advisory Service Report 532. Chicago, IL: American Planning Association.

Smith, Jeffrey J., and Thomas A. Gihring. 2012. *Financing Transit Through Value Capture: An Annotated Bibliography*. 27 December. Victoria, B.C., Canada: Victoria Transport Policy Institute. http://www.vtpi.org/smith.pdf

Tebb, R. G. P. 1993. "Possible Application of Guided Bus Technology in Britain—Operational Design Implications." *Proceedings of the Institution of Civil Engineers: Transport* (November): 203–12.

Vanek, Francis M., and Edward K. Morlok. 2000. "Improving the Energy Efficiency of Freight in the United States through Commodity-based Analysis: Justification and Implementation." *Transportation Research D* 5: 1–29.

Vanek, Jaroslav, and Francis Vanek. 1999. "Systems, Location, Ecology and Society: Theoretical and Empirical Analysis." *Economic Analysis* 2 (3): 209–21.

Further Reading

Burchell, Robert W., and David Listokin. 1995. *Land, Infrastructure, Housing Costs, and Fiscal Impacts Associated with Growth: The Literature on the Impacts of Traditional versus Managed Growth*. Paper prepared for "Alternatives to Sprawl" conference, March 1995, Brookings Institution, Washington, DC.

Bouwman, M. E. 2001. "Changing Mobility Patterns in a Compact City: Environmental Impacts," Chapter 18 in *Compact Cities and Sustainable Urban Development*, edited by De Gert Roo and Donald Miller. Aldershot, UK: Ashgate, 229–40.

Dieper, A. M. L. von. 2001. "Trip Making and Urban Density: Comparing British and Dutch Survey Data." Chapter 20 in in *Compact Cities and Sustainable Urban Development*, edited by De Gert Roo and Donald Miller. Aldershot, UK: Ashgate, 251–62.

ECMT (European Council of Ministers of Transport). 2000. *Strategic Environmental Assessment for Transport*. Paris, France: OECD. http://www.keepeek.com/Digital-Asset-Management/oecd/transport/strategic-environmental-assessment-for-transport_9789 264188174-en DOI: 10.1787/9789264188174-en

European Commission, DG Environment. 2001. *Strategic Environmental Assessment of Transport Corridors: Lessons Learned Comparing the Methods of Five Member States*. London, UK: Environmental Resources Management. http://ec.europa.eu/environ ment/eia/sea-studies-and-reports/sea_transport.pdf

Ewing, Reid, Rolf Pendall and Don Chen. 2003. "Measuring Sprawl and Its Transportation Impacts." *Transportation Research Record* 1831: 175–83.

Forman, Richard T., and Robert D. Deblinger. 2000. "The Ecological Road-Effect Zone of a Massachusetts (U.S.A.) Suburban Highway." *Conservation Biology* 14 (1): 36.

Forman, Richard T. 2000. "Estimate of the Area Affected Ecologically by the Road System in the United States." *Conservation Biology* 14 (1): 31.

Gruen, Victor. 1973. *Urban Environment.* New York: Van Nostrand Reinhold.

Jones, Julia A., Frederick J. Swanson, Beverley C. Wemple, and Kai U. Snyder. 2000. "Effects of Roads on Hydrology, Geomorphology, and Disturbance Patches in Stream Networks." *Conservation Biology* 14 (1): 76.

Levinson, David, and Kevin Krisek. 2008. *Metropolitan Land Use and Transport: Managing Place and Plexus,* New York and Abingdon, UK: Routledge.

Litman, Todd. 2003. "Economic Value of Walkability." *Transportation Research Record* 1828: 3–11.

Lucas, Karen, Greg Marsden, Michael Brooks and Mary Kimble. 2007. "Assessment of Capabilities for Examining Long-Term Social Sustainability of Transport and Land Use Strategies." *Transportation Research Record* 2013: 30–7.

Mohammad, Sari I., Daniel J. Graham, Patricia C. Melo, and Richard J. Anderson. 2013. "A Meta-Analysis of the Impact of Rail Projects on Land and Property Values." *Transportation Research A* 50: 158–70.

National Parking Association. 1990. *Parking: Dimensions of Parking.* 2nd ed. Washington, DC: The Urban Land Institute.

Parendes, Laurie A., and Julia A. Jones. 2000. "Role of Light Availability and Dispersal in Exotic Plant Invasions along Roads and Streams in the H. J. Andrews Experimental Forest, Oregon." *Conservation Biology* 14 (1): 64.

Scot, C., T. Findlay, and Josée Bourdages. 2000. "Response time of Wetland Biodiversity to Road Construction on Adjacent Lands." *Conservation Biology* 14 (1): 86.

Song, Yan, and Gerrit-Jan Knaap. 2003. *The Effects of New Urbanism on Housing Values: A Quantitative Assessment.* College Park: National Center for Smart Growth Research and Education, University of Maryland.

Southworth, Michael, and Eran Ben-Joseph. 2003. *Streets and the Shaping of Towns and Cities.* Washington, DC: Island Press.

Stover, Virgil G., and Frank J. Keopke. 2002. *Transportation and Land Development.* Washington, DC: Institute of Transportation Engineers.

Trombulak, Stephen C., and Christopher A. Frissell. 2000. "Review of Ecological Effects of Roads on Terrestrial and Aquatic Communities." *Conservation Biology* 14 (1): 18.

Chapter 7

Simple and Complex Mathematical Models

Mathematical models are an inescapable part of the analysis of almost any major public transportation project. But the skills required both to use and interpret the results from computerized implementations of mathematical models (computer models) can be quite specialized. Plus, the data collection and validation efforts required in order to build models can be very extensive. Thus, the analyst will often have to accept results from models run by others or even reject them on some occasions.

In order to make determinations about the usefulness and accuracy of computer model results, an analyst must at least understand their strengths and limitations. To assist in this, the analyst can use some simpler methods that give "first-cut" results. These can serve as a test of the reasonableness of results generated by a computer model. Thus, this chapter reviews both simple and complex models.

Technical Purposes for Models

Mathematical models are used for at least five basic technical purposes: 1) as tools for manual quantitative analysis; 2) to provide conceptual understanding of complex relationships; 3) to provide inputs to performance and investment analysis; 4) to allow sensitivity or "what if" analysis of various proposals; and 5) to allow for very detailed computations for various scenarios. The following section describes each in more detail.

Tools for Manual Quantitative Analysis

The analyst does not derive fundamental relationships whenever a quantitative answer is desired. Nor can the analyst resort to collecting large data sets whenever an answer is desired. Instead, one uses a simple mathematical relationship that provides a good approximation.

An illustrative example is modeling traffic speed, a key determinant of transit demand, transit's competitiveness with the auto, and transit operating costs. On the one hand, speed works to increase capacity by decreasing the duration of

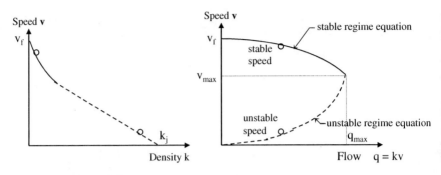

Figure 7.1 Simple traffic speed-density-flow model.

occupancy of a road. On the other, speed works to decrease capacity through disproportionately requiring more separation from other vehicles as speed increases. Two equations capture the essential relations (keep in mind that the curves actually represent an approximate fit to random data). As shown on the left of Figure 7.1, there is a free-flow speed, v_f, when traffic is light, and a jam density, k_j, where traffic is so dense it has come to a standstill. The right half of the figure shows traffic flow as the product of speed times density, $q = kv$ (and which has units of vehicles per hour). It shows that maximum flow, q_{max}, occurs at a speed significantly less than the free-flow speed. It further shows that anywhere except at maximum flow there can be two speeds that deliver equal flow. The dashed line, however, emphasizes that the unstable regime equation begins to be a poor representation for the lower-speed portion of the curve.

Conceptual Understanding of Complex Relationships

There are many interactions among variables occurring within complex phenomena where intuition can fail. A typical example is an electrical network with inductors, capacitors, and resistors. It can be stimulated by a variety of types of inputs using a wide range of amplitudes. The response can be quite different depending upon the combination of signal type and amplitude. In such cases, construction of a model simple enough to numerically evaluate with a hand calculator or spreadsheet helps one begin to grasp which input combinations yield certain outputs, which interrelationships between system components are important, and under what circumstances. Furthermore, one can often identify important overall system characteristics; there may exist maximal or minimal results, there may be "optimal" results in some sense, the system might tend to be stable or unstable, and so on. As systems and their descriptive models become really complex, understanding output becomes more problematic, and the conceptual understanding to be gained becomes more limited.

Figure 3.4 is an example that shows the value of noncomputerized models for preliminary design. It is a mathematical model of line capacity, where only one vehicle size and type operates, but the Transit Unit (TU) size is variable. It reveals a speed that maximizes passenger capacity. The models also showed that if the acceleration and braking rates are the same for any TU size, then the shorter it is, the lower this speed, and vice versa. Thus, in the case of a project where there were both minimal speed and passenger-capacity requirements in a corridor, after inserting preliminary reasonable values, one might preclude solutions using smaller vehicles or shorter trains at the preliminary design stage.

Providing Inputs to Performance and Investment Analysis

Model outputs become inputs to other analyses. This is the main reason non-modelers need to understand models and their strengths and limitations. Estimates for travel times, travel patterns, predicted ridership, land-use impacts near a public transport line, and a host of other variables needed to judge system performance and project viability come from what are often highly complex models. Furthermore, even if the relevance or validity of the model outputs is disputed by an analyst, they often cannot be ignored. For example, a planning authority may be legally responsible for developing and maintaining a regional transportation network model. The public transport project analyst may have neither the technical, financial, or legal means to develop an alternative. Instead, one must critique the existing model and, if necessary, prepare a defense for not using the officially sanctioned model results.

Sensitivity, or "What If" Analysis

The analyst may need to investigate many options. A model can be used to study a large number of possibilities in a relatively short amount of time, once it is constructed and validated. The set of alternatives to be considered for public discussion or for public funding will be the result of extensive study of the trade-offs between conflicting objectives. For example, increasing the fare level could reduce the amount of public operating subsidy required but reduce the number of passengers and, hence, the benefits as well. As another example, an increase in route operating speed may well reduce the fleet required and attract more passengers, but it may raise investment costs in right-of-way and increase negative impacts on surrounding neighborhoods.

Sensitivity analysis is also used to investigate the range of results possible when an input to the model entails some risk or uncertainty. As one example, the interest rate at which construction bonds are issued could change. As another example, huge competing demand for construction firm capacity during a development boom period could drive up costs. Some examples of sensitivity analysis are given in the chapter on engineering cost models.

Final, Detailed Computations

It is sometimes necessary or advantageous to study some aspect of the project in great detail. This is especially true if there is a technology, proposed operating plan, construction technique, or other aspect of the project for which there is little prior experience. In such cases, reassurance might be needed that the project can actually be implemented successfully.

As an example, an elevated right-of-way's structure may have to be almost completely designed in order to verify its strength and construction cost. As another example, novel bus terminal design with a large number of movements within a constrained space could merit a detailed *simulation model* that would investigate operations when irregularities occur. Simulation models show activities in great detail, typically including animation, as opposed to abstract models that provide numerical and static graphical outputs. Another example would be to simulate the signal timing in a series of intersections that are to give priority to transit vehicles in order to optimize performance. Simulation models have become increasingly popular as computer power has increased. As animation and graphics improve, they not only aid the insight of the professional analyst but can help the public visualize end results of a proposed project.

Purposes for Model Application: Projections versus Forecasts versus Plans

The actual applicability of a model, regardless of how technically sophisticated it might be, is always limited by the lack of certainty about the future. Understanding how the future is addressed in the model is always of vital importance. The conclusions that can be drawn from the output of a model depend on it.

Models are usually calibrated and validated by seeing how well they fit with empirical evidence from the past and present. But projects always address future needs as well as the present. The question is how to select an appropriate method of extending the results to the future. It is helpful to define at least three different categories of extension.

Projection is a method that assumes that whatever trends have been occurring in the past will continue into the future. In other words, it is merely extrapolation. Thus, if one plots certain outputs from the model over time and then fit a curve to it, this curve is expected to represent the value of this output into the future. One of the most common examples in transportation modeling is to draw a curve showing an increase in passenger vehicle-miles traveled every year (say, approximately 2 percent) because that increase occurred each year over the last 20 years. This result implicitly assumes the outcome to be independent of changes to factors affecting transportation demand, even though there may be changes to contemplate. If one accepts this projection as inevitable, analysts might conclude that a primary project goal should be to cater to this inevitable 2 percent in some way. But this is ultimately circular reasoning, as one is then assisting a self-fulfilling prophecy.

Forecasting is a more complex method, one that also identifies trends. However, it does not focus upon the trend of a variable in isolation. Rather, it uses many variables that one cannot assume will necessarily change in isolation but, instead, will change through interaction. Forecasting tries to bring order from chaos by tracing how variables change relative to each other and determining which variables are truly independent. Analysts use a variety of filtering, correlating, and other statistical methods to identify patterns and provide insights into the connections between factors. The art and science of forecasting involves including enough variables to provide statistically significant results, but not so many as to make the model unwieldy, difficult, or perhaps even impossible to calibrate and supply with data. It is, of course, necessary that some of the variables be in the control of the project planner or limited by public policy. Otherwise, the model is not helpful for making project decisions.

Forecasting can provide estimates about what particular variables may change in the future. The forecasting ability is often tested by *backcasting*; that is, predicting the past. But even good results are not a guarantee. The future forecast is conditioned on the persistence of certain historical relationships. Thus, returning to the same example about projection, a forecasted increase in vehicle-mile growth might be accurate only when a trend in variables continues (e.g. population and employment continue to grow at a similar rate, fuel prices stay approximately constant, land development patterns continue in the same fashion). There may not even be a clear understanding of what additional data would improve the forecasts if the analyst does not clearly understand the theory behind the model or if the theory itself is inadequate. This must always be borne in mind when interpreting the results.

Planning by objective is less about estimating the future and more about causing it to be. If one finds the output of a model to have an ominous projection or forecast, the focus of planning becomes the study of how a more palatable future can be ensured. Planners might set target values for certain objectives, and models are used to study the effect of changing variables that are influenced by the design factors that planners or public policy control. Decisions are made accordingly.

Planners can deal with the uncertainty of even the best forecasts by plugging in new forecasts as project implementation proceeds or by revisiting the completed project at frequent intervals. If it does not look like a target value is going to be reached by a target date, decision makers adjust investments and public policy accordingly. Active planning and replanning in order to achieve specific targets is only possible where there is either strong public consensus or laws that allow the government to set measurable target values and to implement and to enforce supporting measures. Returning to the vehicle-mile growth example, a publicly supported policy of no further increases in vehicle-miles after a certain date would be established, and any measures required for achieving this objective would be required.

Simpler Models and Quick-Estimate Methods

Analysts always need a starting point for their explorations. They need to establish reasonable ranges of values for resource inputs, design parameters, and project outputs. Simple models can be quite helpful for these purposes. "Simple" in this context means the equations are easily manipulated and can be evaluated with no more than a calculator or spreadsheet program. Simple models appropriate to the project at hand should always be sought. They serve to identify which factors have relatively larger and smaller impact as well as those with virtually no impact at all. They also serve as a "reality check" on more complex model results performed by others. Yet another purpose they serve is to investigate constructive suggestions that, if promising, could then be passed back to the designers/ engineers for more detailed computations.

A particularly important quick-estimate method involves the concept of *elasticity of demand*. It measures the change in passenger demand relative to a percentage change in another variable. If the demand changes with a lower percentage than the percentage change in this variable, the demand is said to be *inelastic*. If the demand changes with a higher percentage than this variable, demand is said to be *elastic*.

Of particular importance are *price elasticity of demand* for the auto mode (*fare elasticity* for the transit mode) and *headway elasticity of demand*. The automobile price could include only fuel and tolls for short-term decisions, with depreciation, maintenance, and insurance considered for long-term decisions. Fares change, not only in absolute terms, but relative to the price of the cost of the competition. Headways are often decreased, and indeed projects that facilitate headway decreases are one of the most effective tools used to increase demand. The basic definitions are:

$$\textit{price elasticity of demand} = \frac{\frac{\Delta d}{d}}{\frac{\Delta f}{f}} = \frac{\Delta d}{\Delta f}\frac{f}{d} \tag{7-1}$$

$$\textit{headway elasticity of demand} = \frac{\frac{\Delta d}{d}}{\frac{\Delta h}{h}} = \frac{\Delta d}{\Delta h}\frac{h}{d} \tag{7-2}$$

These are examples of "arc" elasticities since they are defined over a finite change and become increasingly inaccurate with larger arcs. A "point" elasticity is a unit rate of change defined only at one point. The difference between the two should be familiar from elementary calculus. In fact, point elasticity can be obtained by converting these expressions into differential form.

The actual form of equation used for computing elasticity varies depending upon the nature of the model from which it is extracted. In most demand prediction models, it is usually a simple matter to extract elasticity estimates once the model is complete.

Example 7.1

A bus route carries 10,000 passengers per day with a current fare of $1.50 and headway of 15 minutes. Compute the estimated ridership change a) for a proposed fare increase of $0.30 with a fare elasticity of –0.40 and b) for a proposed headway decrease of 3 minutes with a headway elasticity of -0.30.

a)
$$\Delta d = -0.40\left(\frac{\Delta f}{f}\right)d = -0.40\left(\frac{+0.30}{1.50}\right)10,000 = -800 \ passengers$$
b)
$$\Delta d = -0.30\left(\frac{\Delta h}{h}\right)d = -0.30\left(\frac{+3}{15}\right)10,000 = -600 \ passengers$$

Note that careful attention must be paid to the sign of a change. The fare was increased and the ridership result was thus negative. The headway was decreased and the ridership result was thus positive.

Even at the earliest stage of a project, elasticities can give useful guidance. If the limited information available, including that from peers, suggests a zero or almost zero elasticity with respect to a variable, design efforts to influence this variable are unlikely to have any effect on demand.

A sampling of price elasticities of demand is given in Table 7.1 and headway elasticities of demand in Table 7.2. Observe that off-peak trips tend to be less inelastic, and in some cases even elastic, no doubt because the alternatives to public transport become more attractive during less-congested periods. This explains the common policy of charging significantly higher fares during peak periods; revenue can be enhanced with much less ridership loss than during off-peak periods.

Table 7.1 Sample price elasticities of demand

Mode	Range	No. of Studies
Automobile		
peak	−0.12 to −0.49	9
off peak	−0.06 to −0.88	6
all day (1)	−0.00 to −0.52	7
Intracity Rail		
peak	−0.15	2
off peak	−1.00	1
all day (1)	−0.12 to −1.80	4
Bus		
peak	−0.00	6
off peak	−1.08 to −1.54	3
all day (1)	−0.10 to −0.162	11

(1) Studies did not distinguish between peak and off peak.

Source: Oum and Waters, Chapter 12: Transport Demand Elasticities, p. 205 in *Handbook of Transport Modeling*. Copyright Elsevier 2000. Reprinted with permission.

Table 7.2 Sample headway elasticities of demand

Research Method/Date	Location		Range
Before/after studies 1960–1980	Caen, France		−0.45 to −0.7
	Lille, France		−0.24
	Paris, France		−0.3 to −0.66
	Rennes, France		−0.2 to −1.0
	Portsmouth, England		−0.5
	Massachusetts, USA		−0.2 to −0.8
Logit Model 1985 to 1987	USA	Work trips	−3.37
		Other trips	−1.23
Logit Model 1993	Helsinki, Finland metro area		−0.30
Expressed as Frequency Elasticities of Demand			
Before/after study 1978	Telford, England	Work or school trips	+0.29 to +0.37
Logit Model 1985 to 1987	USA	Work trips	+0.92
		Other trips	+0.33

Original Source: Nevala 2000. Printed in Pursula et al. 2001.

Included studies listed in source.

The use of elasticities based upon information from a peer must be tempered with knowledge about surrounding circumstances. Service can change in more than one attribute, making it difficult to say it was only the price or headway (or any other particular variable) that caused demand to change. For instance, the effect of substitution of larger buses with minibuses based on UK experience shortly after deregulation in the mid-1980s was of wide interest to the world public transport industry. Using a headway elasticity of demand based on using large buses both before and after deregulation would have given an underestimate of the change. Not only were headways decreased, average speed also increased, and walking access distances decreased due to penetration into smaller streets and a hail-stop policy (Morlok, Bruun and Vanek 1997). In such situations, creating and evaluating route indicators, such as those presented in Table 3.3 (see Chapter 3), can be very helpful in deciding whether peers are a close enough match to use them for rough estimates.

For an example of a model specifically designed to estimate fare elasticities, as well as some results for Australian cites, see the study by Hossain et al. (2013). Another model example can be seen in the study by Kennedy (2013) that provides both fare and headway elasticity results for cities in New Zealand. These models both use econometric approaches involving historical travel and socio-economic data.

The interested analyst is referred to Oum and Waters (2000), Oum, Waters, and Young (1992), Goodwin (1992), and Litman (2004, 2013) for more detailed discussion of elasticity concepts and their application as well as numerous sources of estimates. The Transport Research Laboratory of the United Kingdom has also compiled a handbook of demand-related data sources and estimating methodologies (Balcombe et al. 2004). Case studies using elasticities are presented in Evans (2004) and Pratt and Evans (2004), the source of one of the case studies in Chapter 2.

In his highly useful book on the foundations of transportation systems analysis, Manheim (1979) explains several methods, with examples, for use when limited forecasting information is available. His Chapter 4 provides various means for extracting elasticity estimates and other demand-related functions once some variable and parameter values have been established for operating cost, scheduling and operational analyses, and other such planning studies.

There will be situations where no reliable forecast information is available, but there is at least information about the status quo of travel patterns. The sources include manually collected data and information generated by Intelligent Transportation Systems (ITS). Specifically, periodic traffic counts and classifications, periodic user surveys, speed and delay information from public and volunteer vehicles equipped with ITS that are used as traffic probes, and permanently mounted traffic-counting equipment on key arteries and highways are all useful. The idea is to estimate an Origin–Destination matrix (O–D matrix) that summarizes volumes of travel between regional locations. Also needed are travel speeds for each applicable mode along key paths, particularly during congested and high-demand periods of the day. The O–D matrix can be quite detailed when it is associated with precise locations, or it can be quite coarse when the location is better defined as a *zone*. A zone can sometimes be large enough to contain several significant origins and destinations within it. Zones will be discussed further in later sections. For the interested reader, more details of techniques for developing quick-estimate O–D models from limited data are explained in Ortuzar and Willumsen (2011a).

More Complex Methods

When a public transportation project involves a significant portion of a metropolitan region, the resulting changes in travel patterns can be complex. These changes are highly important to identify and quantify as best as possible because many of the cost and benefit estimates of a project depend on them.

Analysts develop regional travel models to provide forecasts of the needed information. Due to the large volume of data needed for such models, very few exist for any given region. Moreover, depending upon the particular laws governing planning, perhaps only one model can be used to provide official estimates. In the United States, this role falls to *Metropolitan Planning Organizations* (MPOs). This does not mean, however, that the analyst cannot use other programs than the official one to inform the analysis. It does mean that any results may be contested, and legal disputes are likely to be settled in favor of the results from the official one.

The actual scope of a model could well be beyond a "region," depending upon circumstances. It may well be that longer-distance traffic significantly interacts with regional traffic. Then the required approach could more accurately be said to be a national model connected to regional models. Such is the case is the case with Norway and Netherlands (Daly 2000).

A highly useful model must forecast well under a variety of scenarios; that is, it must respond in a realistic fashion to the hypothetical changes that the modeler is asked to investigate. In mathematical terms, the model must be specified in such a way that any attributes likely to influence the results must be included. If too few attributes are included, much of the result will be composed of systematic and random error, and the results will be highly inaccurate. In practice, of course, even if it were possible to identify all potentially significant variables, collecting enough data to satisfy such a complete model might be both cost prohibitive and highly problematic. Moreover, some variables may be highly correlated to others, making them inseparable with statistical methods. This requires the use of one variable to act as proxy for others. When interpreting the results, the analyst can recall the fact that the eliminated variables move in proportional to the retained variable. Thus, the final specification must be a compromise between cost, practicality, and versatility of the model.

A distinction is sometimes made between changes in input variables and changes in travel behavior. The distinction revolves around the modeling implications. An input variable might be a transit fare, road toll, parking fee, or other user-related costs facing a user somewhere within an existing regional transportation network. From a mathematical modeling perspective, a change in an input variable simply shifts where an individual's response intersects with an existing functional relationship. On the other hand, examples of changes that might trigger a behavioral response might be a large addition of new, closer job locations relative to housing locations, new travel options due to major new infrastructure, and so on. Such changes are mathematically modeled by actually shifting or altering functional relationships within the model.

Both types of changes are important to the analyst. But changes in policies that can regulate demand, such as pricing, should usually be investigated first. Different use patterns of public infrastructure might be a far more effective public policy than investment in new infrastructure. Unrealistic space requirements within built-up areas, costs of construction in such areas, community opposition to large projects, stricter environmental laws, and so on, limit the opportunities to install new infrastructure in any case. Restated, a regional model should not only forecast changes from new services on new or improved infrastructure, it should forecast the impacts from demand-altering policies (e.g. changes in parking prices, road tolls for auto users, distance-based and peak-hour surcharges for public transport users). Without this capability, a regional network model cannot address all alternatives, some of which may include little or no construction of new infrastructure.

Sequential Four-Step Model with Land Use Appended

Regional transportation network models are built on the concept of *spatial zones*, sometimes also called *transportation analysis zones* (TAZ). These are geographic subareas of the region. These models assume that attributes are concentrated at one point or *node* within this subarea. The node could be at the "center-of-gravity" of the shape of the subarea (in other words, a single point at which the entire population of the subarea is assumed to be concentrated and where links connect to one another). The node may also be at an actual logical location, such as a railway station, motorway interchange, or major intersection. The nodes are connected by *links*, which might carry mixed traffic (right-of-way C), be laterally separated and parallel to another link (right-of-way B), or be totally separated from all other traffic, such as motorways or rapid transit lines (right-of-way A). A real network might have thousands of nodes and links.

The theoretical bases for these models originated in the 1950s and were first implemented on mainframe computers in the 1960s, especially in the United States. As the name implies, the "four-step model" is actually a sequence of models, as shown in the bottom part of Figure 7.2. Sequential models were built to forecast travel demand and travel patterns during a period of rapid population growth and motorway construction (e.g., the U.S. Interstate System). The focus was on capacity requirements during peak periods. Public transportation was in serious decline at the time, and its role in these models was largely an afterthought. Current versions, although now running on desktop computers with many enhancements (including better treatment of public transport), still have fundamentally the same structure. The theory behind each step will be described in the same sequence in which they are executed.

Trip generation   Trip generation, as the name implies, identifies the travel demand the regional network must try to accommodate. Trips can be both produced from and attracted to any given zone. Validation of any theory of trip generation and the starting point for any real application must come from empirical measurements. The types and intensities of activities must be correlated with numbers of trips produced and attracted and the times of day at which they are generated. Tables giving such values can be found in transportation engineering and planning handbooks. Now in its ninth edition, and one of the most comprehensive, is the Institute of Transportation Engineers' *Trip Generation* (ITE 2012). After scaling for the sizes of the particular activities relevant to each zone, this information is loaded into the model.

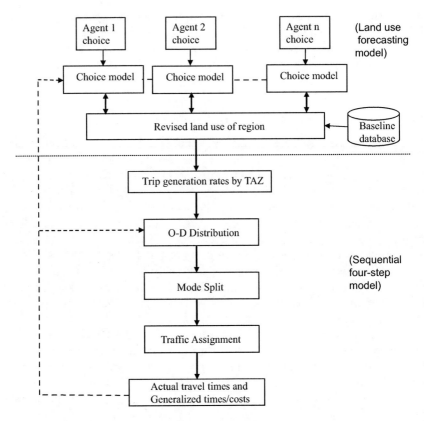

Figure 7.2 Sequential four-step transportation network model using land-use forecasts for trip generation.

If a travel survey was done in the recent past, one may be able to use this directly collected information instead of indirectly computed information based on handbooks. This would include actual numbers of departing and arriving vehicles, types of vehicles, number of persons carried, and numbers of persons using nonmotorized modes. This also has to be broken down by various periods during the day. From historical experience, however, complete and current information usually is not available. Instead, a mix of both empirical information and analytic methods is used.

After analysts gather current information to forecast future trip generation, they need to study how generation can be expected to change with changes in land use and economic development. For each forecast year, the analyst modifies trip generation rates for each zone in accordance with the assumed changes in the socioeconomic character and land use. The generation rate for each zone is typically done with multiple regression analysis of socioeconomic variables (family composition, car ownership, income, etc.) and land-use variables (office, industrial, educational, residential, etc.). The equation takes the form:

$$G_i = a_i X_i + \cdots \cdot b_i Y_i + \cdots + \varepsilon, \qquad (7\text{-}3)$$

where G_i is the traffic generated at zone i, a_i is the coefficient associated with socioeconomic variable X_i, b_i is the coefficient associated with land use variable Y_i, and the final term is the random error.

The forecast of changes in land use is done as an external input to the sequential model. The trip generation remains unchanged during the entire sequence, regardless of what kind of travel conditions are forecast. In reality, at least for nonwork trips, generation would be affected if conditions were highly congested. But one can learn in hindsight by backcasting; that is, comparison of what was predicted for traffic generation versus what really happened.

The need to make the traffic generation part of the model dynamic is the reason that land use interaction models were appended to the four-stop model during the early 1980s. Instead of making only a very limited number of scenarios for which traffic is generated and then running these few cases through the transport model, a dynamic model would allow far more scenarios to be run initially that address the uncertainty in how development actually unfolds over time. Additional scenarios could be developed in response to the forecasted results in order to investigate policies that might promote desired goals and avoid or at least mitigate negative impacts. In an increasing number of regions, development of land use is now coordinated with development of public transportation projects, so such exploration is important for ensuring that project alternatives are robust and for informing public debate.

There is at least one software package in the public domain called *UrbanSim* that is specifically designed to allow alternative scenarios to be studied. The intermediate result of this type of model is a set of traffic generation data for each TAZ. As can be seen in Table 7.3, there are submodels that act upon choices open to households, individual persons, businesses, real estate developers, and the general real estate market condition. Based on the end results from the transport model, the inputs to the submodels can be modified and ran again, even for the same scenario. This might be necessary if the underlying assumptions about speeds, accessibility, and so on, to and from a TAZ that informed the submodel prove to be inconsistent with these results. Thus, there needs to be a feedback loop, as shown in Figure 7.2.

O–D Distribution.   The prevailing theory used to distribute generated trips is *entropy maximization*. (The earlier prevailing theory was the *gravity model* where the relative sizes of attraction between TAZs and the inverse square of the distance between them were the key variables.) Amongst other things, it expresses how particles will tend to disperse randomly, but there is also a highly probable end state when all have been dispersed. Trips too will tend to distribute themselves in the most probable way. The end result is an O–D matrix. Each element T_{ij} is the number of trips produced per hour at origin i traveling to destination j. Summing across the entire row i, the set of trips to all destinations j, gives O_i, the total number of trips per hour produced at i. Summing down the entire column j,

Table 7.3 Agents, choices and models in UrbanSim

Agent	Choice	Model
Household	In- and out-migration	Demographic transition model
Household	Residential moves	Household relocation model
Household	Residential location	Household location choice model
Person	Work at home	Work at home model
Person	Job choice	Workplace choice model
Business	Birth and death	Economic transition model
Business	Business relocation	Business relocation model
Business	Business location	Business location choice model
Developer	Parcel development	Real estate development model
Market	Real estate prices	Real estate price model

Source: Waddell 2011.

the attracted trips from all origins i, gives Dj, the total number of trips per hour attracted to j. The O–D matrix is not symmetric; that is, trips in one direction need not equal trips in the opposite.

There are complications caused by this lack of symmetry. Some generated trips have known origins; for example, journeys to work from places of residence. Others have known destinations; for example, large factories and office complexes. This necessitates that the construction of the O–D matrix be *doubly constrained* to reflect the already known aspects of the distribution. One commonly used entropy maximizing equation that meets these requirements is:

$$T_{ij} = A_i O_i B_j D_j \exp\left(\beta g_{ij}\right) \tag{7-4}$$

The exponential function causes the probability of a trip's distribution from Origin i to Destination j to decay relative to *generalized cost*, g_{ij}. This is defined as a monetized value-of-time for travel between i and j, plus fares, tolls, and other out-of-pocket costs. (An equivalent formulation would be *generalized time*, where out-of-pocket costs are converted to an equivalent time penalty to add to the travel time between i and j.) A_i is a scale factor for the produced trips O_i, and B_j is a scale factor for the attracted trips D_j. For the function given above, these factors are found using the equations:

$$A_i = \frac{1}{\sum_j B_j D_j \exp\left(\beta g_{ij}\right)} \tag{7-5}$$

$$B_j = \frac{1}{\sum_i A_i O_i \exp\left(\beta g_{ij}\right)}. \tag{7-6}$$

Note that B_j is unknown when solving for A_i and vice versa. Thus, these equations must be solved iteratively until mutually satisfied for all A_i and B_j. Then the equations T_{ij} can be computed for all O–D pairs ij. When all the T_{ij} have been computed and the results placed in the proper element, the O–D matrix is complete. The sum of each row i in the O–D matrix equals O_i, the total number of trips originating from node i. The sum of each column j equals D_j, the total number of trips destined for node j.

Example 7.2

Find the completed O–D matrix.

Below is an O–D matrix with four origins and four destinations. Two of the four destinations are known by field data collection to have at least a certain number of trips arriving during the analysis period.

1.0 Starting O–D matrix with known minimum constraints

	j=1	j=2	j=3	j=4	O_i
i=1	0	0	0	0	1200
i=2	0	0	0	0	700
i=3	0	0	0	0	1000
i=4	0	0	0	0	900
D_j	1000 min	0	800 min	0	3800 total

2.0 Final O–D matrix after entropy maximization algorithm (iterative procedure not shown)

	j=1	j=2	j=3	j=4	O_i
i=1	0	300	400	500	1200
i=2	100	0	200	400	700
i=3	700	100	0	200	1000
i=4	500	100	300	0	900
D_j	1300	500	900	1100	3800 total

Note that the two constraints are not violated. The sum of all trips originating from each of the four nodes, O_i, is the same before and after. Also, the sum of all originating trips equals the sum of all trips destined to all four nodes.

Mode split. The dominant technique used for estimating mode split, the fraction of the generated trips that will travel on a given mode, is based on *random utility* *theory.* Utility is an abstract concept. An individual is assumed to have discrete choices and to choose the option that maximizes the utility of that individual. Mathematically, the utility is represented as a linear function of attributes relevant to the decision maker. The higher the value of the attribute, the more it contributes to the utility. An alternative formulation is *disutility.* The disutility function will have negatively valued attributes instead. The higher the negative value, the more it contributes to the disutility of the choice. Opposite to utility, the user picks the option that minimizes the disutility of the choice.

The randomness in a utility or disutility function arises from:

- assumptions about measurement errors;
- using proxies for attributes that are not directly measurable or inseparable;
- attributes not included in the utility function (sometimes called *unobserved* attributes); and
- perhaps, most important, the incompleteness of the model given the diversity of unexplained behaviors of humans facing the same choices.

The utility can be divided into two components, the *systematic component* and the *nonsystematic component*:

$$U_x = V_x + \varepsilon, \tag{7-7}$$

where the subscript x denotes the mode. A well-developed utility function will have a relatively smaller nonsystematic component while including attributes shown to be statistically significant in the decision making process of the target population. A systematic utility (or disutility) function could include many attributes, but these are typical for a simpler one: In-Vehicle Travel Time (*IVTT*), Wait Time (*WT*), Out-of-Vehicle Travel Time (*OVTT*), and out-of pocket costs divided by annual personal income (*Cost/Income*). This latter compound variable has the intuitively attractive property that cost can be expected to decline in importance as income increases. The systematic utility component would then follow as:

$$V_x = bIVTT + cWT + dOVTT + e(Cost/Income) + a_x \tag{7-8}$$

The last term is the *alternative-specific constant*, which is different for each mode choice, even if the equation is otherwise identical. The full utility function is then:

$$U_x = bIVTT + cWT + dOVTT + e(Cost/Income) + a_x + \varepsilon \tag{7-9}$$

By definition, the choice with the higher utility is more likely to occur, or the choice with the lowest disutility is most likely when expressed as a disutility function. But the question that also needs to be answered is: How much more likely? This is answered in terms of the probability of each individual making a given choice. This probability depends in part upon the statistical distribution of the nonsystematic component. To summarize the mathematical derivation, the *logit function* assumes an error distribution (Gumbel) similar to the Normal distribution, which is the most likely distribution to be seen in any large number of random samples. The Gumbel distribution is used because it is much more tractable for use in computations. The logit function has the form:

$$P_j = \frac{e^{U_j}}{\sum_{j=1}^{n} e^{U_j}},$$ (7-10)

where the subscript j refers to each mode choice with a total of n modes. Figure 7.3 shows a binary logit model for the two choices of bus and auto. When the utilities V_B for the bus mode and V_A for the auto mode are equal, the utility difference $V_B - V_A$ is zero, and the choice probabilities will be equal as well. At the opposite extreme, once this utility difference becomes very large, the choice probabilities change very little but are still nonzero. The physical interpretation is that there will always be a few people for whom even a seemingly very unattractive choice for others is still the only one for them.

The logit function gives the probability that an individual will make a particular mode choice for a particular trip. In the utility function given above, the probability will change as a function of the characteristics of the specific trip that could apply to all prospective users and as a function of only one socioeconomic variable: each individual's income. In more complex utility functions, there may be other socioeconomic variables that vary from one individual to the next as well.

This points to an inconsistency in random utility theory. At the same time that economic behavior and, hence, choice making are assumed to be rational for all individuals, there is clearly an unexplained component. This would seem to represent genuinely random behavior. While including more and perhaps better socioeconomic variables can reduce unexplained behavior, it cannot eliminate it. Thus, the development of choice models is always a potential source for introducing

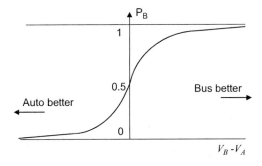

Figure 7.3 Logit probability curve for choice between auto and bus.

incomplete or even erroneous behavioral assumptions. More will be said about this in the forthcoming section on potential sources of error.

Since prospective users of even an identical trip itinerary will have different utilities, the results must be aggregated across a population. Given the nature of the logit function and the diversity of a real population, it would be completely impractical to sum the probability of every individual. Instead, analysts use a variety of feasible *aggregation* schemes, depending on the data available and accuracy desired. One of the simplest, *classification*, is presented as part of Example 7.3, where the population is segmented into large groups with similar characteristics. See Ben-Akiva and Lerman (1985) for explanation of some other schemes.

Example 7.3

A residential area is connected to a major employment area. The trip generation step gave a result of 1,500 trips during the peak hour between the two zones representing these subareas. The persons making the trips are divided into three classes. There are 800 making an average income of $30K, 500 making $60K, and 200 making $90K per year. Find an estimate for the total number of these trips that can be expected by bus.

The random disutility function that describes this market is:

$$U_x = -0.02IVTT - 0.04WT - 0.03OVTT - 2000(Cost/Income) + a_x + \gamma$$

There are two travel choices, auto and bus. The alternative-specific constant plus error term for each is:

$$a_B + \gamma = -0.5$$
$$a_A + \gamma = -1.0$$

The values of the relevant input variables for travel between the two nodes are:

Bus	Auto
$IVTT = 30$ min	$IVTT = 40$ min
$WT = 5$ min	$WT = 0$
$OVTT = 15$ min	$OVTT = 0$
$Fare = \$2.00$	$Gasoline = \$4.00$, $Toll = \$1.00$

The computation of the disutilities for the $30,000 income class gives:

$$U_B = -0.02(30) - 0.04(5) - 0.03(15) - 2000\,(\$2.00/\$30,000) - 0.5 = -1.8833$$
$$U_A = -0.02(40) - 0.04(0) - 0.03(0) - 2000\,(\$5.00/\$30,000) - 1.0 = -2.1333$$

This gives a probability of using the bus of:

$$P_B = \frac{e^{U_B}}{e^{U_A} + e^{U_B}} = \frac{e^{-1.8833}}{e^{-2.1333} + e^{-1.8833}} = \frac{0.1521}{0.1184 + 0.1521} = 0.56$$

If the disutilities are computed again for the other class of user with the middle income, the corresponding probability of taking the bus is $P_B = 0.54$. The corresponding value for the highest income group is $P_B = 0.53$. Summing up the fractions from each class of user gives the estimate of the total number using the bus mode:

$$Total\ bus\ users = 56(800) + 0.54(500) + 0.53(200) = 824\ persons$$

There is a further complication. Logit functions are often also *nested*. In other words, choices proceed down a hierarchy. For example, the first choice might be between auto and public transport. If public transport is chosen, then rail versus bus might be the next choice in the hierarchy. Such a hierarchy is used where there is reason to believe that two choices have similar unobserved attribute(s) in their nonsystematic component (Ben-Akiva and Lerman 1985). To give two examples, commitment to the environment or inability to operate a private automobile would cause favoritism of a large number of individuals for any public transport choice over the auto. At the lower level of the nest, the randomness of the systematic components of the utilities is reduced, and a better probability estimate can be made between the choices. An alternative to nesting, available data permitting, is to include attributes in the utility function that would otherwise end up as unobserved attributes within the nonsystematic component.

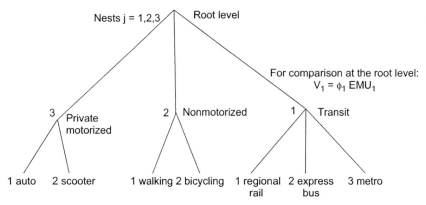

Expected Maximum Utility for Transit: $EMU_1 = \ln(e^{V_1/\phi_1} + e^{V_2/\phi_1} + e^{V_3/\phi_1})$

Figure 7.4 Example of nested logit model.

An example of a two-level nested choice model is shown in Figure 7.4. For the purpose of selecting any mode of transit, nest 1, the combined utility of all three of the transit choices must be represented by the Expected Maximum Utility of this nest (EMU$_1$). The needed value of ϕ_1 must be determined during model calibration. If the transit nest has the highest utility of the three choices at the root level, the second-level logit model selects between the three transit modes.

Traffic assignment. Once the trips have been split into the available modes, the final computational step is to assign them to paths. The term *routes* is sometimes used in the professional literature, but *path* is used here to avoid confusion with public transportation routes, as a path could use segments of several routes.

Wardrop's First Principle states the only paths that will be used are those taking the same time as the path taking the shortest time. In other words, all used paths will have equal and minimal travel times. The theory has to be modified slightly, however, because paths that may not actually be quite as fast might still be chosen. For example, driving conditions could be less stressful for motorists on freeways, highways, or ring roads versus stoplight-to-stoplight driving on a more direct path. There may also be tolls along the fastest route. Likewise, for public transportation users, there may be differences in fares, comfort, and convenience that justify somewhat longer travel times. Thus, analogous to the trip distribution process, analysts must use a generalized time or generalized cost that includes both time and out-of-pocket cost components. They can estimate correction factors by comparing empirical measurements of differences in travel times and driving conditions on alternative paths between the same origin and destination, but only after first verifying that actual times on the used paths are substantially different. This is an important part of the model calibration process.

There could be a dense grid of bus routes, rail lines, arterial roads, and motorways in an area. Therefore, both public transportation and auto users could have multiple combinations of possible paths, especially as cities become large. Finding all paths that have generalized costs equal to the minimum is not easy. There may be an enormous number of candidate path combinations in a large network. Trial and error would not be practical. Fortunately, the assignment problem can be transformed into an equivalent mathematical program that has an *objective function* to be minimized, the so-called Beckmann's transformation, in honor of the originator, Martin Beckmann. But this objective function has no obvious physical interpretation, so it is not shown. The constraints do have physical significance. For each Origin i and Destination j there are constraints expressing the requirement that the sum of the flow on all used paths equals the total flow that the demand forecast predicts will travel between them:

$$\sum_p f_{ij}^p = T_{ij}, \tag{7-11}$$

where f_{ij}^p is flow between i and j with the superscript p denoting the portion on the particular path, p. Additional constraints are that flows must be greater than or equal to zero on all used paths, as negative flows have no physical meaning:

$$f_{ij}^{p} \geq 0 \qquad (7\text{-}12)$$

Finally, there is a *path-link incidence relationship matrix* of zeros and ones describing the network of possible paths between an Origin i and Destinations j for all ij pairs. When premultiplied by the array of generalized costs for all links, a vector, G_a, it gives a vector of the total generalized cost for each path between Origin i and Destination j for all ij pairs:

$$G_{ij}^{P} = G_a \Delta \qquad (7\text{-}13)$$

An array of the flows on all used paths, a vector, F^p, can be multiplied by the transpose of this same relationship matrix. This sums all flows between all ij pairs that use each link a, giving a vector, F_a, of the total volume flowing across each link a:

$$F_a = F^p \Delta^T \qquad (7\text{-}14)$$

The volume for each link a is essential to compute, as it in turn dictates the travel time across the link through the link-performance function. There is a maximum volume that any particular link can support.

Example 7.4

The following network has the incidence relationship matrix shown on the right, as can be verified by using equations 7–13 and 7–14.

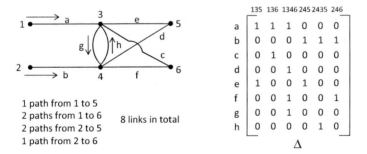

	135	136	1346	245	2435	246
a	1	1	1	0	0	0
b	0	0	0	1	1	1
c	0	1	0	0	0	0
d	0	0	1	0	0	0
e	1	0	0	1	0	0
f	0	0	1	0	0	1
g	0	0	1	0	0	0
h	0	0	0	0	1	0

Δ

1 path from 1 to 5
2 paths from 1 to 6   8 links in total
2 paths from 2 to 5
1 path from 2 to 6

Figure 7.5 Simple network and its path-link incidence relationship matrix.

The generalized cost vector for the six paths is:

$$G_{ij}^{P} = [g_a\ g_b\ g_c\ g_d\ g_e\ g_f\ g_g\ g_h]\ \Delta$$
$$= [g_a + g_e,\ g_a + g_c,\ g_a + g_f + g_g,\ g_b + g_d,\ g_b + g_e + g_h,\ g_b + g_f]$$

The flow vector for the eight links is:

$$F_a = [f_{135}\,f_{136}\,f_{135}\,f_{1345}\,f_{245}\,f_{2435}\,f_{246}]\;\Delta^T$$
$$= [f_{135}+f_{136}+f_{1345},\,f_{245}+f_{2435}+f_{245},\,f_{136},\,f_{245},\,f_{135}+f_{2435},\,f_{1346}+f_{246},$$
$$f_{1346},\,f_{2435}]$$

The resulting equivalent math program formulation is a familiar one and can be readily solved. As Figure 7.2 showed, there is feedback using the outputs of the traffic assignment process. The times or generalized costs computed in the assignment step may contradict those assumed in the O–D Distribution step because the assumed costs in the initial O–D Distribution may have been based on a different level of congestion. Removal of the contradictions requires adjusting the assumed travel times on each link with changes in the assumed flow. (There is more about this in the forthcoming subsection about shortcomings of sequential regional travel models and in the later section about sources of errors.) The capacity of a link may even be exceeded, in which case the network probably has to be modified before running the model again as demand needs to be diverted from this link. (There are other types of algorithms not discussed here that incorporate capacity constraints to prevent this.)

Using Wardrop's First Principle for the traffic assignment rule brings a network to *user equilibrium*. This does not minimize the total generalized time or generalized cost in the network; it only reflects what is best for the individual users. This is sometimes also referred to as a "user optimal" solution. There is also a *system optimum*, which would be the lowest total generalized cost/time possible if everyone were to do what is best for the network as a whole. In this case, analysts assign demand according to *Wardrop's Second Principle*, which says that the generalized cost at the last unit of traffic flow (marginal generalized cost) is the same on all used paths. Unlike the formulation for user equilibrium, the system optimal formulation has an objective function with the logical interpretation; it is the sum of all the generalized costs of the users of all links in the network. The complete model has the same two sets of constraints, Equations 7–11 and 7–12, and the incidence relationships, Equations 7–13 and 7–14, included in the user equilibrium model.

Although not an accurate reflection of reality, solving for the system optimal total generalized time or total generalized cost can be useful for comparison to the user equilibrium total as a measure of how efficiently the network performs. Furthermore, in a highly sophisticated application it would be possible to divide the network into an automobile-mode subnetwork that operates according to Wardrop's First Principle. The public transportation subnetwork operates according to Wardrop's Second Principle because public transportation services could actually be centrally planned and vehicles assigned in such a way as to promote system optimization.

Each mode must be assigned as a separate process using its own link-performance functions and the volumes derived from the previous mode-split step. Thus, the outputs from the traffic assignment step are the actual travel time and generalized costs, $g_{ij}{}^x$, associated with the lowest cost path connecting each ij pair for a particular mode, x. This allows for the easy computation of price elasticity for any O–D pair for any mode using the formula:

$$price\ elasticity\ of\ demand = -g_{ij}{}^x(1 - T_{ij}{}^x / T_{ij}) \qquad (7\text{-}15)$$

where the superscript x indicates the relevant mode. Once a model has been developed, these values can be read from output tables. Note that besides the generalized cost, the elasticity is a function only of the mode split. As explained in the previous section, the elasticity is a good indicator of the potential to attract more riders. If the elasticity is low, service improvements and/or fare changes would be unlikely to make much difference, at least in the short term.

It is useful for analysts studying math program results to be familiar with the *complementary slackness* property of math programs. As an example, for User Equilibrium, its mathematical statement between flow on a path and cost of traveling this path is:

$$f^p (g^p - g_{ij}\ min) = 0 \qquad (7\text{-}16)$$

(For the system optimum case, the idea is the same, except that marginal generalized costs/times along paths are used instead of average.) The structure is such that if generalized cost on any candidate path, g^p, is not equal to the lowest generalized cost found on any possible path, $g_{ij\ min}$, the flow on that path, f^p, must be zero in order for the equation to hold. Conversely, if the generalized costs are equal, the expression in parenthesis is zero, and the flow can be greater than zero, and the constraint is said to be binding. This minimum cost value, $g_{ij\ min}$, is then also called a *shadow price*, as it corresponds to the unit change in the total network cost that can be expected with a unit change in the flow along this path. These shadow prices (also called dual variables) are available as part of the program output.

The interested reader with the requisite mathematical background is referred to the text by Sheffi (1985) for more details about math programming based solution methods for the traffic assignment problem. In particular, Chapter 3 systematically shows how and why the Beckmann transformation works. Chapter 5 explains the Frank and Wolfe algorithm, the historically most important method of computer solution. Chapter 6 refines the model to include public transport and autos that operate independently on separate subnetworks.

For more details about other less involved methods of assignment that can be used, such as all or nothing and the method of successive averages, see Ortuzar and Willumsen (2011b). For situations where data availability is limited, such as in most developing cities, Bedelu and de Langen (2008) have developed a clever, simplified version of the four-step sequential model.

Even More Fully Integrated Sequential Models

Other outputs can be computed as well. Estimates of fuel consumption and pollution emissions, for example, are also of interest. As noted earlier in the book, these outputs can be important to public transportation projects because energy conservation and emissions reductions are now common goals, and such outputs can provide quantitative estimates towards achievement of project objectives. There are several such models available. It is not that difficult to get reasonable estimates because they use the outputs from the transport model quite readily. Total regional fuel consumption and GHG emissions are quite proportional to the distance and hours of travel, to the travel speeds across links, and to delays and bottlenecks. Further additions can be noise prediction submodels, runoff prediction, and so on. The number of additional analyses that should be performed will depend on the initial environmental assessment and how significant impacts are expected to be. In many cases, laws and regulations will specify when and how specific models are to be used.

For any major project, there must be an explicit effort to facilitate analysis of policy-related changes (e.g. fuel prices, tolls, parking prices, fares) and changes in behavior due to a variety of available travel options, development patterns, and changing attitudes towards the environment, automobile ownership, and so on. The effects from these types of changes should also interact between both the land-use and transportation sides of the model, so highly integrated models are an improvement over separate models in this regard, as well. The interested reader should refer to Miyamoto and Vichiensan (2000) for a more detailed comparison of some integrated models that have actually been in use.

Technical Inadequacy of Sequential Models

This section draws heavily from the work of Professor David Boyce. His thesis is that the sequential or four-step procedure as well as the integrated land-use models that use it as a foundation evolved without a firm theoretical basis. The mathematical and behavioral bases of each step are unrelated to one another. This separateness has only been reinforced over the years by academic specialization (Boyce 2002). Any requirements to feedback data between modules does not correct the flawed theoretical basis, it only removes some of the inconsistencies and contradictions between the data sets used in each module.

The fundamental problem with the steps in sequential analysis is that travel decisions are not made sequentially. Individuals do not first decide they are going to a particular destination, then make their mode choice, and then choose their particular path. In reality, they choose to make the trip, their destination, and their mode simultaneously. A more theoretically sound and internally consistent approach is to begin with the traffic assignment problem because the congestion levels on the links that are a part of a candidate path for this trip are central to any travel decisions. The mode(s) used, paths used, and even alternative destinations are all open for consideration. Wardrop's principles would still apply, as would entropy maximization and logit mode choice. But the simultaneous problem is formulated as a constrained optimization program involving an entirely different solution algorithm than the sequential packages. Trip generation, however, is still based on a separate land-use module, which must still generate new forecasts for each year.

This new paradigm is shown in Figure 7.6, where one works outwards from the traffic assignment problem such that the important role of congestion is inherently included rather than forced into consistency through equilibration. (There is more about this in the following section.) The limited application of this approach for forecasting to date in the United States has shown excellent agreement with survey data (Boyce 2002). There is at least one package available, ESTRAUS, developed by researchers and successfully used in Chile (Siegel et al. 2006; Cea et al. 2003). Over time, this new paradigm is likely to provide a more insightful tool for regional transportation modeling, but the techniques and mathematics are not widely understood yet amongst practitioners. To quote Boyce: "This is not Rocket Science. No, it is harder!" (2002: 177).

For further information about the history of land-use models combined with regional transportation network models, written in an accessible fashion, the reader is referred to Miyamoto and Vichiensan (2000). For a comparison of the performance of ESTRAUS with sequential models, see the article by Siegel et al. (2006). The reader with some prior knowledge and advanced mathematical education is referred to Boyce and Williams (2003) for deeper discussion on the theoretical underpinnings of combined regional transportation/land-use network models.

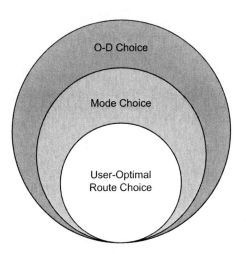

Figure 7.6 Diagram of a new travel forecasting paradigm.

Source: Boyce 2002.

Potential Sources of Error and of Misleading Results

There are many ways in which any particular project can be made to be more or less appealing, depending upon the assumptions and ranges of input values that are used. Most errors are unintentional, and many are even acknowledged to be errors but deemed too difficult to correct. One must also be aware of the possibility of deliberate adjustments to the model so that outputs support a preconceived outcome. The following are some issues to raise or ponder when studying project models and their outputs.

Computed Equilibrium May Not Be Representative (Or Even Exist)

Despite the mathematical sophistication of model construction and of solution techniques, a model is always limited by the simplified scenarios it analyzes. The trip generation rate used is constant, and the trip assignment and trip distribution give fixed values representing constant flow volumes. In reality, there are random fluctuations in traffic from one day to the next. Thus, the "equilibrium" is only a mathematical abstraction used to match infrastructure capacity to assumed volumes. It may never really exist. If it does, once it is reached it must fluctuate with the random variations in flow volumes, which somewhat undermines the concept of equilibrium as a steady state.

These fluctuations in flow reflect the reality that people do not have identical travel patterns from one day to the next, that prevailing conditions affect route choice or even the decision to make a trip at all, and so on. For these reasons, it is prudent to solve the regional model with a range of volumes having the type of distribution seen in practice. It is important to determine if high travel demand and congestion on certain parts of the network are routine or only occasional occurrences; investments should not generally be made to alleviate what are only rare occurrences. If analysts determine that wide fluctuations are an issue, simulation models could be very helpful for visualizing network performance. There will be more discussion of the value of simulation models in a later section.

Peak Hour Is Not the Only Network Design Consideration

Analysts typically use regional network models to study congested periods on the road network. The public transportation subnetwork will also be represented so as to handle peak-hour volumes. This would seem to be a logical way to proceed, as one of the typical goals of public transportation is to divert demand from a saturated private auto network. But it oversimplifies the design problem.

A public transportation system that supports many goals cannot be optimized only for the peak hours. Given a fixed operating budget, one might have to tolerate overcrowding for some duration and even neglect certain market segments in order that adequate service can be provided the remainder of the day. If the regional network model has been set up only for peak-hour scenarios, running it with a different public transportation subnetwork(s) more suitable for all-day service would give more insight into the design tradeoffs. It would be even better if analysts could set up the entire regional model for nonpeak periods. Indeed, the use of such models will only increase over time. There is a more elaborate description of this practice in a later section.

Nonequilibrated Networks

The volume of traffic analysts assign to the various links in the traffic-assignment step of a regional network model is a function of how much traffic is already assigned to it. A link can absorb a certain volume without any impact on speed, but at some point mutual interference between vehicles rapidly deteriorates the speed. This is the upward-curving portion of the *roadway link-performance function* shown on Figure 7.7. As traffic conditions deteriorate, this particular link is no longer as attractive, and the actual volume would be less. Furthermore, the volume on other links would also be affected because vehicles travel on paths that are a series of links. Thus, the network model would need to assume a lower speed along this link. Analysts would need to make such adjustments throughout the network until the assumed speed on each link actually matches the speed implied by the volume assigned to it. In fact, this *equilibration* may require numerous iterations to produce a stable solution. However, this is not always done. Equilibration has little consequence if the vast majority of links have traffic volumes not in the congested range, but it can be a major source of error when they are.

For example, if a nonequilibrated highway link runs parallel to a proposed commuter rail line, but the analyst assumes the highway has higher vehicle speeds than it really does, the analyst would be making a significant error. The too-high speed would incorrectly lower the demand estimates for the rail line. Continuing, the analyst might incorrectly assume connecting roads to the rail line have

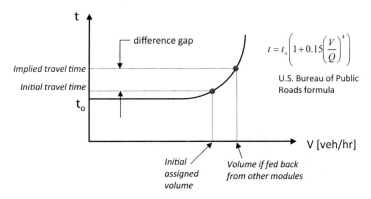

$$t = t_o \left(1 + 0.15 \left(\frac{V}{Q} \right)^4 \right)$$

U.S. Bureau of Public Roads formula

Figure 7.7 Roadway link-performance curve contradiction when model steps are not equilibrated.

higher speeds than they actually do because heavy auto traffic might build as one approaches a park-and-ride lot. On the other hand, increased local transit feeder service and better accessibility by nonmotorized modes might decrease traffic. Therefore, each step of the model may have to be resolved with numerous iterations before demand estimates reflect changed travel conditions on all modes and traffic assignment is such that there is equilibration on all links.

Transit link-performance functions also bear attention. The important characteristic for public transport is that performance can improve with increasing passenger volumes, just the opposite of private autos. Its ability to absorb more passengers without an increase in right-of-way width means that shifting persons to transit along the same path could actually improve the situation for both transit users and auto users.

A transit link-performance function is shown in Figure 7.8. Below a certain passenger volume, travel time is constant as a fixed maximum policy headway is provided. Above this threshold, travel time will decrease due to shorter wait times as a consequence of the shorter headways used when accommodating higher demand. At some point, the transit vehicle operating in mixed traffic (ROW C) will encounter increased congestion, and travel time will begin to increase again, in the same manner as autos. Higher demand justifies investment in ROW B or A, resulting in a further reduction in travel time without the same congestion effect. As will be discussed in detail in the section on the value of time, reducing wait time has a disproportionate effect over travel-time reduction measures, further stimulating demand. Theoretically, the vehicle operating on a separated right-of-way can continue to show decreases in travel time until the minimum headway defined by safe separation of vehicles is reached. As a practical matter, random disturbances usually prevent running near theoretical minimums, especially because of passenger-induced delays under crowded conditions. The reader interested in details about the development of performance curves is referred to Morlok (1979).

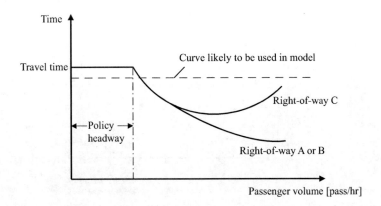

Figure 7.8 Transit link performance curve—actual versus modeled.

In practice, use of actual transit link-performance functions is rare. Instead, a constant headway and travel time is assumed, also shown on Figure 7.8. Thus, proper equilibration by a mathematical algorithm is not even possible. At most, the modeler might shift the performance curve by changing the assumed headway if there proves to be a glaring contradiction between the supply implied by the headway and the forecasted demand. The analyst should always look for such contradictions; but to really model public transportation correctly would require the introduction of proper link-performance curves so that the operating costs shown in the objective function of the mathematical program automatically change with headway.

The analyst should bear in mind that just because the network is equilibrated, it is still no guarantee that the forecast is accurate. If not equilibrated, however, it has no chance at all. It is also possible that the actual amount of service supplied is less than that assumed within the model. Demery (1994) found that a few new LRT lines had such few cars when they opened that it would be physically impossible to carry the forecasted demand.

Cost and Price Elasticities Can Change

Analysts use cost inputs in models that can significantly change output results. The inputs might very well change substantially over the planning horizon. A large change in fuel prices, tolls, public transport fares, and parking prices do more than just change terms in equations having monetary cost components. These collectively can cause large changes in demand, performance, and cost recovery by the various transport modes. In fact, because of the interdependency of variables, they might actually profoundly influence travel behavior by individuals in the long run as they adapt their lifestyles.

Recall also that analysts can base elasticities in some simpler, quick-estimate methods on observed values from peer locations. If conditions change enough from those employed to justify the peer selection, using such peer conditions may no longer be justified. Analysts might also derive them from discrete choice models or elsewhere within the sequential model. Yet there may be variables omitted from the model specifications, particularly having to do with the change in the quality of service, which should be included for better estimation (Oum and Waters 2000). Point elasticities are usable only over small changes in variables, making them suspect when analysts use models to investigate large changes in costs and travel behavior. Arc elasticities provide better estimates for larger changes but can also be erroneous when there are significant changes in costs or travel behavior.

Therefore, analysts need to check the plausibility of the values used as inputs and generated within complex models because one can often expect large changes over time. Indeed, large changes in travel patterns are the entire point of many proposed investments. As is shown in Table 7.4, elasticity tends to increase over time. The explanation is that individuals need time to change their behavior, and institutions providing complementary or competitive services need time to adjust their offerings.

Table 7.4 Sample fare elasticities of demand related to time period (transit bus)

Research Method	Time Period	Avg. Elasticity	Std. Dev.	No. of Studies
Before/after	6 months	−0.21	0.12	3
Explicit short term	0 to 6 months	−0.28	0.13	8
Unlagged time series	0 to 12 months	−0.37	0.18	24
Explicit long term	4 years	−0.55	0.20	8
Equilibrium models	5–30 years	−0.65	0.18	7

Source: Goodwin 1992.

Included studies listed in source.

The Value of Time

The value of time individuals save in travel is often the largest contribution to the monetized benefit from an investment. The generalized cost for a trip is typically the fare, F, plus the monetary value of time spent underway, vT, which is shown on the vertical axis of Figure 7.9. If a trip becomes faster and d_1 persons were previously taking it, the cross-hatched area between 0 and d_1 is the savings benefit to existing riders. The reduced generalized cost attracts additional riders who would have been willing to pay more. Their benefit is the cross-hatched triangle between d_1 and d_2. The total savings benefit represented by the entire cross-hatched area is known as the *consumer surplus*. There can be a corresponding value for the competing modes as well because conditions can improve for all choices.

Equating travel times on all used routes is a clear quantitative criterion. By comparison, the generalized cost is a mathematical concept, where the time spent has to be monetized so that it can be added to fares and tolls. Requiring that the generalized cost be the same for all path choices actually used creates a calibration criterion for the model. The calibration can be based on empirical information about revealed behavior of travelers using different paths between selected O–D pairs. The idea is that analysts can deconstruct the various popular paths to ascertain what types of facilities and conditions cause people to be willing to spend extra time in travel; the value of time for travelers on such links can be reduced accordingly.

Even with these corrections, however, there are many concerns about the precise nature of the time saved and the appropriateness of monetizing travel times from computerized models in order to include them as monetary costs and benefits. These are discussed here.

-Are the time savings permanent?   If there are no supporting measures, public transport investments that relieve auto traffic congestion are likely to have only temporary impact. In this case, it is incorrect to assume a continuous benefit to motorists. Instead the time savings should taper off with time. Furthermore, any time savings to an individual user may well be translated into a longer driving

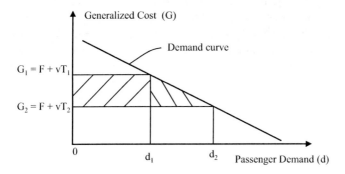

Figure 7.9 Consumer surplus as benefit from time savings.

distance over the long run. There is ample evidence that the average journey-to-work time has remained at about 30 minutes for centuries across all cultures, although the distribution of travel times has widened (Kenworthy et al. 1997). Even with the widely different levels of wealth and technology in use across the world, it still seems to hold:

> Journey to work time is remarkably consistent across all the different city types. Australian and North American cities average 26 minutes, European cities average 28 minutes, and Asian cities average 33 minutes. These differences hardly seem significant when compared to the massive difference in use of cars, especially when cars are facilitated and promoted on the basis they are faster and save time. (Kenworthy et al. 1997, 21)

This throws into question whether public transportation projects with the goal of reducing commuting time are really promoting sprawl instead. Perhaps only time savings for individuals who were previously forced by circumstance, instead of choice, to travel for lengths of time at the high end of the distribution should be counted as permanent. The exception is if another requirement is met: serious measures are taken in tandem to suppress the increases in trip length that would tend to reconsume the time savings.

The likely permanence of any time saving should be factored into the evaluation of each future year. Models are supposed to account for the fact that traffic grows when congestion is relieved, but this needs to be confirmed. There is a corollary as well: the disruption and time delays caused by construction should be subtracted from the future benefits of any project. One study found that the years of major delays caused by a massive freeway interchange widening would never make up for it by the decreased congestion after its completion (Surface Transportation Policy Project 1999).

-Can time savings be aggregated?   Savings may come in the form of many individuals saving a few minutes instead of a smaller target population receiving larger savings. The savings may be of no practical significance in the former case, especially if travel times are unreliable and force people to make larger allowances for the random variation in travel times than the average time savings in any case. Yet, analysts have traditionally held that the aggregation of small savings is equivalent to an equal aggregation made up of fewer but larger savings. It is argued here that the conventional analysis should be revised to discount the alleged benefit from small savings to many users. See Strand (1993) for a more detailed discussion of the issue.

-Are all travel conditions of equal value? Surely standing on a crowded bus that stops repeatedly (like the poor are likely to use) is more odious than riding on a train with comfortable seating, that stops infrequently, and where one can do productive work or sleep. While this comparison is extreme, this is not an academic issue. Most investment studies take little account of actual travel conditions in valuing time, either regarding comfort or the possibility of productive use of travel time. Ignoring travel conditions can be discriminatory by income class.

-Is the use of wage rates to monetize time savings valid? The neoclassical economic concept called *willingness to pay* or *contingent valuation* usually justifies the use of wage rates to monetize time savings. The idea is that, by studying analogous situations (but ones in which people have an opportunity to save time) or by asking the right questions, one can estimate what time is worth to individuals. Not surprisingly, people who earn more money are willing to pay more. Thus, projects that serve wealthier regions or wealthier corridors will always appear to accrue larger benefits, given the same number of projected beneficiaries and the same total time savings. Saving an upper-middle-class contingent earning $40 per hour only 5.5 minutes each would be of equal value to saving the working poor earning $6 per hour a full 30 minutes each. The implication of using monetized time in an analysis outcome is highly discriminatory in favor of upper-income classes and regions.

Treating time saved as equal for all income levels is wrong for another reason founded in neoclassical economic theory as well. If indeed time can be treated as equal to money, saving an equal amount is not of equal value to people of different incomes. The concept of *marginal utility* applies, which argues that saving a dollar (or whatever denomination) means much less to a wealthy person than a poor person.

Many projects hinge upon the monetized value of time saved, in many cases stated as the consumer surplus. Model outputs using summed monetary benefits should be viewed with skepticism, and the analyst must be prepared to challenge the results. For some projects, the analyst could even argue for the total exclusion of monetary "off-the-clock" time savings (meaning any trips made by travelers not explicitly on paid duty). This could drastically reduce the monetized benefits to both transit users and users of autos who were intended to benefit from reduced traffic. See Metz (2008) and the commentary he elicited for more on this important subject.

Standard practice typically requires monetization. As will be discussed in Chapter 8, there are often official guidelines or regulations to be followed. Even so, it can be insightful to do a supplementary analysis. The quantity of time saving, its distribution geographically, demographically, by length of time increments saved, and by impact on comfort of travel should all be listed. These should be considered as nonmonetary benefits and measured against the objectives of the project.

Finally, it is especially difficult to place monetary values of time on people who earn very little money and perhaps don't even participate much in the cash economy. For such cases, I. T. Transport (2005) has given some helpful guidance.

Transfer Penalties

The transfer penalty issue was discussed in detail in Chapter 3, in particular, in the section regarding the complex interaction between networks and individual routes. To summarize, Transfer Time is considered more onerous than In-Vehicle Travel Time and is therefore weighted with a factor greater than 1. So, all else being equal, a break in a journey will negatively affect demand. However, the whole point of a well-designed transfer-based network is not for all else to be equal, but to provide offsetting advantages (e.g. more frequent connections). If time penalties are used within the forecasting model, the model must also include the countervailing time saved due to more frequent departure possibilities and, perhaps, multiple routing possibilities. Thus, mode-choice models should be adjusted for improvements in frequency when services are restructured to improve them.

The penalty factor must also take into account the comfort and convenience of the transfer facilities. As discussed in Chapter 5, the quality of connections matter. Guo and Wilson (2004) developed several choice models that use available detailed Geographic Information System (GIS) data to include detailed aspects of the transfer conditions at particular stations and the walking environment, which simpler models could not capture. They have derived some penalties expressed in equivalent walking access or egress time that capture transfer behavior in the Boston area. In a further study they modeled commuter rail to subway connections and found that the penalty in central area stations was between 8.5 to 17 minutes, compared to an average of 7.3 minutes between subway lines (Guo and Wilson 2007).

With some caution, similar penalty times can perhaps be added to existing models in other regions to simulate the effect of transfers under a variety of conditions. Guo and Wilson (2004) include a useful listing of transfer penalty results from various studies around the world. It would desirable to do a penalty analysis, preferably similar to their more modern technique, in any region that was contemplating a major project, in order to improve the larger sequential model.

Given the subject's importance, there have been some large-scale studies whose purpose was to improve understanding both theoretically and empirically. See, for example, Gunn (1991) about the Netherlands study and Bates (1991) for the United Kingdom study. Two conclusions are that the trip purpose and the circumstances giving rise to the wait are both important. As can be seen in Table 7.5, a commuter forced to wait because of a "failed schedule" will find it highly objectionable as reflected in the very high penalty weighting factor of 3.0. A business traveler arriving at a stop a random time can expect to wait a "half headway." The penalty of only 1.3 suggests a higher tolerance for waiting than the rule of thumb of 2.0 used by many modelers, and so on for other situations.

The general lesson is that weighting factors used in regional models should be reviewed for their applicability on a project-specific basis. This should include transfers to and from the auto mode as well. See Gunn (2000) for more on the basic techniques used for the valuation of time.

Table 7.5 Transfer penalty weighting factors

	Factor on In-Vehicle Travel Time		
	Commuting	*Business*	*Other*
Walk time	1.0	1.6	1.3
Interchange time	2.1	1.6	1.6
Failed schedule	3.0	1.4	1.4
Half headway	1.3	1.4	1.7

Source: Gunn 1991, Netherlands Value-of-Time Study 1985–1991.

Spatial Zones That Are Too Coarse

As noted above, spatial zones, sometimes also called transportation analysis zones, are geographic subareas of the region. Attributes are all concentrated at one point or node, either at the center of gravity of the shape or at a logical location like an intersection or rail station. In other words, analysts represent travel within the zone only as travel leaving the node and returning to the node. In the O–D matrix, this is reflected in the zero values along the diagonal. Furthermore, given the design of the model, modelers might have little choice but to represent what is actually short-distance travel just over a zonal boundary as a much longer journey from node to node. Such an approach is useless for analyzing local travel. Thus, most regional models are usable only for studying the travel behavior and decisions for longer trips. The size of the spatial zone can also be too small to trace diverted traffic when there are changes to the network, which is discussed in the section on traffic degeneration. The analyst should confirm that, given the nature of activities that occur within the subarea, a reasonable number of trips, especially for nonmotorized modes, are occurring within the zone rather than being ignored or being misrepresented as longer zone-to-zone travel. Fortunately, recent modeling package upgrades might allow assignment at the parcel level instead of the zone level.

Lack of Pedestrian/Bicycle Modes

In addition to the inadequacy of network models for short trips because of the lack of detail, they can also neglect modes frequently used for short trips (i.e. walking and bicycling). As was discussed in Chapter 5 on characterizing and influencing modal relationships, if walking and bicycling are neglected in the mode-split analysis, travel characteristics can look very different from what they should be. In locations where walking and bicycling are safe and attractive, these modes might be possible as feeders to the long trips, but their contribution would be underestimated. In most regional transportation models, the quality of the walking experience is not considered, only the time based on walking distance. The fact that a bicycle extends the access distance is usually not considered at all.

The lack of nonmotorized modes also makes it impossible to estimate mode splits for short trips within any spatial zone where walking and bicycling are realistic options. It may not be realistic to build a new regional model with smaller spatial zones. One solution instead might be to build a separate subregional model for local shorter trips, at least for those spatial zones where there is a major transportation hub and/or employment center with adjacent shopping or residential areas and, consequently, the possibility of the significant use of nonmotorized modes. Such models are not easy to construct, however, because the traffic flows entering and leaving the boundaries of the subregional model must be made to match those of the larger model if data are to be shared between them.

Traffic Degeneration

Recently there have been numerous proposals for projects that involve taking away substantial capacity from automobiles and freight vehicles in order to give the space instead to public transport and to nonmotorized modes. Examples include creation of a pedestrian zone on a downtown street or the conversion of a general-purpose lane into a bus lane. These, in turn, elicit warnings of gridlock or other dire consequences. But there are other possibilities. One is that trips of marginal value are simply not taken, at least at the same time of day. Another is that densification has occurred (e.g., building on what used to be gas stations and parking lots), building taller buildings, and so on. Densification can reduce auto capacity in the affected subarea but can offset these reductions by individuals switching to nonmotorized modes for short trips and public transport for longer trips (Holtzclaw et al. 2002).

The seemingly logical way to shed light on the actual likely results is to use a regional transportation network model; however, most regional transportation models were designed in an era where traffic volumes were expected only to increase over time. Moreover, analysts were not accustomed to situations in which transport capacity might be reduced rather than increased. For example, the auto trip generation rates may not yet reflect the offset possible by switching to nonmotorized modes. The new situation suggested that adjustments to modeling techniques were necessary.

In order to establish the credibility of model results and to make suggestions for corrections as necessary, Bates et al. (1998) performed a worldwide survey of capacity reductions. The key data collected included changes in traffic flow after capacity reductions as a percentage of previous traffic in the affected areas. These reductions stemmed from both temporary, incidental closures (e.g. for bridge repair or replacement) as well as permanent, intentional total road closures or lane removals. They did not generally find the dire consequences predicted by some. Some of the traffic was diverted, but on average about 16 percent simply disappeared, although there was wide variation. The explanation seems to be that certain trips are of such a marginal nature that people will simply forego them, take them at a less congested time, or consolidate with another trip. Thus, accurate behavioral response prediction on the demand portion of the model is important, and improvements to the model may be necessary before predictions improve. Even though most current regional models have limited ability for behavioral response for anything other than peak trips, models are already evolving to consider the entire day. As the models become more sophisticated about travel patterns and behavior, changing their trip generation rates and times accordingly, their predictions about traffic degeneration will also improve.

In the meantime, Bates et al. (1998) recommend the use of simulation models of sufficient local detail to include junction (intersection) movements instead of the link-performance functions typically used to describe longer distance segments on regional network models. Simulation creates a section of a road with intersections, where an appropriate mix of vehicles types pass through them, based on lane configurations and signal timings. Bates et al. also suggest that the analyst will have to make a detailed estimate of how large the area to be analyzed should be. The area must be large enough that one can actually include possible diversion paths for traffic but not so large that the affected area represents only a small portion of the total traffic activity within it.

After analyzing local flow conditions assuming existing demand prior to closure or removal, the question is whether existing demand can be accommodated at a tolerable level of congestion. If not, the forecasting elements of the model must also be changed in order to estimate the demand reduction likely in the face of significantly changed travel conditions. The revised demand must then be reassigned to the revised traffic network.

Impact of and Upon Freight Vehicles

One must remember that freight and other commercial vehicles can make up high percentages of the traffic on certain parts of a regional network. Such traffic can affect the speed and capacity of the network. The analyst should determine that the model's link-performance functions and trip generation rates are realistic when the demand forecasts reveal a large amount of activity associated with large vehicles and commercial vehicles.

The contribution of freight activity to economic activity is sometimes a very important consideration. Decision makers are likely to evaluate and justify an investment in passenger transport in monetary terms, at least in part, by economic development benefits. But if a project has an adverse impact on freight activity, surely these costs will be subtracted from the benefits to the passenger side of the network. However, determining the right amount can be very problematic. Surely the time of the driver can be included and any direct cost changes from changes in fleet size due to speed changes (can be either higher or lower), but the value of the cargo is not as clear. Just because it arrives at a destination earlier or later does not always make a difference to the cost of running a supply chain; it depends on the specific situation. Moreover, as with passenger travel, higher speeds may just result in relocation of assembly, warehousing or distribution facilities farther away, a form of "freight sprawl."

Insufficient Data—The Noise Factor

Any model based on statistical methods will be subject to sampling errors and to variables that were omitted but whose inclusion would explain the influence of additional factors. When the size of the combined nonsystematic error from these errors and omissions rival the size of the variables the model is trying to estimate, one can speak of the output values dropping into the *noise floor* of the model. A good analogy to explain this phenomena is election polling. When the "margin of error" of a poll is plus or minus 3 percent, how would it be possible to estimate the popularity of a candidate where the actual popular support is less than 3 percent? In the same way, transit use can be so small relative to private auto use that the samples and consequently the model equations are not sufficiently accurate to predict transit use.

Where transit use is significant, nonmotorized mode use is likely to be as well. Inclusion of both nonmotorized modes and transit in a comprehensive data-collection effort prior to running the regional model will decrease the dominance of the auto mode in the data set, benefiting the accuracy of forecasts for all modes.

In practical terms, some regional models may still be incapable of estimating transit-related outputs in a statistically valid sense because too little data has been collected relative to the auto option. Where the auto is the only realistic option for all but a handful of trips, there may no correction possible as the sample size relative to auto trips is simply too small. In this case, the regional model is unusable for public transportation forecasts.

Revealed Preference and Stated Preference Methods and Model Calibration

Modelers need to set their model's parameters and populate them with data specific to the region. Some data are directly measurable, such as link speeds and traffic counts, albeit randomly distributed and therefore in need of statistical estimation. Others involve predicting human behavior and are much less directly measurable. The process of assessing the "goodness of fit" of data, the estimation of statistical descriptors of random data, and the selection of model parameters is known as *calibration*.

There are two primary types of approaches for the collection of information to calibrate models involving human behavioral responses. Revealed Preference (RP) is a class of approaches that try to predict travel behavior based upon choices that can be observed in real life. Stated Preference (SP) is a class of approaches that also tries to predict travel behavior but is based upon experimental or hypothetical situations and carefully designed questions about choices between the situations.

The complexity of RP and SP methods makes it exceptionally difficult for the nonexpert to use them. It is not easy for the uninitiated to challenge the psychological theories, the statistical procedures, and experimental designs appropriate to specific circumstances in such methods. SP in particular bears suspicion by its very nature; one is trying to ascertain what persons will do in hypothetical circumstances. Nevertheless, the nonspecialist can still ask searching questions if the strengths and limitations of these methods are understood.

RP clearly has the advantage because it is based on events that have either occurred already or can be observed in the future. It would seem to have the advantage that it accords with neoclassical economic theory that people are "rational" actors. Being rational, their behavior would be a sound guide to the project planner. Yet, this is not always the case. One reality is that individuals do not always make their choices based on perfect information. They might have chosen differently had they known or maybe even thought more about other options. (This is also true for SP choice.) There is also evidence that individuals have "impulse control" problems; that is, they make hasty decisions not in their own best interest. If they would have been more patient and done a thorough calculation, their choice might be different (Frank 2001). Furthermore, when risks need to be factored into a decision, researchers have concluded people are "generally muddled and incoherent" (Broome 2001).

RP methods cannot be used where individuals have no possibility for making actual relevant choices. This is often the case with proposed rail projects in regions currently without any rail service, for example. SP overcomes the fundamental problem that RP faces when observations are not possible. SP can also be used to fill gaps in data often seen at the end of RP exercises. SP also has the theoretical advantage over RP of allowing for systematic testing of nuanced alternatives in a project. Indeed, SP methods perform best when investigating marginal changes (Polak and Jones 1997). When changes become too remote or hypothetical, it raises issues about validity.

One of the theoretical foundations of SP is that asking individuals to make the aforementioned willingness-to-pay or contingent-valuation decisions is the appropriate way to measure the public will. While such theory has a certain logic and again accords with a belief in rational actors, it must be viewed with skepticism. Consider what happens when asking about investment decisions that would have negative implications for some communities and individuals. Planners may tell residents that the project considers these negative impacts; but how can one infer the willingness to pay accurately from responses when compensation to the community and individuals to offset the negative impact does not actually occur?

The responses might well be different if the beneficiaries of the project were literally going to have to pay those hurt by a project (Richardson 2001).

Consider, also, that people tend to be concerned, and rightly so, about the effectiveness and equity of any contribution they make. Thus, how much people are willing to pay also depends upon what others are willing to pay (Sen 2000). Yet, this information is not necessarily available. Consider further that surveys in almost any field show "asymmetries"; that is, respondents are usually far more willing to pay to prevent something harmful from happening than to undo it after the fact (Boyce 1992). This especially pertains to environmentally related questions, and such questions are often relevant to public transportation projects.

Then there is the "imbedding effect" where the sum an individual is willing to pay is less for a total package than if asked about each component separately. Moreover, in SP questioning, one can find that an individual will give similar prices for a wide range of quantities. Sen (2000) gives the example in which the respondents gave equal value to the saving of the lives of 2,000, 20,000, and 200,000 birds. People were, in effect, indicating a wide range of unit prices for each bird saved. Their understanding of the question (or lack of it) meant they did not give rational answers, and their responses are useless. If, instead, they had been indicating their willingness to spend whatever it takes to preserve a threatened species, the same price regardless of the number of birds actually saved would have been a rational response. This shows how the validity of an answer depends on the individual's perception of what they think the project is achieving.

SP methods are being steadily improved. One way to address some of SP's shortcomings is for analysts to develop questionnaires based on actual choice sets; that is, basing questions on clearly defined project alternatives that are still genuine candidates after preliminary analysis. Another is to unambiguously phrase any questions, making clear what assumptions are being made and what the project is trying to achieve. Analysts are also widening the focus of SP methods so that they can learn about more complex forms of behavioral responses (Polak and Jones 1997). More knowledge is needed about what will cause trips to be shifted away from the peak period, multiple destination trips, elimination of trips of marginal value, and so on. In turn, this should improve the modeling of traffic degeneration, improve transfer-weighting factors, the value-of-time estimates, and so on. This should also improve the calibration of models, making them usable for predicting travel over the whole day, not just during peak periods.

The current state-of-the-practice is to use both RP and SP techniques and combine the data. Combining is done to obtain the advantages of both, which can expand the range and usefulness of results (Bradley and Daly 1997; Cherchi and Ortuzar 2002). But this can also be problematic. For example, random values generated by each method can have different variances and other statistical difficulties impeding the merging of data. For a concrete example of difficulties, the interested reader is referred to a study that used SP data to update an RP-based travel-demand model in the Helsinki, Finland region (Kurri, Mikola and Karasmaa 2001).

Trends in Model Development

Urban transportation network models were developed in an era when the most pressing issue was the provision of capacity to handle ever-growing peak demands. In the developed nations, the relevant issue is increasingly often the best use of existing capacity, especially for the modes sharing right of way. Thus, ways to spread demand over the day and to influence travel behavior to reduce demand on overtaxed links and corridors are of increasing interest. Better understanding and, consequently, modeling of travel behavior by individuals is necessary to achieve these ends. This does not mean that analysts must literally examine the behavior of every individual separately within the model, but it does mean that they must choose parameters and specify equations that will permit a wider range of responses by individuals.

Models that solve the equilibrium process simultaneously rather than sequentially are a step in the direction of better behavioral modeling. To reiterate, sequential models have weak theoretical justification in the first place. For instance, individuals do not first select their destination and then their mode per the sequential model, but make those choices simultaneously, nor do simultaneous models depend on equilibration procedures that force consistency between program modules built upon unrelated theoretical foundations.

Also helpful to the analyst is the ever-increasing amount of RP and SP information as additional public transportation projects are completed. There can be both more information about the region in question as well as information that can be transferred from suitable peers (after some appropriate tests). Moreover, SP methods are being refined and questions are being modified for the changed purposes of projects. Specifically, modelers are trying to reach a better understanding of all-day household activity patterns, schedules, and other factors underlying travel decisions (Polak and Jones 1997).

Historically, regional models used separate databases from models for more local study, such as traffic simulation models used to study optimum traffic-signal timing, bus-stop placement, and so on. In other words, analysts had to collect either separate data or they would need special expertise to reformat and move data from one level of modeling to the next. Furthermore, different analysis teams were likely to be working on models from one level to the next.

The most advanced modeling packages now share their databases far more effectively. For example, data collected by field sensors to monitor real-time traffic flows can be read from an archive and then used to compute summary statistics, which, in turn, can be used to develop link-performance functions and parameters for the regional model. For another example, models can use predicted flows on a link or corridor to develop traffic-flow functions suitable for simulating traffic through a series of intersections. The end result of database integration can only be broadening of expertise by professional modelers, increased participation in different levels of modeling, and wider use of each level of modeling.

Data collection through the sensors integral to ITS is widespread and continually increasing. On the private vehicle front, a variety of traffic sensors continuously collect information about traffic composition, volume, and speed. In public transportation, Automatic Vehicle Location (AVL) provides continuous data about a vehicle's location at fixed time intervals and time spent at specific locations. Public vehicles so equipped can also act as general traffic probes. Automatic Passenger Counters (APCs) provide continuous data about boarding and alighting linked to time and location. Analysts can use archived data from the various systems to load models, eliminating the need for periodic manual counting and the installation of temporary field sensors.

The importance of continuously collecting data should not be underestimated. Project planning efforts often suffer from a lack of current data. Historically, attempts to collect such data could be costly and time-consuming, creating pressure to accept less-than-optimal input information. As a result of continuously available data, current trip generation and trip distribution modeling steps may not be necessary at all when investigating the status quo or very near future, as the current O–D matrix is known with sufficient detail and accuracy. Furthermore, forecasts of trip generation and distribution of future forecast years will require less preparation effort and thus not cost as much. They will also be less error-prone due to the fact that as databases increase in sample size and in scope, the noise component shrinks. In summary, the data quality and hence the prediction qualities of models can be expected to increase.

Regional modeling packages are also generally developing more user-friendly interactive formats and display options. Earlier generations of regional demand forecasting models and other such predication could be awkward to debug and run, and algorithms could take a long time to execute. GIS maps now provide the visual connection between a location and all attributes associated with it. When done well, graphical outputs can be easier to interpret than tabular and narrative formats. Similarly, analysts can more easily modify input values and see the consequences much quicker. This includes assistance in construction and specification of intermediate models, such as logit models, or trip distribution matrices that have incomplete information, into the larger model. This will no doubt increase the use of such programs in university courses and continuing education programs and, over time, increase the number of practitioners with some familiarity with them.

A likely consequence of the aforementioned improvements is increased accessibility to modeling for planners with a wider array of responsibilities, and perhaps even for citizen activists and others who have little modeling expertise. It will allow analysts other than the "official" regional modelers to create and run their own scenarios and, especially, to investigate and to challenge results that affect investment analysis. This can only increase the transparency and intellectual honesty of complex modeling efforts.

Summary

Models are an inescapable part of any major project analysis. An analyst must at least understand enough about them to accept or reject their outputs. This requires being able to ask the right questions and to be able to do independent "back of the envelope" calculations to test the reasonableness of the results.

Analysts use models for several different purposes. Simpler models allow analysts a range of reasonable values for preliminary project analysis, as well as the tools to perform independent calculations testing the plausibility of more complex models. The accepted results from complex models are then used as inputs to investment and performance analyses. Once confidence is developed in a model, it can be further used for "what if" analysis to investigate project alternatives and likely impacts from events not within the control of project implementers. Models are also used to fine tune results and perform final, detailed computations.

Sometimes it is difficult to understand what a specific model is really computing, and consequently, whether it is even a valid exercise. Projections simply extrapolate current trends and should be rejected almost automatically. The reasoning is that attempts to accommodate projections ignore the possibility of influencing trends. Instead, accommodation only helps to create self-fulfilling prophecies. Forecasts are more useful because they are designed to estimate the results from different design and policy choices in project alternatives. Planning by objective involves the continual adjustment of a project based on comparison of actual results during implementation versus the project's objectives.

There are some particularly useful types of simple models, defined as those that can be done without special software, large data sets, or special expertise. Models to estimate travel conditions are relevant because speed and capacity are important to both public transportation and its competition. Models for estimating demand as a function of socioeconomic class classes are relevant to tailoring services for particular users. Those for estimating demand as a function of headway are important for service improvements and as function of price for estimating ridership and revenue. When a computerized regional model is not available or is suspect, being able to establish at least the status quo of travel patterns in the form of an O–D matrix can be highly useful.

Regional travel models are almost always used as important input sources for evaluation of major projects. These are central for forecasting key results from an investment, such as ridership on public transport, congestion levels on roads in the same corridor, and ability of a corridor to absorb intensified land use. Moreover, there is often a legal or planning regulatory requirement that such forecasts be performed by an officially sanctioned organization.

Sequential four-step regional models go through the following steps. First, the trips get generated. Generation is usually based upon empirical information about traffic that results from particular types and intensity of land uses. The modeler treats trip generation as an exogenous input, meaning that the results are not fed back into the solution process to modify the trip generation for any given scenario, although later forecast years might merit such modification. Second, the modeler distributes trips from origins to destinations, typically using a doubly constrained entropy model that operates on the principle of the most likely outcome. Third, the modeler selects the mode choice, typically with logit models based on random utility theory where the probability of making a particular choice is based on the socioeconomic attributes of the individual. Fourth, the modeler assigns the traffic using Wardrop's First Principle, which says that all used routes have the same generalized costs, defined as a combination of monetized time and other out-of-pocket costs. The output from the fourth step is then fed back to a lesser or greater extent, to remove contradictions between assumed travel times and flows on links.

As models become more integrated, land development is a function of the types of available transportation links and services. When it is public policy to integrate transportation and land-use planning, modelers can study specific corridors where development can be encouraged and transport capacity and performance can be upgraded in complementary fashion. Such models can be linked to further submodels to provide estimates of energy consumption and emissions. These results can also be very important inputs to any performance and investment analysis.

The sequential models have a weak theoretical basis, particularly in their understanding of travel patterns and the psychology of individuals. In reality, travelers' destinations are not selected first, then the mode, then the particular path. Furthermore, the destination can be changed, as it too is a function of the assignment of volumes assigned to various routes and the resulting travel conditions. Therefore, individual travelers make all of these decisions simultaneously.

Feedback is just a method to try to force consistency between steps and only partially addresses the shortcomings of the four-step sequential model. Moreover, expertise in the various steps has historically developed largely separately, impeding a deep understanding of the whole process by any one analyst. Because simultaneous models address these shortcomings, they will eventually displace sequential models, even though they require more mathematical prowess to solve.

Analysts need to investigate a lot of potential sources for error and potentially misleading results when choosing to accept or reject both the inputs and outputs for complex regional models. These include nonequilibration of link flows, changing prices and elasticities over time, numerous issues with the monetization of the value of time, transfer penalties assessed, spatial zone coarseness, treatment of nonmotorized modes, traffic degeneration phenomena, interaction with the freight system, data noise levels, and more. Particularly opaque to the nonexpert is the art and science of SP and RP for modeling of human behavioral responses and for calibrating models. Nevertheless, an analyst can learn to ask searching questions and contribute to the modeling process.

Understanding complex all-day travel behavior, not just peak-commuting-trip behavior, is becoming ever more necessary to make better use of existing network capacity. SP and RP methods will become more reliable as methods for forecasting behavioral responses, while increasing numbers of projects and, hence, volumes of data will allow more transfer of findings from peers. Highly detailed GIS databases of walking and accessibility conditions are also enabling more localized understanding of transfer penalties so that mode-split and ridership predictions can be improved.

Models will also benefit from better quality and quantity of data collected by ITS. For example, databases will be shared more from stand-alone modal systems such as AVL for buses and traffic-management centers for autos and freight vehicles. These will pass much more current and complete data to complex regional models than has historically been the case. In turn, the regional models can pass their results along to localized models, such as corridor traffic simulators. Finally, models are certain to become easier to modify and to rerun because of integrated databases and more user-friendly GIS-based interfaces.

A likely consequence of improvements is increased accessibility to modeling for planners with a variety of responsibilities, and perhaps even for citizen activists who are not modeling specialists, especially with the steady improvement in visualization tools. This can only increase the transparency and intellectual honesty of complex modeling efforts.

References

Balcombe R., R. Mackett, N. Paulley, J. Preston, J. Shires, H. Titheridge, M. Walman and P. White. 2004. *The Demand for Public Transport: A Practical Guide*. TRL Report 593. Berkshire, UK: TRL Limited. http://www.demandforpublictransport.co.uk/TRL593.pdf

Bates, J. J. 1991. "The British Value of Time Study." Paper presented at the Nordic Seminar on the Value of Travel Time, 2–3 December, Masala, Finland.

Bates, John, Denvil Coombe, Martin Dale, Mike Maher, S. Cairns, C. Hass-Klau and P. B. Goodwin. 1998. *Traffic Impact of Highway Capacity Reductions: Assessment of the Evidence*. London, UK: Landor.

Ben-Akiva, Mosha, and Steven R. Lerman. 1985. *Discrete Choice Analysis: Theory and Application to Travel Demand*. Cambridge, MA: MIT Press.

Bedelu, Binyam, and Marius de Langen. 2008. "Simplified Travel Demand Modeling for Developing Cities: The Case of Addis Ababa," *World Transport Policy & Practice* 14(2): 47–73.

Boyce, David. 2002. "Is the Sequential Travel Forecasting Paradigm Counterproductive?" *Journal of Urban Planning and Development* 128 (4): 169–83.

Boyce, David E., and Huw C. W. L. Williams. 2003. *Urban Travel Forecasting Models in the USA and UK: States of the Art and States of the Practice*. Presented at 43rd Congress of the European Regional Science Association, Jyvaskyla, Finland, 27–30 August.

Boyce, Rebecca R., Thomas C. Brown, Gary H. McClelland, George L. Peterson and William D. Schulze. 1992. "An Experimental Examination of Intrinsic Values as a Source of the WTA-WTP Disparity." *American Economic Review* 82 (5): 1366–73.

Bradley, M. A., and A. J. Daly. 1997. "Estimation of Logit Choice Models Using Mixed Stated Preference and Revealed Preference Information." Chapter 9 in *Understanding Travel Behavior in an Era of Change*, edited by Peter Stopher and Martin Lee-Gosselin. Oxford, UK: Pergamon Press, 209–29.

Broome, John. 2001. "Cost-Benefit Analysis and Population." In *Cost Benefit Analysis: Legal, Economic, and Philosophical Perspectives*, edited by Matthew D. Adler and Eric A. Posner. Chicago: University of Chicago Press, 117–34.

Cea, Joaquim de, J. Enrique Fernandez, Valerie Dekock, Alexandra Soto and Terry Friesz. 2003. *ESTRAUS: A Computer Package for Solving Supply-Demand Equilibrium Problems on Multimodal Transportation Networks with Multiple User Classes*. Presentation at (January) 2003 Transportation Research Board Annual Meeting, Washington, DC.

Cherchi, E., and Juan Ortuzar. 2002. "Mixed RP/SP Models Incorporating Interaction Effects." *Transportation* 29: 371–95.

Daly, Andrew. 2000. "National Models." Chapter 25 in *Handbook of Transport Modeling*, edited by D. A. Henscher and K. J. Button. New York: Pergamon, 421–32.

Demery, Leroy W., Jr. 1994. "Supply-Side Analysis and Verification of Ridership Forecasts for Mass Transit Capital Projects." *Journal of the American Planning Association* 60 (3): 355–71.

Evans, John E. 2004. *Traveler Response to Transportation System Changes: Chapter 9—Transit Scheduling and Frequency*. Report 95. Washington, DC: Transit Cooperative Research Program, National Academy Press. http://www.tcrponline.org

Frank, Robert H. 2001. "Why Is Cost-Benefit Analysis So Controversial?" In *Cost Benefit Analysis: Legal, Economic, and Philosophical Perspectives*, edited by Matthew D. Adler and Eric A. Posner. Chicago: University of Chicago Press, 77–94.

Goodwin, P. B. 1992. "A Review of New Demand Elasticities with Special Reference to Short- and Long-Run Effects of Price Changes." *Journal of Transport Economics and Policy* 26 (May): 155–65.

Gunn, Hugh. 2000. "An Introduction to the Valuation of Travel Time Savings and Losses." Chapter 26 in *Handbook of Transport Modeling*, edited by D. A. Henscher and K. J. Button. New York: Pergamon, 433–47.

———. 1991. *Research into the Value of Travel Time Savings and Losses: The Netherlands 1985 to 1991*. Summary report material presented at The Nordic Value of Time Seminar, Helsinki, December, Hague Consulting Group (now Rand Europe), The Hague, Netherlands.

Guo, Zhan, and Nigel H. M. Wilson. 2007. "Modeling Effects of Transit System Transfers on Travel Behavior: Case of Commuter Rail and Subway in Downtown Boston, Massachusetts." *Transportation Research Record* 2006: 11–20.

———. 2004. "Assessment of the Transfer Penalty for Transit Trips: Geographic Information System–Based Disaggregate Modeling Approach." *Transportation Research Record* 1872: 10–18.

Holtzclaw, John, Robert Clear, Hank Dittmar, David Goldstein and Peter Haas. 2002. "Location Efficiency: Neighborhood and Socio-Economic Characteristics Determine Auto Ownership and Use—Studies in Chicago, Los Angeles and San Francisco." *Transportation Planning and Technology* 25 (1): 1–27. http://www.tandf.co.uk/journals/online/0308-1060.html

Hossain, Afzal, David Gargett and David Cosgrove. 2013. *Public Transport use in Australia's Capital Cities: Modelling and Forecasting*. Research Report 129. Canberra, Australia: Bureau of Infrastructure, Transport and Regional Economics, Department of Transport and Infrastructure.

I. T. Transport, Ltd. 2005. *How to Manual: The Valuation of Rural Time Savings in Least Developed Countries*. Arlington, Oxfordshire, UK: U.K Department of International Development.

ITE (Institute of Transportation Engineers). 2012. *Trip Generation*. 9th ed. Washington, DC: Institute of Transportation Engineers.

Kennedy, D. 2013. "Econometric Models for Public Transport Forecasting." Research Report 518. NZ Transport Agency. http://www.nzta.govt.nz/resources/research/reports/518/

Kenworthy, Jeff, Felix Laube, Peter Newman and Paul Barter. 1997. *Indicators of Transport Efficiency in 37 Global Cities: A Report for the World Bank*. Perth, Australia: Institute for Science and Technology Policy, Murdoch University.

Kurri, Jari, Juha Mikola and Nina Karasmaa. 2001. "Stated Preference Study of Mode Choice in the Helsinki Metropolitan Area." Chapter 13 in *Mathematical Methods on Optimization in Transportation Systems*, edited by Matti Pursula and Jurkko Nittymaki. Dordrecht, Netherlands: Kluwer Academic Publishers, 203–23.

Litman, Todd. 2013. *Transport Elasticities: Impacts on Travel Behavior, GIZ-SUTP Technical Document 11.* GIZ (Deutsche Gesellschaft fur Internationale Zusammarbeit GmbH. http://www.sutp.org/index.php/en-dn-tp

———. 2004. *Transit Price Elasticities and Cross-Elasticities.* http://www.nctr.usf.edu/jpt/pdf/JPT%207-2%20Litman.pdf

Manheim, Marvin. 1979. *Fundamentals of Transportation Systems Analysis.* Cambridge, MA: MIT Press.

Metz, D. 2008. "The Myth of Travel Time Savings." *Transport Reviews* 28 (3): 321–36.

Miyamoto, Kazuaki, and Varameth Vichiensan. 2000. "A Review of Land Use Model Applications in Transportation Demand Forecasting." In *Urban Transportation and Environment*, edited by Oscar Diaz Gonzalez Palomas and Christian Jamet. Rotterdam: A. A. Balkema, 449–54.

Morlok, Edward K. 1979. "Types of Transportation Supply Functions and Their Applications." *Transportation Research* 13: 1–19.

Morlok, Edward, Eric C. Bruun and Francis Vanek. 1997. Chapter 2 in *The Advanced Minibus Concept: A New ITS-Based Service for Low Density Markets.* Report PA-26-700D. Washington, DC: U.S. Federal Transit Administration.

Nevala, Riku. 2000. *The Effects of Low-Floor Vehicles, Service Headway and Travel Time on the Demand of Urban Bus Transportation* [In Finnish.] Master's Thesis, Helsinki University of Technology, Espoo, Finland.

Ortuzar, Juan de Dios, and Luis G. Willumsen. 2011a. "Simplified Transport Demand Models." Chapter 12 in *Modelling Transport.* 4th ed. Sussex, UK: John Wiley and Sons, 395–427.

———. 2011b. "Assignment." Chapter 10 in *Modelling Transport.* 4th ed. Sussex, UK: John Wiley and Sons, 349–90.

Oum, Tae Hoon, and W. G. Waters II. 2000. "Transport Demand Elasticities." Chapter 12 in *Handbook of Transport Modeling*, edited by D. A. Henscher and K. J. Button. New York: Pergamon, 197–210.

Oum, Tae Hoon, W. G. Waters II and Jong-Say Yong. 1992. "Concepts of Price Elasticities of Transport Demand and Recent Empirical Estimates." *Journal of Transport Economics and Policy* 26: 139–54.

Polak, John, and Peter Jones. 1997. "Using Stated Preference Methods to Examine Preferences and Responses." Chapter 8 in *Understanding Travel Behavior in an Era of Change*, edited by Peter Stopher and Martin Lee-Gosselin. Oxford, UK: Pergamon Press, 177–97.

Pratt, Richard, and John E. Evans IV. 2004. "Bus Routing and Coverage." In *Traveler Response to Transportation System Changes.* Report 95. Washington, DC: National Academy Press, Transit Cooperative Research Program, 62–66. http:// www.tcrponline.org

Pursula, Matti, Riku Nevala and Jari Kurri. 2001. *Estimating the Effect of Shorter Service Headway and Low-Floor Vehicles on Bus Patronage.* Presentation at the 80th Annual Meeting of the Transportation Research Board, Washington, DC.

Richardson, Henry. 2001. "The Stupidity of the Cost–Benefit Standard." In *Cost Benefit Analysis: Legal, Economic, and Philosophical Perspectives*, edited by Matthew D. Adler and Eric A. Posner. Chicago: University of Chicago Press, 135–68.

Sen, Amartya. 2000. "The Discipline of Cost-Benefit Analysis." In *Cost Benefit Analysis: Legal, Economic, and Philosophical Perspectives*, edited by Matthew D. Adler and Eric A. Posner. Chicago: University of Chicago Press, 95–116.

Sheffi, Yosef. 1985. *Urban Transportation Networks: Equilibrium Analysis with Mathematical Programming Methods.* Englewood Cliffs, NJ: Prentice Hall.

Siegel, Justin D., Joaquin de Cea, Jose Enrique Fernandez, Renan E. Rodriguez and David Boyce. 2006. "Comparisons of Urban Travel Forecasts Prepared with the Sequential Procedure and a Combined Model." *Networks and Spatial Economics* 6: 135–48.

Strand, Sverre. 1993. "Time in Transport: A Perverted Problem? Arguments for a Fresh Look at Time Utility Research and Its Applications." *Transportation Research Record* 1395: 10–14.

Surface Transportation Policy Project. 1999. *Road Work Ahead: Is Construction Worth the Wait?* http://ntl.bts.gov/lib/7000/7400/7476/road_work_pr.html

Waddell, Paul. 2011. "Integrated Land Use and Transportation Planning and Modelling: Addressing Challenges in Research and Practice." *Transport Reviews* 31 (2): 209–29.

Further Reading

Abrantes, Pedro A.L. and Mark R. Wardman. 2011. "Meta-analysis of UK Values of Travel Time: An Update." *Transportation Research* A 45: 1–17.

Barra, Tomas de la. 1989. *Integrated Land Use and Transport Modeling: Decision Chains and Hierarchies.* Cambridge, UK: Cambridge University Press.

Beimborn, Edward, Rob Kennedy and William Schaefer. 1996. *Inside the Black Box: Making Transportation Work for Livable Communities.* Washington, DC: Environmental Defense Fund.

Jansson, Kjell, and Reza Mortazavi. 2000. "Models for Public Transport Demand and Benefit Assessments." Chapter 31 in *Handbook of Transportation Modeling,* edited by D. A. Henscher and K. J. Button. New York: Pergamon, 509–25.

Lam, William H. K., and Michael G. H. Bell. 2003. *Advanced Modeling for Transport Operations and Service Planning.* New York: Pergamon. See especially Chapters 4–8 and 11.

Marchetti, C. 1994. "Anthropological Invariants in Travel Behavior." *Technological Forecasting and Social Change* 47: 75–88.

McFadden, Daniel. 1998. "Measuring Willingness-to-Pay for Transportation Improvements." In *Theoretical Foundations of Travel Choice Modeling,* edited by Tommy Garling, Thomas Laitila, and Kerstin Westin. New York: Pergamon, 339–64.

Polydoropoulou, A., and Moshe Ben Akiva. 2002. "Combined Reveals and Stated Preference Nested Logit Access and Egress Mode Choice Model for Multiple Mass Transit Techniques." *Transportation Research Record* 1771: 38–45.

Putman, Stephen H. 1983. *Integrated Urban Models: Policy Analysis of Transportation and Land Use.* London, UK: Pion Ltd.

Southworth, Frank. 1995. *A Technical Review of Urban Land Use-Transportation Models as Tools for Evaluating Vehicle Travel Reduction Strategies.* Report 6881. Oak Ridge, Tennessee: Center for Transportation Analysis—Oak Ridge National Laboratory. http://ntl.bts.gov/DOCS/ornl.html

Vuchic, Vukan R. 2007. "Transit System Performance: Capacity, Productivity, Efficiency and Utilization." Chapter 4 in *Urban Transit: Systems and Technology.* Hoboken, NJ: Wiley, 149–201.

Vuchic, Vukan R. 2005. "Modeling and Optimization in Transit Systems Analysis." Chapter 3 in *Urban Transit: Operations, Planning and Economics.* Hoboken, NJ: Wiley, 158–84.

Wardman, Mark. 2012. "Review and Meta-analysis of U.K. Time Elasticities of Travel Demand." *Transportation* 39: 465–90.

Chapter 8

Methods to Evaluate a Transit Project in Monetary Terms

Comparative evaluation of performance generally involves using summaries of outputs from the analyses of several alternative project solutions, each of which the modeler has analyzed at a similar level of detail. There are two basic types of comparisons. The first type is for the purpose of selecting a particular solution amongst two or more alternatives (e.g. How does BRT compare to LRT in Seattle?). The second involves using data from a similar peer application elsewhere in order to learn more about the costs and benefits of particular potential solutions at the project location (e.g. How would LRT perform in Seattle based on experience in Portland?).

This chapter begins with some important issues raised by attempting to summarize and evaluate the worthiness and performance of a transit project in monetary terms. The chapter continues with a detailed discussion of the type of project cost-related inputs required for monetary evaluations and much briefer introduction to the types of benefits that must be estimated. It then reviews the basic evaluation tool of Net Present Value (NPV) and its close relative, the Benefit to Cost Ratio (BCR), and provides some examples. It continues with a discussion of the assumptions behind the monetary approach to project evaluation and its inherent limitation that it pays little heed to how the costs and benefits are distributed. It concludes with commentary about further shortcomings to the monetary approach from the standpoint of long-term sustainability.

Chapter 9 presents a cost-estimating method that modelers can use to provide inputs to these the evaluation tools presented in this chapter. All of the cost estimating methods discussed in both this chapter and Chapter 9 are sophisticated enough to allow for sufficiently detailed analysis to compare relatively minor differences between various alternative project solutions, but still simple enough to do with a hand calculator.

Issues in Comparative Evaluations

There are three issues to address before modelers can develop evaluation methods and interpret the results. One is that modelers should not compare costs between alternative project solutions without considering the difference in service attributes; in other words, benefits must also be compared. A second issue is that alternatives must be realistic, not ones so far apart as to be incomparable. If one is comparing performance to a peer elsewhere, the peer again must be a realistic one. Chapter 3 suggested some indicators that can be used for identifying realistic peers. The third issue is that there are attributes inherent to a specific project location that should not be confused with the attributes of the modes and technologies included within the alternative project solutions. This third issue will be elaborated upon.

It is easy to oversimplify comparisons. In popular discussion and debate, modelers often use only one or two values to summarize alternatives. For example, some major cost (e.g. total operating cost or total capital cost) might be divided by a number of hours of service for which vehicles operate, number of miles (kilometers) associated with this operation, or some other measure of service output or consumption. One or two values is never enough to characterize anything other than the most simple of projects. When there are too few values for comparison, one cannot visualize the tradeoffs. One service might cost significantly more per vehicle-hour but have a higher operating speed or a higher comfort standard to offset that cost. One service might look impressive when measured by cost per vehicle-hour, yet still perform poorly when judged by cost per vehicle-mile (vehicle-kilometers) if the operating speed is low.

In addition to vehicle-hours or vehicle-miles (vehicle-kilometers), other measures of service output are commonly used in evaluations. Space-hours or space-miles are found by multiplying vehicle-hours or vehicle-miles by the number of spaces for passengers. This is supposed to correct for vehicle size. At some point in any comparison, however, the fraction of this space actually consumed by passengers becomes relevant. But one cannot simply divide a cost by vehicle occupancy to compute the lowest cost mode per passenger because the number of passengers by each alternative project solution is not the same. For example, a noisy bus with plastic seats and no air-conditioning will cost less to own and operate than a quiet bus having upholstered seats and air-conditioning. In a hot climate, the former will not attract many people who have access to a car. This point was missed in one of the landmark books on urban transportation in the United States in its era. Meyer, Kain and Wohl wrote *The Urban Transportation Problem* (1965). In Chapter 9, it presented curves purporting to show a passenger-volume breakeven point between modes. It is a mistake that is still sometimes made. In actuality, different services have different levels of passenger attractiveness and thus different numbers of passengers. Furthermore, since an increase in cost per space can be offset by an increase in ridership, the deficit per passenger and the total deficit could actually be less, despite a more expensive service.

Summary indicators of performance can give a misleading impression when modelers presume that they relate primarily to modal or technological characteristics. As was shown in Chapter 3, the specific alignment and characteristics of the service area also have implications for performance. For example, a radial route inherently has lots of unused capacity at its outer end, regardless of mode or level of technology. In contrast, the tangential lines 2 and 6 of the Paris Metro are not particularly fast or modern. But because of their high turnover of passengers, high ridership for their entire lengths, and high demand over most of the service day, their capacity usage and cost-efficiency indicators will surely exceed virtually all of the newer radial-oriented lines, even those using the latest rapid-transit technologies.

As this Paris example shows, it is necessary to try to identify those service attributes inherent to the alignment and service area and those inherent to the modes and technologies involved in the particular project solution being analyzed. A list of commonly relevant attributes of alignment and service area is given in Table 8.1. Planners can design service configuration alternatives that employ a mode or perhaps more than one mode to try to better apply the abilities of each particular mode(s) to offset any inherent limitations of the available alignments and service area. Comparing these initial configurations leads to other more refined configurations, perhaps employing modes in an innovative matter to best respond to the limitations. Planners should discard unrealistic possibilities when attempts at refinement still leave major flaws.

After developing possible project solutions, planners should subject each to the same evaluation procedures. In addition to the monetary values, there needs to be indicators that will reveal which solutions, if any, better overcome the inherent limitations of the project location. As an example, use of short-turn routes along the inner sections of a long radial route will improve capacity-utilization indicators. Although rail and bus modes can both use a short-turn configuration at a particular project location, one of them might prove more efficient, or an unusual combination might prove most efficient. In this case, the indicator serves to reveal that selection of the project solution with a slightly lower NPV might well be justified due to higher operational efficiency. Another example might be that

Table 8.1 Some important service attributes influenced by alignment and service area

○ Station or stop spacing

○ Ease of passenger access

○ Cruising speeds

○ Acceleration/Deceleration rates

○ Transfer facilities

○ Frequency of services

○ Frequency of connections

○ Origin–Destination patterns

○ Demand profile along routes (spatial demand profile)

○ Demand profile by time of day (temporal demand profile)

○ Congestion conditions for autos

one project solution gives more convenience to the passengers despite a slightly lower NPV, and so on.

The Required Inputs

Monetary evaluation requires essentially two types of information to be assembled. The first type is related to the physical construction and ongoing operation and maintenance costs that will be created by a project. The second type is the array of benefits and external costs that will arise from it. These are discussed separately.

Project Construction and Ongoing Operation and Maintenance

This concerns actual monetary costs and revenues and does not include any monetized values generated for the purpose of cost-benefit evaluation. It typically includes any land acquisition required, the estimated cost of the design effort, information about investment quantities and schedules, operating and routine maintenance costs (usually on an annual basis), major maintenance costs and their schedules, anticipated revenues (again, on an annual basis), and any salvage revenues, or their opposite, decommissioning costs.

Planners must prepare one or more *engineering cost models* in order to supply some of these inputs. These models allow an analysis of costs on the basis of the resources consumed to support a given scenario. These cost models are also useful for a second important purpose: allowing *sensitivity analysis*, which means exploring the effects from differences in technology, wages, operating practices, financial constraints, and more. Chapter 9 will deal with the topics of engineering cost model development and sensitivity analysis in more detail.

A description of methods for evaluating transit project performance in monetary terms requires a review of how time affects analysis. Evaluations can be short term, medium term, or long term. The defining principle is that more of the factors driving costs become amenable to change over time. Given enough time, even seemingly permanent and essential fixtures can be made redundant as travel patterns change and new travel options emerge. For example, numerous elevated railways have been torn down, sometimes without direct replacement with either at-grade or underground rights of way.

Short-term models include costs as reflected in the current state and technical capabilities of the supporting infrastructure and equipment affecting the proposed investment. Typically, only direct operating and maintenance costs and the ownership costs of vehicles are included in these costs because they are the main ones that can be influenced in the short term. Modelers often ignore ownership costs in short-term analyses on the grounds that these are *sunk costs* (i.e. once owned, such costs no longer factors into the decision to use an asset). They are not ignored here because one can assume that 1) the lives of many assets (e.g. buses) really are dependent on how much they are used, and 2) many assets could immediately find use elsewhere and thus have an opportunity cost. This is discussed further in a later section.

In the medium term, more can be changed. Transportation planners can change network connections, substitute modes, and upgrade or relocate facilities as they require renewal. Demand between origins and destinations could change, either by design or by factors beyond the control of transportation planners. In the longer term, every aspect of a network, physical and operational, is subject to change. Rarely is a long-term scenario truly the product of a clean state, but it remains a real possibility nonetheless. Table 8.2 lists some common components included in cost models as a function of time.

As time periods become longer, results become more uncertain. In addition to inflation, which can be problematic since it does not affect all cost inputs equally, technology and relevant public policy can be unpredictable. Some emerging technologies meet expected performance, while others do not. A policy such as competitive contracting might drastically reduce labor costs. Indeed, there is always the risk of something unforeseen. For these reasons, sensitivity analysis is used to explore the consequences of hypothetical deviations from some base values. Through this process, planners can identify changes that could have the largest impact on the outcome of an analysis.

The distinction regarding lengths of time periods is ultimately arbitrary, of course, since there is no natural definition for short term, medium term, or long term. Nonetheless, conceptually setting a period is of vital importance. Planners should make comparisons using cost models that span similar lengths of time and are consistent in scope. As an example, if a medium-term scenario regarding a proposed busway includes expired-life bus replacement, the corresponding

Table 8.2 Components commonly included in cost models

Short Term
Operating and maintenance costs (including administration)
Vehicle ownership
Medium Term
Operating and maintenance costs
Vehicle ownership
Vehicle overhaul or replacement
Infrastructure improvements affecting performance
Mode substitution in selected areas
Network reconfiguration in selected areas
Demand changes in network
Long Term
All items under medium term plus redesign and replacement, up to and including entire infrastructure

proposed scenario of a rail line should include any rolling-stock replacements or overhauls that would occur during the same time period (although adjustments might be required to account for unequal vehicle lives). When capital investments are involved, models should span sufficient lengths of time so that the commonly sought trade-offs between higher capital cost and lower operating costs are evident. A common example would be a comparison between purchasing new buses with lower maintenance and fuel costs versus a cheaper life-extending overhaul with maintenance and fuel costs similar to the present. The analysis time period must be long enough to reflect a period in which the overhauled buses will have to be replaced and new ones purchased.

Benefits and External Costs

The point of a project is to create benefits, of course, but these are not necessarily all monetary and will therefore need to be monetized. Similarly, byproduct costs may not be directly billable to the project but are nevertheless real and need to be included. Other chapters discuss these costs and benefits in detail, so only some of the most major ones that may require research are highlighted here.

One of the most dominant benefits is usually the time saved by users of the finished product. Perhaps others will see time savings as well if the overall transport network sees reduced congestion. Estimates of the total time saved for each alternative must be prepared and the value(s) of time (VoT) must be selected. In many countries, there will be mandated procedures or at least guidance. See, for example, the letter by Belenky (2011) with suggestions to U.S. Department of Transportation employees what percentages of hourly salaries should be used under which circumstances. Interestingly, he makes no recommendations about the VoT for freight vehicles and drivers but acknowledges the VoT is nonzero. See I.T. Transport's study (2005) for recommendations to the UK central government about VoT in developing countries. See also Chapter 7 for an extended discussion on VoT.

Predictions about increases or decreases in accidental deaths, shortened or extended lifespans, loss of hearing, and other health-related impacts must be assembled for each alternative. Noise can be both a nuisance that degrades the value of an area and a health issue. There are new studies continually being released that can influence health analyses. There are many other potential items to include, depending upon the specific nature of a project. Some may have far-reaching accessibility improvement implications, others may not; some may have major impacts on the ecosystem, others may not, and so on. Their inclusion will usually be determined in the course of doing the U.S. Environmental Impact Assessment, or its equivalent elsewhere. See the report by van Essen et al. (2007) for a fairly comprehensive listing of impacts and some best practices in monetization.

Tools for Performing Monetary Evaluations

This section reviews evaluation tools that planners can use once they have developed alternative project solutions, using the resulting costs and benefits that are either monetary or can be monetized. The analyst should always keep in mind one point: the ultimate evaluation and the selection of proposed investments depend upon more than just these numerical indicators.

All models used to estimate future costs and benefits require *discounting* to reflect the time value of money. Money earns interest to justify saving it rather than using it today. A corollary is that money tomorrow is worth less than money today, hence the term *discounting*. How much less depends upon the purpose of the expenditure and the type of institution pondering the investment. The rate used for public investments is generally lower than for profit-seeking investments.

The basic discounting relationships use a few conventions. One is that compounding occurs only at discrete periods. Another is that the compounding period closest to the present is time period 0. The basic relationships are then:

$$F = P(1+i)^n \quad \text{or} \quad P = \frac{F}{(1+i)^n} \qquad (8\text{-}1)$$

where F is the future value, P is the present value, i is the discount rate, and n is the number of compounding periods. In general, P (and F) can be either positive or negative. In this book, both benefits and costs will have positive values. The negative relationship of costs to benefits is reflected in a formula convention in which the analyst subtracts costs from benefits.

Example 8.1

A transit agency gets the following terms from a bus manufacturer. It can pay $300,000 now or $350,000 at the time of delivery, three years from now. It earns 7 percent interest on money stored in its capital fund. Which terms are more advantageous?

The future value of the $300,000 if stored is:

$$F = \$300,000(1+0.07)^3 = \$367,500$$

The higher future value means paying at the time of delivery would leave the agency with $17,500 more than paying at the time of purchase. An alternative approach is to start with the future value and see which purchase cost has the lowest present value:

$$P = \frac{\$350,000}{(1+0.17)^3} = \$285,700$$

The present value of the purchase cost is $14,300 lower by paying at the time of delivery. Once again, the conclusion is the same.

An economic analysis of a public transport project will generally include a stream of investments, operating and other monetizable costs, and revenues and other monetizable benefits. Figure 8.1 shows a *cash-flow diagram*, a highly useful method for visualizing and organizing income and expenditure streams. Some typical elements of such diagrams are labeled. The subscript *j* refers to the period at which at an event occurs. The nomenclature shown includes *P* for the initial investment in year 0, C_j for costs incurred in year *j*, R_j for revenues received in year *j*, and *S*. *S* represents the *salvage value*, the value that one can recover in year n, when the investment's physical assets are sold or scrapped and any other assets are recovered for reuse.

Now, introduce nomenclature specific to the transit industry. Cost is in two components, OC_j for operating costs, and C_j for other costs. Revenues are in two components as well, R_j for operating revenues, and B_j for additional benefits. When the analyst inserts these additional costs and benefits, some of which may not even accrue to the transit agency, a similar diagram to the cash-flow diagram can be made instead, a *cost-benefit stream diagram*, as shown in Figure 8.2. When one is analyzing only what is best for the agency or firm from a monetary standpoint, cash-flow is considered. When one is analyzing what is best for the community as a whole, the entire cost-benefit stream that includes monetized costs and benefits is considered instead.

The sum of all operating costs plus other costs after discounting is the *Cost Present Value*, or *CPV*:

$$CPV = \sum_{j=1}^{n} \frac{OC_j + C_j}{(1+i)^j} + P. \tag{8-2}$$

Looking at the expenditures for the entire life of an investment in a capital good, one will typically see an investment stream with an initial large expenditure for construction or purchase, a series of smaller expenditures for operation and maintenance, and occasional large expenditures for major repairs or refurbishments.

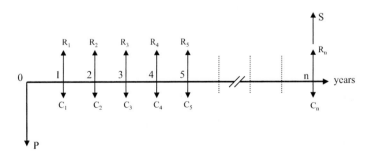

Figure 8.1 Cash flow diagram.

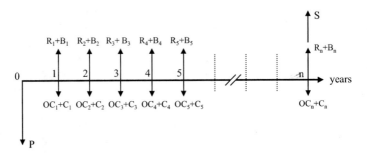

Figure 8.2 Cost-benefit stream diagram.

Similarly, the discounted sum of all revenues plus all monetizable benefits is the *Benefit Present Value*. Its form is analogous to the *CPV* but with one separate term for the salvage value:

$$BPV = \sum_{j=1}^{n} \frac{R_j + B_j}{(1+i)^j} + \frac{S}{(1+i)^n}. \qquad (8\text{-}3)$$

Selecting the investment with the lowest *CPV* is *life-cycle costing*. But it may not necessarily be the best choice, as the benefits may not be the same from each choice. Thus, an analyst should use it only for situations where the benefits are approximately the same for each investment. In the vast majority of situations, it is the difference between the costs and benefits that counts in the end. This difference is the *NPV*:

$$NPV = BPV - CPV = \sum_{j=1}^{n} \frac{(R_j + B_j) - (OC_j + C_j)}{(1+i)^j} + \frac{S}{(1+i)^n} - P. \qquad (8\text{-}4)$$

The particular discount rate selected is hereafter referred to as the *Minimum Allowable Rate of Return* (MARR). If the economic results are satisfactory using the MARR, the project is said to be *feasible*. If the results are not satisfactory at the MARR, the project is *infeasible*, the money is better used elsewhere, or should be held to earn interest at the MARR or above. The test of a feasible project (i.e. one that pays for itself after due consideration of the money VoT) is that the NPV must be greater than zero when the discount rate equals the MARR:

$$NPV = \sum_{j=0}^{n} \frac{(R_j + B_j) - (OC_j + C_j)}{(1 + MARR)^j} + \frac{S}{(1 + MARR)^n} > 0 \qquad (8\text{-}5)$$

Example 8.2

A small-town transit agency wants to install a passenger information system expected to last six years. The system will cost $1,000,000 to purchase and integrate into their existing infrastructure. The field equipment (e.g. signs and radio links) will need maintenance and an upgrade at three years costing $250,000, and replacement with new technology at six years. The vendor has also promised to buy back the bus-stop signs, however, for $50,000 at the end of the six years. The system is estimated to increase ridership at 2 percent per year, compounded annually. The current ridership is 3 million per year paying a fare of $1 each. The Minimum Allowable Rate of Return is 7 percent. Find the Net Present Value of the project proposal.

The ridership and therefore the revenue compounds by 2 percent each year. The additional revenue above the baseline revenue of R_0 for each year j can be calculated by the formula:

$$\Delta R_j = R_0(1.02)^j - R_0$$
$$\Delta R_1 = \$3.0M (1.02)^1 - \$3.0M = \$0.06M$$
$$\Delta R_2 = \$3.0M (1.02)^2 - \$3.0M = \$0.1212M$$
$$\Delta R_3 = \$3.0M (1.02)^3 - \$3.0M = \$0.1836M$$
$$\Delta R_4 = \$3.0M (1.02)^4 - \$3.0M = \$0.2473M$$
$$\Delta R_5 = \$3.0M (1.02)^5 - \$3.0M = \$0.3122M$$
$$\Delta R_6 = \$3.0M (1.02)^6 - \$3.0M = \$0.3785M$$

The resulting cash-flow diagram is shown in Figure 8.3. The calculation is then straightforward:

$$NPV = \frac{\$0.06M}{(1.07)^1} + \frac{\$0.1212M}{(1.07)^2} + \frac{\$0.1836M - \$0.25M}{(1.07)^3} + \frac{\$0.2473M}{(1.07)^4}$$
$$+ \frac{\$0.3122M}{(1.07)^5} + \frac{\$0.3785M}{(1.07)^6} + \frac{\$0.05M}{(1.07)^6} - \$1.0M = -\$0.195\ M$$

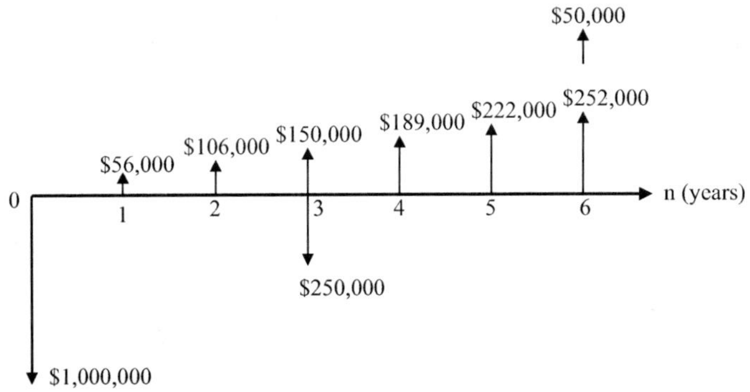

Figure 8.3 Cash flow diagram for proposed passenger information system.

Example 8.2 (continued)

Is the investment feasible?

Since −$0.195M is less than zero, the answer is no.

What amount of revenue R_0 would the agency have to be collecting at the start of the project for the project to have been feasible?

The threshold for feasibility is when the NPV reaches zero. This is determined by setting the NPV equal to zero and solving for R_0:

$$NPV = R_0 \left(\frac{\$0.02M}{(1.07)^1} + \frac{\$0.0404M}{(1.07)^2} + \frac{\$0.0612M}{(1.07)^3} + \frac{\$0.0824M}{(1.07)^4} + \frac{\$0.1041M}{(1.07)^5} \right.$$
$$\left. + \frac{\$0.1262M}{(1.07)^6} \right) - \frac{\$0.25M}{(1.07)^3} + \frac{\$0.05M}{(1.07)^6} - \$1.0M = 0$$

Solving for R_0 gives a value of $3.6 million. Thus, the base revenue would have to start at 20 percent higher. Thus, the base revenue would need to have been 20 percent higher.

If alternative investments are being compared, the best one is the one with the highest positive NPV. If all are negative, all should be rejected. Recall that this test implicitly ignores all costs and benefits not expressed in monetary form and which therefore are not captured in this analysis.

One particularly important pattern deserves more detailed discussion. It involves the spreading of ownership costs over the useful life of an investment. An investment P made in year 0, the present, needs to be converted to a nominal value constant over n years, yet one that reflects both the steadily declining worth of an asset and the money VoT. Derivations are shown in numerous texts, so only the results will be repeated here. If the initial capital cost is spread over these n years, this annualized cost, commonly referred to as a *Capital Recovery Factor*, or CRF, is given by

$$CRF = \frac{i(1+i)^n}{(1+i)^n - 1}. \tag{8-6}$$

To understand this concept, one should recognize that it is totally analogous to computation of a constant periodic repayment amount for a bank loan in the face of an ever-declining principal as the loan is repaid. The investment repayment is thus spread out in equal amounts, A, using the relationship:

$$A = P(CRF). \tag{8-7}$$

When n tends to infinity, the CRF asymptotically reaches a lower bound given by:

$$CRF = i \qquad n \to \infty.$$

CRF can be interpreted as the annualized cost of a long-lived investment when the analysis period becomes very long. It can also be interpreted as saying that,

---

Example 8.3

If a bus costs $350,000 and the MARR is 7 percent, what is the annualized amount A for which the bus should be amortized if the bus is assumed to have a useful life of 12 years? The situation is shown in Figure 8.4.

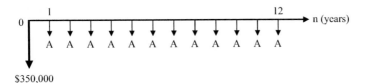

$350,000

Figure 8.4 Equivalent annualized cost A over 12 years.

Each year should have a nominally equal amount, which when the sum of them is discounted back to the present should P = $350,000. Since this is just the NPV, A is found indirectly by using the definition of NPV:

$$P = \$350,000 = \frac{A}{(1+0.07)^1} + \frac{A}{(1+0.07)^2} + \frac{A}{(1+0.07)^3} + ---- + \frac{A}{(1+0.07)^{12}}$$

Rather than sum every term, reference to a table in any engineering economics textbook will show that an equivalent form that does not require a tedious calculation for the case of equal values in every year is:

$$A \sum_{i=1}^{n} \frac{1}{(1+i)^n} = A \left(\frac{(1+i)^n - 1}{i(1+i)^n} \right) = A \left(\frac{1}{CRF} \right).$$

Upon substitution the equation becomes:

$$P = \$350,000 = A \left(\frac{(1.07)^{12} - 1}{0.07(1.07)^{12}} \right).$$

Solving for A gives an annualized amount of $44,070 per year.

if the repayment rate on an initial investment P is not higher than iP per compounding period, the loan would never be repaid. Restated more simply, a long-lived capital good should be seen as imposing a perpetual annual cost equal to the income the money could earn with interest equal to the discount rate.

BCRs are often cited in policy and investment analyses in many sectors of society. Thus, the public may expect that project analyses be reported in this fashion. The inclination to comply should be resisted for at least two reasons. First, the resulting ratio is ambiguous. The BCR is essentially the ratio BPV/CPV, whereas the NPV method uses BPV − CPV. This difference raises the issue of whether certain items are increases in benefits or decreases in costs. The difference is not always obvious, yet the resulting ratio depends upon the decision, as one choice will add benefit to the numerator while the other will subtract cost from the denominator. Although the BCR will always identify whether a project is feasible (by having a value greater than 1), the higher ratio that might indicate a "better" project might not be the result of an equally reliable calculation.

Example 8.4

A project alternative currently has a BPV of $60,000 and a CPV of $50,000 giving a CBR of 1.2. Another alternative is investigated which can reduce costs by $10,000.

If the alternative cost reduction is viewed as a benefit, in that perhaps lesser subsidy is required, the ratio is computed as

$$\frac{\$60,000 + \$10,000}{\$50,000} = 1.4$$

If, on the other hand, the cost reduction is viewed as only a reduction in operating costs, the ratio is computed as

$$\frac{\$60,000}{\$50,000 - \$10,000} = 1.5$$

Two different results arise, depending upon whether the change is viewed as a cost or benefit.

One cannot assume, however, that such techniques have been used if their use is not documented. This makes comparisons to projects evaluated by others hazardous without first looking closely at the methodology. Usually it is possible to find and adjust some of the intermediate values of CPVs and BPVs of another study in order to put them on a consistent basis with one's own methodology. An analyst can then use the incremental benefit to incremental cost ratio method to accurately rank alternatives. Two alternatives that both have BCR over 1 can be systematically compared by selecting the one with the higher CPV and subtract the lower one from it, that is, $CPV_1 - CPV_2$. Then find the corresponding difference, $BPV_1 - BPV_2$. The one with the higher ratio $(BPV_1 - BPV_2)/(CPV_1 - CPV_2)$ is unambiguously the higher-ranked alternative. For more details, see Sullivan et al. (2008) or other contemporary books on engineering economics.

A second reason to avoid BCRs is because they are also prone to abuse and misunderstanding in the public arena. Often cited as a definitive measure of the worth of a project, a ratio is, just like the NPV, only one indicator that needs to be weighed along with nonmonetary factors included in this performance or project analysis that are not always possible to use in this evaluation tool. Moreover, a BCR actually contains less information than the NPV. The NPV also gives indication of the size of the net monetary benefit or cost to the taxpayer.

On the other hand, there can be arguments in favor of using the incremental BCR instead of NPV. The NPV by itself does not state the size of the investment involved, and in many cases this is very relevant. For example, if all alternatives are limited to a maximum investment amount, ranking them by BCRs could be better indicator of "bang for the buck." Again it needs to be borne in mind that the list of costs and benefits included is incomplete.

Finally, as a practical manner, as Example 8.3 showed, calculation of the CPV, BPV, and NPV need not always require a tedious summing of individual terms for each year. Rather, formulae for common patterns, such as nominally equal values for multiple years, can be found in texts and reference books. Some business and statistical calculators also have preprogrammed functions.

Incidence of Costs and Opportunity Costs

The *incidence* of the costs and benefits matter. The validity of the use of monetary analyses (e.g. NPV comparisons) is a much easier argument to make for one who is not actually living close to a proposed project and who will not be affected much by the costs it imposes on the nearby community. It is an even easier argument to make by persons who might further receive a major benefit from the project but none of its adverse impacts. The trade-off of the benefit for many at the expense of fewer is not expressed in the formulation of an overall NPV or BCR for a project. The incidence of the benefits and costs of the project can often be better understood, however, if the modeler performs subanalyses that try to cordon the benefits and costs and the nonmonetary costs into local groupings, which is central to questions of *environmental justice*. Continual improvement in Geographic Information System technology is making this task easier (Klein 2007).

Restating the definition of MARR, it reflects the opportunity cost of using money on a particular investment instead of on one of the alternatives. The investment gives a positive NPV only when the investment yields at least the MARR. The important point is that the opportunity cost implied by this method is only that of using money. Yet, this is simply not the only consideration in many cases, a point that keeps recurring in this text. For example, one can approximately monetize the value of the land purchased along a right of way and the change in value of any adjacent property, but not some of the other impacts. These might defy monetary value. What is the value of the disruption to a community that is severed or must live with any noise or shadows cast by elevated structures or other unpleasing impacts? What about the loss of a park or open space for children? What about destroying a view for many people? These examples show that the potential loss of what already exists can be an opportunity cost just as much as the potential loss of a foregone investment alternative.

A serious limitation of monetary analysis is that it cannot make a conclusive comparison or ranking of alternatives when the opportunity costs are not monetary. There may even be attempts to monetize the worth of community severance or park removal, anyway, in order to maintain the validity of this approach. But as long as some elements of the population disagree about whether the numerical values the modelers select are reasonable, it does not really change the fact that there are significant nonmonetary opportunity costs. Indeed, the community might even refuse to agree to negotiate a price, saying that, to them, some aspects of their community are irreplaceable and they reject the entire utilitarian viewpoint. Can one really say they are wrong and one can put a price on everything?

Disputes over what the opportunity costs really are for a project are only becoming more heated over time. Conservationists and ecologists are increasingly demanding that fuller consideration be made of the value of what already exists and they are not accepting traditional methods of monetary calculations as the means of dispute resolution. This is one of the reasons for the development of *sustainable economics* or *ecological economics* as a branch of economic analysis that seeks to overcome limitations of traditional economic evaluation methods. Because of the limitations of monetary methods, Chapter 12 describes some methods of decision making that reflect the reality that society cannot always agree on the overall validity of a monetary method as the best way for describing costs and benefits.

Changing the Results by Taking Ownership of Certain Costs

The German federal government allows removal of cost items from cost-benefit analysis if the lower level of government or public agency applying for the funds chooses to cover this expense itself. It will improve a project's ranking in the competition for funding (Bundesminister für Verkehr 1996). This has several advantages. First, it allows specific local or regional costs to be covered by specific local or regional beneficiaries of the project such that the costs have a better correspondence of incidence to benefits. It may also allow this lower-level government or agency to request funds locally that are focused on the most politically acceptable items (although this may undo the first advantage if the acceptable source of payment for this cost ends up bearing no relation to the largest beneficiaries of the project.) Finally, it demonstrates a commitment to the project because the applicant for competitive funds believes that there are benefits not monetized and captured by the NPV or BCR. This approach has a lot of merit and is worth considering elsewhere.

The Issue of Sustainable Development

So far this discussion has been a review of conventional engineering economics. Its monetary evaluation tools give fully valid results for profit-seeking firms because they usually consider only costs incurred and benefits received by their own firm. They are not expected to take the long view by considering public costs and benefits. (Nor need their competitors.) Monetary evaluation is also correctly applied to public-sector investment analysis when certain conditions are met. Project costs and benefits should have finite life, attempts must be made to include any nonmonetary items that can be monetized, and due consideration must also be given for factors not captured in the monetary analysis. These factors must be permitted to temper or perhaps even override the numerical results.

As the life of public investments becomes longer, however, the use of discounting raises serious issues that have not been satisfactorily resolved. The emerging field of sustainable economics takes as an axiom that the welfare of future generations is equally important to the current one. It also claims that the ecosystem has many benefits not reflected in market prices. The loss of these benefits would need to be accounted for as real costs when the ecosystem degrades. Yet, unless taxes or other mechanisms are used to intervene in the market, the market will tend to reflect only short-term monetary costs. One of the most important examples is oil; despite the fact that oil is nonrenewable and that the peak of production is likely to occur early in the twenty-first century, prices actually declined in the late 1990s. This happened despite widespread knowledge that production might decline at the same time worldwide demand increases. Pretax prices primarily reflect short-term refining capacity and storage capacity of the worldwide production and distribution system, not the long-term consequences of its use.

Discounting implies by definition that future costs and benefits are worth less than those that occur today. Using this prevailing concept, the market signals that a resource should be consumed towards exhaustion as long as the increase in its price is less than the discount rate. Also, any monetary costs representing depletion of nonrenewable resources and permanent environmental damage tend towards zero within 15 to 30 years, depending upon the MARR used. Ultimately, any real discount rate greater than zero eventually reduces any cost, no matter how significant, to zero. Figure 8.5 shows the decline in value of one monetary unit for 2, 7, and 15 percent.

The declining annual CRF with increasing life would suggest that annual benefits can also be less than they appear for a longer-lived investment. Thus,

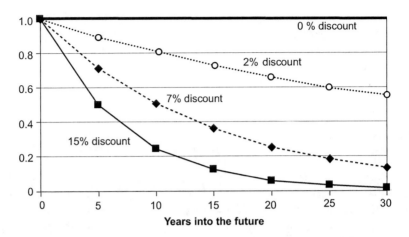

Figure 8.5 Effect of the discount rate on future value of one monetary unit.

discounting also implies that the annual benefits need not be as high to justify a longer-term investment; but surely for consistency, if long-term costs should not be discounted, we should not discount long-term benefits to future generations either. If costs persist, so should some benefits; otherwise, the project is likely to be unattractive.

In practice, the difference between benefits and costs sometimes increases over time. For example, the value of London's or Paris's subway tunnels since the turn of the twentieth century have a higher utility to the present generation than to the one that financed and built them. These cities are far larger in population and area today, while the transport capacity required to support the higher level of activity in a modern society has also increased. Meanwhile, the annual cost of the tunnels today is only maintenance. Should this benefit to the current generation have been discounted when the investment decisions were being made?

Not to overstate the case, benefits can dissipate as well. As a contrary example, the Broad Street subway in Philadelphia has a four-track tunnel, complete with express tracks, yet the area it serves has been undergoing steady population and employment loss for years.

Whether costs and benefits to future generations change in tandem, whether benefits persist while costs decrease, or whether costs persist while benefits decrease are extremely interesting questions for long-term analyses. Conventional evaluation tools, however, are not designed to answer questions whose outcome is relevant to future generations. See Stiglitz (1994) for a deeper discussion of the role of the discounting concept in cost-benefit analysis, and Partridge (2003) and Howarth (2003) about the differences between philosophical and neoclassical economic approaches in policy analysis.

Difficulties in the application of conventional economic analysis tools does not necessarily argue for their total abandonment for long-term analysis, but it does argue for modification of procedures and for additional decision criteria beyond discounted NPV. Pioneers in the field of sustainable economics, Daly and Cobb discussed intellectual efforts to adjust discount rates, showing that the problem cannot be reconciled by an adjustment to rates. Instead, they proposed "that any reduction in economic welfare in the future below the level currently enjoyed should be counted as if the cost occurred in the present" (1989, 410). Hampicke argues, "it is adequate to discount whenever there is a well-founded expectation that these problems will *in fact become* less severe because of an increase in problem solving capacity of future generations. (2003, 99). Neither of these ideas is mainstream practice as of this writing, but they are likely to become so in the future. When they are, many analyses will have very different outcomes than they would have using today's conventional practices.

Summary

Monetary evaluations compare either several alternative project solutions or one project solution with the performance of peers elsewhere. To be an insightful comparison, one must distinguish as best as possible what is inherent to the alignment or service area and what is inherent to the modal or technological attributes of the particular proposed alternatives. This helps define realistic alternatives and guides selection of additional nonmonetary indicators to be used in the evaluation.

Project construction and ongoing operation and maintenance costs must be assembled for each project alternative. The estimated time saved for users of the greater transportation network must also be assembled and values put on this time. This value may not necessarily be the same for all system users. Similarly, health and relevant environment impacts must be estimated by project and values placed on them. Often there are official procedures, or at least guidance, available. Depending upon the project, additional impacts many also need to be included, such as major changes in job accessibility across a region, or ecosystem restoration or deterioration.

Monetary performance and investment evaluation is greatly assisted by the development of cash-flow diagrams and cost-benefit-stream diagrams. The former contains only direct monetary costs and benefits while the ladder also includes monetizable costs and benefits. Both diagrams require discounting in order to reflect the present value of money. NPV computations are used both to assess feasibility and for comparison of alternatives. A project alternative is feasible if the NPV is greater than 0. The "best" alternative is the one with the highest NPV.

BCRs can reliably identify feasible projects but are not recommended for comparative evaluation unless they are done in an incremental fashion due to definitional ambiguity between reduced costs and increased benefits. Furthermore, they can imply unwarranted conclusions in the public mind that all costs and

238   Methods to Evaluate a Transit Project in Monetary Terms

benefits are included when they are not. On the other hand, if all project alternatives have the same upper limit to investment allowed, the BCR might be more appropriate for internal evaluation.

NPV analyses based strictly on monetary considerations are valid for private firms and for short-term public sector projects where nonmonetary costs are not significant. It may also be appropriate for public investment decisions, but subject to certain conditions. Project costs and benefits should have finite life, should include nonmonetary items that can be monetized, and due consideration should be given for factors not captured in the monetary analysis. These factors must be permitted to temper or perhaps even override the numerical rankings.

The incidence of the costs and benefits from a project are of importance. Depending upon location and personal situation, one can perceive the costs and benefits very differently. Opportunity costs must also always be weighed in any decision. What could have been done instead and what that already exists might be lost if a project proceeds are both of vital interest. Many of the most contentious political fights and hearing debates stem from differences of opinions on how to value the opportunity cost. There will be many situations where no monetary value is acceptable to some portion of the population. When there is competition for funding, the incidence of costs to benefits could be improved by allowing the applicants to remove specific costs from their computations that are covered by specific beneficiaries. This is already the official practice in Germany.

Medium-term and long-term analyses raise issues from a public-policy viewpoint over the appropriateness of discounting of ecosystem- and resource-related items since they imply that costs and benefits to future generations are zero. As an alternative, Daly and Cobb (1989, 410) proposed "that any reduction in economic welfare in the future below the level currently enjoyed should be counted as if the cost occurred in the present." Revised analysis tools to reflect sustainable principles, not just from neoclassical economics but from other disciplines, are not yet in widespread use, but they will change the analysis outcomes significantly when compared to current conventional practices when they are.

References

Belenky, Peter. 2011. *The Value of Travel Time Savings: Departmental Guidance for Conducting Economic Evaluations*. Revision 2. Washington, DC: Office of the Secretary of Transportation, U.S. Department of Transportation. http://www.dot.gov/sites/dot.dev/files/docs/vot_guidance_092811c.pdf.
Bundesminister für Verkehr. 1996. *Anleitung für die Standartisierte Bewertung von Verkehrswegeinvestitionen des ÖPNV und Hinweise zum Rahmenantrag Schriftreihe des Bundesministers für Verkehr*, Heft 51. (in German) Berlin: Federal Transport Ministry.
Daly, Herman E., and John B. Cobb, Jr. 1989. *For the Common Good*. Boston, MA: Beacon Press.
Hampicke, Ulrich. 2003. "The Capacity to Solve Problems as a Rationale for Intertemporal Discounting. *International Journal of Sustainable Development* 6 (1): 98–111.

Howarth, Richard B. 2003. "Discounting and Sustainability: Towards Reconciliation," *International Journal of Sustainable Development* 6 (1): 87–97.

I. T. Transport, Ltd. 2005. *How to Manual: The Valuation of Rural Time Savings in Least Developed Countries.* Arlington, Oxfordshire, UK: U.K. Department of International Development.

Klein, Nicholas. 2007. "Spatial Methodology for Assessing Distribution of Transportation Project Impacts with Environmental Justice Framework." *Transportation Research Record* 2013: 46–53.

Meyer, John, John Kain and Martin Wohl. 1965. Chapter 9 in *The Urban Transportation Problem.* Cambridge, MA: Harvard University Press: 196–249.

Partridge, Ernest. 2003. "In Search of Sustainable Values." *International Journal of Sustainable Development* 6 (1): 25–41.

Stiglitz, Joseph. 1994. "Discount Rates: The Rate of Discount for Cost-Benefit Analysis and the Theory of the Second Best." In *Cost Benefit Analysis,* 2nd ed., edited by Richard Layard and Stephen Glaister. Cambridge, UK: Cambridge University Press, 116–59.

Sullivan, William G., Elin M. Wicks and C. Patrick Koelling. 2008. *Engineering Economy.* 14th ed. Englewood Cliffs, NJ: Prentice Hall.

van Essen, H. P., B. H. Boon, M. Maibach and C. Schreyer (INFRAS). 2007. *Methodologies for External Cost Estimates and Internalization Scenarios.* Discussion paper for the workshop on internalisation on March 15, 2007. CE Delft Oplossingen voor milieu, economie en technologie. http://www.ce.nl/4288_Inputpaper.pdf

Further Reading

Adler, Matthew D. and Eric A. Posner, eds. 2000. *Cost Benefit Analysis: Legal, Economic, and Philosophical Perspectives.* Chicago: University of Chicago Press.

Bayer, Stefan. 2003. "Generation-Adjusted Discounting in Long-Term Decision-Making." *International Journal of Sustainable Development* 6 (1): 133–49.

Beukers, Els, Luca Bertolini and Marco Te Brömmelstroet. 2012. "Why Cost Benefit Analysis is Perceived as a Problematic Tool for Assessment of Transport Plans: A Process Perspective." *Transportation Research Part A* 46: 68–78.

Layard, Richard, and Stephen Glaister, eds. 1994. *Cost Benefit Analysis.* 2nd ed. Cambridge, UK: Cambridge University Press.

Chapter 9

Cost Model Development

Engineering cost models are widely accepted methods to compute the total cost of a technical project element or service over convenient time periods, typically increments of one year. It need not be on an annual basis, but it is usually convenient to use one-year increments because of data availability. These models consist of cost-component terms that are proportional to consumed resources. These resources are not directly financial but are rather other measurable or calculable resource input quantities and asset commitments needed to deliver a given service. Cost models then relate the consumption of these inputs to the financial resources required. The interested reader can find numerous texts describing their development and application in detail. See, for example, Sullivan et al. (2008) for a comprehensive reference in engineering economics and Chapter 9 of Morlok (1978) for a detailed treatment of cost models in particular. Only applications specific to ground passenger transportation are discussed here.

Constructing Cost Models

When applied to public transportation for the purposes of service planning, *Vehicle-Hours*, *Vehicle-Distance*, and peak *Fleet Size* are typical *resource variables* driving the estimated operating cost of various scenarios, although others may be used as well. Unit coefficients, c_{VH}, c_{VD}, and c_{FS} represent the unit cost attributed to each vehicle-hour, vehicle-distance, and the maximum number of vehicles in peak service, fleet size, respectively. The capital letters are used to distinguish these as resource variable quantities to be input by the analyst. The final term represents the asset commitment, represented by annualized ownership cost of vehicle(s) costing P in year 0. The result is a model for estimating total operating costs in the short term.

$$AC_T = c_{VH}(\text{Vehicle-Hours}) + c_{VD}(\text{Vehicle-Distance}) + c_{FS}(\text{Fleet Size}) + P(CRF), \tag{9-1}$$

where AC_T signifies an *annualized total cost*. Table 9.1 gives an example of a systematic method for assigning the total short-term expenditures to the various resource variables. All expenditures are allocated to the appropriate elements in the matrix. For example, tires and most other expendables are consumed in direct proportion to *Vehicle-Distance* operated. As another example, operator pay (wages and fringe benefits) is directly proportional to *Vehicle-Hours* operated. It may be that some costs are not sufficiently well approximated as proportional to only one input resource variable. In Table 9.1, vehicle maintenance and fuel consumed are both a function of both *Vehicle-Hours* and *Vehicle-Distance*, in recognition of how the frequency of stopping and starting (the duty cycle) influences these vehicle costs. Thus, the fractions X and Y and their complements 1-X and 1-Y are both introduced to prorate these costs.

Once the analyst has assigned all expenditures, each column is totaled to get the total expenditure associated with each particular input resource variable, designated using capital letters as C_{VH}, C_{VD}, or C_{FS}. Finally, each of these is divided by their corresponding total annual resource consumption, using the abbreviated nomenclature *VH* for *Vehicle-Hours*, *VD* for *Vehicle-Distance*, and *FS* for peak *Fleet Size* to arrive at the unit coefficients.

One important variation on this cost model is the *annualized operating cost*, AC_O. It is similar to AC_T except that the vehicle ownership cost is not included:

$$AC_O = c_{VH}(\textit{Vehicle-Hours}) + c_{VD}(\textit{Vehicle-Distance}) + c_{FS}(\textit{Fleet Size}) \qquad (9\text{-}2)$$

There is no fundamental reason why this cost should be excluded from a short-term cost model, given that vehicle depreciation is an important component of real-life public transport operations. Due to financing methods where an operator may not be responsible for this cost but instead receives a grant for almost the entire purchase cost, or is provided with vehicles by the public agency with which it contracts, it is often customary to ignore it. A second reason analysts often ignore

Table 9.1 Typical cost-allocation matrix

	Vehicle-Hours	Vehicle-Kilometers	Fleet Size
Vehicle Operators	C_o		
Fuel	$(1\text{-}X)C_f$	XC_f	
Tires and other expendables		C_t	
Vehicle Maintenance	$(1\text{-}Y)C_m$	YC_m	
Facility Maintenance			Cf_m
Administration			C_a
Supervision and Control Center	C_s		
Other			
TOTAL	C_{VH}	C_{VD}	C_{FS}
Unit coefficients:	$c_{VH} = C_{VH}/VH$	$c_{VD} = C_{VD}/VD$	$c_{FS} = C_{FS}/FS$

it is that vehicles no longer needed for a particular route or depot are not usually sold or discarded, but simply put to use elsewhere in the system or stored for use when other vehicles wear out. Thus, vehicle ownership is often treated as a sunk cost, not as a variable cost.

Analysts need to decide several things about the scope of the model and the precise definitions of the resource variables. The model can represent a single route or line, a group of routes or lines serving the same area or operating from the same terminal, a whole depot of one mode, or even an entire network. If the variation in vehicles and services is large, however, the cost model takes on highly averaged properties, and the accuracy regarding particular aspects of the network diminishes.

In practice, the available descriptive data has a strong influence on cost modeling decisions. Analysts can use budgets and service statistics for an entire network if better information is not available, but the more specific and confined the model, the closer it can represent an existing operation or a proposed operation having similar characteristics. On the other hand, there is little point trying to isolate a subsystem too completely, as the increased precision about operating particulars will be offset by the decreased precision with which one must allocate joint costs (e.g. shared terminals, maintenance facilities, control centers). Joint costs raise difficult questions, such as:

- How much should one prorate nonvehicle maintenance costs like depot upkeep?
- How many of the reserve fleet should be included in costing if the reserves are shared with operations external to the subsystem in question?
- How much of the capital investments additional to vehicle ownership should also be prorated if the benefits and costs are shared outside of the project in question?

These are the kinds of questions one can answer better over time. Unless one is in possession of good information about joint-use issues, it is best to use either depot-wide or system-wide figures for one mode as a starting point for the analysis. One can refine models down to subsystems later as one gains better insight into the cost structure of the larger system.

There are two ways to define the *Vehicle-Hours* and *Vehicle-Distance* input variables: on a revenue basis and a total basis. *Revenue-Vehicle-Hours* and *Revenue-Vehicle-Distance* are defined as those revenues consumed while vehicles are actually in service (i.e. while available for passenger occupancy). *Total-Vehicle-Hours* and *Total-Vehicle-Distance*, on the other hand, include the revenue service plus deadheading operations. To review from Chapter 3, these vehicle movements occur outside of revenue service. These could be movements to and from depots, repositioning to different routes, or empty reverse runs during peak periods whose purpose is to place the vehicle back in the high-demand direction as soon as possible. Once an analyst chooses a definition, the cost coefficients are based upon it, and all subsequent input resource values inserted in the model must be consistent with it.

There are advantages and drawbacks to each definition. The total basis has an advantage inasmuch as it uses data readily available to existing systems; vehicle odometer readings can be summed to provide total distance, and the blocks of work assigned to vehicle operators can be summed to determine total operating hours. The total basis has its drawbacks as well. While it uses data convenient for analyzing existing services, it requires extra steps for estimating deadheading vehicle-hours and deadheading vehicle-distance, and adding these to the revenue values when investigating new alternatives. By comparison, the revenue basis has the desirable property of making the cost of resource inputs directly proportional to the service provided to the public instead of to total vehicle movement, but it also implicitly assumes a fixed ratio of total-to-revenue values and therefore introduces error if the service being analyzed has a substantially different ratio from the average. A further drawback of using revenue-vehicle-hours and revenue-vehicle-distance, as explained in Chapter 3 on transit routes and networks, is that deadheading is a somewhat arbitrary definition. A vehicle can be "on-route" primarily to be repositioned, not to supply revenue service. Thus, differences in policy between operator entities regarding permission to stop for passengers while repositioning could complicate comparisons by blurring the distinction between repositioning and revenue service. Whichever is chosen, the results must be labeled as such to avoid direct comparison with costs computed on the other basis.

The operating cost data needed for computation of the unit-cost coefficients can be gathered from several sources. The objective is to find the best possible baseline values to insert in the cost-allocation matrix. Accounting records and budget exercises are a rich source of cost-allocation data if one has access to them. In the United States, all agencies receiving aid from the federal government must submit extensive information that is then formatted into various cost-allocation schemes and made available to the public through the *National Transit Database* (FTA 2011). In the European Union, there is a data standard known as *TransModel* (EU 2001). Its purpose is to facilitate data sharing and software interoperability. Making data available to the public, however, is not mandatory. The preferable source is data from similar experiences at the same entity that will be responsible for operation once in service. Lacking this, one can use data from carefully selected peers. Key indicators (e.g. such as those listed in Table 3.3) should be used to guide selection of a similar operation.

When new equipment is to replace old, analysts can modify their estimates of these costs by comparing existing performance with manufacturers' specifications for the new equipment. In the case of leading-edge designs unproven in revenue service, only manufacturers' specifications and service design criteria may be available. The analyst must use this data to adjust what else is known about the cost structure of the organization that will manage the capital investments or operate the services. Failing to verify the truth of an organization's performance claims leads to uncertainty. The analyst needs to assess the monetary cost significance and any other significant risks to the project from a failure to meet the claimed performance. A method to do so will be discussed as follows.

Example 9.1

A depot operates 100 buses in peak service; the budget breakdown is given in Table 9.2. Each bus has a 12-year life. Construct the total operating cost-estimating equation if the average annual Vehicle-Hours per bus is 4,000, annual vehicle-kilometers per bus is 64,000 and the annual ownership cost per bus is $40,000.

From the table below:

$$AC_T = \$33.40(VH) + \$0.47(VK) + \$21,000(FS) + \$40,000(FS)(CRF)$$

Table 9.2 Cost-allocation matrix for 100 bus depot example

	Vehicle-Hours	Vehicle-Kilometers	Fleet Size
Operators	12,000,000		
Fuel	(1–0.75)800,000	(0.75)800,000	
Tires and other expendables		400,000	
Vehicle Maintenance	(1–0.75)2,700,000	(0.75)2,700,000	
Facility Maintenance			900,000
Administration			1,200,000
Supervision/ Control Ctr	500,000		
TOTAL	$13,375,000	$3,025,000	$2,100,000
Unit coefficients:	c_{VH} = 13,375,000/ 4×10^5 = $33.40/hour	c_{VK} = 3,025,000/ 64×10^5 = $0.47/km	c_{FS} = 2,100,000/100 = $21,000/bus

Infrastructure and other permanent facility construction costs can be very site specific. These can depend on property acquisition costs, soil and hydrologic conditions, regional availability of desired building materials, contractor market conditions, speed of construction schedule, and other factors. Investigating then requires caution and maybe even special expertise. Aesthetic standards deserve special mention; elegant buildings and high-quality landscape architecture can be highly valued by the community yet viewed as nonessential to a project narrowly conceived as one limited to transportation. In seeking peers for cost estimates, it is necessary to ensure that enhancements not germane to the community's desires are deducted and that others that might be relevant for a given location are incorporated in their place.

As fleet size grows, analysts typically add capital investments in maintenance, storage, administrative, and supervision/control facilities to the cost-estimating model that will increase absolute operating costs. They can incorporate growth (or shrinkage) in the model by changing coefficient(s) at the appropriate year(s) by estimating the additional costs on an annual basis, starting with year i, the year the investment becomes operational. The analyst then adds this *incremental cost*, or *IC*, to the appropriate coefficient for all subsequent years. Thus, the model changes after each incremental investment increases the operating cost. For example, if a bus depot is expanded when fleet size exceeds FS_1 it will then cost an additional *incremental cost*, IC_{fm}, to operate per year. The corresponding fleet size coefficient C_{fm} changes for all subsequent years. Referring again to the *Fleet Size* column in Table 9.1 and modifying it for an increase in nonvehicle maintenance:

$$c_{FS} = \frac{C_{fm} + C_a}{FS} \leq FS_1 \qquad (9\text{-}3)$$

$$c_{FS} = \frac{C_{fm} + C_a + IC_{fm}}{FS} > FS_1 \qquad (9\text{-}4)$$

This incremental or "lumpy" nature of many investments can create large discontinuities in the coefficients. A jump occurs when a threshold is reached, but then the coefficient can again decrease steadily with increasing resource input until perhaps another investment threshold is reached. Continuing with the same example, this discontinuous nature of the coefficient is shown conceptually in Figure 9.1. For analyses involving system expansion over time, different coefficients can cross different thresholds at different periods so that the entire cost model evolves over time with system expansion (or contraction). A cell entry changes at each threshold so that the table changes over the years. Example 9.2 shows an example computation.

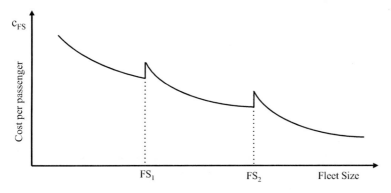

Figure 9.1 Example of discontinuities in unit cost when investment threshold is reached.

Example 9.1 (continued)

After 100 vehicles, a new storage area will be built to hold another 30. After 130, another new area will be built for the next 30. The incremental facility maintenance cost of each expansion is $300,000. Find the cost coefficient associated with Fleet Size both just before and just after the first expansion.

Using the total costs associated with Fleet Size from Table 9.2 in Equation 9-3 gives the current cost coefficient:

$$c_{FS} = \frac{900,000 + 1,200,000}{100} = \$21,000/bus$$

Just before an expansion is needed, the cost coefficient would be:

$$c_{FS} = \frac{900,000 + 1,200,000}{130} = \$16,150/bus$$

In any year a threshold was crossed, a new value for the total amount spent on facility maintenance would have to be entered in the cell for this item. Using Equation 3-4 just after the area expansion with a fleet now at 131 buses, the cost coefficient jumps instead of continuing to steadily descend with each additional bus:

$$c_{FS} = \frac{900,000 + 1,200,000 + 300,000}{131} = \$18,320/bus$$

If the incremental cost is the same for each unit of expansion, then the cost coefficient will continue to trend downward, demonstrating economies of scale. The final curve is shown in Figure 9.2.

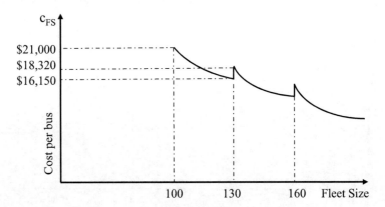

Figure 9.2 Example of change in Fleet Size coefficient with expansion.

Recall that the cost-allocation process sometimes requires fractional division of costs between more than one resource variable. If the financial and operating budget data do not clearly indicate what an appropriate fraction of cost might be, an analyst can do more analysis (e.g. regression analysis of cost component versus resource variables). As an example, corresponding to the breakdown in Table 9.1, fuel consumption of buses is likely to be better represented as a function of the *Vehicle-Hours* and *Vehicle-Distance* together rather than simply Vehicle-Distance. The form would be:

$$C_f = A\,(Vehicle\text{-}Hours) + B(Vehicle\text{-}Kilometers) + \varepsilon, \qquad (9\text{-}5)$$

where A corresponds to $(1\text{-}X)C_f$, and B corresponds to XC_f in the cost allocation table, and ε is a combined unexplained component and error term regularly used for regression equations. When data are not available, then it is best to borrow these prorating factors from a peer operator that uses similar vehicles on similar duty cycles.

Sensitivity Analysis

To reiterate, once an analyst constructs a cost model, it should only be considered as a baseline value. It is prudent to investigate the possible consequences of estimating errors, miscalculations, or unanticipated changes that might occur over the course of a project. Not all deviations from the baseline will be significant, but one might prove to be so crucial that the economic feasibility of a project hinges upon it. Sensitivity analysis is performed in order to investigate these deviations. Analysts can then consider the magnitude of this risk, whether it is excessive, and whether it can be mitigated.

Sensitivity analysis can do more than investigate uncertainty; analysts can use it to investigate trade-offs between elements (e.g. lower labor costs might be offset by higher automation acquisition costs, or higher vehicle purchase price might be offset by lower maintenance costs). For an example that focuses on labor costs due to vehicle operators, C_o in Table 9.1, consider how the analyst can introduce varying fractions of the baseline value, Z, into the affected unit-cost coefficient, c_{VH}:

$$c_{VH} = \frac{Z\,C_o + (1 - X)C_f + (1 - Y)C_m + C_s}{VH}. \qquad (9\text{-}6)$$

Z equals 1.0 at the baseline value. In addition to labor, other major drivers of cost and benefit uncertainty, which analysts could investigate are listed here, supported by a few clarifying examples.

Labor Costs

Labor costs are particularly important to scrutinize, as public transportation is a labor-intensive endeavor. Typically between 60 and 80 percent of short-term costs are labor costs, generally at the higher end for all bus transit systems. (Labor costs may be a far lower percentage of costs in some developing countries) These costs may vary within the same network for the same vehicle type if there is more than one service provider. There may also be cost trade-offs between corresponding required fleet sizes if the organization pays different labor rates to operators of larger vehicles. In the case of guided modes, there may also be trade-offs between purchasing automation features versus using operators.

Example 9.1 (continued)

Modify the equation if operator labor is reduced to 80 percent of the baseline value.

When operator labor is 80 percent of the baseline value, note that only c_{VH} is affected. The modified coefficient is then computed using a multiplier $Z = 0.8$ for C_o:

$$c_{VH} = \frac{0.8(12,000,000) + (1 - 0.75)(800,000) + (1 - 0.75)(2,700,000) + 500,000}{4000(100)}$$

$$= \$27.40/hour$$

To extend this example, if mechanic labor was also reduced to 80 percent, this would require the further breakdown of the vehicle maintenance cost into labor costs plus a fixed component, as it is currently an aggregate of all maintenance costs. The approach would be the same; introduce a multiplier in front of the labor portion of the maintenance costs.

System Technological Elements

System technological elements may not perform as billed. This is particularly true for equipment based on technologies lacking an extensive record of revenue service. Operators can minimize risk but not eliminate it by using proven equipment; even proven technologies, especially electronics, tend to be supplanted in the market at an increasing pace and replacements or repair become unavailable.

Example 9.2

The same depot with 100 buses in peak service is to be equipped with Automatic Vehicle Location (AVL) technology that costs $8,000,000 and adds $100,000 per year for electronics maintenance. But it is argued that it will allow them to do the work of 106 buses that do not have the benefit of AVL. This is because of reduced bunching and fewer buses needed to fill gaps during service disruptions. Based on experience at a peer property, the better service is also estimated to increase ridership by 3 percent. If the current total fare revenue collected by this depot is $6,000,000 per year and the Minimum Allowable Rate of Return is 7 percent, is this investment

feasible based only upon the financial considerations to the agency, neglecting any other benefits to the community?

One benefit is the avoided cost from needing to operate six fewer buses to perform the same amount of service. Since the difference in vehicles is only six, the cost-estimating equation from the previous example can be used in a different form as a close approximation:

$$\Delta AC_0 = \$33.40(\Delta VH) + \$0.47(\Delta VK) + \$21{,}000(\Delta FS)$$

The *Vehicle-Hour* savings is 4,000 per bus, the *Administration* required is also reduced, but the *Vehicle-Kilometers* remains unchanged since the same quantity of service is offered as before. Thus

$$\Delta AC_0 = \$33.40(6(4000)) + \$0.47(0) + \$21{,}000(6) = \$928{,}000 \ per \ year$$

A second benefit is additional revenue equal to $0.03(\$6{,}000{,}000) = \$180{,}000$. The initial capital investment in year 0 is equal to $\$8000(100) = \$8{,}000{,}000$.
The total annual benefit B = $\$928{,}000 + \$180{,}000 = \$1{,}108{,}000$ per year.
The annual cost C = $\$100{,}000$ per year.

The resulting cash-flow diagram is shown in Figure 9.3. The Net Present Value (NPV) can then be computed by referring to the diagram:

$$NPV = -8{,}000{,}000 + \sum_{i=1}^{12} \frac{1{,}108{,}000 - 100{,}000}{(1+0.07)^i}.$$

Rather than sum every term, one can recognize that, because the values are equal for every year, the alternative, computationally less-tedious form introduced in Chapter 8 can again be used:

$$A\sum_{i=1}^{n} \frac{1}{(1+i)^n} = A\left(\frac{(1+i)^n - 1}{i(1+i)^n}\right).$$

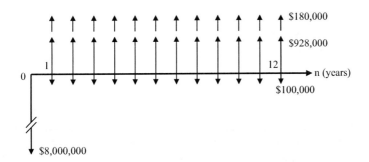

Figure 9.3 Cash-flow diagram for bus depot with Automatic Vehicle Location (AVL) investment.

Upon substitution, the equation becomes:

$$NPV = -8,000,000 + (1,008,000)\left(\frac{(1.07)^{12} - 1}{0.07(1.07)^{12}}\right) = +\$6,200.$$

The answer is yes. The project is financially feasible, barely.

As an example of sensitivity analysis, note how the project becomes infeasible if ridership increases only by 1 percent. The benefit is now reduced to B' = $928,000 + (0.01)(6,000,000) = \$988,000$. The NPV is recomputed as:

$$NPV = -\$8,000,000 + (\$988,000)\left(\frac{(1.07)^{12} - 1}{0.07(1.07)^{12}}\right) = -\$153,000.$$

This shows the riskiness of investments based primarily on estimates derived from peer experience.

Construction Costs

Construction costs can vary a great deal, depending upon the business cycle. During boom times, contractors extract a premium price, and demand for popular construction materials may increase prices. In recessionary periods, these costs can be much lower. Timing of projects is crucial. Delays in the start date or changes in the pace of construction can cause large differences in the Cost Present Value (CPV) of a project. In some places, organizations defer projects until a low period in construction activity in a process known as *countercyclical spending*. The point is not only to save costs but also for government to stimulate demand and employment in a slack economy. However, this approach requires a further, separate analysis: Do the construction cost savings from waiting outweigh the foregone benefits from completion at an earlier date?

Energy Costs

Energy costs can be a substantial portion of costs for high-capacity modes, as stations and buildings consume energy as well as vehicles. They are nowhere near as large a fraction for the bus mode, but they can be subject to large fluctuations over the course of a few years. Depending on tax policy and the mix of energy sources, there can be large disincentives or incentives to switch from one energy source to another. In the short term, service design and networks can be reconfigured to increase average vehicle loadings, reduce deadheads, use more short feeders to fewer large vehicles, and so on. In the medium to long term, vehicles of different propulsion technologies can be substituted.

The Minimum Allowable Rate of Return

The *Minimum Allowable Rate of Return* (MARR) can change with the policy of the organization(s) selecting and financing the project due to governmental economic conditions and fiscal policy. The rate will increase when there are fewer spending resources available and decrease when more are available. Restated, when the opportunity cost of money is higher, it is more difficult for a project to pass a financial feasibility test. Furthermore, a privately funded project will almost always have to satisfy a higher MARR than a public one because private investors demand a higher rate of return.

Example 9.3

If a project has a net benefit of $1.2 million per year for 12 years, and the initial investment is $8 million, how does the Net Present Value (NPV) vary with the Minimum Allowable Rate of Return (MARR)? At what interest rate does the project become infeasible?

Using the following equation with a range of interest rates, the analyst constructs the list of results. The feasibility point (i.e. where the NPV becomes zero) can be found using trial and error.

$$NPV = -\$8,000,000 + \sum_{i=1}^{12} \frac{1,200,000}{(1+MARR)^n}$$

MARR	NPV
5%	+$2,636,000
7%	+$1,531,000
9%	+$593,000
10.45%	$0
11%	−$209,000
13%	−$899,000

Inflation

Inflation is a hazard to any medium- or long-term cost-estimating exercise. Due to compounding, it can have a profound effect. It also requires care to address correctly because there are two different methods that can easily be confused. One is to express monetary values in their *actual* or *nominal* sense, defined as the value in dollars (or other denomination) of the particular year they occur. The other method is to express monetary values in their *real* sense, defined so that all values are expressed in terms of the buying power of a reference year. The resulting Net Present Value (NPV) is the same with either method as long as care is taken to use appropriate discount rates. The real method is helpful when comparisons are being made between time periods within the same project, but it is not convenient when computing and comparing cost and benefit streams across several projects, as these are usually expressed in actual terms. Since it is easy to do conversions for real-cost comparisons after completing an actual analysis, only the actual method is discussed further here. Many texts provide a detailed comparison of both methods for the interested reader. See for example, the text by Sullivan et al. (2008).

Each component in the cost and benefit stream can inflate at different rates and over different time periods. In the United States during the decade of the 1990s, it was not atypical for agencies to see deflating fuel costs, stagnant wages, and inflating construction costs. Indeed, it is often the case in real-life situations that some cost components might actually increase in value while others decrease. One must still estimate an underlying general inflation rate over the length of the investment analysis period. Strictly speaking, using an estimated underlying general rate is not correct; rather, the analyst should use the average for the particular project's cost and benefits streams. The difference is probably slight, however, and the analysis can become quite intractable if the analyst tries to compute a more exact project inflation rate. The analyst should make such an effort, however, if there is reason to believe inflation will have a large difference in impact on overall project costs compared to overall project benefits.

There are a variety of data sources for use in forecasting inflation. In most nations there is statistical information available about cost trends for a wide variety of commodities, production inputs, and consumer goods and services (e.g. the Producer Price Index and Consumer Price Index in the United States). This index provides historical data, but there is of course no guarantee that any trend will continue. In addition, useful cost studies specifically tailored to an industry exist (e.g. a cost index study specific to the US public transportation industry that gives trends of various components likely to be included in projects; consult Schneck, Laver and Mothersole 1995).

An analyst can investigate each cost or benefit component separately for each year. Care must be taken to ensure against double counting because inflation might already be imbedded in some values. Also, one must be sure not to inflate components fixed in nominal value (e.g. some contractual agreements and annuities). Let k index the particular cost or benefit component and j the particular year. Once the analyst selects component inflation rates, e_{kj} (some might have a negative value for deflating prices), each cost and benefit component in the stream is then adjusted using the relations:

$$B_{k'j} = B_{kj} (1 + e_{kj}) \tag{9-7}$$
$$C_{k'j} = C_{kj} (1 + e_{kj}) \tag{9-8}$$

In later years, the inflation rate for some components may have been compounded by using more than one differential rate. Once all the values in the stream have been adjusted, the NPV is found by algebraically summing all the cost and benefit components for each year and discounting the total for each year back to the present. But a *combined MARR*, $MARR_c$, is used instead of the real *MARR*. It is defined by:

$$1 + MARR_c = (1 + MARR)(1 + f), \tag{9-9}$$

where f is the underlying general inflation rate. Note that when there is no underlying inflation rate, the relationships simplify. The combined $MARR_c$ becomes equal to the real *MARR*.

Example 9.4

An analyst investigates a depot operating a peak of 100 buses to see whether it is economically feasible for a prospective contract operator to assume operations of the depot. It would require signing a five-year contract. It includes provision by the contracting public agency of new vehicles of improved reliability and efficiency. The operator retains all untaxed revenues plus a subsidy. The underlying inflation rate is assumed to be 3 percent and the Minimum Allowable Rate of Return (MARR) is 12 percent. The initial costs and revenues and expected component inflation rates are given.

Using Equation 9-9, the combined MARR, $MARR_c$, is $(1.12)(1.03) - 1 = 0.154$. Revenues = \$11.0M no increase in passengers, but 2 percent fare increases in the second and fourth years

Subsidy = \$10.0M	constant for all 5 years
Op. & Maint. = \$15.0M	−4 percent for 3 years, −2 percent for two years
Vehicle Lease = \$4.0M	3 percent per year for all 5 years

The computations are shown in Table 9.3. Because the Net Present Value is \$1.14 million, it is feasible. Note how the net positive values in the first two years of operation more than offset the net negative values during the last three years of the contract.

Table 9.3 Net Present Value (NPV) computation table for Example 9.4

	Year 0	Year 1	Year 2	Year 3	Year 4	Year 5
Revenues	0	11.0	11(1.02)	11(1.02)	$11(1.02)^2$	$11(1.02)^2$
Subsidy	0	10.0	10.0	10.0	10.0	10.0
Ops. & Maint.	0	15.0(1.04)	$-15.0(1.04)^2$	$-15.0(1.04)^3$	$-15.0(1.04)^3$ (1.02)	$-15.0(1.04)^3$ $(1.02)^2$
Leasing	0	−4.0(1.03)	$-4.0(1.03)^2$	$-4.0(1.03)^3$	$-4.0(1.03)^4$	$-4.0(1.03)^5$
Subtotals	0	\$1.28M	\$0.75M	−\$0.24M	−\$0.268M	−\$0.747M

NPV = $1.28/1.154 + 0.75/(1.154)^2 - 0.24/(1.154)^3 - 0.268/(1.154)^4 - 0.747/(1.154)^5 = +$ \$1.14M.

Investigating the consequences of higher or lower underlying general inflation rates as well as a range of individual component inflation rates is important for sensitivity analysis. Once an analyst creates a spreadsheet to do the initial calculation, recomputation with changes in values takes little time. Particular attention is usually paid to construction costs of major projects because the CPV could change enormously. Because financing mechanisms such as bonds are predicated on these estimates, the range of estimates can be very important. Revenue bonds in particular require careful anticipation of inflation, not only of construction costs but also of revenue sources. The revenue stream will be used to pay back the investment.

Probability in Cost Estimating

Recall from Example 9.2 in this chapter that one must have an estimate for the change in the quantity of input resource variable(s) in order to compute a change in the engineering cost models. This example used single values for changes in each of the three input resource variables. In the probabilistic approach, the analyst samples each variable from the range of values and recomputes the total cost (or benefit) with each new sample. Instead of one value, the computations yield a range within which the cost or savings likely resides. Such analysis is necessary when the amount of input resources consumed is not known with great accuracy. As an example, experience shows that signal priority for public transport vehicles does not give equal time savings on every run. Another example is that the amount of hours spent on maintenance may vary.

Empirical studies using data assembled from numerous applications in different locales are one source of probabilistically distributed data. Another source could be a model that does random simulation. Continuing with the traffic-signal priority example, a corridor simulation for a bus operating in mixed traffic with some traffic-signal priority investments would make numerous runs. The result would be a range of values for the decrease in travel time.

The analyst can use the range of changes seen in the input resource variable to form a histogram. The histogram of each data set is first rescaled so that the total area under the histogram is equal to one. This is done to convert the data set to a probability distribution. The histogram can then further be overlaid with a triangle, as shown in Figure 9.4. The left-most data point is the minimum value, the right-most point the maximum value, and the apex the most likely value. The triangle need not be symmetrical. Using the sides of the triangle, algebraic relationships can then be written for the probability and cumulative probability relationships. (Cumulative probability is the probability of any outcome up to and including a given value.)

In order to determine the most likely resulting cost (or benefit) value and the probability distribution of outcomes, the analyst must sample the distribution for each variable numerous times. The cost equation is recomputed with each

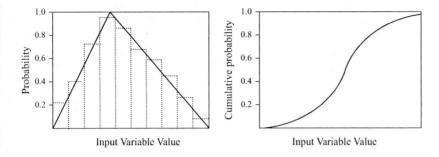

Figure 9.4 Triangular distribution of input resource variable.

iteration until the distribution of the possible outcomes is established. The output will be an *expected value* (most likely outcome) as well as statistical descriptors such as the standard deviation of the range of outcomes. It is straightforward to use desktop computers to perform these calculations because there are commercial software programs (e.g., *@Risk*) that will provide assistance in developing the appropriate probability distributions and the sampling techniques (Vose 2008). There are also software tools specifically designed for application to project evaluation in the transport sector, such as those developed at the Technical University of Denmark (Salling and Leleur 2011, 2012). These tools were used in the Öresund case study discussed in Chapters 2 and 12.

As always, there are cautions required when doing statistical analysis. First, one should have sufficient data to have confidence the sample size is adequately large and unbiased. Second, the approach presented here assumes that the input resource variables are independent; that is, a change in one does not directly correspond to a change in another. In fact, they might be related. The analyst must perform tests to ensure the variables are independent. If not, somewhat more complicated techniques would be involved. See the manuals for the commercial software for more details.

Summary

Engineering cost modeling is an established method that can provide needed values for the cost, benefit, and revenue streams in an NPV analysis. It can also form the nucleus of financially related performance analysis. The method is to create cost-estimating equations proportional to the key resources consumed in support of particular services. An analyst can construct a cost-allocation matrix to organize categories of costs such that unit-cost coefficients can be computed for input resource variables. These include *Vehicle-Hours*, *Vehicle-Distance*, peak *Fleet Size*, and perhaps others.

Discontinuities in the cost coefficients are created when resources can only be added in discrete quantities (e.g. when bus depots are expanded in large increments). Analysts can accommodate these discontinuities by applying appropriate incremental changes to cell entries for the year that they occur and recompute the cost coefficients in accordance with the changes in total resource quantities consumed.

Similar experiences at the institutions responsible for project implementation and for operations once in service should provide the most appropriate data. Even within the same agency, different routes may have very different duty cycles, so cost coefficients should be used from services with similar cycles. Lacking such data, one can use data from carefully selected peers. Analysts should use manufacturer and system design specifications for proven designs, but not exclusively when unproven technologies or concepts are involved, as they may not perform as billed.

Engineering cost models lend themselves readily to sensitivity analyses. It is prudent to perform these in most any project analysis but especially when there are unproven technological or conceptual aspects, major construction, or the analysis is of a long-term nature. Analysts can incorporate inflation estimates in computations, preferably applying them to particular components rather than applied uniformly. The "real" method expresses values relative to a reference year. The "actual" or "nominal" method uses values expressed in the current year. But when there is underlying inflation, care must be taken to use a combined MARR rather than the real MARR.

In some cases, instead of a range of possible coefficient values, there may be a wide range of possible input resource values. For example, the actual savings one might anticipate in vehicle-hours and vehicle-distance required may not be deterministic but instead are inferred from experience elsewhere. In this case, one can assign a distribution to the variable and use a simulation package to estimate a range of likely outcomes.

References

EU (European Union). 2001. *Transmodel*. Brussels, Belgium. http://www.transmodel.org/en/cadre1.html. Accessed July 2013.

FTA (U.S. Federal Transit Administration). 2011. *National Transit Database*. Washington, DC: U.S. Department of Transportation. http://www.ntdprogram.gov

Morlok, Edward K. 1978. Chapter 9 in *Introduction to Transportation Engineering and Planning*. New York: McGraw-Hill, 345–410.

Salling, Kim Bang, and Steen Leleur. 2012. "Modelling of Transport Project Uncertainties: Feasibility Risk Assessment and Scenario Analysis." *European Journal of Transportation Infrastructure Research* 12 (1): 21–38. http://www.ejtir.tbm.tudelft.nl

_____. 2011. "Transport Appraisal and Monte Carlo Simulation by Use of the CBA-DK Model." *Transport Policy* 18: 236–45.

Schneck, Donald C., Richard S. Laver and John Mothersole. 1995. *Transit Capital Cost Index Study*. Washington, DC: U.S. Federal Transit Administration, Office of Planning.

Sullivan, William G., Elin M. Wicks and C. Patrick Koelling. 2008. *Engineering Economy.* 14th ed. Englewood Cliffs, NJ: Prentice Hall.
Vose, D. 2008. *Risk Analysis—A Quantitative Guide.* 3rd ed. Oxford, UK: John Wiley and Sons.

Further Reading

Golder Associates, and Keith Molenaar. 2011. *Guide for the Process of Managing Risk on Rapid Renewal Projects.* Renewal Project R09. Washington, DC: National Academy Press, Strategic Highway Research Program 2.

Chapter 10

Average and Marginal Costs of Services[1]

The cost of adding a bus, an additional car to a train, or an entire additional train into service is an important consideration in many planning and operations analyses. This chapter first describes basic concepts and gives a few examples of how marginal costs might be used. It then derives marginal-cost formulas based on the average annualized cost equations described in Chapter 9. It continues by using both the average and marginal-cost equations in examples. This chapter then develops a methodology for estimating operating costs for entire bus routes and rail lines. It concludes by addressing two other important questions: How much does it cost to accommodate *linked trips* (i.e. trips involving connections)? Do particular trips improve or detract from financial performance of a transit network?

Basic Concepts and Example Applications

The cost models in the previous chapter were based on system-wide total costs for a modal fleet. These average cost values have limits to their usefulness. True marginal cost provides additional information about the cost of providing one more unit of input into the service production process or supplying one more unit of output. Incremental cost is the analog for inputs that cannot be provided or outputs that cannot be expanded in just one unit but rather in a minimum number of units. For example, consider a bus purchase; fleet-depot capacity is not expanded for just one bus, but for many at once. This incremental effect was shown in Figure 9.1. The "lumpiness" in total cost per passenger was created when total passenger volume reached a level such that it required the addition of another depot.

Three examples in which marginal costs provide insight into operational performance and investments that are not available with average costs are outlined here.

Marginal Cost Versus Marginal Revenue Test

The test is summarized in Table 10.1. Per passenger fare should ideally be set such that it generates sufficient revenue to cover the cost of the last unit of service

Table 10.1 Marginal cost versus marginal revenue test

MR > MC service generates more revenue than it consumes
MR = MC efficient pricing; revenues cover costs
MR < MC service costs more than it generates; service requires subsidy

provided. This is the neoclassical economics definition of *efficient pricing*—marginal revenue (MR) should equal marginal cost (MC). Such pricing cannot always be used in practice, but when it can, it does guarantee there will be no adverse impact on other services. If MR exceeds MC, it begins to reduce the operating subsidy requirement or increases profit, in the case of nonsubsidized services. An example where this might occur is a premium express service. More typically, MR will be less than MC, indicating that each additional passenger actually increases the subsidy requirement or reduces profit, in the case of nonsubsidized services. This points to a dilemma. Public transport agencies are generally expected to increase ridership. On the other hand, attracting some types of riders will only increase the subsidy requirement, which is something the agency may not be able to afford if it has a fixed operating budget.

Marginal-cost information can be used to rank individual services so operators could tell whether the fares collected would cover the actual costs of existing services and proposed expansions in service. It can also be insightful for studying the combined effect of more than one increase in service. If service intensification within an existing area causes marginal costs per passenger to decrease, there are *economies of density*. If expansion of the area in size causes marginal costs to decrease, there are *economies of scale*.

Operating Versus Investment Cost Test

Economists often base their investment estimates on the rationale that the higher initial cost will be offset by lower ongoing operating costs. But revenue will also be affected as the quality and/or level of service changes; in other words, changes in revenue must also be estimated, Any annual operating savings and increased revenue can be evaluated against the initial investment in a Net Present Value (NPV) analysis by annualizing all monetary costs and revenues. As per the discussion in Chapter 8, an NPV greater than zero indicates an investment whose monetary benefits exceed its monetary costs.

If an operation is intended to be able to fluctuate in capacity over the course of a day or to expand in future years, the marginal cost of expansion can also weigh heavily in project evaluation. Indeed, one of the main reasons for using rail technology is to increase capacity at low marginal cost by simply adding cars to a train. Unlike buses, there is no additional operator cost. Therefore, frequency can remain constant or close to constant over a wide range of passenger

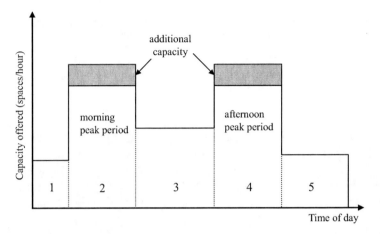

Figure 10.1 Capacity supply profile.

demands without incurring what is generally the largest portion of vehicle operating costs—labor. As an example, Figure 10.1 is a simple *capacity supply profile*, showing five discrete time periods during the day having different supply requirements. There are two peak time periods (2 and 4) where additional capacity is being considered, shown by shading. It might be possible to leave the number of Transit Units (TUs) and frequency unchanged if sufficient capacity can be met by adding train cars. When trains are at maximum length or higher frequency is desired, additional trains must be added instead.

Optimum Reserve Fleet Analysis

Reduction of marginal cost with increasing use of each existing vehicle and with the avoidance of expanding the fleet is another basic concept of public transport operations. The fewer vehicles needed, the fewer costs associated with ownership, operation, maintenance, and storage. At some point, however, costs will start to increase again when vehicles suffer from inadequate time for maintenance. The reduction as a function of vehicle usage is shown conceptually in Figure 10.2.

The engineering cost model presented in the previous chapter, which assigns the components of total annual operating cost to be a function of one of several resource variables, is the basis for the approach explained here. For buses, the three variables were *Bus-Hours*, *Bus-Distance*, and *Fleet Size*. For trains, the three variables were *Train-Hours*, *Car-Distance*, and car *Fleet Size*. Direct operating and supervisory labor costs were assumed to be proportional

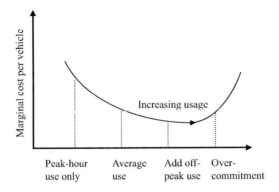

Figure 10.2 Marginal cost decreases with increasing vehicle use.

to hours. Support services, expendables consumption, and insurance were assumed to be proportional to distance. Energy for propulsion and maintenance were assumed to be a function of both hours and distance. Remaining costs (e.g. administration and facility upkeep) were assumed to be proportional to car *Fleet Size*.

Slightly modifying a result from the previous chapter to make the unit-cost coefficients bus-specific, the average operating cost per bus on an annualized basis using system-wide statistics is:

$$AC_o = c_{BH} \, \textit{(Bus-Hours)} + c_{BD} \, \textit{(Bus-Distance)} + c_{FS} \, \textit{(Fleet Size)} \quad [\$/\text{year}] \, (10\text{-}1)$$

As before, the analyst must insert the specific values of the necessary quantities of the inputs, expressed as *Bus-Hours, Bus-Distance,* and *Fleet Size* in order to study the existing or proposed service.

Capital costs of vehicle acquisition can easily be included if desired. The modification requires including a Capital Recover Factor (CRF) term in the average annualized cost equation, as was shown in the previous chapter. But the details are not presented here.

Marginal cost can also be derived by first changing each input variable to an increment of the variable. Then one divides the entire equation by an incremental change in the variable for which the marginal cost is sought, in the finite difference form. The marginal cost with respect to a unit of resource is (actually an incremental cost if not strictly divisible into one unit):

$$MC_{unit} = \frac{\Delta AC_o}{\Delta unit} \quad [\$/\text{unit}] \tag{10-2}$$

The marginal cost with respect to *Bus-Hours* follows as:

$$MC_{bus\text{-}hour} = c_{VH} + c_{VK}\left(\frac{\Delta Bus\text{-}Distance}{\Delta Bus\text{-}Hours}\right) + c_{FS}\left(\frac{\Delta Fleet\ Size}{\Delta Bus\text{-}Hours}\right) \quad [\$/hour] \quad (10\text{-}3)$$

Similarly, the marginal cost with respect to *Bus-Distance* is:

$$MC_{bus\text{-}distance} = c_{VH}\left(\frac{\Delta Bus\text{-}Hours}{\Delta Bus\text{-}Distance}\right) + c_{VK} + c_{FS}\left(\frac{\Delta Fleet\ Size}{\Delta Bus\text{-}Distance}\right) \quad [\$/km] \quad (10\text{-}4)$$

The discussion of trains is slightly more complicated and appears in the Train Costs section.

The evaluation involves estimating the difference ratios at the last increment of resource input. Precise determination of these values is not the purpose here because unraveling the cost relationships to eliminate all uncertainty is very difficult. Instead, the purpose is to determine a reasonable range of values.

There are several implicit assumptions in the derivations in the Appendix:

1   The system-wide ratios of total-distance to revenue-distance and total-hours to revenue-hours remain unchanged with increases in service.
2   When additional fleet is acquired, physical plant, support staff, and overhead increase in proportion with fleet size.
3   When additional fleet is acquired, it is assumed it will be used at the same average rate as the existing stock, except where otherwise noted.
4   When additional fleet is acquired, any capital investment in maintenance and storage facilities is not included.

There is usually a reserve fleet, and some equipment will be withdrawn for repairs or maintenance. Thus, there can be ambiguity as to whether fleet really needs to be added. The analyst should first investigate the possibility of reducing reserves or expediting maintenance procedures before making the assumption that more fleet really is needed.

Marginal-cost formulae have been derived in Appendix 10.A. based on operating costs under a range of conditions but subject to the listed assumptions. Recall that the annualized average cost equation typically uses the "peak *Fleet Size*," defined by the number required to operate the maximum service during a weekday schedule.

Bus Costs

The finite difference ratios needed to evaluate the marginal cost formulas for a range of cases are shown in Table 10.2. These can be inserted into the formulas to develop appropriate estimates.

Table 10.2 Bus marginal cost equation multipliers

a. *Marginal cost per bus-hour* $MC_{b-k} = c_{BK} + c_{BH}\left(\dfrac{\Delta bh}{\Delta bk}\right) + c_{FS}\left(\dfrac{\Delta fs}{\Delta bk}\right).$

Condition	Multiply c_{BH} by	Multiply c_{BK} by	Multiply c_{FS} by
system-wide average	I	$\dfrac{BD}{BH} = v_{avg}$	$\dfrac{FS}{BH}$
route-specific average	I	$\dfrac{BD_r}{BH_r} = v_{avgr}$	$\dfrac{FS_r}{BH_r}$
peak use for X hours per weekday (must acquire buses)	I	v_{peak}	$\dfrac{I}{X254}$
off-peak (no extra buses needed)	I	$v_{off-peak}$	0

b. *Marginal cost per unit bus-distance* $MC_{b-d} = c_{BH}\left(\dfrac{\Delta bh}{\Delta bd}\right) + c_{BD} + c_{FS}\left(\dfrac{\Delta fs}{\Delta bd}\right)$

Condition	Multiply c_{BH} by	Multiply c_{BD} by	Multiply c_{FS} by
system–wide average	$\dfrac{BH}{BD} = \dfrac{I}{v_{avg}}$	I	$\dfrac{FS}{BD}$
route-specific average	$\dfrac{BH_r}{BD_r} = \dfrac{I}{v_{avgr}}$	I	$\dfrac{FS_r}{BD_r}$
peak use for X hours per weekday (must acquire buses)	$\dfrac{I}{v_{peak}}$	I	$\dfrac{I}{v_{peak}X254}$
off-peak (no extra buses needed)	$\dfrac{I}{v_{off-peak}}$	I	0
service increase w/o additional bus-hours	0	I	0

Example 10.1

A bus system has the financial values given in Table 9.2. Find the system marginal costs for three cases:

1   off-peak service;
2   newly acquired vehicles that get used the same amount as existing vehicles; and

3   newly acquired vehicles that get used only for six hours of peak service per day.

The values are repeated here:

$c_{BH} = \$33.40/bus\text{-}hour,$
$c_{BK} = \$0.47/bus\text{-}kilometer,$
$c_{FS} = \$21,000/bus\text{-}year$
$Bus\text{-}Hours\ (BH) = 4 \times 10^5$
$Bus\text{-}Kilometers\ (BK) = 64 \times 10^5$
peak $Fleet\ Size\ (FS) = 100$

The marginal cost on a per bus-kilometer basis is:

$$MC_{b-k} = c_{BK} + c_{BH}\left(\frac{\Delta bh}{\Delta bk}\right) + c_{FS}\left(\frac{\Delta fs}{\Delta bk}\right).$$

Since no mention was made of different operating speeds for the three cases, nor was any route-specific data provided, assume change in bus-hours with respect to bus-kilometers is the average for all three cases:

$$\left(\frac{\Delta bh}{\Delta bk}\right)_{avg} = \frac{BH}{BK} = \frac{1}{v_{avg}} = \frac{4 \times 10^5}{64 \times 10^5} = \frac{1}{16}$$

The change in fleet size with respect to bus-kilometers will be different for each case. For the first case of off-peak service:

$$\left(\frac{\Delta fs}{\Delta bk}\right)_{off-peak} = 0$$

The second case is for average usage:

$$\left(\frac{\Delta fs}{\Delta bk}\right)_{avg} = \frac{FS}{BK} = \frac{100}{64 \times 10^5}$$

The third case is peak-use only:

$$\left(\frac{\Delta fs}{\Delta bk}\right)_{pk} = \frac{1}{v_{avg} \times 254} = \frac{1}{(16)(6)(254)_1}$$

Inserting these values:

$$\textit{Off-peak: } MC_{b\text{-}k} = 0.47 + 33.40\left(\frac{1}{16}\right) + 21,000(0) = \$2.56/bus - km$$

$$\textit{Average: } MC_{b\text{-}k} = 0.47 + 33.40\left(\frac{1}{16}\right) + 21,000\left(\frac{100}{64 \times 10^5}\right) = \$2.89 / bus - km$$

$$\textit{Peak only : } MC_{b\text{-}k} = 0.47 + 33.40\left(\frac{1}{16}\right) + 21,000\left(\frac{100}{(16)(6)(254)}\right)$$
$$= \$3.42/bus - km$$

The marginal cost on a per bus-hour basis is:

$$MC_{b-h} = c_{BH} + c_{BK}\left(\frac{\Delta bk}{\Delta bh}\right) + c_{FS}\left(\frac{\Delta fs}{\Delta bh}\right)$$

Since no mention was made of different operating speeds, nor was any route-specific data provided, assume the change in bus-kilometers with respect to bus-hours will be the average value for all three cases:

$$\left(\frac{\Delta bk}{\Delta bh}\right)_{avg} = \frac{BK}{BH} = \frac{64 \times 10^5}{4 \times 10^5} = 16$$

The change in fleet size with respect to bus-hours will again be different for all three cases:

$$\left(\frac{\Delta fs}{\Delta bh}\right)_{off-peak} = 0$$

$$\left(\frac{\Delta fs}{\Delta bh}\right)_{avg} = \frac{FS}{BH} = \frac{100}{4 \times 10^5}$$

$$\left(\frac{\Delta fs}{\Delta bh}\right)_{pk} = \frac{1}{X\,254} = \frac{1}{(6)(254)}$$

Inserting these values:

$$\textit{off-peak: } MC_{b-h} = 33.40 + 0.47(16) + 21,000(0) = \$40.92/bus - hour$$

$$\textit{average: } MC_{b-h} = 33.40 + 0.47(16) + 21,000\left(\frac{100}{4 \times 10^5}\right) = \$46.17/bus - hour$$

$$\textit{peak: } MC_{b-h} = 33.40 + 0.47(16) + 21,000\left(\frac{1}{(6)(254)}\right) = \$54.70/bus - hour$$

Note the relationship between the two sets of solutions. By multiplying by the ratio of bus-kilometers to bus-hours one can convert the marginal cost on a per-hour basis to the marginal cost on a per-kilometer basis. Using the inverse ratio, one can convert in the opposite direction. Thus, it was not necessary to do both sets of calculations.

Train Costs

The annualized total operating cost equation for trains is slightly different from the bus model presented in Chapter 9 due to the possibility of some trains having more cars than others. One of the resource input variables is associated with entire trains, the other two with individual cars:

$$AC_o = c_{TH} \ (Train\text{-}Hours) + c_{CD} \ (Car\text{-}Distance) + c_{FS} \ (Fleet \ Size)$$
$$[\$/ \ year] \tag{10-5}$$

The marginal cost with respect to train-hours follows as:

$$MC_{train\text{-}hour} = c_{TH} + c_{CD} \left(\frac{\Delta Car\text{-}Distance}{\Delta Train\text{-}Hours} \right) + c_{FS} \left(\frac{\Delta Fleet \ Size}{\Delta Train\text{-}Hours} \right)$$
$$[\$/train\text{-}hour] \tag{10-6}$$

And the marginal cost with respect to car-distance is:

$$MC_{car\text{-}kilometer} = c_{TH} \left(\frac{\Delta Train\text{-}Hours}{\Delta Car\text{-}Distance} \right) + c_{CK} + c_{FS} \left(\frac{\Delta Fleet \ Size}{\Delta Car\text{-}Distance} \right)$$
$$[\$/km] \tag{10-7}$$

The change of *Train-Hours* with *Car-Distance* is more complicated than the change in *Bus-Hours* with *Bus-Distance*. Unlike buses, train-costing conditions must also distinguish between adding cars (increasing train length) and adding an entire train (increasing the number of trains). Because a train can vary in size, the difference ratios of *Train-Distance* with *Car-Distance* and *Train-Hours* with *Car-Hours* can also vary. There can be considerable differences in the increase in *Fleet Size* with an increase in service, depending upon conditions. Adding service in off-peak hours, when cars are available, involves no increase in peak *Fleet Size*. At the other end, if entire trains must be added during the peak periods, causes the highest cost increases. In the latter case, new equipment must be acquired in order to provide additional service (unless there is a preexisting surplus of reserve equipment).

Some useful definitions are presented before proceeding further. The system-wide average consist size is:

$$m_{avg} = \frac{\text{total } \textit{Car-Distance}}{\text{total } \textit{Train-Distance}} \quad [\text{cars}/\text{train}] \tag{10-8}$$

The system-wide average speed is defined by:

$$v_{Tavg} = \frac{\text{total } \textit{Train-Distance}}{\text{total } \textit{Train-Hours}} \quad [\text{distance}/\text{hour}] \quad (\text{Total basis}) \tag{10-9}$$

or:

$$v_{Ravg} = \frac{\text{revenue } \textit{Train-Distance}}{\text{revenue } \textit{Train-Hours}} \quad [\text{distance}/\text{hour}] \quad (\text{Revenue basis}) \tag{10-10}$$

As with buses, the terminology v_{avg} will generally be used in further discussion. The "total" and "revenue" distinctions are dropped with the understanding that once one or the other is selected, it will be used consistently.

Figure 10.3 shows the difference between adding a given number of cars as a complete m-car long train or adding the same number individually, one per existing train. When m cars are added as an entire train, the marginal cost on a per car basis decreases as m gets larger. This is because each additional car added to a train spreads the costs proportional to train-hours (a large fraction of which is train driver cost) over a larger number of cars. By contrast, the marginal cost is always the same when each of the m cars is added individually to an existing consist.

Finite difference ratios for the two train marginal cost formulas are derived in Appendix 10.A and collected for a range of conditions in Table 10.3. These can be inserted into the formulas to develop appropriate estimates.

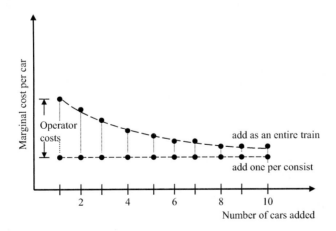

Figure 10.3 Marginal cost of adding train cars.

Table 10.3 Train marginal cost equation multipliers

a. Marginal cost per train-hour $MC_{t-h} = c_{TH} + c_{CD}\left(\dfrac{\Delta cd}{\Delta th}\right) + c_{FS}\left(\dfrac{\Delta fs}{\Delta th}\right)$

Condition	Multiply c_{TH} by	Multiply c_{CD} by	Multiply c_{FS} by
system average	1	$\dfrac{m_{avg}TD}{TH} = m_{avg}v_{avg}$	$\dfrac{FS}{TH}$
route-specific average	1	$\dfrac{m_r TD_r}{TH_r} = m_r v_r$	$\dfrac{FS_r}{TH_r}$
peak use for X hours per weekday (must acquire cars)	1	mv_{peak}	$\dfrac{m}{X254}$
off-peak (no extra cars needed)	1	$mv_{off-peak}$	0
Δm cars added to existing train for peak use only (must acquire cars)	0	Δmv_{peak}	$\dfrac{\Delta m}{X254}$
Δm cars added to existing train for off-peak (no extra cars needed)	0	$\Delta mv_{off-peak}$	0

b. Marginal cost per unit car-distance $MC_{c-d} = c_{TH}\left(\dfrac{\Delta th}{\Delta cd}\right) + c_{CD} + c_{FS}\left(\dfrac{\Delta fs}{\Delta ck}\right)$

Condition	Multiply c_{TH} by	Multiply c_{CD} by	Multiply c_{FS} by
system-wide average	$\dfrac{TH}{m_{avg}TD} = \dfrac{1}{m_{avg}v_{avg}}$	1	$\dfrac{FS}{CD}$
route-specific average	$\dfrac{TH_r}{m_r TD_r} = \dfrac{1}{m_r v_r}$	1	$\dfrac{FS_r}{CD_r}$
peak use only for X hours per weekday (must acquire cars)	$\dfrac{1}{mv_{peak}}$	1	$\dfrac{1}{v_{peak}X254}$
off-peak (no extra cars needed)	$\dfrac{1}{mv_{off-peak}}$	1	0
Δm car addition to existing train, peak use only	0	1	$\dfrac{1}{v_{peak}X254}$
Δm car addition to existing train, off-peak	0	1	0
any service increase w/o added train-hours or car-hours	0	1	0

Example 10.2

A rapid transit system has cost coefficients and input resource consumption given below:

c_{TH} = $95.70/Train-hour
c_{CK} = $1.29/Car-Mile
c_{FS} = $226,000/Car-Year
Train-Hours (TH) = 167,800
Train-Miles (TM) = 5,932,000
Car-Hours (CH) = 1,239,000
Car-Miles (CM) = 43,853,000
Peak Fleet Size (FS) = 406

A) Find the marginal cost of adding a car to an average-sized consist (train) for these four cases:

1   **off-peak service;**
2   **add peak service using reserve fleet;**
3   **acquire new vehicles that get used the same amount as existing vehicles; and acquire new vehicles that get used for six hours of peak service per day.**

The average consist size is:

$$m_{avg} = \frac{43,853,000}{5,932,00} = 7.4 \; cars/train$$

The average speed is:

$$v_{avg} = \frac{TK}{TH} = \frac{5,932,00}{167,800} = 35.4 \; miles/hour$$

The marginal cost on a per car-mile basis is:

$$MC_{c-m} = C_{TH}\left(\frac{\Delta th}{\Delta cm}\right) + C_{CM} + C_{FS}\left(\frac{\Delta fs}{\Delta cm}\right)$$

The change in *Train-Hours* with respect to *Car-Miles* will be zero, since total Train-Hours remain unchanged when cars are added:

$$\left(\frac{\Delta th}{\Delta cm}\right)_{avg} = 0$$

The change in *Fleet Size* with respect to *Car-Miles* for the first case is zero, since no additional cars are required: The first is for the off-peak:

$$\left(\frac{\Delta fs}{\Delta cm}\right)_{off-peak} = 0$$

Since reserves are used, no additional cars are required for the second case either:

$$\left(\frac{\Delta fs}{\Delta cm}\right)_{reserves} = 0$$

The third case is for average usage:

$$\left(\frac{\Delta fs}{\Delta ck}\right)_{avg} = \frac{FS}{CM} = \frac{406}{43,853,000}$$

The fourth case is for peak-use only:

$$\left(\frac{\Delta fs}{\Delta ck}\right)_{peak} = \frac{1}{v_{avg} \times 254} = \frac{1}{(35.4)(6)(254)}$$

Inserting these values:

$$Off\text{-}peak \ and \ reserves: \ MC_{c-m} = \$95.70(0) + \$1.29 + \$226,000(0)$$
$$= \$1.29/car\text{-}mile$$

$$Average: \ MC_{c-m} = \$\ 95.70\ (0) + \$1.29 + \$226,000\left(\frac{406}{43,853,000}\right)$$
$$= \$3.38/car\text{-}mile$$

$$Peak \ only: \ MC_{c-k} = \$\ 95.70\ (0) + \$1.29 + \$226,000\left(\frac{1}{(35.4)(6)(254)}\right)$$
$$= \$5.48/car\text{-}mile.$$

The results show how relatively little it costs to add capacity during the off-peak periods or if reserve vehicles are available for scheduled use versus having to acquire additional rolling stock.

B) Now find the marginal cost on a per-Train-Hour basis for the following two cases:

1 acquiring an average-sized consist that will have average usage; and
2 an average-sized consist that will be used only for six peak hours per weekday.

The marginal cost on a per train-hour basis is:

$$MC_{t\text{-}h} = c_{TH} + c_{CM}\left(\frac{\Delta cm}{\Delta th}\right) + c_{FS}\left(\frac{\Delta fs}{\Delta th}\right)$$

The change in *Car-Miles* with respect to *Train-Hours* for an average-sized consist is estimated by:

$$\left(\frac{\Delta cm}{\Delta th}\right)_{avg} = \frac{43,853,000}{167,800}$$

The change in *Fleet Size* with respect to *Train-Hour* ratio estimates are:

$$\left(\frac{\Delta fs}{\Delta th}\right)_{avg} = \frac{FS}{TH} = \frac{406}{167,800}$$

$$\left(\frac{\Delta fs}{\Delta th}\right)_{peak} = \frac{m}{X\ 254} = \frac{7.4}{(6)(254)}$$

Inserting these values:

$$average:\ MC_{t\text{-}h} = \$\,95.70\,(0) + \$1.29\left(\frac{43,853,000}{167,800}\right) + \$226,000\left(\frac{406}{167,800}\right)$$
$$= \$978/train\text{-}hour$$

$$peak:\ MC_{t\text{-}h} = \$95.70\,(0) + \$1.29\left(\frac{43,853,000}{167,800}\right) + \$226,000\left(\frac{7.4}{(6)(254)}\right)$$
$$= \$1530/train\text{-}hour$$

The large difference shows the financial consequences of purchasing vehicles and expanding facilities, staffing, and administration only to provide additional peak services. (On a long rail line, six hours represents at most only two round-trip runs each during the morning and evening peak periods.)

C) Now find the marginal cost per train-hour to operate a four-car consist (train) in the off-peak period.

The change in *Car-Miles* with respect to *Train-Tiles* is adjusted for a four-car consist:

$$\left(\frac{\Delta cm}{\Delta th}\right)_{avg} = \frac{4(TM)}{TH} = \frac{4(5,932,000)}{167,800}$$

The change in fleet size is zero, since cars are available:

$$\left(\frac{\Delta fs}{\Delta th}\right)_{off\text{-}peak} = 0$$

Inserting these values:

$$MC_{t\text{-}h} = \$95.70 + \$1.29\left(\frac{4(5,932,000)}{167,800}\right) + \$226,000\,(0) = \$278/train\text{-}hour$$

The relationship between marginal costs on the two bases of *Car-Miles* and *Train-Hours* is not quite as direct as with *Bus-Miles* and *Bus-Hours*. Due to variability of consist size, one cannot simply multiply through by a ratio to convert between them. There is a fixed component that represents operator/supervision/control costs independent of train size. This component is not included in the per-car calculation because the assumption of adding four cars individually to four different trains is not the same as adding one four-car train.

It is always possible to convert a per-train-hour marginal cost to a per-car-hour marginal cost by dividing through by the consist size. However, if this is done, it must be clearly stated that this is based on adding an entire consist, and not on adding a car.

D) Now find the marginal cost on a per-mile basis instead for adding the same four-car train.

One approach is to convert the results from Part C) using the fleet average speed:

$$\frac{\$278/train\text{-}hour}{35.4\,miles/hour} = \$7.85/train\text{-}mile = \$1.97/car\text{-}mile$$

The second approach is to use the formula for *Car-Miles* directly. Because a whole train is added, the change in *Train-Hours* with respect to *Train-Miles* is no longer zero. Instead:

$$\left(\frac{\Delta th}{\Delta cm}\right)_{avg} = \frac{TH}{4(TM)} = \frac{167,800}{4(5,932,000)}$$

The result is again the same:

$$MC_{c\text{-}m} = \$95.70\left(\frac{167,800}{4(5,932,000)}\right) + \$1.29 + \$226,000\,(0) = \$1.97/car\text{-}mile.$$

Costs of Operating Routes

Annual Operating Cost Estimates

The annual operating cost of providing service during subperiod i may be estimated with:

$$OC_i = N_i AC_i, \quad [\$/\text{year}], \tag{10-11}$$

where OC_i is the annual cost of operating service during period i of the schedule. N_i is the number of TUs required to maintain a given constant headway during subperiod i, which was shown in Figure 10.1 represents a constant service over certain time period(s) over the course of the day and certain days of the week. AC_i is then the annualized cost of operating one TU during subperiod i. It is computed using the hours and distance that one TU would operate over the course of one year for subperiod i.

The annual cost of operating a specific route or line, r, requires summing up the cost of all of the service subperiods on this route. In general, an analyst can produce a close enough estimate for project analysis purposes by dividing the service into subperiods of time i that have uniform headways (similar to Figure 10.1) and constant hourly wage rates. One then adds the contribution of these discrete periods:

$$OC_r = \sum_i OC_i, \quad [\$/\text{year}] \tag{10-12}$$

where OC_r is the annual cost of operating all scheduled service on route r. This particular formulation is a convenient one because it is often the case that only changes to one specific subperiod i is of interest. Thus, the grand total for all periods might not need to be computed. Instead, only the difference between the before and after costs of proposed changes to service needs to be computed. The before and after costs of the unchanged periods will cancel to zero. Thus, once the cost coefficients have been calculated, the only additional information required is the difference in resource variable consumption.

For very high accuracy, all the details of the transitions between service subperiods are also required. In other words, the analyst must evaluate every movement of every TU. This may also be necessary in the case of sparse and irregular service that cannot be divided into repeating operations. A graphical presentation of the entire schedule showing all movements can be helpful for computing more accurate totals for resource consumptions (Bruun, Vuchic and Shin, 1999).

Example 10.3

A) Two three-hour peak service subperiods for a bus route each supply 60 kilometers of additional service. Find the incremental resource inputs.

The two three-hour periods can be combined to one six-hour period per day for five days of the week with each bus accumulating 120 kilometers per weekday in this service. The resulting incremental unit resource consumption values are:

Incremental Bus-Hours = 3 × 2 × 5 × 52 = 1,560 per year
Incremental Bus-Kilometers = 2 × 60 × 5 × 52 = 31,200 per year
Incremental Fleet Size = 1

B) The weekend service period for a train line using four-car trains operates 18 hours per day for two days of the week with each train accumulating 400 miles per day. Find the incremental resource inputs.

In this case there is only one sub-period per day, so the incremental unit resource consumption values are:

Incremental Train-Hours = 18 × 2 × 52 = 1,872 per year
Incremental Car-Miles = 4 × 400 × 2 × 52 = 166,400 per year
Incremental Fleet Size = 4

C) What is the annual cost savings from using one bus less if the service change is as described in Part A? Use the cost coefficients from Example 10.1.

Incremental values can be used because we are concerned only with the cost difference. The unit cost for subperiods 2 and 4 combined is:

$$OC_{2\&4} = \$33.40 \, (1,560) + \$0.47 \, (31,200) + \$21,000 \, (1)$$
$$= \$87,800 \, / \, bus\text{-}year$$

Verification of Fleet-Size Requirements and Schedule Feasibility

The proper value for N_i, the number of TUs assigned during period i, should be verified. It is important to check for the possibility of a change in the number of TUs required because it may have major implications for the cost of providing service. It may also be the primary justification for some investments.

The basic scheduling relationship from Chapter 3 for service during operating subperiod i is slightly modified by introducing a subscript i for each subperiod.

$$T_i = N_i \, h \qquad\qquad\qquad (10\text{-}13)$$

Furthermore, if the headway is fixed, T_i must change in increments, as can be seen by this algebraic manipulation:

$$\Delta T = \Delta (N_i\, h) = (\Delta\ N_i\ )\ h \quad \text{(if h is fixed)} \qquad (10\text{-}14)$$

This equation requires that, because the change in N_i must be an integer, the change in cycle time, T, must also change in integer multiples of the headway:

$$\Delta T = 0, \pm 1h, \pm 2h \ldots\ldots \qquad (10\text{-}15)$$

Another scheduling relationship from Chapter 3 states that the cycle time equals round-trip operating time plus two terminal times. This is also slightly modified so that it applies to each operating period i:

$$T_i = \frac{2L}{v_0} + tt_1 + tt_2 \qquad (10\text{-}16)$$

In practice, a minimum terminal time, tt_{min}, is set by agreement with employees, for operational reliability, or both. This introduces the additional constraint:

$$tt_1,\ tt_2 \ge tt_{min} \qquad (10\text{-}17)$$

The set of relationships 10–13 through 10–17 define *feasible* changes to a schedule. Violating any of these relationships would make the schedule either technically inoperable or institutionally unacceptable. In practice, the feasible solution set(s) will usually be dictated by specific circumstances. Changes in route length may not be possible, increases in operating speed may not be practical, and terminal times may already be close to their minimums.

Example 10.4

Due to a traffic-signal improvement, the average operating speed on a route is to be increased from 11.2 miles/hour to 11.8 miles/hour. It has a headway of six minutes, and a one-way length of 10 miles. The minimum layover by agreement with the operators is eight minutes and is equal at both ends. Can a bus be saved with this increase in speed?

First, find the current layover time. The three relationships 10-16, 10-13 and 10-17:

$$T_i = \frac{2(10)}{11.2/60} + 2tt$$

$$T_i = N_i\ (6.0)$$

$$tt \ge 8.0$$

The lowest value of T_i that satisfies all three is 126 minutes. It follows that $N_i = 21$ and $tt = 9.43$ minutes. For a vehicle to be saved if v_o' is 11.8/hour, the cycle time must be reduced by one headway:

$$T_i' = (N_i - 1)h = (20)6 = 120$$

The next step is to solve for the revised terminal time, tt', to ascertain that the minimum of 8.0 minutes is not violated:

$$T_i' = \frac{2(10)}{11.8/60} = 2tt' = 120$$

Solving for tt' gives 9.15 minutes. All three relationships are satisfied. A reduction of one bus is possible. The value $N_i' = 20$ should be used accordingly for evaluating the operating cost.

The reduction (or increase) of the *Fleet Size* needed to serve a route can already represent a major savings (or cost). It is possible, however, to further refine the cost-estimating coefficients for a specific route once it is recognized that its characteristics deviate significantly from the average. This will often be the case because it is the purpose of many investments to alter performance characteristics. Reiterating from the previous chapter, an analyst must keep in mind that the increased accuracy of employing more route-specific values in the cost-allocation matrix used to compute the coefficients can be offset by the decreased accuracy of trying to isolate joint costs to this same specific route. The coefficients associated with *Vehicle-Hours* or *Vehicle-Distance* may better represent the specific route, but the accuracy of the coefficient associated with *Fleet Size* may deteriorate instead.

Example 10.5

A key element in a proposed 16-kilometer-long trunk line is the relative operating costs of an LRT solution versus a Bus Rapid Transit (BRT) solution. The capacity profile required of the service is as in Figure 10.1. Both options can operate at 30 km/hour. The base headway cannot exceed 15 minutes. The terminal time at each end must be a minimum of 15 percent of the travel time. Each BRT bus has a capacity of 120 persons, each LRV a capacity of 186 persons.

The cost coefficients for LRT are:
$c_{TH} = \$93.27\ per\ Train\text{-}Hour$
$c_{CK} = \$2.06\ per\ Car\text{-}Kilometer$
$c_{FS} = \$362,600\ per\ Car\text{-}Year$

The corresponding coefficients for BRT are:

c_{BH} = $55.93 per hour
c_{BK} = $2.14 per kilometer
c_{FS} = $184,800 per Bus-Year

A) What is the annual operating cost of providing base service with a single-car LRT consist?

First, the base *Fleet Size* must be determined. The off-peak levels are the same so that the capacity can be broken into 18 hours daily at a base level with two three-hour weekday peak periods requiring additional increments. The constraints for the base service that must be satisfied are:

$$T = Nh = \frac{2\,L}{v_o} + 2tt$$

$$2\,tt \geq 0.15\,\frac{2\,L}{v_o}$$

Inserting values:

$$T = N(15/60) = \frac{2(16)}{30} + 2tt$$

$$2tt \geq 0.15\frac{2(16)}{30}$$

The lowest integer value for N that satisfies the first and second constraints is 5. The corresponding value for $2tt$ is 11.0 minutes. The third constraint requires that $2tt$ be greater than 9.6 minutes, so it is satisfied as well.

The operating cost of one single-car train in base service 18 hours per day for one year is found using the annual operating cost equation with a peak *Fleet Size* of one:

LRT Base Cost Increment = $93.27((18)(365)) + $2.06((18)(365)(30))
+ $362,600(1) = $1,381,400 *per year*

The total cost of operating the LRT trunk line is estimated by multiplying the single-car cost by the fleet required for 15-minute headways:

Annual LRT Trunk Line Base Cost = ($1,381,400)(5) = $6,900,000 *per year*

B) What is the annual cost to add one car to each LRT train during peak periods?

Inserting both the appropriate difference ratios from Table 10.3b and applicable numerical values into the marginal cost equation on a per Car-Kilometer basis gives:

$$MC_{car\text{-}kilometer} = \$93.27(0) + \$2.26(1) + \$362,600\left(\frac{1}{(30)(6)(254)}\right)$$
$$= \$10.19 \ per \ car\text{-}kilometer$$

Multiplying this per-kilometer value by the operating speed converts the cost to a per-hour basis. Multiplying in turn by the number of peak hours annually gives the annual additional operating cost for one car:

$$LRT \ Peak \ Cost \ Increment = (\$10.19) \ (30)[(6)(254)](1)$$
$$= \$465,000 \ per \ peak \ car\text{-}year$$

The annual cost of adding one car to all trains on the trunk line is simply five times this amount:

$$Annual \ LRT \ Trunk \ Line \ Peak \ Cost = \$465,000 \ (5) = \$2,325,000 \ per \ year.$$

To add two cars to all trains would simply double this amount.

C) What is the annual cost to add one complete three-car train?

Once all trains on a line have been lengthened to their maximum, the term proportional to Train-Hour costs in the marginal cost equation is no longer zero. Referring to Table 10.3b and inserting appropriate values:

$$MC_{car\text{-}kilometer} = \$93.27\left(\frac{1}{3(30)}\right) + \$2.26(1) + \$362,600\left(\frac{1}{(30)(6)(254)}\right)$$
$$= \$11.23 \ per \ car\text{-}kilometer$$

The annual cost for one three-car train is then found by first multiplying by operating speed to convert to a per-hour basis, then multiplying by the number of peak hours annually, and then by the number of cars:

$$Annual \ Three\text{-}Car \ LRT \ Peak \ Cost = (\$11.23)(30)[(6)(254)](3)$$
$$= \$1,540,000 \ per \ year$$

D) If the base operating budget is equal for BRT and LRT, what is the frequency of service that can be provided using BRT?

This is done in two steps. The first is to use Equation 10-1 to determine the annual cost of operating one BRT vehicle in base service:

$$BRT\ Base\ Cost\ Increment = \$55.93(18)(365) + \$2.14(18)(365)(30)$$
$$+ \$184,800(1) = \$974,000\ per\ year$$

If the operating budget is the same for BRT as for LRT, the fleet size affordable using BRT follows by dividing Annual LRT Trunk Line Base Cost by the BRT Base Cost Increment:

$$Base\ BRT\ Fleet = \$27,600,000/\$974,000 = 7.08$$

It is impossible to exactly match operating costs due to the integer constraint on fleet, so the low cost estimate fleet is rounded to 7. This compares with five vehicles using LRT technology. The corresponding headway is then 10.6 minutes.

E) What is the annual cost of doubling BRT trunk-line capacity only during the peak periods?

Inserting both the appropriate difference ratios from Table 10.2a and applicable numerical values into the marginal-cost equation on a per-hour basis gives:

$$MC_{BRT-hour} = \$55.93(1) + \$2.14(30) + \$184,800\left(\frac{1}{6(254)}\right)$$
$$= \$241.0\ per\text{-}hour$$

Multiplying by the number of peak hours annually per vehicle and by the Fleet Size increase of seven then gives the annual cost estimate:

$$Annual\ Additional\ BRT\ Peak\ Cost = \$241.0[6(254)](7)$$
$$= \$2,570,000\ per\ year$$

F) What is the annual cost if single cars are added to each LRT train for six hours during the off-peak instead? What is the corresponding cost if BRT service is doubled during the off-peak instead?

Referring to Table 10.3b for LRT, the last term in the marginal-cost equation associated with Fleet Size can be dropped since the change in *Fleet Size* is now zero. The marginal cost becomes only $2.26 per car-kilometer. The additional cost is recomputed using this new value:

$$Annual\ Additional\ LRT\ Off\text{-}Peak\ Cost = \$2.26(30)(6)(254)(5)$$
$$= \$517,000\ per\ year$$

Referring to Table 10.2a for BRT, the last term can be dropped from its corresponding equation as well. The marginal cost is reduced to only $120.30 per vehicle-hour. The additional cost is recomputed using this new value:

$$Annual\ Additional\ BRT\ Off\text{-}Peak\ Cost = \$120.30(6)(254)(7)$$
$$= \$1,280,000\ per\ year$$

G) Make a table of headways, fleet sizes, and trunk-line capacities of both LRT and BRT for the following conditions: base service, doubling of capacity, tripling of capacity, adding a three-car train after all trains reach full length (LRT only), and adding three more buses (BRT only).

Trunk Line capacities can be computed using Equation 3-1:

$$Trunk\ Line\ Capacity = mC_v\ (60/h)\ \ [spaces/hour],$$

where C_v is the sum of both seated and standee capacity for the particular vehicle design. The computation is straightforward.

Service Condition		h (min)	N	Capacity (spaces/hour)
LRT				
	Base	15	5	744
	Double	15	10	1,488
	Triple	15	15	2,232
	Add three-car train	12.5	18	2,678
BRT				
	Base	10.6	7	679
	Double	5.3	14	1,358
	Triple	3.5	21	2,037
	Add three buses	3.1	24	2,334

Note that the LRT headway does not decrease until after all consists reach full length. The BRT headway decreases directly with each unit addition of capacity.

Other Route Costing Sources

Cost estimates based on hypothetical performance improvements using untested approaches or technologies are not as reliable as ones based on proven performance of existing systems. If untested improvements are the focus of the analysis, one must use the values provided by the designer or vendor, with appropriate consideration of the risk. Otherwise, if such improvements are only one small aspect of the project, one might want to use conservative (meaning higher rather than lower) estimates that are based on proven approaches or technologies.

If the project is an expansion, extension, speedup, or other modification to an existing public transportation network, output from a commercial scheduling software package using advanced operations research and optimization techniques may be available. These packages do not analyze routes only as separate lines; rather, they analyze an entire network simultaneously. They look:

- for opportunities to *interline* between routes to reduce layovers;
- to shift route assignments between depots to reduce deadheading;
- to relocate operator relief points to reduce unproductive time;
- for efficient transition plans between peak and non-peak services; and
- to change vehicle or train size and other measures to improve efficiency.

They also divide the scheduled service into efficient blocks of work to be performed by individual operators and then assign that work to particular individuals based on whatever scheme has been arranged between labor and management. Particularly with larger agencies, such programs are essential. Even small gains in efficiency can translate into large sums (e.g. millions of dollars or euros) in operating savings on an annual basis. But the permutations of possible changes are far too numerous for even an experienced scheduler to consider them all.

These programs provide very accurate average costs for existing routes. Analysts can readily adapt these estimates to routes having similar characteristics. Furthermore, such techniques generate marginal cost figures for adding service at particular times of the day on particular routes. These too can be adapted to particular projects.

Costs of Connecting Services

The costs of traveling on a network are additive with each link. Each term must therefore have a common basis for the results to make sense. But using a common basis can be problematic in practice. If the cost is per vehicle or per TU, the analyst must specify the particular type and size of the vehicle or unit. It should be clear that one link is using a minibus, the other a 40-foot (12-meter) long bus, or one a three-car consist, the other a six-car consist. To make comparisons more direct, costs are often normalized to a per-seat basis. This is an improvement, but it is still possible that even vehicles of similar size and design might have different numbers of seats, reflecting different levels of comfort and convenience. If standees are allowed, a per-space rather than a per-seat basis is required. An assumption about how much space to allow per person is needed, which again reflects differences in service standards. Thus, comparisons must include service standards (e.g. crowding levels) as well as cost. For this reason, the analyst should always make clear the assumptions about service standards and vehicle characteristics.

The previous examples pertained to the service offered and are independent of the service actually consumed. When the consumption of service by a passenger over the course of a trip is of interest, one passenger should be the unit of normalization. The analyst can use seats or spaces occupied instead of seats or spaces offered. This then gives a unit cost per passenger.

Formulas for average cost, marginal revenue, and marginal cost are presented here, assuming a two-link trip. Let Link 1 be the one being investigated and Link 2 a connecting service. The equations are readily extended to an n-link trip.

From an operator's perspective, the average cost of a trip, AC, on any unit basis, is just the sum of the two individual costs on each link:

$$AC_{unit} = AC_{unit1} + AC_{unit2} \qquad (10\text{-}18)$$

However, there is also a value to a passenger's travel time. If one is concerned only about the cost to the operator, this cost can be neglected. If the total cost is desired (i.e. the social cost), it includes both the user and the operator. A term that converts passenger travel time into a monetary cost must then be included:

$$AC_{passenger} = AC_{pass1} + AC_{pass2} + V(T_{O\text{-}D}), \qquad (10\text{-}19)$$

where V is the monetized value per unit of passenger travel time and $T_{O\text{-}D}$ the travel time from origin to final destination. For the reasons discussed in the section about potential sources of errors and misleading results in Chapter 7, I do not recommend using this third term in many types of cost-benefit analyses. To reiterate those reasons, use of this third term will tend to downplay all investments that benefit lower-income communities and shorter trips, and to enhance those for higher-income communities and longer trips.

An expression that includes value-of-time is valuable, however, for analyzing the trade-offs between operating cost and travel time for a range of assumed values-of-time. In some cases, $AC_{passenger}$ might increase with improved service and reduced travel times. In others, it might be the reverse. This was seen in the network analysis done by Lee discussed in Chapter 3. His analysis varied both the travel time and the value of passengers' time in order to investigate how network structure should be changed depending upon the relative magnitude of users' costs and operators' costs.

The Marginal Revenue (MR) on a per-passenger basis is simply the additional revenue provided by additional passengers. If one additional TU-hour attracts j additional passengers per hour, the MR is the sum of all the j additional fares collected on both links:

$$MR = \sum_j F_{1j} + \sum_j F_{2j}, \qquad (10\text{-}20)$$

where F_{1j} and F_{2j} are the fares collected, the first subscript refers to the link, and the second the individual passenger. If all passengers pay the same fare, or an average value is used for each link, the formula becomes:

$$MR = \Delta P_1 F_1 + \Delta P_2 F_2, \tag{10-21}$$

where ΔP_1 is additional passengers attracted per hour on link 1. ΔP_2 is the passenger increase for link 2. The formula on a per TU-distance basis would be similar, except that the additional passengers and the fares collected are expressed on a unit per-distance instead of per-hour basis.

Calculating the marginal cost of connections is not as conceptually straightforward as calculating MR. The very existence of a marginal cost depends on the perspective. Here are three sample perspectives:

1 If a service exists or will continue to exist, regardless of any analysis outcome, the monetary marginal cost to the operator of accommodating any additional user is virtually zero.
2 If a service's existence is in doubt, the marginal cost is non-zero and any monetary cost imposed on the operator for adding this service should be attributed only to the additional passengers it attracts.
3 If one is investigating the possible elimination of service, the cost should be attributed to those who would stop riding transit if the service should disappear.

For improved accuracy, the analyst should deduct any per-passenger cost reduction on the connecting link due to the sharing of the cost with more passengers. Or, for possible elimination of service, the analyst should add to the unit cost on the connecting link because fewer passengers will be riding the connector. This value may be very small in comparison, particularly if the connecting link is of high capacity, but this should not be assumed *a priori*. There can be situations where the connecting link has a comparatively high cost per passenger.

The marginal cost equation, including the correction for the deduction to average cost on the connecting link, can be formulated such that it uses commonly available information. It is developed from this defining expression:

$$MC_{passenger} = \frac{MC_{TU-hour1}}{\left(\dfrac{\Delta passengers}{TU-hour}\right)_1} - \frac{AC_{TU-hour2}}{\left(\dfrac{passengers+\Delta passengers}{TU-hour}\right)_2}. \quad [\$/\text{pass}] \tag{10-22}$$

This can be recast in a form convenient for the data usually available:

$$MC_{passenger} = \frac{MC_{TU-hour1}}{\left(\dfrac{P}{f}\right)_1\left(\dfrac{\Delta P}{P}\right)_1} - \frac{AC_{TU-hour2}}{\left(\dfrac{P}{f}\right)_2\left(1+\dfrac{\Delta P}{P}\right)_2}, \quad [\$/\text{pass}] \tag{10-23}$$

where f is the frequency before the addition of any service (or after the elimination of any service). $\Delta P/P$ is the ratio of new trips attracted after addition of service to the previously existing trips (or the ratio of reduced trips to remaining trips after the elimination of service).

Example 10.6

The rapid transit network described in Example 10.2 has an overcrowding problem on its longest line during the peak period. It carries 6,000 passengers per hour in one direction and 2,000 in the other with an average headway of 12 minutes using 10-car trains, each car having 125 spaces. It takes three hours to make a round trip, so one additional train uses six hours to make two round trips per day. Demand estimation procedures suggest that adding one more train in the peak hour will attract 20 percent more passengers, partly because of the improved frequency, but mostly because of the provision of more capacity. It connects with three other lines. They all use the average train size, carrying a combined total of 20,000 persons per hour in both directions and provide 24 connections per hour. About 75 percent of the newly attracted passengers on the long line will make a connection. The average fare paid is $3.20 based on a $0.26 per mile rate.

A) What are the marginal cost and marginal revenue estimates for a trip of average length? Assume that new equipment must be purchased and service will not be similarly increased in the off-peak hours.

Some preliminary computations for use in Equation 10.23 are:

$$\left(\frac{P}{f}\right)_1 = \frac{6000+2000}{5+5}, \quad \left(\frac{P}{f}\right)_2 = \frac{20000}{24}, \quad \left(\frac{\Delta P}{P}\right)_1 = 0.20, \quad \left(\frac{\Delta P}{P}\right)_2 = 0.75(0.20)$$

The 10-car train is to be used only to add frequency to the peak hours and can make only one round-trip during each peak period. Thus, using Table 10.3b, the marginal cost estimate will be:

$$MC_{10car-hour} = \$95.70 + \$1.29\left(\frac{10(5,932,000)}{167,800}\right) + \$226,000\left(\frac{10}{6(254)}\right)$$

$$= \$2034/train\text{-}hour$$

The fleet-wide average cost per TU-hour was not given in Example 10.2 but can be computed from the available data. First, compute the total annual operating cost, AC_o, using Equation 10-5:

$$AC_o = \$95.70(167,800) + \$1.29(43,853,000) + \$226,000(406)$$
$$= \$164,385,000/year$$

Then the fleet-wide average cost is found by dividing AC_o by total Train-Hours operated:

$$AC_{TU-hour} = \frac{AC_o}{TH} = \frac{\$164,385,000}{167,800} = \$980/TU\text{-}hour$$

Inserting all of these values into Equation 10-23, the hour-based marginal cost, gives:

$$MC_{pass} = \frac{\$2034}{\left(\dfrac{8000}{10}\right)(0.20)} - \frac{\$980}{\left(\dfrac{20000}{24}\right)(1+0.75(0.20))} = \$12.71 - \$1.02$$

$$= \$11.69/passenger$$

The marginal revenue per passenger is the sum of the revenue collected on both lines. The difference between marginal cost and marginal revenue is:

$$MC - MR = \$11.69 - \$3.20 = \$8.49/passenger$$

Because the average fare is $3.20 and the rate is $0.26 per mile, the average trip length must be 12.3 miles.

Note one serious deficiency with this hour-based estimator. There is no trip-length variable, making it only an estimate for an "average" trip. If a trip with specific characteristics is of interest, some information about trip-length distribution is also needed. If the space-averaged load factor, ξ, as was defined in Chapter 3 is available, the analyst can develop an estimate that prorates the marginal cost with trip length on each link. This is useful because it assigns the cost according to how much capacity a passenger consumes. *This is not the full cost that could be assigned if one argues that empty capacity must be carried on this passenger's account.* Whether this freed capacity can be turned over with other passengers or trimmed to match demand along the route or line depends on the specific situation. If it cannot, the full length of the line can be used instead of the actual distance traveled.

The development of a distance-based (using kms as an example) marginal cost equation starts from this defining expression:

$$MC_{passenger} = \frac{MC_{TU-km1}}{\left(\dfrac{\Delta pass-kms}{TU-kms}\right)_1} L_1 - \frac{AC_{TU-km2}}{\left(\dfrac{pass-kms+\Delta pass-kms}{TU-kms}\right)_2} L_2, \quad [\$/\text{pass}] \tag{10-24}$$

where L_1 is the distance traveled by a passenger on link 1, and L_2 is the distance traveled by the same passenger on Link 2. This can be recast in a form more convenient for the data usually available:

$$MC_{passenger} = \frac{MC_{TU-km1}}{\xi_1 m_1 C_v \left(\dfrac{\Delta pass - kms}{pass - kms} \right)_1} L_1 - \frac{AC_{TU-km2}}{\xi_2 m_2 C_v \left(1 + \dfrac{\Delta pass - kms}{pass - kms} \right)_2} L_2 \quad [\$/\text{pass}]$$

$$(10\text{-}25)$$

Example 10.6 (continued)

Better information is now available about the same situation. The two-way space-averaged load factor during the peak-hour for the long line is 0.28 pass-miles/space-miles, for the others it is 0.40 pass-miles/space-miles. (If these values seem low for a crowded service, recall that, in this service, only one-third as many passengers travel in the off-peak direction, meaning there will be spare capacity at the outer end even in the peak hour.)

B) What is the marginal-cost estimate for an average length trip if the increase in passenger-miles is 15 percent for the long line? (The percentage can be less than for simple passengers if many of the additional trips are short). The increase in passenger-miles is also expected to be 15 percent for the combination of the other three lines.

The marginal cost on a per-TU-mile basis can be easily computed by conversion from a per-hour basis:

$$MC_{10car-km} = \frac{MC_{10car-hour}}{v_{avg}} \frac{\$2,034/TU-hour}{35.4\,miles/hour} = \$57.46/TU - mile$$

The average cost on a per-TU-mile basis is also straightforward since AC_o is already computed:

$$AC_{7.4car-km} = \frac{\$164,385,000 \,/\, year}{5,932,000 \; TU - mile/year} = \$27.71 \,/\, TU - mile$$

Inserting the appropriate values into Equation 10-25 for marginal cost based on passenger-miles:

$$MC_{pass} = \frac{\$57.46}{0.28(10)(125)(0.15)} L_1 - \frac{\$27.71}{0.40(7.4)(125)(1+(0.15))} L_2 = \$1.09 L_1 - \$0.065 L_2$$

It was not specified how much of the trip was on the long line. If all of it is:

$$MC_{pass} = \$1.09 \,(12.4) - \$0.065 \,(0) = \$13.50/passenger$$

the difference between marginal cost and marginal revenue is then:

$$MC - MR = \$13.50 - \$3.20 = \$10.30/passenger$$

If instead, the trip involves 9.2 miles on the long line and 3.1 miles on one of the others, the difference is:

$$MC_{pass} = \$1.09 \ (9.2) - \$0.065 \ (3.1) = \$10.00 - \$0.20$$
$$= \$9.80/passenger$$

Note that the per-unit distance formula prorates the marginal cost to particular trips based on their total length and the fraction traveled on each link.

C) If the estimate for the increase in passenger-miles is now given as only 10 percent for the long line, what is the marginal cost estimate assuming 9.2 miles of travel on the long line and 3.1 miles on one of the others?

$$MC_{pass} = \frac{\$57.46}{0.28(10)(125)(0.10)}(9.2) - \$.065(5) = \$15.10 - \$0.20$$
$$= \$14.90/passenger$$

The smaller increase in passenger-miles drives up the cost attributed per passenger because the same additional increment of service is added, but less service is being consumed.

One more important observation will complete this example. It is usually possible to carry some short trips at the outer end of radial lines at virtually zero marginal cost because there is significant unused capacity. This can cause some confusion as to the point of these calculations. It must be remembered that the reason for the analysis is the crowding at the section close to the connection point. This is where passengers need to be accommodated.

The analyst must always consider the quality-of-service implications at the same time as the monetary implications. The analyst should be aware that the monetary costs act opposite to the nonmonetary costs perceived by the passengers. The extra service added on Link 1, while its creation is attributed to only the additional riders it attracts, in reality also relieves any overcrowding and improves frequency, thus benefiting other passengers as well. On the other hand, the connecting link will see additional riders without adding any frequency or capacity, thus contributing to increased crowding. The improved service to existing passengers might be an additional justification for adding service despite the expense. Conversely, contributing to overcrowding on connecting links might be a reason to postpone adding service.

Summary

The MC versus MR test indicates the financial impact of carrying one additional passenger. If MC is greater than MR, additional subsidy will be required. If MC equals MR, efficient pricing has been achieved. If MC is less than MR, then less subsidy is required, or in the case for-profit operations, profit is increased.

The costs generated and revenues collected by adding a unit of service can be estimated using marginal-cost and marginal-revenue concepts. Marginal cost is important for analyzing many situations, including optimization of Fleet Size, expansion of existing service, selecting modal technologies for new services, and others. Lower marginal costs can often justify higher capital investment costs.

Estimating formulas for both bus and train modes can be derived applying a finite difference approximation method to engineering cost models. Different formulae for each mode are necessary because trains, unlike buses, can vary in capacity without adding an operator. A range of estimates can be computed, one of the crucial factors being whether additional vehicles are available from the existing fleet or whether they must be purchased. If it is the latter, additional support facilities and staff will add to the operating cost. Furthermore, the fewer hours per day vehicles are used, the higher the marginal cost.

Estimates for the annual cost of operating a bus route or rail line can be developed with a formulation convenient for focusing on only the changed periods of the daily schedule. It is often only the change in cost due to service that is of interest to the analyst. The cost of operating a route or line is proportional to the fleet required, but this can change as the result of investments affecting operating speed and other performance aspects that might permit more efficient schedules. Therefore, whether the Fleet Size can be reduced is something that should be verified. It involves mutually satisfying three relationships:

1   The number of TUs assigned must be an integer, and its product when multiplied with headway must equal the cycle time.
2   The round trip travel time plus terminal times must also equal the cycle time.
3   Both terminal times must be greater than or equal to a minimum value.

If the project involves extension, expansion, speedup, or other modification to an existing service, the output from an advanced scheduling software package might be available. Such a program might be able to provide accurate annual average cost figures and marginal-cost estimates from the same route or line or from routes or lines having characteristics similar to the project. These might be usable with no or slight modification.

The analyst sometimes takes a look at a trip involving more than one route. Thus, formulas for investigating the cost of these linked trips were also developed. The average cost is straightforward because it is simply additive as long as both costs are expressed in the same units (e.g. per seat, per space, per passenger).

The marginal cost of adding service is more complicated, particularly on a per-passenger basis because it should be attributed to only the newly generated passengers, not to persons who may be on the vehicle and who would have been traveling in any case. Furthermore, a correction is required to average cost per passenger on the connecting link because any newly attracted passengers who also use an existing connecting service spread this cost over more users. Formulas can be used that deduct this saving from the marginal cost. The formulas can be recast to be usable with data in a form that agencies are likely to have available.

If only a simple passenger-per-hour statistic is available, the marginal cost estimate can be based on average trip length. If the space-averaged load factor is available, cost can be better prorated to a multilink trip having a specific travel length on each link.

Increasing service on one link to attract additional passengers adds expense for the operator, but it also improves frequency and adds capacity to the benefit of existing passengers as well. At the same time, it lowers the cost on the unchanged connecting link on a per-passenger basis by increasing the number of persons transferring to it, but it could also exacerbate any crowding to the detriment of the existing passengers.

Appendix 10.A

Derivation of Marginal Cost Estimates

Bus Costs

It is convenient to begin with some definitions. The system-wide average speed is given by:

$$\frac{total\ Bus\text{-}Distance}{total\ Bus\text{-}Hours} = v_{Tavg}, \quad (\text{Total basis}) \tag{10-26}$$

where the subscript T in v_{Tavg} is used to denote a calculation based on total values. Similarly:

$$\frac{revenue\ Bus\text{-}Distance}{revenue\ Bus\text{-}Hours} = v_{Ravg}, \quad (\text{Revenue basis}) \tag{10-27}$$

where the subscript R in v_{Ravg} denotes a calculation based on revenue values. The terminology v_{avg} will generally be used in further discussion. As with average costs, either total-hours and total-distance (includes deadhead moves) or revenue-hours and revenue-distance can be used, but the "total" and "revenue" distinctions are dropped with the understanding that once one or the other is selected, it will be used consistently.

The finite difference ratios needed to evaluate the marginal-cost equations will now be analyzed for a range of conditions.

Ratio I. Estimate Change in Bus-Distance with Change in Bus-Hours and Its Inverse

An average estimate, based on system-wide statistics, for the likely increase in Bus-Distance with an increase in Bus-Hours is:

$$\left[\frac{\Delta Bus\text{-}Distance}{\Delta Bus\text{-}Hours}\right]_{avg} = \frac{\text{total } Bus\text{-}Distance}{\text{total } Bus\text{-}Hours} = \frac{BD}{BH} = v_{Tavg}, \quad \text{(Total basis)}$$

(10-28)

where the nomenclature BD is introduced for more compact denotation of system-wide *Bus-Distance* and BH for *Bus-Hours*. The average estimate for the required increase in *Bus-Hours* with an increase in *Bus-Distance* is simply the inverse of the previous estimate:

$$\left[\frac{\Delta Bus\text{-}Hours}{\Delta Bus\text{-}Distance}\right]_{avg} = \frac{\text{total } Bus\text{-}Hours}{\text{total } Bus\text{-}Distance} = \frac{BH}{BD} = \frac{1}{v_{Tavg}} \quad \text{(Total basis)}$$

(10-29)

The average estimates for a specific route r can be improved by replacing BH and BD based on system-wide statistics with those for this specific route:

$$\left[\frac{\Delta Bus\text{-}Distance}{\Delta Bus\text{-}Hours}\right]_{r} = \frac{(Bus\text{-}Distance)_r}{(Bus\text{-}Hours)_r} = \frac{BD_r}{BH_r} = v_{avgr},$$

(10-30)

where the subscript r denotes only for route r. An estimate specific to a route r for the likely increase in Bus-Hours with an increase in Bus-Distance is simply the inverse of the previous estimate:

$$\left[\frac{\Delta Bus\text{-}Hours}{\Delta Bus\text{-}Distance}\right]_{avgr} = \frac{1}{v_{avgr}}$$

(10-31)

Averages should be used only where more detailed information is not available. If the proposed service is to be operated only during the peak periods, use v_{peak} instead. If it is to be operated during only the off-peak periods, use $v_{off\text{-}peak}$ instead.

To analyze further conditions, the initial expressions are first rewritten as:

$$\left[\frac{\Delta Bus\text{-}Distance}{\Delta Bus\text{-}Hours}\right]_{r} = \frac{\Delta bd_r}{\Delta bh_r},$$

(10-32)

and:

$$\left[\frac{\Delta Bus\text{-}Hours}{\Delta Bus\text{-}Distance} \right]_r = \frac{\Delta bh_r}{\Delta bd_r}, \tag{10-33}$$

where the more compact nomenclature Δbh_r denotes any additional bus-hours needed for the proposed service being investigated. Similarly, Δbd_r denotes the additional bus-distance needed. Both Δbh_r and Δbd_r must be determined under each case of interest.

Analysts often investigate service changes that require no change in an input resource. For example, a route can be extended (within limits) if terminal time is correspondingly shortened or operating speed increased; in either case, no increase in bus-hours is required. Since there is no difference in service hours, the numerator is zero. Expressed in mathematical terms:

$$\left[\frac{\Delta Bus\text{-}Hours}{\Delta Bus\text{-}Distance} \right] = \frac{0}{\Delta bd} = 0 \quad \text{if change has no impact on bus-hours.} \tag{10-34}$$

Ratio 2. Estimate Change in Fleet Size with Change in Bus-Hours

An average estimate, based on system-wide statistics, for the required increase in *Fleet Size* with increase in *Bus-Hours* is:

$$\left[\frac{\Delta Fleet\ Size}{\Delta Bus\text{-}Hours} \right]_{avg} = \frac{\text{peak }Fleet\ Size}{\text{total }Bus\text{-}Hours} = \frac{FS}{BH} \tag{10-35}$$

where the more compact nomenclature FS is introduced for system-wide peak *Fleet Size*. An average estimate specific to route r for the increase in *Fleet Size* with an increase in *Bus-Hours* is given by:

$$\left[\frac{\Delta Fleet\ Size}{\Delta Bus\text{-}Hours} \right]_r = \frac{(\text{peak }Fleet\ Size)_r}{(Bus\text{-}Hours)_r} = \frac{FS_r}{BH_r}, \tag{10-36}$$

where, as before, the subscript r denotes only for route r.

Averages should be used only when more detailed information is not available. To analyze other conditions, the initial expression is first rewritten as:

$$\left[\frac{\Delta Fleet\ Size}{\Delta Bus\text{-}Hours} \right]_r = \frac{\Delta fs_r}{\Delta bh_r}, \tag{10-37}$$

where, similar to previous terms, the more compact Δfs_r denotes any additional fleet required for a proposed service. Both Δfs_r and Δbh_r must be determined under the conditions of interest.

The increase in fleet size with increase in bus-hours is 0 if the peak fleet size does not need to be increased. This is usually the case for additional service in the off-peak periods. Expressed in mathematical terms:

$$\left[\frac{\Delta Fleet\ Size}{\Delta Bus\text{-}Hours}\right]_{off-peak} = \frac{0}{\Delta bh} = 0 \quad \text{if change has no impact on fleet size.} \quad (10\text{-}38)$$

A higher-range estimate based on the assumption that additional buses are acquired for use only X hours per day during peak periods is:

$$\left[\frac{\Delta Feet\ Size}{\Delta Bus\text{-}Hours}\right]_{pk} = \frac{1}{\left(X\dfrac{hours}{weekday}\right)\left(254\dfrac{weekdays}{year}\right)} \quad \text{for peak use only.} \quad (10\text{-}39)$$

Ratio 3. Estimate Change in Fleet Size with Change in Bus-Distance

An average estimate, based on system-wide statistics, for the required increase in *Fleet Size* with increase in *Bus-Distance* is:

$$\left[\frac{\Delta fleet\ size}{\Delta bus\text{-}kilometers}\right]_{avg} = \frac{peak\ fleet\ size}{total\ bus\text{-}kilometers} \quad \text{(Total basis)} \quad (10\text{-}40)$$

An average estimate specific to route r for the increase in *Fleet Size* required with an increase in *Bus-Distance* is given by:

$$\left[\frac{\Delta Fleet\ Size}{\Delta Bus\text{-}Distance}\right]_r = \frac{(peak\ Fleet\ Size)_r}{(Bus\text{-}Distance)_r} = \frac{FS_r}{BD_r}, \quad (10\text{-}41)$$

where the subscript r once again denotes statistics only for route r.

Averages should only be used when more detailed information is not available. To analyze other conditions, the initial expression is first rewritten with the more compact nomenclature:

$$\left[\frac{\Delta Fleet\ Size}{\Delta Bus\text{-}Distance}\right]_r = \frac{\Delta fs_r}{\Delta bd_r}. \quad (10\text{-}42)$$

As with previous ratios, these two values must be determined under each condition of interest.

The increase in fleet size with increase in *Bus-Distance* is 0 if the peak *Fleet Size* does not need to be increased. This is usually the case for additional service in the off-peak periods. Expressed in mathematical terms:

$$\left[\frac{\Delta Fleet\ Size}{\Delta Bus\text{-}Distance}\right]_{off-peak} = \frac{0}{\Delta bd} = 0 \text{ if change has no impact on fleet size.} \quad (10\text{-}43)$$

A higher-range estimate on the assumption that newly acquired buses are used for only X hours per day during peak periods is:

$$\left[\frac{\Delta Fleet\ Size}{\Delta Bus\text{-}Distance}\right]_{pk} = \frac{1}{v_{peak}\left(X\ \dfrac{hours}{weekday}\right)\left(254\ \dfrac{weekdays}{year}\right)} \quad \text{for peak use only.} \quad (10\text{-}44)$$

Train Costs

The finite difference ratios needed to evaluate the marginal cost equations will now be analyzed for a range of conditions.

Ratio 1. Estimate Change in Car-Distance with Change in Train-Hours and Its Inverse

An average estimate, based on statistics, for the likely increase in *Car-Distance* from an increase in *Train-Hours* is:

$$\left[\frac{\Delta Car\text{-}Distance}{\Delta Train\text{-}Hours}\right]_{avg} = \frac{total\ Car\text{-}Distance}{total\ Train\text{-}Hours} = m_{avg}\ v_{Tavg}, \quad \text{(Total basis)} \quad (10\text{-}45)$$

where *CD*, *TD*, and *TH* are introduced to more compactly denote system-wide *Car-Distance*, *Train-Distance*, and *Train-Hours*. An average estimate for the likely increase in *Train-Hours* from an increase in *Car-Distance* is simply the inverse:

$$\left[\frac{\Delta Train\text{-}Hours}{\Delta Car\text{-}Distance}\right]_{avg} = \frac{TH}{m_{avg} TD} = \frac{1}{m_{avg}\ v_{avg}}. \quad (10\text{-}46)$$

An average estimate for a specific rail line r can be improved by replacing Train-Hours and Car-Distance based on system-wide statistics with those for this specific line:

$$\left[\frac{\Delta Car\text{-}Distance}{\Delta Train\text{-}Hours}\right]_{r} = \frac{m_r (Train\text{-}Distance)_r}{(Train\text{-}Hours)_r} = \frac{mTD_r}{TH_r} = m_r v_r, \quad (10\text{-}47)$$

where, as before, the subscript r denotes only for route r. Similarly:

$$\left[\frac{\Delta Train\text{-}Tours}{\Delta Car\text{-}Distance}\right]_{r} = \frac{1}{m_r v_r}. \quad (10\text{-}48)$$

As with buses, averages should be used only when more detailed information is not available. If the proposed service is only to be operated during the peak periods, use v_{peak} instead. If it is to be operated only during the off-peak periods, use $v_{off\text{-}peak}$ instead.

To facilitate analyzing other conditions, the initial expressions are first rewritten as:

$$\left[\frac{\Delta Car\text{-}Distance}{\Delta Train\text{-}Hours} \right]_r = \frac{\Delta cd_r}{\Delta th_r}, \tag{10-49}$$

and:

$$\left[\frac{\Delta Train\text{-}Hours}{\Delta Car\text{-}Distance} \right]_r = \frac{\Delta th_r}{\Delta cd_r}, \tag{10-50}$$

where again the more compact Δth_r denotes any additional train-hours for the proposed service being investigated and Δcd_r denotes the additional car-distance. Similar to buses, these two values must be determined under each condition of interest.

As with buses, analysts often investigate service increases that require no increase in one or more of the resource inputs. For example, a rail line can be extended (within limits) if terminal time is shortened to compensate or if operating speed is increased, in either case, with no increase in train-hours. Expressed mathematically:

$$\left[\frac{\Delta Train\text{-}Hours}{\Delta Car\text{-}Distance} \right]_r = \frac{0}{\Delta cd_r} = 0 \quad \text{if change doesn't affect train hours.} \tag{10-51}$$

Furthermore, unlike buses, car-distance can increase without an increase in train-hours by adding cars to trains instead of adding trains. Expressed mathematically for an increase in consist size by Δm cars:

$$\left[\frac{\Delta Train\text{-}Hours}{\Delta Car\text{-}Distance} \right]_{\Delta m} = \frac{\Delta th}{\Delta cd} = \frac{0}{\Delta cd} = 0 \quad \text{if cars are only added to existing trains.} \tag{10-52}$$

This result holds true for both peak and off-peak conditions. On the other hand, the inverse is not zero, as *Car-Distance* must always increase with *Train-Hours* (unless, of course, the number of train cars is reduced). Expressed mathematically:

$$\left[\frac{\Delta Car\text{-}Distance}{\Delta Train\text{-}Distance} \right]_{\Delta m} = \frac{\Delta cd}{\Delta th} = \frac{\Delta m \Delta td}{\Delta th} = \Delta mv. \tag{10-53}$$

If the proposed service is to be operated only during the peak periods, use v_{peak}. If it is to be operated only during the off-peak periods, use $v_{off\text{-}peak}$ instead.

An analyst must use caution when interpreting the difference ratios for a change involving Δm cars. When calculating on a per train-hour basis, the "change" refers to distinguishing those train-hours where the Δm cars are added from those where they are not.

Ratio 2. Estimate Change in Fleet Size with Change in Train-Hours

An average estimate, based on system-wide statistics, for the required increase in *Fleet Size* with increase in *Train-Hours*, is:

$$\left[\frac{\Delta Fleet\ Size}{\Delta Train\text{-}Hours} \right]_{avg} = \frac{\text{peak } Fleet\ Size}{\text{total } Train\text{-}Hours} = \frac{FS}{TH} \quad \text{(Total basis)} \qquad (10\text{-}54)$$

where the compact notation FS is again introduced to denote system-wide peak *Fleet Size*. An average estimate specific to line r for the required increase in *Fleet Size* with an increase in *Train-Hours* is given by:

$$\left[\frac{\Delta Fleet\ Size}{\Delta Train\text{-}Hours} \right]_{r} = \frac{(\text{peak } Fleet\ Size)_{r}}{(Cars\text{-}Hours)_{r} / m_{r}} = \frac{FS_{r}}{TH_{r}}, \qquad (10\text{-}55)$$

where the subscript r denotes only for line r. Again, averages should only be used when more detailed information is not available.

To analyze further conditions, the initial expression is rewritten as:

$$\left[\frac{\Delta Fleet\ Size}{\Delta Train\text{-}Hours} \right] = \frac{\Delta fs_{r}}{\Delta th_{r}}, \qquad (10\text{-}56)$$

where Δfs_{r} denotes the increase in Fleet Size required to support the proposed service increase on line r. As with the other difference ratios, the values of the numerator and denominator must be determined under each condition of interest.

The increase in fleet size with increase in train-hours is zero if the peak Fleet Size is unchanged. This is usually the case when service is added in off-peak periods. Expressed in mathematical terms:

$$\left[\frac{\Delta Fleet\ Size}{\Delta Train\text{-}Hours} \right]_{off-peak} = \frac{0}{\Delta th} = 0 \quad \text{if change doesn't affect fleet size.} \qquad (10\text{-}57)$$

This result holds true whether complete m-car trains are added, or Δm cars are added to an existing consist. A higher-range estimate based on acquiring a complete m-car train for use X hours per day during peak periods, is:

$$\left[\frac{\Delta Fleet\ Size}{\Delta Train\text{-}Hours}\right]_{peak} = \frac{m}{\left(X\dfrac{hours}{day}\right)\left(254\dfrac{days}{year}\right)} \qquad \text{using m-car train only X hours per day.}$$

$$(10\text{-}58)$$

If the existing trains are below their maximum consist length, and Δm cars are added to one of these instead, then:

$$\left[\frac{\Delta Fleet\ Size}{\Delta Train\text{-}Hours}\right]_{\Delta m} = \frac{\Delta m}{\left(X\dfrac{hours}{day}\right)\left(254\dfrac{days}{year}\right)} \qquad \text{if lengthened for X hours per day.}$$

$$(10\text{-}59)$$

As before, some caution is required in interpreting the difference ratios for a change involving Δm cars. When calculating on a per train-hour basis, the "change" refers to distinguishing those train-hours where Δm cars are added from those where they are not.

Ratio 3. Estimate Change in Fleet Size with Change in Car-Distance

An average estimate, based on system-wide statistics, for the required increase in *Fleet Size* with increase in *Car-Distance*, is:

$$\left[\frac{\Delta Fleet\ Size}{\Delta Car\text{-}Distance}\right]_{avg} = \frac{\text{Peak } Fleet\ Size}{Car\text{-}Distance} = \frac{FS}{CD}.$$

$$(10\text{-}60)$$

Once again, system averages should be used only when more detailed information is not available. An average estimate for line r only for the required increase in *Fleet Size* with an increase in *Car-Distance* is given by:

$$\left[\frac{\Delta Fleet\ Size}{\Delta Car\text{-}Kilometers}\right]_{r} = \frac{(\text{Peak } Fleet\ Size)_{r}}{(Car\text{-}Distance)_{r}} = \frac{FS_{r}}{CD_{r}},$$

$$(10\text{-}61)$$

where once again the subscript r denotes specific to line r.

To analyze further conditions, the initial expression is rewritten using more general nomenclature:

$$\left[\frac{\Delta Fleet\ Size}{\Delta Car\text{-}Distance}\right]_{r} = \frac{\Delta fs_{r}}{\Delta cd_{r}}.$$

$$(10\text{-}62)$$

As with previous ratios, the values of the numerator and denominator must be determined under each condition of interest.

The increase in *Fleet Size* with increase in *Car-Distance* is zero if the peak *Fleet Size* is unchanged. Again, this is usually the case when service is added in off-peak periods. Expressed in mathematical terms:

$$\left[\frac{\Delta Fleet\ Size}{\Delta Car\text{-}Distance}\right]_{off-peak} = \frac{0}{\Delta cd} = 0 \quad \text{if change doesn't affect peak fleet size.}$$

(10-63)

This result holds true whether complete m-car trains are added, or Δm cars are added to an existing consist. A higher-range estimate for the same ratio, assuming the newly acquired rolling stock is used for only X hours per day during peak periods, is:

$$\left[\frac{\Delta Fleet\ Size}{\Delta Car\text{-}Distance}\right]_{peak} = \frac{1}{v_{peak}\left(X\ \dfrac{hours}{weekday}\right)\left(254\ \dfrac{weekdays}{year}\right)} \quad \text{if used only X hours per day.}$$

(10-64)

This result also holds true whether complete m-car trains are added or Δm cars are added to an existing consist.

Note

1 Part of this chapter is based on previously published material from *Transportation Research Record* 1927 (2005): Table 3, p. 15; Table 4, p. 17, text sections, pp. 14, 16, 18, 19. © 2005 by Transportation Research Board. Reprinted by permission.

References

Bruun, Eric. 2005. "Bus Rapid Transit and Light Rail: Comparing Operating Costs with a Parametric Cost Model." *Transportation Research Record* 1927: 10–20.
Bruun, Eric, Vukan Vuchic and Yong-Eun Shin. 1999. "Time-Distance Diagrams: A Powerful Tool for Service Planning and Control." *Journal of Public Transportation* 2 (2): 1–24.

Further Reading

Ceder, Avishai. 2007. *Public Transit Systems Planning and Operations*. Oxford, UK: Elsevier.
———. 2003. "Public Transport Timetabling and Vehicle Scheduling." Chapter 2 in *Advanced Modeling for Transport Operations and Service Planning*, edited by William H. K. Lam and Michael G. H. Bell. Bingley, UK: Emerald, 31–58.
Friedrich, Rainer, and Peter Bickel. 2001. "Marginal Costs." Chapter 13 in *Environmental External Costs of Transport*. New York: Springer-Verlag, 169–91.
Poehl, Joern. 2002. "Scheduling." Chapter 6 in *Railway Operations and Control*. Mountlake Terrace, WA: VTD Railway Publishing.
Vuchic, Vukan. 2005. "Transit Operations and Service Scheduling." Chapter 1 in *Urban Transit: Operations, Planning and Economic*. Hoboken, NJ: Wiley, 3–77.

Chapter 11

Organizational Structures and Contract Models

The organization of public transportation planning, financing, management, and delivery has implications for the evaluation of its performance and for evaluation of any investment. Organizational structures can vary in the institutional incentives they entail and in the appropriate measures for evaluation. They also vary widely in the latitude they provide planners towards meeting particular goals. Furthermore, partial or total reorganization of public transport can be a possible substitute for investments, particularly if the primary goal is making existing services more efficient. Therefore, there may be cases where reorganization could be posed as a project alternative in lieu of capital investment.

Public versus Privately Owned Firms

There is a spectrum of organizational possibilities, with public versus private ownership being a fundamental distinction. One obvious difference between private and public firms is that private firms expect a profit, which means that private firms have higher Minimum Allowable Rates of Returns. The two classes of firms are also subject to different rules regarding taxation and financing, but the differences can go much further.

Privately owned or operated systems will perceive a different set of goals than will publicly owned ones. As a result, they will respond to different incentives and disincentives and will use different measures and criteria to evaluate themselves. In situations where there are public goals to be executed through a private entity, analysts should identify any and all incentives and disincentives because an organization is unlikely to do anything to hurt its own self-interest.

Just because an organization is "publicly" controlled, it does not automatically follow that it will behave in the public interest. It may be either incapable or unwilling to assist in the achievement of even officially stated public policy. It may have such limited funding that it would be impossible to comply with a new policy. There can even be conflicting mandates (e.g. to both simultaneously maximize ridership and minimize public subsidy).

A public organization may even have a board of directors or management that feels immune from outside influence. In extreme cases, the extent of public control, either directly or through elected representatives, could be virtually nonexistent. In his biography of Robert Moses, Robert Caro (1975) describes how Moses managed to construct an empire of ostensibly public authorities in both New York City and New York State. Beginning shortly after World War II, for decades, not one single mile of rail transit was completed in New York City. Meanwhile, hundreds of miles of freeways and auto tunnels were built. Such an outcome would have been extremely unlikely with genuine public participation. To the extent it existed, public involvement was in the form of resistance.

In modern times, it is increasingly common to have a substantial redistribution of traditional responsibilities between public and private organizations to set the stage for a successful project. This might include a redistribution of capital funding and revenue streams. Indeed, an entire project could hinge on private funding sources. As an example, if the completed project were to create significant added monetary value to nearby landowners, it might be financially linked to nearby private investment so that some of this value can to be recaptured as a funding source. Another example would be that the private operating firm invests in improved vehicles and Intelligent Transportation System technology, while the public agency invests in complementary infrastructure.

Typology of Organizational, Financial, and Regulatory Structures

The following are intended only as helpful categorizations. There is, in reality, a spectrum of possibilities that might include something in between.

Unlicensed, Unregulated, and Unsupported Private Operations

Unlicensed, unregulated, and unsupported private operations are literally laissez faire approaches in which public transport is offered only in a manner analogous to a farmer's market. There is no preset level of service, being based strictly on the immediate market judgments and financial abilities of any entity interested in providing service. Nor is there any preset fare structure, the fares being based strictly on the judgment of the provider. This type of system is generally seen where the government is very weak. The government is either incapable of regulation or disinterested because regulation has costs and requires enforcement.

Such operations are typically seen in low-income nations, but they can also be seen in fast-growing fringe areas near cities with more formal public transport organizations. An example is the Mexico City region, where millions live in fringe cities to which the metro lines have not yet been extended. Service by thousands of unregulated minibuses and midibuses is a market response to unmet mobility needs.

Licensed but Unsupported Private Operations

Licensing is the first step government can take when it decides disorder is excessive, perhaps even chaotic. The licensing is intended to either limit the number of operators, to impose some standards upon them, or both. The revenue from license fees also provides the means for enforcement.

Because there is no financial incentive to comply beyond the ability to remain in business, regulators are likely to exert minimal influence on the service provider. Furthermore, attempts to impose significant costs upon operators are sometimes met with resistance. It could perhaps even cause political unrest if the costs translate into higher fares for passengers or monetary losses for operators.

Such problems commonly occur in developing nations. The only example in the developed nations is the United Kingdom, outside of the London metropolitan region. Buses were deregulated by the central government in 1986. The government would allow a few limited services to be deemed socially vital by local governments and consequently eligible to receive public support. Such routes were usually rural or for the elderly and disabled. The vast majority was truly unsupported and minimally licensed operations (e.g. limited to driver standards, insurance requirements, and vehicle condition.)

Licensed and Publicly Supported Private Operations

Public financial support can have impacts across the whole planning and operating environment. It might raise the income of persons involved in service provision, cause the quality and condition of vehicles to improve, and cause the numbers of vehicles in operation to change dramatically. It may also lead to tiers of operators, with some remaining underground and foregoing any support.

There may still be wide latitude remaining for operating firms to select their own routes and schedules, but once financial support is provided, some measure of control of the operation is usually expected in return. This might mean monitoring of service volumes to ensure the public money is going into the expected service and not simply being consumed in corruption or excess profit. It might also mean the imposition of crowding limits to improve safety and the quality of service given to passengers. It might also require that service hours be expanded to guarantee that service is provided at times when it is not profitable.

Publicly Planned and Supported Private Operations

The planning of routes and schedules are probably the single most significant organizational distinction that can be made between public and private systems. The nature and stability of the service a community receives can be profoundly different depending upon whether the selection of services is made by a public agency or private firm. When these are publicly planned, private operators primarily play the role of deliverers of service. Their competitive nature then focuses on being awarded what they judge to be the most lucrative routes and/or on efficient operations to control costs. This is the dominant model in South America.

This structure places the responsibility for meeting the travel needs of the riding public squarely on the planning authority and, in turn, on those who set the planning agency's priorities and budget. The question of how much public support to provide usually has to be answered on a case-specific basis. It might well be that a private firm is willing to operate one route at what the planners deem an acceptable level of service, based only on the fare revenues that can be generated. For other routes, the public support may have to be substantial. Routes can be bundled such that operators have a set of routes with a range of cost recovery potential.

Bundling might even be an imperative for complicated rail networks. Otherwise, there would be too many conflicts over use of joint sections of track, as evidenced by the early days of the UK rail privatization. There were numerous technical problems with the "bid and offer" method of allocating service slots because the software and bureaucratic procedures required to investigate the downstream and upstream consequences of any particular allocation were not adequate (Watson 2001). Although the initial technical problems were overcome, the fact still remains that capacity needs to be distributed in a systematic and repeating fashion between routes for the convenience of passengers and for equity between communities on different lines. Furthermore, as a consequence of these scheduling constraints, the possibilities for direct "on-rail" competition of more than one firm providing service between identical Origin–Destination Pairs will probably always be limited (Shaw 2001).

Publicly Planned, Supported, and Operated Network

A publicly planned, supported, and operated network is the predominant model in most of North America and the Cold-War-era Eastern European countries, and until recently, most of the European Union countries as well. This is akin to a public monopoly in electricity or water. Usually, no private operator can create potentially competing services without permission. Even other governmental units that have also established fully public systems in surrounding jurisdictions may still require intergovernmental agreements just to cross into another's territory.

An argument in favor of such an arrangement is that services had to be coordinated in order to maximize the benefits from major investments in multimodal public transport systems. But it is also prevalent at simpler systems having only one or two modes.

This arrangement is often an historical legacy of public takeovers of private systems that were no longer financially viable, especially in North America during the 1960s and early 1970s. Preserving the system often meant a complete and rapid transfer, without the practical possibility of finding private operators for parts of the system. New financial, legal, and organizational arrangements involving private firms could not be developed and stabilized. Even decades after public takeovers, there is still a widespread assumption that history would just repeat itself in the financial failure of the next private firm if operational responsibility was given back to private firms.

Organizational Structure of Authorities Responsible for Public Transportation

An organization with the legal task of implementing public transportation policies is not necessarily the same one that will deliver the service. The tasks it actually performs may be more limited. It might use internal contracts with its own operating division(s), or it might delegate actual service provision using external contracts. In either case, the responsible organization must balance conflicting objectives when developing its contracts, as shown in Figure 11.1. Authorities are organized using one of several basic structures, as discussed in the following sections.

Service Allocation and Operation by a Local Authority

When a local authority allocates and operates service for a transit system, one public agency takes the responsibility for the provision of all service as well as the design of all routes and schedules. Its domain is most likely restricted to the same geographic boundaries as all other public services provided by the local government. This agency may be organized simply as one more division of the

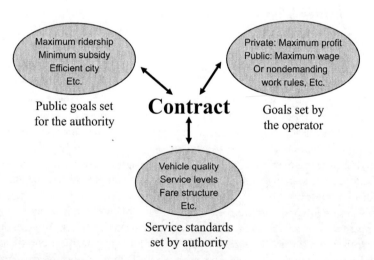

Figure 11.1 The balancing act facing the public authority.

Source: Ringqvist 2001.

government or as a publicly owned corporation with an independent board providing oversight and direction.

Service Allocation and Operation by a Region-Wide Authority

When services will be operated by a region-wide authority, one public agency still takes the responsibility for the provision of all service as well as the design of all routes and schedules. Furthermore, it decides the basis for allocation of service throughout a region consisting of many jurisdictions. It may have internal allocation rules that could reflect equity considerations or a mission/vision statement that it uses to rank the goals it is trying to meet with its network of services. But it may also be subject to whims of directors or elected officials, or even of its own employees.

Coordinating and sharing services between local jurisdictions depends upon the often difficult and unwieldy joint cooperation of numerous units of governments. A region-wide authority is intended as an alternative solution for organizing a public transport system to meet regional needs that do not respect local political boundaries. At the same time, it can create a new problem: the service is not necessarily accountable to local governments and individual neighborhoods. Moreover, it can lead to the provision of a "plain vanilla" brand of service that is uniform across the service area instead of reflective of particular characteristics and needs of subregions.

Municipal Contracts with a Region-Wide Authority

When municipalities contract with a regional authority, one public agency again takes the responsibility for the provision of all service and the design of routes and schedules. But the allocation of service is decided at least partially on the basis of contributions from local governments. In a variation of the model, a *service district* that consists of all or part of several municipalities allocates service according to a formula based on population, usage, financial contributions or some combination of these.

This structure may make the region-wide authority more accountable to its subregions. It also guarantees a degree of equity because subregions are likely to get service proportional to their contributions. On the other hand, regional goals may not be best served by equity. Some areas may call for disproportionate service due to mitigate higher costs or to deliver greater benefits. For example, a less wealthy service district may not be able to contribute an adequate amount of money for services to cover all its population. Such an area is likely to have a concentration of passengers highly dependent upon public transport. As another example, a central business district typically has slower travel speeds due to congestion and heavier volumes of boarding and alighting, and consequently its operating costs are higher as are its service needs. It simply must receive a disproportionate share of service for the network to function effectively.

Implementing a set of municipal contracts may be problematic. It is not realistic, for instance, to have a route that connects two towns but that operates express through a town that has not opted to participate in the service. Nor is it realistic if the most centrally located municipalities with the most popular origins and destinations decline to participate. However, there is at least one way to address outlying nonparticipants. In the Helsinki metro area, persons living in such a municipality must pay a higher price for a pass to compensate for lack of tax contribution by their local government. This type of solution can only work where there is a legal requirement to register one's address as a condition of getting a reduced-rate pass. This approach has the merit of making transparent the connection between taxes and services rendered.

Contracting Models for Operations and Maintenance

Gross Contract Models

Gross contract models are planned and administered by a public agency separate from both public and private operating entities. The public subsidy is set through competitive proposals to operate the services. The winning operator commits to a specific level of service by time of day and by route, complying with minimum reliability and quality standards. The revenues collected are in no way connected to the amount paid to the operator. The primary incentive to the operator is to cut costs to the extent possible without jeopardizing service quality to the point of contract renewal. A contract could even be cancelled in the middle of its term when there is egregious underperformance.

While the positive side from the funding agency's perspective is the strong incentive for cost control in order to maximize profit, the negative side is the lack of an incentive to either improve service or attract additional passengers. Operation of a service under such a model may result in work rule changes and wage concessions for the service to remain competitive. From labor's perspective, the cost control may well seem to come primarily at their expense.

Such a situation can also turn into a negative from the public authority's perspective if it leads to high employee turnover rates. When the turnover becomes high enough, quality of service suffers and some service may never be delivered. It is not necessary to do formal research to notice high turnover environments. A sufficiently large number of cancelled runs on any particular route would quickly manifest itself in numerous complaints from the riding public. It is also apparent from advertising campaigns. For example, casual observation in London shows large numbers of buses adorned with signs continually recruiting more drivers. When high turnover persists, it suggests that gross contracts may need to be modified into what is known as a *composite contract model* in order to specify minimum wage levels. There is more discussion about composite models below.

Net Contract Models

A separate public agency is typically in charge of net contracting. But this model provides public subsidy calculated to be sufficient only to guarantee a minimum level of service with the remainder of financial support coming from operating revenues. The combined subsidy and revenues must generate a profit great enough to attract a willing operator. It shifts some of the responsibility for the overall financial (and ridership) performance from the public authority to the private sector. In this model, the contract operator has an incentive to deliver higher-quality service to maintain ridership and revenue, and to perhaps even innovate in order to attract yet more ridership.

While the positive side from the public authority's perspective is the strong incentive for the operator to participate in the creation of additional ridership, the negative side is the potential loss of control. Once the contract terms are set, the operator may find ways to improve profitability other than the service improvements envisioned by the public authority. For example, a contractor might simply create an austere, minimal, but highly profitable service. It is a balancing act because too little latitude will constrain the ability of the contractor to innovate in the attempt to attract passengers.

Composite Contracting Models

As Figure 11.2 shows, the gross and net contract models reflect differing degrees of public influence and levels of integration of public transport. The experience in Sweden with privatization engendered the development of models that can capture some of the positive aspects of each. For example, the gross contract model can have a "quality bonus" based upon a periodic, structured survey of customers. The bonuses in Sweden have ranged from 2 percent to 5 percent of the gross amount (Ringqvist 2001). Another way of integrating the two approaches is to add a percentage of revenues collected to the gross amount paid in the contract because this bonus creates an incentive to increase ridership. Or consider Sao Paolo, Brazil. It creates greater latitude for the operator but still allows a high degree of public control by requiring customer polling before any change. "Operators can add, delete or modify service offerings as long as it meets with public approval via the polling mechanism" (ITSP 1999). Contracts may also be modified with minimum wage requirements to reduce staff turnover or to raise the minimum level of staff training. Experimentation worldwide is ongoing. The analyst needs to stay abreast of trends to identify relevant best practices. The effectiveness of the contracting model one chooses will depend on the flexibility the service authority can give to contractors given the local situation.

Figure 11.2 also shows the situations of concessions and total deregulation that, except in the case of the United Kingdom, are rare in the richer countries. Concessions are usually granted when the government is not funding public transport but is still trying to maintain some control over the volume of vehicles

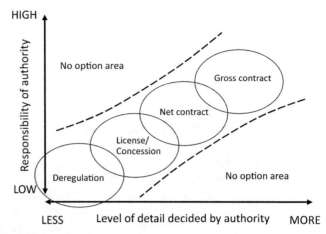

Figure 11.2 Different operating contract regimes.

Source: Ringqvist 2010.

serving particular streets and districts. There is little evidence of public satisfaction with transit in deregulated environments, so deregulation is usually just a default, or *de facto*, result when the government is either unwilling or unable to control public services or the streets.

Contracting Models for Capital Projects

What follows is a description of some of the most common models. In practice, there is a spectrum of models in use, to suit particular situations.

Traditional Model—Separation of Project Phases

Historically, the most popular way to conduct projects requiring major capital investments in physical construction of machinery and infrastructure is to separate the project into phases. The first phase, basic design and specification, is performed by the first party, who is also providing the funding. Next, proposals are accepted and a contract is awarded to a second party for the physical implementation. A third party may also be involved as the public's representative for oversight during implementation.

The historical reasons for phasing are several. One key reason is that the expertise to develop a system to meet a variety of societal goals is different than the expertise to manage manufacturing and construction. Another key reason is to remove conflicts of interest. The total value of the design and specification portion of a project is usually a small fraction of the physical construction and manufacturing portions.

Thus, designers could be tempted to use more capital-intensive approaches if their company is involved in later phases. Yet another key reason is so that the funding authority(s) are able to control the progress of the project, an important consideration for what are often high-profile, publicly scrutinized endeavors.

Design–Build Model

The Design–Build model combines the two phases. The firm that does the design also does the construction and equipment procurement. Having the firm who does the design also do the construction creates certain synergies. For instance, the firm can design for its' own construction practices, and the firm can optimize the project phasing based on its internal resources rather than having to respond to an externally imposed schedule; such efficiency might reduce costs. Furthermore, designers and constructors from different firms will often debate the practicality and wisdom of particular design solutions, possibly causing project delays and cost overruns. Thus, Design–Build removes delays due to the need for negotiation and the threat of litigation about change orders and scope-of-work changes; these disputes are instead settled internally between the prime contractor's own internal divisions and its subcontractors.

From the funding agency's perspective, the Design–Build model shifts much of the project cost risk and completion date risk to a *turnkey* provider, meaning that one firm is responsible for "handing over the keys" to a finished product. The contract can provide bonuses for early completion and penalties for late completion as well as financial rewards for completion under budget. The benefits of this approach are increasingly seen to outweigh the disadvantages. This model has been used with success in Asia for decades (ITSP 2002).

Design–Build–Operate–Maintain Model

The Design–Build–Operate–Maintain (DBOM) model extends a single firm's responsibility into the operational phase. If a firm's long-term profitability is going to be based upon efficient, low-cost operation for many years and not just on the construction phase, it will strive to design the capital features to support it. A firm will try to minimize the life-cycle cost of an investment rather than deal with the capital and operating costs separately.

The DBOM model is not suitable for extensions to existing rail lines or to highly integrated networks because the particular completed project cannot be operated in isolation from the existing services or infrastructure.

The DBOM model should not be confused with an organizational structure that requires no public financial support. The case of the Bangkok Skytrain, a rapid-transit line that opened in 1999, is illustrative. It was initially more precisely a "finance plus DBOM" project where both capital investment and operating expenses were supposed to be repaid entirely through fare revenues collected. As a result, the fares were set too high for the majority of commuters and capacity.

From the public authority's perspective, paying no public subsidy was central, but from the riding public's perspective, the public authority did not fully support what should no doubt be central goals of their first rapid transit line: congestion reduction and provision of increased travel options to escape the congestion. In retrospect, Bangkok should have considered using a gross contract or composite contract model in order to reduce fares at the outset; this might have eliminated the need for later reorganization (Maryon 2004).

Build–Operate–Transfer Model

As its name implies, in the Build–Operate–Transfer (BOT) model, the construction firm operates the system for an interim period, at which time it reverts to public ownership and operation. If the period before transfer to the public authority is lengthy, there is little difference from a DBOM model. If it is only for a few years, BOT functions as a training mechanism. It can provide for administrative, supervisory, operating, maintenance, and repair training. This can add a second class of potential benefits from a major investment project—the technology transfer brings skills applicable to other parts of the economy to local workers.

Issues When Considering Appropriate Organizational Structures and Contract Models

There are some generalizations that can be made about deciding which organization and structure and contract model to use, but as always, there will be exceptions.

Arguments for and against Change

One reason for switching organizational structures is simply to break up existing relationships, be they public or private. The details of the new arrangements are not as important as the fact that new institutions are involved. Existing organizations may have evolved in a way that makes them less responsive to public-transport-related project goals. They may be politically influenced in their employment practices or directing contracts to favored vendors. In such cases, investment funds will not provide as much benefit as the public has the right to expect. In some extreme cases, it may deliver no product at all. Some researchers have concluded that total reorganization is virtually a prerequisite to making progress in some situations. See, for example, the analysis of public transport in India's cities by Pucher et al. (2004) and by Russell and Anjum (1997) about transport in cities in Pakistan. As an example of how total reorganization might bring success, see also the companion article by Anjum and Russell (1997) about a successful reorganization into an NGO that regulates service in Faisalabad, Pakistan, in a manner similar to a cooperative. This system is called Faisalabad Urban Transport System and all vehicles that belong carry its logo. It remains in operation as of this writing.

Cultural traditions, preexisting infrastructure, the financial state of the region and nation, and the political power of those who would be affected will all influence public investment policy. Whatever contract model(s) the authority uses should reflect these realities. For example, if cost reduction is more important than diverting auto users by providing a more attractive service, a net contract model might be sufficient. Or, if a key public goal is to rationalize services from several providers in order to increase public transport use through the creation of a multimodal network, the authority should use something closer to a gross contract model. Otherwise, there would be little incentive for operators to participate in timetable coordination and the joint-fare structures needed to optimize a network.

The nature of a large project is such that the full array of public goals cannot be made to fully align with those of a private firm contracted to carry out the project. By dividing the project into smaller packages for different contractors, private firms can be made to focus on those aspects where their goals and the goals of the public authority align. As an example, if a new terminal is intended to be a source of civic pride, perhaps a Design–Build competition should be held on the basis of cost versus aesthetic quality. If instead the project were to be a DBOM contract for the next 30 years, the competing private firms would likely all propose more austere, less-appealing facilities designed for minimal operating and maintenance costs.

The details of the contract can have unintended consequences. If the payment is expressed as a rate per-unit-distance of service delivered (e.g. dollars per bus-kilometer) or per-passenger-carried the incentives are different than if the payment is for a fixed amount of service hours (e.g. dollars per day for providing X hours of service). Paying on a per-unit-distance basis would create a preference for long routes that can be operated at a reliable, relatively high speed, regardless of the fact that most passengers might be concentrated on a shorter section of that route in an area with congested traffic. On the other hand, payment on a per-passenger-carried basis would create the opposite preference; namely, for shorter trips only where the majority of passengers are found. As an example, when a per-unit-distance contract was switched to a per-passenger contract in Sao Paolo, Brazil, there was a dramatic swing in the type of route bundles that operators preferred (Golub and Hook 2003).

With the release of the European Commission's review of public policy for contracting for public transport services (Commission of the European Community 2000), it had become apparent that competitive contracting of one form or another would become the norm in the European Union. These issues went to the core of the question of the legitimate role of government spending to support and promote public transport. The eventual outcome would establish legal precedents. The resulting impact on public transport service contracting would be of interest outside the EU as well.

A particularly pressing question was the legal interpretation of what constitutes "state aid" to private business. Such aid must be approved not only by local/regional/national government but also by the European Commission (European

Union Committee 2004). The Commission used generic arguments against state aid that perhaps do not pertain equally to all public services. The Commission is generally concerned about economic efficiency and about unfairly favoring domestic or local firms. One counter-argument to permit state aid is the need to bridge the gap between what a service costs and the fares necessary to support the service given the goals set for the public transport system. In this view, this difference does not represent a subsidy to the operator, but rather to the users and the community at large. Another counter-argument is that the higher level of service enabled by the subsidy can be justified by the manifold benefits the community receives in return. In other words, the indirect benefits are said to justify the direct monetary costs.

The resolution for regions with multiple operators led to the current EU practice of allowing subsidy, but not such that it creates a windfall profit to an operator. For example, private operators cannot receive noncompetitive contracts directly but must bid (tender) to operate routes in competition with other firms. Additional payments such as bonuses are acceptable, but only as a reward for meeting additional service requirements. (Maluses are also acceptable.) Publicly owned operators, such as city-owned rail systems, may receive compensation for services from a public authority without competitive bids, but only sufficient to cover their actual costs. It is also to permissible to compensate operators for extra investments in the public interest, such as accelerated replacement of older, more polluting vehicles.

Another important question that seems to have been settled as of this writing is whether there should be broader exceptions to the competitive contracting rule for large, highly integrated, multimodal systems. One counter-argument to competition is that the operations and physical infrastructure are so intertwined that they cannot be coordinated effectively except as single entities. The degree to which this is actually true would have to be investigated on a case-by-case basis, but one can certainly envision situations where coordination ceases to exist. Seemingly persuaded by this argument, the very large, multimodal *Régie Autonome des Transports Parisiens (RATP)* organization serving the Il-de-France (Paris) region and a few other large organizations are exempt from the competitive contracting requirements.

Another counter-argument relates to the technological advances that come from large multimodal agencies. Decision makers need to consider the effect dissolution will have on innovations in technologies applicable to multimodal integration. For example, the aforementioned *RATP* has a reputation for being one of the industry leaders in ITS applications. Would unimodal organizations continue this tradition? If not, funding agencies may have to initiate and fund multimodal technology projects themselves (e.g. regional fare smartcards). This cost will offset some of the savings from competitive contracting. As will be discussed shortly, another possibility might be that the technology investment vacuum will be filled by a for-profit firm to meet their particular needs instead of the broader community's needs.

Yet another counter-argument to competition has to do with the nature of work provided by large integrated transport organizations. Public transport systems that get broken up tend to lose many of their career-path employees and opportunities for cross training. Central workshops that completely rebuild vehicles, in-house engineering departments (such as the one at London Transport that designed the famous Routemaster double-decker bus), and testing facilities and apprentice training programs disappear to reduce costs. Instead, maintenance work is likely to be outsourced to specialist firms (McGuinness, Gillingwater and Bryman 1994; White 1997). The lack of career-path opportunities may well have exacerbated the aforementioned high rate of turnover seen in London and elsewhere in the United Kingdom.

Indeed, many other continental Europe operators that have been bidding (tendering) for operating contracts have also found high turnover to be a problem. As have paratransit operators in the United States, where contracting has been normal practice for decades. This is no doubt due to setting the highest weight on low costs and much less on the potential to attract employees who could be promoted from within to increasing levels of responsibility.

Under the right circumstances, it may be possible to expose persons to the transit industry who might never have thought about and create career path opportunities at the same time. Universities that have a local transit system, or closely coordinate with a local system due to their location in a small city or rural setting, can initially offer part-time driving positions to students. Some of those drivers will become interested in other aspects of the field, even to the point of enrolling a certificate program with the aim of joining the industry upon graduation. At one such program, both the university operator and a nearby private contract manager/operator assigns students to internships and provide workshops on a variety of topics (Collura et al. 2012).

Investment When There Are No Contractual Obligations to Provide Service

The ability of unregulated, unsupported operators to invest in a system will depend on the competitiveness and profitability of their operating environment. If the financial condition of an operator is marginal due to competition that brings excess capacity, that operator might be unable to finance various investments to improve or expand service. Or their board of directors may not want to suppress current meager profits in the hope of future gains. Ironically, it might be that less competition and market dominance by one or two companies actually facilitates investment in service improvements. As an example, the dominant operator in deregulated Bradford, UK, developed an "overground" system, a set of routes with special branding and service features (Jack 2001). It also invested in a smartcard fare-payment system that can provide discounts to steady users. Such enhancements reinforce passenger loyalty and impede entry into the market by other firms.

Perhaps the best reason for licensing previously unregulated and unsupported operators to encourage investment is the degree to which licensing restricts entry to the market. High standards for vehicle safety, insurance and driver training, for example, would not only address safety issues, it could suppress the number of small, casual operators that could reduce profitability to all because of over-capacity. An operator might even have decided that some investment in public infrastructure could make its service more attractive at minimal cost. But if there is no ownership of the rights to use specific routes and to use specific stops, there are two strong disincentives. The first is that competitors will also use it (the classical "free rider" problem). The second is that road or market conditions might change, making the roads where the infrastructure was placed no longer the best ones to use and the investment redundant. The aforementioned operator in Bradford did not make investments in road infrastructure.

One solution used by local authorities worried about insufficient infrastructure investment in their public transport systems in this climate of limited authority was to develop *public-private partnerships* (*PPPs*). Indeed, the Bradford Council and the regional planning authority invested in a laterally separated (right-of-way B) guided bus facility to complement the aforementioned private improvements (APTA 2002). Since then, other cities in the United Kingdom have followed with so-called "quality bus" contracts of a similar nature. Most recently, the central government has further strengthened these efforts by providing competitive grants requiring matching funds from the local authority, bus operators, or both (Baker 2011).

The need for and creation of such PPPs could have been predicted from the early results of deregulation. The United Kingdom has been a living laboratory for investigating the impact of changes in both organizational structures and contract models for public-transit systems. When transit (non)-systems operate in the same country, where economic and cultural differences are less pronounced, comparative analysis was made simpler. After privatization, Greater London followed a gross contracting model for delivering a service that remained publicly supported and planned. The remainder of the United Kingdom was deregulated and largely unsupported, with net contract models used for those services deemed still socially necessary.

In the United Kingdom, bus operating and maintenance costs were reduced everywhere, but otherwise the results were very different between London and the rest of the United Kingdom. London saw steady increases in ridership, whereas most of the remaining regions saw stagnation or decline, despite increases in service hours. It is worthwhile for the analyst to read various interpretations and debates over the available performance results, as well as various conclusions. There are suggestions for improving organizational structures and contracts in order to remedy perceived shortcomings and reinforce perceived successes (Pickup et al. 1991; McGuinness et al. 1994; Fawkner 1995; Pucher and Lefevre 1996; White 1997; Banister and White 1997; Gomez-Ibanez and Meyer 1997). Only a brief summary of the results for the bus mode after the first eight years is given in Table 11.1. A more recent review by the UK central government indicates continuing dissatisfaction by the public at the state of bus services (U.K. Department for Transport, 2006). Doing full justice to this discussion would be the subject of its own book.

The situation for rail privatization in the United Kingdom was far more complicated. Railroads are traditionally almost always vertically integrated, with one firm controlling all functions. In the UK, the railroad was split functionally as well as geographically. Infrastructure was separated from train operations and train maintenance. Franchises were awarded to train operating companies (TOCs) for specific networks. There were also companies that leased rolling stock to the TOCs. Then there was RailTrack, an infrastructure ownership company that was to reinvest rail-use charges into improvements on the joint infrastructure. Overseeing it all was a regulating authority, intended to resolve conflicts and maintain competition in an unbiased manner.

In general, fares stayed high. After the initial years of privatization, it could be concluded that two important public policy goals were not met: 1) enhancing the competitive position of rail against auto, and 2) reduction of public investment. Again, justice cannot be served by a brief discussion. A more detailed summary and insights into the future prospects and limitations of privatizing large rail networks is given by Shaw (2001).

RailTrack ultimately failed, and public investment had to be increased. The overall costs of its successor, Network Rail, are currently 30 to 40 percent higher than European peers (House of Commons 2011). Part of this is due to the legacy of underinvestment and consequent problems with worn-out equipment and obsolete technologies, but much of it is due to the complexities of trying to conduct

Table 11.1 Results from the first eight years of bus privatization in the United Kingdom

Expectation	Effect of Deregulation	Effect of Contracting (London)
Encourage innovation	Mixed—increased use of minibuses only important service innovation	Mixed—some service innovations from more enterprising operators
Encourage cost reductions	Yes—25% reductions or more	25% reductions
Provide a service which better corresponds to the need of the customer	No—worsened regularity and poor information have offset the benefit of a substantial increase in service provided	Yes—large improvement in quality
Reductions in fares	No—fares up 30%	No—fares up 6%
Arrest reduction in bus travel and reduce reliance upon the private car	Mixed—traffic down 30%, although in a few areas with only one operator there have been large increases	Yes—ridership maintained

Source: Fawkner 1995.

work under such fragmented responsibilities and numerous operators. By comparison, the German railway (DB) was not broken into many fragments like the United Kingdom. Instead, the system was re-organized to incentivize better performance through a process of regionalization of decision-making about purchasing of services, not necessarily from the pre-existing provider. The results have been positive, with DB responding with productivity improvements and ridership increasing substantially in many regions (Buehler and Pucher 2011).

Based on the UK experience, many persons have come to the conclusions that government-planned services give the best results and any competition should be restricted to operations and maintenance. Yet one important point should be borne in mind before drawing definitive conclusions from this debate about regulated versus deregulated and privately versus publicly operated transport systems. When appraising performance, there is always the question of the "counterfactual" results (i.e. results the analyst did not get to investigate because the chosen public policy precluded seeing the alternative results that might have otherwise happened). Henscher and Beesley (1997) make the observation that one does not really know what kind of innovation might have been stimulated with a relaxation of rules in regulated locations. For example, they point out that the use of high-frequency minibuses in the United Kingdom upon deregulation may well have slowed the decline in ridership in some regions.

Furthermore, Henscher and Beesley point out that fully publicly planned services also benefit by learning from innovations at less regulated locations because their current contractual and organizational arrangements often provide little or no incentive for exploratory ventures and innovations in their own service environment. Extending their line of reasoning, the appearance of unauthorized services in a region with entirely publicly planned services merits close attention. Their very existence in a highly regulated environment might well be interpreted as a failure to meet travel needs by the officially sanctioned organizational structures that do exist.

One example was the jitney service in Miami. It provided service that met travel needs not well served by the official system. It also provided employment for an ethnic community (Urban Mobility Corporation 1992). It was eventually incorporated into the regular transit organization including many of the drivers. Another example was an informal van service in Queens, New York City. It provided local community-connector service where official service was thin as well as employment within an ethnic community. Efforts to put it out of business through enforcement were mostly unsuccessful (Mitchell 1992; Faison 1992). Only years later, when the MetroCard was introduced that provided free transfers to and from the subway system, did demand subside.

One can also find examples of services catering to a more professional demographic. Large IT-related companies located in the San Francisco and Seattle suburbs, for example, have their own bus-route networks to connect their campuses with districts where there are clusters of employees residing (Fowler 2012; Dickey 2012; Long 2009; Microsoft 2009). They feature comfortable seats and Wi-Fi and are no doubt an effective recruiting tool. Such services would probably not be necessary in most major European metro regions.

It must also be pointed out that the inability to address markets or to innovate can also often be attributed to union resistance. In the United States, there is very little contracting of fixed-route operations at larger agencies. Their unions have opposed reduced pay for driving smaller buses. This is perhaps myopic, since it could be a way to expand the system, expand the workforce and eventually have even more positions for large vehicle drivers. Due to a public monopoly, private firms will also be denied permission to operate or receive any subsidies even if they identify an unserved market niche. (The aforementioned IT-related firms get around this by carrying only their own employees, and not the general public.) The end result is that route and service planners tend to focus their limited resources for expansion on large bus services that have better labor productivity.

Even with a general consensus that competitive contracts, or even the threat of competitive contracts, can reduce operating costs by promoting efficiency, it cannot be concluded that private operations are always more efficient. The ambiguity arises because one cannot always separate what characteristics are simply inherent to the service area and the type of service from what characteristics are amenable to influence by management. McCullough, Taylor, and Wachs (1998) performed a regression analysis of cost-efficiency, as measured by the cost-per-revenue-hour indicator, against many variables and applied it to an array of US transit systems. They did not find that the degree of contracting, as measured by the ratio of privately operated revenue-hours to entire system revenue-hours, was the most significant variable. Instead, they found vehicle scheduling, as measured by the ratio of total vehicle-hours to revenue-hours (deadhead ratio) and labor use, as measured by total paid-hours to total vehicle-hours, were far more significant.

An example may help to understand this research result. While the relaxation of union work rules under a competitive contracting regime are generally expected to translate into higher labor use rates, such opportunities might be limited. The analyst can take a close look at particular route-performance indicators, such as those shown in Table 3.3, and at service attributes that can be influenced by characteristics of the route alignment and service area, such as those in Table 8.1. One might then find that there is little any management can do without discarding key service goals. For instance, a high deadhead ratio could be the result of a public-policy emphasis on serving peak-direction, peak-hour-only, commuting trips. It might also be due to an inability to raise capital funds for an additional depot closer to these routes. Whatever the reason, neither a public nor a private operator would be able to improve this inherently inefficient use of vehicles and paid operator hours without addressing either publicly set service priorities or infusing significant public capital.

Summary

Private firms seek profit and thus have a higher Minimum Allowable Rate of Return. They are also subject to different rules regarding taxation and financing. As a result, privately owned or operated system will perceive different goals and objectives and use different measures and criteria for evaluation.

There are a variety of organizational, financial and regulatory structures:

- Unlicensed, unregulated, and unsupported private operations are such that there is no preset level of service or fare. This type of system is generally seen where the government is very weak but can also be seen in fast-growing fringe areas.
- Licensed but unsupported private operations are a first step that can be taken against chaotic conditions. The revenue from license fees also provides the means for enforcement.
- Licensed but publicly supported private operations may still have wide latitude in selecting routes and schedules. But some measure of public control is usually expected in return.
- Publicly planned and supported private operations can make a large difference in the nature and stability of service. This structure places the responsibility for routes, schedules, and other service design issues squarely on the planning authority. This model is dominant in much of South America.
- A publicly planned, supported, and operated network is the predominant model in North America and, until recently, in most of the European Union. It is akin to a public monopoly in electricity or water.

If the organizational structure involves public financial support, it can be rendered in different ways:

- Allocation and operation by a local authority means one public agency plans and operates all service. Its domain is restricted to the same as the local government.
- Allocation and operation by a region-wide authority is similar, but now it must also decide the basis for allocation of service throughout a region. It is intended to meet regional needs that do not respect local political boundaries. A negative is that such an entity can also be less accountable to local governments.
- Municipal contract with a region-wide authority is a similar model, but the allocation of routes and service is decided, at least partially, on the basis of contributions from local governments or service districts. This restores some accountability as well as equity.
- Under a gross contract model, a public agency gives a subsidy set through competitive proposals to a private operator. The revenues collected are in no way connected to the amount paid. A negative is the lack of an incentive to improve service.
- Under a net contract model, the public subsidy is only sufficient to guarantee that a minimum essential level of service is provided, or what is necessary to attract a willing operator, or both. The firm receives the operating revenues. A positive side is the incentive to improve and innovate.
- Composite contracting models are designed to capture some of the positive aspects of both net and gross contract models. An example of a modification in such a composite is a "quality bonus." Another incentive is to add

a percentage of revenues collected to the gross amount of the contract. Yet another modification is to allow an operator to add, delete, or modify service offerings, as long as these changes meet with public approval via polling.

There is a variety of contracting models for capital projects as well:

- Separating by project phases is the traditional model.
- Under the Design–Build model, the firm that does the design also does the construction and equipment procurement. It shifts much of the project cost risk to a turnkey provider.
- Under the DBOM model, a single firm's responsibility extends into the operational phase as well. It is based on the concept of minimizing the life-cycle cost of an investment.
- Under the BOT model, the firm that did the construction operates the system only for an interim period. It transfers skills needed to operate and to other parts of the economy.

The authority granting the contract should consider cultural traditions, preexisting infrastructure, the financial state of the region, and political power, which all influence public investment policy.

One reason for switching organizational structures is simply to break up existing relationships, be they public or private. Some researchers have concluded that reorganization is virtually a prerequisite to making progress in some situations.

The full array of public goals cannot be made to align with the goals of a private firm. By dividing projects into smaller packages, private firms can be made to focus where they do align.

If contracted public payments are expressed as a rate, such as per-unit-distance or per-passenger-carried, the incentives are different than if the payment is for a fixed amount of service hours.

Competitive contracting of one form or another will become the norm in the European Union. But as of this writing, there are contentious issues that must be settled. One is the amount of "state aid" that can be given to private operating firms. Another is the dissolution of multimodal operating agencies, where operations and physical infrastructure are intertwined.

The importance of licensing for encouraging investment stems from the degree to which licensing restricts entry to the market. High standards would suppress the number of small, casual operators that could reduce profitability to all because of overcapacity.

The ability of unregulated, unsupported operators to invest will depend on profitability. Ironically, it might be that less competition and market dominance by one or two companies actually facilitate investments that might reinforce passenger loyalty and impede entry into the market by other firms.

If there is no ownership of the rights to use specific routes and to use specific stops, there are two strong disincentives to invest in infrastructure. The first is the classical "free rider" problem. The second is that road and market conditions might change, making the infrastructure redundant.

The United Kingdom has been a living laboratory for investigating the impact of changes in both organizational structures and contract models. For the bus mode, greater London followed a gross contracting model. In the rest of the country, bus service has been deregulated and largely unsupported, with net contract models being used for services deemed socially necessary. While costs were reduced everywhere, ridership outside of London also decreased.

In the United Kingdom, the rail mode was split functionally as well as geographically into many fragments. The goal of stimulating increased competition against the car was not met because fares stayed high. The private company in charge of infrastructure, RailTrack, ultimately failed, and the UK government had to create and inject public capital into a new company, Network Rail, whose costs remain far above its peers in continental Europe. Regionalization of choice about purchase of services, but without breaking up the national railway, as was done in Germany, has met with much greater success.

Many analysts have come to the conclusion that government-planned services give the best results and any competition should be restricted to operations and maintenance. But there is always the question of the counterfactual results. For example, the use of high-frequency minibuses in the United Kingdom upon deregulation may well have slowed the decline in ridership that was occurring before deregulation.

The appearance of unauthorized services in a region with publicly planned services merits close attention. Their very existence might well be interpreted as a failure to meet travel needs by the officially sanctioned organizational structures. It must also be pointed out that the inability to address markets or to innovate can also often be attributed to union resistance. In the United States, the unions at larger agencies will oppose reduced pay for driving smaller buses. The end result is that route and service planners tend to focus their limited resources for expansion on large bus services that have better labor productivity.

Even with the general consensus that competitive contracts can reduce operating costs, it cannot be concluded that private operations are always more efficient. One cannot always separate what characteristics are simply inherent to the service area and service type from what characteristics are amenable to influence by management. For example, peak-hour, peak-direction-only services and routes far from depots are inherently inefficient no matter what type of operator or contract.

References

Anjum, G. Abbas, and John R. E. Russell. 1997. "Public Transport Regulation Through a Government Organized NGO: The Faisalabad Experience in Pakistan." *Transport Reviews* 17 (2): 105–20.

APTA (American Public Transportation Association). 2002. "Britain's Guided Busway Gets Underway in Bradford." *Passenger Transport* 4 (March): 12.

Baker, Norman. 2011. "Investment in Bus and Community Transport." Statement to Parliament, U.K. Department for Transport. http://www.dft.gov.uk/news/statements/baker-20111207

Banister, D., and P. R. White. 1997. "Deregulation of Buses in Great Britain: Editorial Suggestions for Further Reading." *Transport Reviews* 17 (1): 31–35.

Buehler, R., and J. Pucher. 2011. "Making Public Transport Financially Sustainable." *Transport Policy* 18 (1): 126–38.

Caro, Robert A. 1975. *The Power Broker: Robert Moses and the Fall of New York.* New York: Vintage.

Collura, John, Donald Fisher, Michael Knodler and Allan Byam. 2012. *Graduate Certificate in Transit Management and Operations.* Program revision application form, Amherst: University of Massachusetts. http://www.umass.edu/senate/councils/Grad_Proposals/TRANSIT_MGMT_AND_OPERATIONS_CERT.pdf

Commission of the European Community. 2000. *Proposal . . . On Action By Member States Concerning Public Service Requirements and Award of Public Service Contracts in Public Transport by Bus, Rail and Inland Waterway.* Proposal 2000/0212 (COD). http://europa.eu.int/eur-lex/en/com/pdf/2000/en_500PC0007.pdf

Dickey, Megan Rose. 2012. "Here's a Map to Silicon Valley's Cushy Private Buses." *Business Insider* (October 12). http://www.businessinsider.com/silicon-valley-private-buses-2012-10

European Union Committee. 2004. *Policy Issues: Legal Framework for Public Transport.* Brussels, Belgium: Union International des Transport Publics. http://www.uitp.com/eupolicy/policy.cfm

Faison, Seth. 1992. "Bus Fare Cuts Fail to Lure Queens Riders." *New York Times* (November 29): 41–43.

Fawkner, J. 1995. "Bus Deregulation in Britain: Reforms or Loss?" *Public Transport International* 95 (6): 18–23.

Fowler, Geoffrey A. 2012. "Map Reveals Corporate Bus Routes Tech Workers Take." *The Wall Street Journal* (October 10). http://online.wsj.com/article/SB10000872396390443982904578044520776395486.html

Golub, Aaron, and Walter Hook. 2003. "Sao Paolo's Bus Reform Leads to Turmoil." *Sustainable Transport* (Fall). New York: Institute for Transport and Development Policy, 14–16. http://www.itdp.org

Gomez-Ibanez, Jose A., and John R. Meyer. 1997. "Alternatives for Urban Bus Service: An International Perspective on the British Reforms." *Transport Reviews* 17 (1): 17–29.

Henscher, David, and Michael Beesley. 1997. "Market, Politics and Environmental Policy Issues for Public Transit." *Journal of Public Transportation* 1 (4). Tampa, FL: Center for Urban Transportation Research, 81–99.

House of Commons: Committee of Public Accounts. 2011. "Office of Rail Regulation: Regulating Network Rail's Efficiency." *Forty-first Report of Session 2010–12.* London, UK: The Stationery Office Limited. http://www.publications.parliament.uk/pa/cm201012/cmselect/cmpubacc/1036/1036.pdf

ITSP (International Transit Studies Program). 2002. *Design–Build Transit Infrastructure Projects in Asia and Australia. Research Results Digest* 53. Washington, DC: Transit Cooperative Research Program, National Academy Press. http://www.tcrponline.org

_____. 1999. *Private Urban Transit Systems and Low Cost Mobility Solutions. Research Results Digest* 33. Washington, DC: Transit Cooperative Research Program, National Academy Press, 31. http://www.tcrponline.org

Jack, Doug. 2001. "All Change in Bradford." *Urban Transport International* 36 (Jul/ Aug): 32–34.

Long, Katherine. 2009. "Microsoft Connector: 19 Routes, 53 Buses Later." *Seattle Times* (April 12). http://seattletimes.com/html/microsoft/2009025535_msshuttle12m.html

Maryon, John. 2004. "Restructuring of Bangkok's Transport." *Urban Transport International* 53: 25–26.

McCullough, William S., III, Brian D. Taylor and Martin Wachs. 1998. "Transit Service Contracting and Cost Efficiency." *Transportation Research Record* 1678: 69–77.

McGuinness, Iain, David Gillingwater and Alan Bryman. 1994. "Organizational Responses to the Deregulation of the Bus Industry in Britain." *Transport Reviews* 14 (1): 341–61.

Microsoft Real Estate and Facilities. 2009. *Microsoft Connector Commute Fact Sheet.* Olympia: Washington State Transportation Commission. http://wstc.wa.gov/Meetings/AgendasMinutes/agendas/2010/July13/documents/20100713_BP8_MicrosoftCon nectorCommuteFactSheet.pdf

Mitchell, Allison. 1992. "Illegal Vans in Battle for New York Streets." *New York Times* (January 24): B1–B2.

Pickup, Laurie et al. 1991. *Bus Deregulation in the Metropolitan Areas.* Aldershot, UK: Avebury/Gower.

Pucher, John, Nisha Korattyswaroopam and Neenu Ittyerah 2004. "The Crisis of Public Transport in India: Overwhelming Needs but Limited Resources." *Journal of Public Transportation* 7 (4): 1–20.

Pucher, John, and Christian Lefevre. 1996. "Great Britain: Failure of Free Market Policies." Chapter 7 in *The Urban Transport Crisis in Europe and North America.* New York: MacMillan, 117–37.

Ringqvist, Stenerik. 2010. "The Swedish Experience" Presentation. Six months experience of the PSO regulation, Joint UTP/UITP Conference. Paris: 7 June.

_____. 2001. *Scandinavian Solutions: A Model of Cooperation.* Proceedings of Public Transport "EU Special." Linz, Austria, 5–6 March.

Russell, John R. E., and G. Abbas Anjum. 1997. "Public Transport and Urban Development in Pakistan." *Transport Reviews* 17 (1): 61–80.

Shaw, John. 2001. "Competition in the UK Passenger Rail Industry: Prospects and Problems," *Transport Reviews* 21 (2): 195–216.

U.K. Department for Transport. 2006. *Putting Passengers First: The Government's Proposals for a Modernised National Framework for Bus Services.* December. London, UK: http://webarchive.nationalarchives.gov.uk/20090806013054/http:/www.dft.gov.uk/pgr/regional/buses/secputtingpassengersfirst/pdfputtingpassfirst.pdf

Urban Mobility Corporation. 1992. *The Miami Jitneys.* Washington, DC: U.S. Federal Transit Administration.

Watson, Robert. 2001. "Railway Privatization Effects on UK Train Planning." *Transport Reviews* 21 (2): 181–93.

White, Peter R. 1997. "What Conclusions Can Be Drawn About Bus Deregulation in Britain?" *Transport Reviews* 17 (1): 1–16.

Further Reading

Anderson, Bjoern. 1992. "Factors Affecting European Privatization and Deregulation Policies in Local Public Transport: The Evidence from Scandinavia." *Transportation Research A* 26 (2): 179–91.

Camara, P., and D. Banister. 1993. "Spatial Inequalities in the Provision of Public Transport in Latin American Cities." *Transport Reviews* 13 (4): 351–73.

Daduna, Joachim R. 2001. "Impacts of Deregulation on Planning Processes and Information Management Design in Public Transit." Chapter 2 of *Computer Aided Scheduling of Public Transport*, edited by Stephan Voss and Joachim Rolf Daduna. Berlin: Springer-Verlag, 429–51.

Diaz, Rodrigo, and Daniel Bongardt. 2013. "Financing Sustainable Urban Public Transport: International Review of National Urban Transport Policies and Programs." Bonn, Germany: GTZ/EMBARQ. http://sustainabletransport.org/financing-sustainable-urban-transport-international-review-of-national-urban-transport-policies-and-programmes/

Finn, Brendan, and Corinne Mulley. 2011. "Urban Bus Services in Developing Countries and Countries in Transition: A Framework for Regulatory and Institutional Developments." *Journal of Public Transportation* 14 (4): 89–107.

Girnau, Gunter. 2005. *Restrukturierung von OPNV-Unternehmen fur den Wettbewerbsmarkt— eine Zwischenbilanz und Dokumentation*. Cologne, Germany: Verband Deutscher Verkehrsunternehman (VDV). (in German) http://www.vdv.de

Holvad, Torben. 2009. "Review of Railway Policy Reforms in Europe." *Built Environment* 35 (1): 24–42.

International Transit Studies Program. 2002. *Emerging Trends in European Public Transport*, *Research Results Digest* 54. Washington, DC: Transit Cooperative Research Program, National Academy Press. http://www.tcrponline.org

Leinbach, T. R. 1995. "Transport and Third World Development: Review, Issues, and Prescription." *Transportation Research A* 29 (5): 337–44.

Muñoz, Juan Carlos, and Louis de Grange. 2010. "On the Development of Public Transit in Large Cities." *Research in Transportation Economics* 29: 379–386.

Munoz, Juan Carlos, and Antonio Gschwender. 2008. "Transantiago: A Tale of Two Cities." *Research in Transportation Economics* 22: 45–53.

TCRP (Transit Cooperative Research Program). 2005. *Innovations in Bus, Rail and Specialized Transit. Research Results Digest* 70. Washington, DC: Transit Cooperative Research Program, National Academy Press.

UITP (Union Internationale des Transport Publics). 2003. *New Possibilities for Regional Railway Operators in Europe*. UITP Focus Paper. http://www.uitp.org

———. 2001. *Position of the UITP-EU Committee in Regard to the Proposal of the European Commission Concerning the Award of Public Service Contracts*. UITP Focus Paper. http://www.uitp.org

U.K. Department for Transport. 2012. *Reforming our Railways: Putting the Customer First*, Presented to Parliament by the Secretary of State for Transport, March. https://www.gov.uk/government/uploads/system/uploads/attachment_data/file/4216/reforming-our-railways.pdf

Vuchic, Vukan. 2005. "Transit Ownership, Regulation and Organization." Chapter 9 in *Urban Transit: Operations, Planning and Economics*. Hoboken, NJ: Wiley.

White, Peter, and S. Tough. 1995. "Alternative Tendering Systems and Deregulation in Britain." *Journal of Transport Economics and Policy* 29 (3): 275–90.

Wirth, C. J. 1997. "Transportation Policy in Mexico City: The Politics and Impacts of Privatization." *Urban Affairs Review* 33 (2): 155–81.

Chapter 12

Simultaneous Evaluation of All Factors

The ultimate purpose of any project evaluation is to select a course of action. If the project is a major one affecting many people, not everyone will agree about which course is "best." Opponents might feel the process was flawed and their particular concerns have not been properly considered, or they might feel inequitably burdened with the negatives or costs of the projects while others receive the benefits. Therefore, those charged with making the decisions should have a basis for defending them. This is not only out of concern for the democratic principle that decision makers should reflect the public will, it is also needed to reach closure of the analysis process and to move on with implementation.

There usually is no process where one just "turns the crank" to generate the "right" or "best" answer between complex project alternatives. There simply is no way to combine monetary and nonmonetary factors, and then evaluate them jointly in a way everyone will agree is satisfactory. Some nonquantitative factors cannot be expressed in terms of units. For instance, there are no "livability" units. Even if there were, they would have to be converted to an equivalent monetary unit if a monetary evaluation method were being used. This issue of *incommensurability* of factors is something that plagues the decision process.

Despite these difficulties, a way must be found to perform the evaluation. This chapter outlines several typical approaches. Some can serve to initially screen alternatives and others to further differentiate them. Still others can help to make a final selection. One highly useful method that incorporates all available information and types of evaluation expertise is presented, but there are others as well. Indeed, a separate book would be required to explain most of them in detail. Here, only some of the major theoretical and practical issues, as seen from both my and a couple of other prominent researchers, can be presented.

Appendix 12.A concludes the chapter with a brief description of a few more of these methods that are less accessible to a lay audience or even to most public transport decision makers. Nevertheless, analysts should be aware that a variety of methods exist so that they can be explored when faced with a challenging project.

Assembling and Organizing the Information

A recurring theme of this book has been that analysts must develop and compare discrete project alternatives, perhaps including a "do-nothing" case as well. Comparing the universe of possibilities for every element of the project with every other feasible set of combinations of other elements is not practical. The resulting number of combinations quickly becomes astronomical. Readjusting and forming promising new sets of elements can always be used to create and delete new project alternatives as the project analysis proceeds. Analysts should consider each promising project alternative, even those that are far stronger in pursuit of some goals at the expense of being far weaker in others, but no alternative can neglect commonly agreed-upon key goals.

The ultimate project actually implemented will rarely be identical to the formally chosen project alternative. Detailed final design may reveal unanticipated difficulties with that alternative. The final project design almost always involves further changes in elements as it reaches the procurement stage. Proposals from vendors may show higher- or lower-than-estimated costs. Vendors sometimes present possibilities that analysts had not contemplated. Nevertheless, selecting a discrete alternative is still the focus of the evaluation process, with the understanding that this choice probably is not really and truly the "final" design, especially if the implementation phases take many years. Moreover, if management-by-objective was the planning philosophy used to develop the project in the first place, there will be checkpoints along the way that require revisiting project goals and objectives.

Once the analyst narrows the choice of possible project alternatives, the next step is to assemble all available information for each. While this may seem obvious, in practice it is not always easy. Different groups may have participated in different steps of the analysis. It may turn out that they used different assumptions or had conflicting information available. It is also quite likely that some alternatives have better and more reliable information than others. For instance, a proven elevated right-of-way design will have a more reliable cost estimate than will tunneling under a river with unknown soil properties. Analysts need to judge when they need to further study an alternative. It can be particularly difficult to know when enough research has been done when critics challenge monetary values that are placed on incommensurable elements. Perhaps a range of values needs to be used instead of only one value to represent a particular element, or maybe monetary valuation gets rejected altogether.

Displaying Information for Comparison

Analysts can organize information in a variety of ways. One of the most common is to put key goals into a matrix. There should be a list of objectives associated with each goal because these were the objectives analysts deemed to be measurable. Each project alternative is then rated for each objective with a score on some type of scale: numerical, high-low, weak-strong, important-unimportant, and so on. An example of such an evaluation matrix that relied only upon numerical scores was given in Table 2.2 in connection with the case study involving the analysis performed by SEPTA, the transit agency serving the Philadelphia region. It is also possible to explicitly add negative impacts to the matrix if one is certain that no alternative will be viewed as positive with respect to this criterion. (Otherwise, it should be added as an objective.)

A variation on the matrix is to focus on more limited comparisons. Rather than try to summarize and absorb everything at once, specific objectives (and perhaps negative impacts) are studied one by one. These can, in turn, be investigated by pairwise comparisons instead of all project alternatives at once. This has the advantage of ensuring that no criterion and no project alternative are skipped. It has the disadvantage that it can be tedious and time-consuming when there are many decisions. Examples using this technique are shown later.

Another way to organize information is to graphically portray data for two or more indicators simultaneously. This enables comparison in a way that simple numbers do not. One can study how alternatives that may be similar in one respect vary in other respects, or how one individual compares against a group. The graphics are not confined to two dimensions; a third dimension can also be portrayed, even on two-dimensional paper. In this case, a slice through a plane representing one value for one element becomes a plane showing how two other elements vary. An example was shown in Figure 3.15, where a section X-X was cut through the Location axis, which then defined a plane of Ridership versus Time of Day applicable only to this particular location.

If the data are being used in the context of an investment analysis, the indicator the analyst chooses for comparison is plotted versus other project alternatives. Peers can also be included to further enhance the comparison. If the data are used in the context of performance analysis, the comparison is of services with one another. These services can be either within the same region, with peers from elsewhere, or both. Each route is represented by one point on the graph. Routes are also grouped into families: CBD Local, Urban Local, Suburban Local, Rail, Metro (regional bus routes), and Call-n-Ride (demand-responsive), using a different type of marker for each. This grouping is done because each type of subarea is subject to different service expectations and standards within the organization. As an example, Figure 12.1 shows a graph actually used by the Regional Transit District (RTD), the agency serving the Denver, Colorado, metropolitan region to compare bus routes against standards used to justify a given frequency of service. The graph plots an efficiency indicator on the y-axis (Subsidy per Boarding) against a productivity indicator on the x-axis (Boardings per Vehicle-Hour) for the Suburban Local and Call-n-Ride groups. Note that the -axis is plotted as increasing downwards. In this format, any point farther that is to the right and higher up represents unambiguously better performance than a point to its left and lower down. No performance trade-offs are involved since both get better.

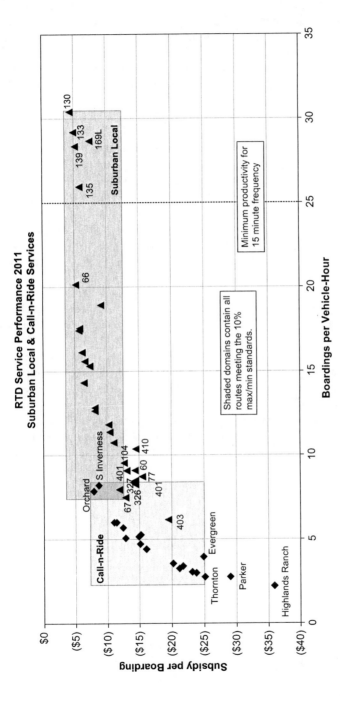

Figure 12.1 Performance evaluation comparison graph.

Source: RTD 2013.

Another basic type of graphical display is the trend plot. These graphs require consistent data collection over time, so they cannot be used with new operations. The purpose is to reveal whether the indicator is improving or deteriorating over time. Several routes can be shown at the same time. As an example, Figure 12.2 shows the average-operating-speed indicator for two hypothetical routes. A point is plotted every two years. Even though both started out at the beginning of data collection at the same speed, clearly Route 1 has been deteriorating much faster.

Some factors cannot be portrayed accurately using a scale because of their "nonlinear" nature. Small differences between values from one project alternative to the next could have significant implications. For example, there might be matching investment-fund restrictions that give one alternative a huge financial contribution for which others cannot qualify, trigger levels at which provisions become applicable and maximum amounts can be received annually, and other such rules that constrain project design and implementation.

In such cases, a small difference in investment capital requirements can affect project feasibility. The end result could be that two otherwise similar project alternatives with respect to the goals they are intended to meet have far different financial or schedule implications. If one decides to express such constraint information by assigning a score or a monetary value, it requires supporting details explaining the tentativeness and the relevant restrictive conditions. Persons reviewing the alternatives need to bear these in mind when reviewing the scores and financial aspects.

One particular type of nonlinear information deserves special mention in the context of evaluations that include environmental factors and sustainable development. That is the concept of *weak sustainability* versus *strong sustainability* factors. The weak sustainability approach "does not take account of any thresholds in critical natural assets or limits to the substitutability between natural and produced assets" (Friedrich and Bickel 2001, 102). Thus, while monetization may sometimes be acceptable for the weak approach, strong sustainability

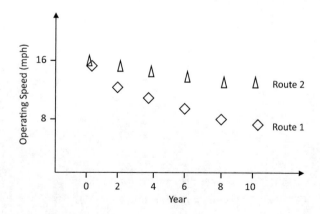

Figure 12.2 Trend comparison graph.

would instead set a firm, quantifiable limit on the allowable impact on a natural asset. Thus, strong sustainability forms a hard constraint on all project alternatives, meaning any such constraint cannot be violated, no matter how high a value would be placed on exceeding the constraint. In this case, the applicable alternative(s) could still otherwise be scored, but an explanation would also be given as to why the alternative must be rejected.

Compliance with Public Policies

Analysts must also consider public policies during the evaluation. In some cases, a simple "complies/does not comply" might suffice for each alternative with respect to each policy. In others, it may not be immediately clear. It could require further research or perhaps a legal ruling. As an example, a Build–Operate–Transfer project solution may never have been done in a jurisdiction before, and its legality may not be clear. In this case, the comment needs to be added that legislation may be required. As a more drastic example, one of the more expensive public transport project alternatives could be predicated on diverting funds from popular highway projects. In this case it should be made clear that the applicable alternative precludes this entirely unrelated project unless additional funding is found. Thus, a public-policy decision as to the importance and priority of this other project would need to be made.

The process of identifying relevant policies can prove important for at least two reasons. The first is that a project goal may be shown to conflict with other governmental goals. If these other goals are promoted or defended through official public policies, challenges to the project alternative may be expected, both from within government and without. The more emphasis a particular alternative puts on a particular conflicting goal, the more intense the opposition is likely to be. The second is that a risk element must be added to any alternative that depends upon political resolution of conflicts among goals or changes in laws. Ideally, analysts will identify and address such issues early in the project, not when the final selection is near.

Methods of Ranking Alternatives

Initial Ranking

At first, the project alternative selection process proceeds along similar lines to those used by project managers in general, regardless of the field. Based on the all of the scaled results in hand, analysts classify each project alternative to the degree possible through an informal screening process. This classification into a group depends upon how the alternative performs on the indicators used to measure achievement of objectives. This is also done for the other information that is nonquantitative or nonlinear in nature, adds risk, may require enabling legislation, and so on.

Table 12.1 shows a very general example. There are six different hypothetical outcomes from this initial classification process into groups for "Scaled Results" and for "Other Information." One alternative could prove to be superior in every respect, in which case it is said to be *dominant*. This would mean that no further evaluation was necessary, but this rarely happens in reality. At the opposite extreme, an alternative inferior in every respect is said to be *dominated* and can be dropped from consideration. This is also rare, but analysts can usually readily identify inferior alternatives. Thus, an initial screening can at best identify a clear winner and, at worst, reduce the number of alternatives left for further consideration.

Continuing with this example, the alternatives in the second through fourth classifications still need a closer look. While it may seem that only project alternatives classified as mostly superior in both Scaled Results and in Other Information need a closer look, this is probably imprudent. The initial screening is usually too informal to jump to such conclusions. In order to address the concern that alternatives might get prematurely eliminated before adequate consideration, a systematic exploration is required. One technique is *SWOT (Strengths and Weaknesses, Opportunities and Threats)*. As the name implies, it involves listing and comparing strong and weak points of an alternative and attempting to identify and list unforeseen opportunities and threats. In this way, projects that have possibly fatal flaws can be eliminated or, conversely, that open up additional possibilities for positive impacts can be retained, despite earlier impressions. Steen Leleur (2012) lists a variety of such "soft" methods, including brainstorming, mind mapping, critical systems heuristics, soft systems methodology, stakeholder analysis, and futures workshops.

At this point, the alternative evaluation turns more difficult. How important is meeting each objective? How important is each particular Scaled Result and item of Other Information? Furthermore, who gets to decide the answers to these questions? Perhaps there is some scientific methodology that could synthesize all of the information and unambiguously reveal the best alternative. If this were the case, the decision could be left in the hands of appropriate experts. But for projects with longer-term, broad consequences, and with alternatives laden with

Table 12.1 Some hypothetical outcomes for a project alternative

Scaled Results	Other Information	Decision
All superior	All superior	Dominant—Select
Mostly superior	Mostly superior	Likely one of the best choices
Mostly superior	Mostly inferior	Must weigh further
Mostly inferior	Mostly superior	Must weigh further
Mostly inferior	Mostly inferior	Likely one of the worst choices
All inferior	All inferior	Dominated—Reject

incommensurable information, such a method does not exist. This does not mean that all alternatives should be treated as equal, either. It just means there needs to be a defensible logic for how the choice is made.

Trying to Find an Optimal Project Alternative

The conventional economic analysis of investment decisions usually speaks in terms of optimization. One seeks to maximize the Net Present Value (NPV) of a project, subject to constraints on the investment budget available each year. This maximum is found by solving a *mathematical program* that includes these constraints. The alternative with the highest NPV that does not violate any constraints is selected.

In reality, the analysis is further complicated by both the timing and duration of all incurred costs and by the timing and duration of the completion of each usable part of the project. Despite the fact that projects might otherwise have equal NPV, the distribution of costs over the course of the project could be quite different and affect the attractiveness of an alternative. As an example, the commercial disruption caused by construction could prove to be unacceptable in one or more years. Similarly, project attractiveness might depend upon how quickly benefits are received. As an example, a rapid transit project may take five years to complete the first usable part while a fully completed bus project may take only two years. Project timing and duration limitations can be accommodated by additional constraints that express requirements about when the first benefits are desired, the maximum duration for construction expenditures, maximum expenditure allowed in any one year, and so on.

Figure 12.3 is an example mathematical program that shows the concepts. The math program always includes an *objective function* to be maximized. The objective function is the sum of discounted benefits minus costs for all n years of the project life, plus any discounted salvage value recovered in the year n, S_n. The first constraint says that the total cost in any year j is the sum of both monetary and monetized costs. The second constraint says that the monetary expenditures in any year j must be less than or equal to the residual amount left over from the previous year, plus any newly available capital in year j, plus any net interest. (Net interest is defined as any interest income earned from unused funds less any interest or bond payments due in year j.) The third constraint places a maximum allowable monetized cost in any year j. The fourth constraint places a minimum benefit in any year j. The fifth constraint simply says that benefits and costs must both be defined as positive values.

Sixth are any hard sustainability constraints that the analyst must verify for compliance. These constraints are not expressed as monetary units. If any of these constraints is violated, the project is already infeasible. An example might be that consumption of wetlands is beyond the maximum allowed. The violating alternative must either be modified to get under the maximum or else be discarded.

If the numerical values of these costs and benefits and the various constraints are known with relative certainty, these types of multiyear programs can be readily

Maximize

$$\sum_{j=1}^{n}(B_j - C_j) + S_n$$

Subject To:

$$C_j = Monetary\ Costs_j + Monetized\ Costs_j \tag{1}$$

$$Monetary\ Costs_j \leq Residual_{j-1} + NewCapital_j + NetInterest_j \tag{2}$$

$$Monetized\ Costs_j \leq Max.Allowable\ Monetized\ Costs_j \tag{3}$$

$$B_j \geq Minimum\ Benefits_j \tag{4}$$

$$B_j, C_j > 0 \tag{5}$$

$$+ any\ hard\ sustainability\ constraints \tag{6}$$

Figure 12.3 Net Present Value taking into account time, monetary and sustainability constraints.

formulated and solved using a manual calculator for small problems or with the assistance of spreadsheet software for larger problems. It can happen that a project alternative is timed to unfold such that constraint(s) would be violated. In such a case, the computations will reveal the amount of that violation and how the project must be modified in order to be feasible. At this stage, such a computation might already lead to deleting a project alternative or making modifications to address the constraint violations. In some such situations not having too much uncertainty, the NPV maximization approach can find the best alternative. See, for example, Winston (2003) for an introduction to formulating programs involving capital budgeting and cash flow constraints and their methods of solution.

If there are no constraint terms (except for nonnegativity), the math program simplifies down to just an NPV equation. Note the similarity of the objective function to the NPV equations presented in Chapter 8. As before, the solution with the highest NPV is, by definition, the "best" one and should be chosen. Simplifying even further, if the analyst can clearly define and delimit the benefits and nothing additional is sought, the alternative that achieves those benefits at minimum cost would be the best one. Thus, it becomes a simpler *cost-minimization program*, where the benefits drop out of the math program since they are the same for all alternatives. Many short-term to medium-term business and operational decisions are of this nature. For example, as long as candidate bus designs all meet the same high reliability and comfort standards, the best bus choice would be the one with the lowest life-cycle costs. The situation where the cost is fixed instead for all alternatives would be similar. It becomes a simpler *benefit-maximization program*, where the costs drop out because they are the same for all alternatives.

Distinct project alternatives with longer-term and far-reaching impacts will each represent a different bundle of additional benefits and costs, each with different degrees of incommensurability. So these simpler cost-minimization or benefit-maximization approaches are clearly not applicable to such projects. Even the more comprehensive NPV method that takes into account both monetary and monetized costs and benefits, will only lead to the best choice amongst several distinct alternatives without consideration of the incommensurable costs and benefits. The NPV-related methods analyze what Steen Leleur (2012) describes as the "core performance" of a project, that is, those traditionally associated with an NPV-related cost-benefit analysis. In principle, optimization of the core performance can be done, keeping in mind that further analysis would be required afterwards to include the noncore items.

These distinct project alternatives are very often sample combinations out of what might be a continuum of combinations of elements that can be used to make up a specific design alternative. As a rail example, train (consist) sizes, signaling versus automation, track network layout and length, percentages of tunnel and elevated sections, station spacings, and service frequencies might all be derivative from some basic design elements common to several alternatives.

Furthermore, there are often controversies regarding valuation of monetary and monetized estimates associated with these design elements. The source of the controversy may stem from the use of uncertain coefficients (unit cost, unit production rate, construction speed, etc.) that represent construction uncertainty, revenue uncertainty from ridership forecasting imperfection, the value of time for various affected travelers, wage rates of vehicle operators and mechanics, and so on.

In the analytic optimization approach, functional relationships expressing the relationships between the design elements are used in the objective function and the constraints. These may be similar for most project alternative, but, generally, some alternatives can be expected to require some functional relationships that differ (e.g. those alternatives with bus technology instead of rail). It would be ideal to have one math program that could represent all alternatives, but if different ones are required, it only means that each one that represents a group of alternatives must be run separately and their optimal values compared.

The resulting math program(s) are possibly quite intractable to solve for the inexperienced analyst. However, once completed and successfully executed, an analytic model has a very important property. It transforms the analysis from one where there are discrete alternatives of which one must be selected to one where a composite solution might be found that outperforms all of the discrete alternatives. It may blend project components (e.g. train sizes, structures, network layout, station spacings, service frequency) in such a way that was never envisioned.

Such a math program has the further advantage of permitting sensitivity analysis that provides additional insight. Sensitivity analysis means that the functional relationships are adjusted by using a range of coefficients and by different values on the right-hand side of the constraint equations and inequalities. This will reveal which project components could greatly influence outcomes if the initial coefficient and constraint value estimates are wrong and which components would not affect outcomes too much, a highly useful result for optimizing designs and minimizing risks. Furthermore, the solving algorithm can search for values of variables at which the various constraints become *binding*. The *shadow price* associated with a binding variable is often a useful marginal cost indicator. See Forst and Hoffman (2010) for a detailed explanation.

Even if an advanced analyst has the mathematical prowess to solve a genuinely well-formulated and complete mathematical program, critics would find it easy to attack. "Black box" evaluations (i.e. evaluations done using mathematical methods and procedures that the nonexpert cannot follow) are rightly distrusted because it is unclear to the nonexpert what the mathematical statements really say and what assumptions are imbedded. To address the concerns of nonexpert decision makers and concerned citizens, the results would have to be displayed in such a fashion that nonexperts can understand.

To accommodate these concerns, the math program would have to be rerun numerous times to map out a "solution space." This is defined as a set of results where, for each input variable, a range is systematically tried while holding other inputs constant to assess the contribution and importance of each, using the aforementioned sensitivity analysis techniques. Perhaps this can also be done with a complementary analysis using Monte Carlo simulations, as mentioned in Chapter 9, that give probabilities for particular values for comparison. For both techniques, the NPV would then have to be expressed in a range rather than as one simple result. There would also need to be supporting information about most likely outcomes, which design elements are key to controlling project costs and delays, and so on. This is what the statement "There is no crank that one can turn to evaluate major projects and select a clear winner" means.

Analytical optimization has yielded some very useful system and network design solutions in the context of private-sector investments where the incommensurable social costs and benefits need not be taken into account. They also might provide great insight into the pros and cons of discrete alternatives and help convergence towards new alternatives that improve upon the initial candidates. But the lack of satisfactory inclusion of incommensurable items motivates the search for additional project evaluation and selection techniques.

Satisficing as an Alternative to Optimizing

The result of NPV analysis may be either one highly disputable number or a range of values too wide to be conclusive. When optimization techniques cannot select the best discrete project alternative, or find an optimal combination of components, then what? The economist Herbert Simon (1916–2001) noted that even smaller decisions quickly become too complicated for an individual to optimize. The information to make the optimal choice among alternatives is not necessarily available, and the individual may not have the technical skills to do the computation. While it would be possible to gather more information, it may simply not be worth the effort, or there may not be sufficient time. It would also be possible to sharpen an individual's evaluation skills, but this is not realistic for every decision. Rigorous evaluation skills can only be learned over time. Thus, Simon argued that, in reality, people are "satisficers"; in other words, people select the "good enough" solution rather than continuing to analyze until they reach the optimal solution. There is an axiom that says it simply: the perfect is the enemy of the good. This is not a minor point, as conventional economic analysis posits that when people make decisions, they are "welfare maximizing," an optimization process.

There is by no means universal agreement by academic theorists that satisficing should replace optimizing as the model for individual decision making. See Byron et al. (2004) for an expert debate on this point. It does suggest, however, an approach to project decision making when the computation of NPV is either not possible or can be established only within a wide range. An analogous argument to the individual can be made for institutional decisions. The research and alternative design work done for any major project guarantees that more information is available than it would be to an individual, and the evaluation skills that can be brought to bear are usually far higher. However, the decision to be made is also far more complex than individuals are asked to make. Perhaps the best real-life strategy is to find the project that is "good enough," giving up on the quest to find the project with the highest net benefits. Additional support for this strategy stems from the realization that every attempt to adjust elements within project alternatives, to increase their net benefits, risks a new round of debate and renewed opposition, perhaps this time from a different quarter.

If one accepts the satisficing approach, all of the information is jointly evaluated to see if there is at least one good-enough project alternative. If several seem close to each other in overall "goodness," the analysis can go further to distinguish between the candidates that have not been eliminated.

Some Accessible Methods for Further Ranking

This section describes several more assessment methods. Their ranking results may well differ. But trying more than one method and then determining why their rankings differ might, in itself, give additional insight into the arguments for and against the various project alternatives. Certainly, if all methods pointed to the same alternative, that would also be compelling information.

Breakeven analysis.   The breakeven analysis concept is based on NPV analysis but modified to incorporate benefits that cannot be readily monetized or whose valuation is controversial. These benefits are referred to as the *Unmonetized Benefits, UB_i,* for alternative i. The known discounted monetary costs are subtracted from the known discounted monetary benefits for alternative i to get the preliminary *Net Benefit, $(B-C)_i$*. If this is positive, the project is already feasible by the NPV $> = 0$ criterion. But it is made even more attractive because of the additional *Unmonetized Benefits, UB_i*. If, on the other hand, $(B-C)_i$ comes out to be negative, the question is whether UB_i is large enough to close the gap and make it at least zero or positive? If UB_i is large enough, the project is still feasible. If UB_i is not large enough, the NPV stays negative, and the project is infeasible. This review process is sometimes known as the *Krutilla-Fischer algorithm.* It has been incorporated into European Union public investment decision-making processes regarding environmental issues (Friedrich and Bickel 2001).

At first glance it might seem that the Krutilla-Fischer algorithm solves nothing, as the question of valuation of the unmonetized items remains. What it does, however, is set a minimum threshold for the benefit. It might well be that the unmonetized benefit is large enough that it easily meets the criterion, even using the lowest and least controversial valuation from a range of valuations. It helps in another way as well. By adding the UB_i estimate to $(B\text{-}C)_i$ to get a revised NPV, it might also change the relative ranking of project alternative i.

Example 12.1

Three rail transit project alternatives were designed with three goals in mind that could be expressed with reasonable monetary estimates: 1) reduction in street congestion to allow freight commerce to move more quickly, 2) recovery of some street space that can then be sold to developers for nontransport use, and 3) reduction in private expenditures for commuting. The only differences between them is that one crosses a large wetland area at grade by usurping an existing highway right-of-way, the second crosses it on an elevated section, allowing the roadway to be removed entirely to fully restore the wetlands, and the third goes around the wetlands. The first has a preliminary net benefit of +$200M, the second –$300M, the difference stemming from the $500M cost of constructing the elevated section. The third is at -$600M due to the high cost of the much longer route. Which one is the best choice?

$$(B\text{–}C)_1 = \$ + 200M,\ UB_1 = \$0$$
$$(B\text{–}C)_2 = \$ - 300M,\ UB_2 = ?$$
$$(B\text{–}C)_3 = \$ - 600M,\ UB_3 = ?$$

The first project alternative is clearly feasible. The second depends upon the size of UB_2. If the lowest noncontroversial valuation for the contribution of wetlands to the economy is something less than $300M, the second alternative is infeasible and can be eliminated. If it is equal to $300M, the second alternative becomes feasible, but it is still inferior to the first alternative. If the wetland's economic services are valued at $500M, the two alternatives become equal. If these services are valued at greater than $500M, the second alternative becomes superior. The value of totally avoiding the wetland would have to be at least $600M for the third alternative to be feasible.

A second stage could be added to this evaluation. So far, only included in the valuation is the economic value of the services that wetlands perform for the economy, as estimated by ecological economists. If this turned out to be below the $300M to reach feasibility, the question can be asked, How much are the recreational and aesthetic values to the community, value to tribal nations who are in proximity, and so on, worth? If the gap is small, it might easily be closed with a noncontroversial decision.

Benchmarking   Benchmarking is a comparison method based on establishing reference points for one or more performance indicators. It can be helpful for distinguishing alternatives in at least a couple of different contexts.

First, benchmarking can be useful for investment situations where each alternative is to be subject to similar performance standards. Returning to Figure 12.1, one can see that 24 boardings per hour is the threshold at RTD for 15-minute headway service, and 40 per hour for 10-minute headway service. Hence, any forecast that shows the project alternative unable to meet the standard after the investment means the project is inferior. If two or more alternatives meet the standard, these can be further differentiated by a comparison of their incremental Benefit to Cost Ratios (BCRs) with respect to various objectives. As an example, assuming that increasing ridership is an objective, the incremental ratio would be additional boardings per hour forecast for the project after it is completed divided by the investment cost. (Although not strictly necessary, analysts can convert the investment from a total or annual basis to an hourly basis to make the indicator values larger and perhaps easier to appreciate.)

Second, in performance-analysis situations, benchmarking is useful for identifying which of the project objectives might already be met well and which not so well. Returning to Figure 12.1, there are boxes enclosing each set of routes belonging to one family of services. Clearly, members towards the top and right of a box are already excelling in the two indicators, Boardings per Hour and Subsidy per Boarding. Thus, any objective whose achievement these indicators are supposed to measure is also being met better than for those members that are to the left and down. Returning to Figure 12.2, the achievement of any objective associated with operating speed is steadily eroding on Route 1 but only slightly on Route 2.

Another graphical technique for making comparisons is to use a *radar plot*, which conveys somewhat different information. Instead of only two indicators at a time, it displays many. More importantly, for each indicator, it compares an individual performance to the median of the set and the best of the set. This allows a ready comparison of strengths and weaknesses. Figure 12.4 shows such a radar plot using indicators similar to those used by CoMET, a consortium of the world's largest rapid transit operators. In this case, entire systems instead of single routes or lines are being compared to one another. The individual system shown in this figure can be seen to have the best space-averaged load factor indicator (passenger-distance per space-distance offered) but is below the median for two other indicators. This technique has been used by its members with some success to identify where improvement is needed in relation to their peers (Bata 1999; RGI 2003; RTSC 2009, 2011).

As the two examples suggest, benchmarking can be used for internal comparison as well as external comparison. It was used for comparing individual services within a set at the RTD and for comparison of entire networks with one another at CoMET. Because it is important that networks be peers, somewhat smaller metro systems form another peer group called NOVA. There is at least one consortium for regional rail operators, the International Suburban Rail

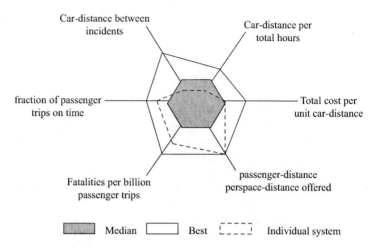

Figure 12.4 Radar plot comparing rapid transit system performance to peer operators.

Benchmarking Group (ISBeRG, 2013). Another example is the International Bus Benchmarking Group, a consortium of operators of large bus fleets. Yet another is the more recently created American Bus Benchmarking Group, or ABBG (2011), a consortium of midsized bus fleet operators in the United States.

Mageen, Mulley, and Nelson (2001) suggest three possible levels of comparison. Level 1 is a self-assessment using only internal data. Level 2 is a comparison with a database that can include external peer information. Level 3 is partnering, which is distinguished by actively working with other organizations in order to identify best practices and means of implementation, possibly even exchanging confidential information.

External comparisons are more difficult to organize as they require agreement about which indicators to track about uniform, consistent data-collection and processing methods to maintain comparability. Fortunately, suitable groups of peer operating firms often already exist. Where they do not, the establishment of a successful benchmarking program can be accelerated by reference to existing programs. See, for example, the detailed description of EQUIP, a European Commission–sponsored benchmarking program (Mulley, Mageen and Nelson 2001). Unfortunately, details about the aforementioned groups are restricted because of the confidential data being shared, but newsletters do release some selected results, examples being the CoMET/NOVA newsletters cited above. Academic publications may also release useful information about issues related to selection of performance indicators (Trompet, et al. 2011) and characteristics of members (Trompet, Anderson and Graham 2009). Thus the analyst not participating in such consortia should continually monitor publications.

The RTD and CoMET examples show how performance analysis relates to the investment cycle. The benchmarks suggest the goals that should have priority and what types of projects are needed next in a process of "continuous improvement." Logically, there is probably less need to improve already excellent aspects of a service than those that are substandard. Furthermore, it usually is much more difficult to further improve something already at or near the best-of-breed than to improve something to a standard most other peers have already been able to achieve. Restated, there are diminishing returns to investment towards improving performance when performance is already at a high standard.

Professional panel.   A professional panel employs a group of experts to do the evaluation, each contributing their own special experience to the mix. The theory behind this technique is that the best solution will eventually be filtered out from the mass of information. Individuals with a set of oddball or extreme views will tend to be countered by opposite views and dominated by the majority views. A variation on the professional panel is the *Delphi method*, in which each individual does the evaluation independently without consultation or input from other reviewers.

The actual format of the evaluation can vary. It can range from an informal roundtable discussion in which the aim is to reach a consensus, to a formal matrix completion in which the applicable factors are preselected based on the category of project.

An advantage of more informal processes is that experts can learn from each other's viewpoints and perhaps revise their evaluations accordingly. Another advantage is that the group can develop compromise project alternatives sometimes if it agrees that such compromise overcomes problematic issues identified during the discussion. On the other hand, an informal process reduces comparability with similar projects.

A formal process has the advantage that the exact same factors are evaluated for each project of a similar nature. This approach would be applicable where a project is expected to meet the same criteria as similar projects that have gone before it and that will come after it. It would also be applicable where the project alternatives are similar with respect to technology and goals, with the main difference being the geographic locations. For example, a project might involve investing a fixed budget for Transit Signal Priority equipment procurement and installation. This budget is sufficient only to equip one corridor. The evaluation issue then becomes which corridor would get the most benefit, all things considered.

The Finnish government's guidelines for Intelligent Transportation System (ITS) evaluation (Kulmala et al. 2002) provides a good example of a formalized process applied to these types of situations. The panel is to divide each type of major ITS into a list of functions it performs. Each function has a row within a matrix. Each column represents an impact the panel will evaluate. The result is a matrix of evaluation cells. These impacts are divided into three major groups: Target of Impacts, Main Impacts, and Transport and Information Society Policy Objectives. A few of the cells are highlighted to indicate they are not pertinent to the particular function. The results submitted by different experts can be statistically analyzed, both in comparison to each other for the current project and in comparison to previous projects.

Sole reliance upon such methods may be appropriate for selecting a project alternative where deep technical expertise is required, but not where the public implications are huge. If the public must live with the decision for a long time and its impact will be far-reaching into aspects that help define the city to its citizens, it is unlikely the public will allow "experts" to make the decision without public input.

Public participation.   Public transportation projects are ultimately supposed to serve the public, reflecting the public's needs and desires. Furthermore, the public is usually the source of most, if not all, of the investment capital and will have to pay any operations and maintenance subsidies. For all of these reasons, it is right for the public to participate in the project selection process. Indeed, it is the law in the United States and in many other countries that there is public participation when federal funds are used. The question is when and how to involve them. There are many steps in the process, and there are many levels of detail.

It can happen that there is no practical "fix" to some public concerns. It is unrealistic to think there will ever be an alternative for a complex, major project that satisfies everyone or treats everyone perfectly equitably. But the public input at least raises the issue to public officials that some form of compensation should be considered to those who are the most negatively affected. This would be done not only out of a sense of justice but also to remove potential obstacles to project advancement.

Any public outreach must be preceded by research on the most effective ways to contact a cross-section of society, not just those who initiate contact or respond to formal opportunities. If done fairly and in good faith, public outreach will quickly make clear who thinks they are getting an inequitable deal or have other serious concerns about a given project alternative. This information can then be fed back into the alternatives development process to modify alternatives to correct flaws, increase equity, and address unmet needs.

Projects that involve physical redesign of the urban landscape should always involve public opinion. Not only do project directors need to respond to concerns about aesthetic impacts, but they need to consider the potentially revolutionary changes to the character and livability of neighborhoods. Rights-of-way may impede pedestrian travel and split communities. Street-level changes will affect driving and parking conditions. If a corridor is to have high-capacity transit at frequent intervals, there may be safety and air and noise pollution issues. Logically, this participation should come early in the alternatives development process. *Charettes* are an effective means to this end. They allow the public to visualize alternatives, discuss them, and perhaps even improve upon them. *Focus groups* might be given similar information to discuss but are not self-selected through their own interest, being selected instead by project team members to meet some specific demographic criteria. *Public hearings* are more formal, so there cannot be the same degree of interaction to discuss and suggest modifications to alternatives. *Public comment periods* allow people who cannot physically be present to also state their views. Written public comments have the advantage that they leave a written record to which others can respond. This is particularly valuable when the testimony involves numerical analysis or reference to multiple documents.

As the project moves forward and project lenders refine discrete project alternatives, the same outreach techniques can be used more than once. The public should be provided with additional detail when it becomes available. In the United States, the National Environmental Policy Act requires that an environmental impact statement be issued for major projects. There likely will be regulations from lower levels of government requiring documentation of anticipated impacts and any planned mitigations as well. The law may well mandate public hearings or a public comment period to allow response before the project can proceed further.

Outreach techniques are greatly enabled by the widespread use of the Internet. Images and analysis results can be posted beforehand so that people have time to contemplate them before attending a *charette* or public hearing. People can even participate remotely through video links, thereby expanding the numbers. Comments can be immediately shared with the whole population. The public participation and outreach process is rapidly evolving and can only improve as a result of improved communications media. One noteworthy example is from the Portland, Oregon area, where the regional government created an internet exercise where concerned citizens could pick and choose their priorities for projects and corridors subject to a budget constraint (Metro 2009). As this example, shows, developers of project alternatives can expect to get ever more frequent and detailed feedback in the future.

There are also limits to the type of information one can expect from the public. First, it is only natural that most residents will tend to focus on the impacts on their own immediate community more than on others. Second, people who lead busy lives cannot possibly be up to date on every aspect of a project. Reiterating the point about individuals being unable to reach an optimal solution, even the best-intentioned and selfless citizen or elected official will not be able to pick the alternative with the highest net benefit for the community at large. However, what they can do is reveal unanticipated flaws, impacts, and needs. Long-time residents and current regular transport system users can identify these much better than planners or engineers who shift from one project to the next.

There are exceptions to this rule about the public not being expected to do a comprehensive analysis. One of the roles of professional planners in larger regions is to design project alternatives that attempt to reconcile differences between districts within a city, between adjacent cities, and so on, while also considering equity. But smaller cities might be able to do without this assistance. They might well be able to develop a community involvement process that generates a transportation investment plan genuinely driven by the public. Ithaca, New York, is an example of a city where "the final ITCTC [Ithaca-Tompkins County

Transportation Council] planning document accurately captures the spirit and values of the broader community" (Boyd and Gronlund 1995, 61). The authors of this quote have one more point to make as well: "One of the clear lessons is that it is not advisable to attempt to satisfy the desires of all of the members of the public" (1995, 61). Even in the smaller city, there will never be one perfect alternative that satisfies everyone.

One other mode of public participation is to hold a public vote. These stem from a referendum by elected officials or in response to a citizens' mandated initiative. If it is an advisory on the selection between several alternatives, it is like an expanded version of a public comment period. If it is a binding vote, it actually undercuts the public participation process by cutting off all further discussion. If it is a large project involving construction, it might well be the single most expensive investment with the most far-reaching impacts the region has ever considered. In my opinion, a small turnout in an off-year election would hardly seem to be an unbiased reflection of the public's will and a poor basis for making such a decision.

Even a simple go/no-go vote on the recommended final project alternative raises serious issues. The public may react, not to the qualities of the alternative, but to their perceived fairness of the proposed funding. For example, in the United States, using property taxes generally creates resistance because it puts this proposal in competition with public schools and other public services. The chosen tax might also have a regressive impact on persons with fixed incomes or other particular interest groups, perhaps raising new objections from yet another quarter. Thus, it can tie the decision to a particular funding formula, rather than to the merits of the project relative to its alternatives.

Second, a funding vote puts public transportation at a disadvantage with other transportation investments that don't require a vote. In the United States, funding of particular highway projects, seaport improvements, or airport improvements are rarely voted upon. (Or, if they are, they are through bond approval measures that obscure the specific nature of projects they will fund.) Instead, funding is often simply appropriated from general taxation for both investment and operations and maintenance due to a low gasoline tax. Meanwhile the vast majority of new transit projects require a public vote on funding both for capital and for ongoing operational subsidies (Beimborn and Puentes 2003). Even projects that appear to be self-financing have environmental and social impact, while the remainder of the transportation system might see new costs imposed through intermodal linkages.

Restated, major projects may be self-sufficient in terms of capital investment and repayment, but they are rarely self-contained without externalities. In the interest of the development of a balanced multimodal transportation system, all types of major investment proposals should be subject to evaluation processes that consider the full range of both benefits and costs and where decision makers are equally accountable for money spent on any mode (Puentes and Bailey 2003). As always, the process should also consider the opportunity cost of investing elsewhere instead.

Somewhat Less-Accessible Methods that Require Weighting

What is still missing from the aforementioned methods is the *relative weight of importance* of each Scaled Result and each item of Other Information. The relative ranking of each could change if items where an alternative performs in a superior fashion are of little consequence and items where it performs in an inferior fashion are of great consequence, or vice versa. It is this attempt to put some analytic rigor into the ranking process that characterizes more "hard" methodologies.

There is no perfect means of assigning weights. Any method in use has its detractors who can point to its shortcomings, but this cannot be an argument not to use weighting factors, as the alternative of assigning no weighting factors is implicitly assigning equal weights to all criteria included in the evaluation. This is itself an arbitrary decision. The SEPTA case study in Chapter 2 was a typical example of a flawed process in wide use. For a quite sophisticated and current exploration of the theoretical issues associated with establishing weights in the context of projects intended to contribute to a sustainable economy, see "The Use of Weights in an SMCE Framework" in Munda (2008).

Each newer method has some features meant to address shortcomings in older methods of weighting. Thus, multicriteria evaluation is a work in progress and the analyst should stay abreast of trends. The techniques emphasized here are presented because they have what, in my opinion, a reasonable combination of rigor and comprehensibility and acceptability to decision makers and the interested public.

Analytic Hierarchy Process.   The Analytic Hierarchy Process (AHP) is a versatile evaluation tool with wide application possibilities. It involves systematically tracing, weighing, and comparing all impacts for each proposed alternative. There are many ways in which AHP has been used in the past for making decisions. See, for example, the volume edited by Golden, Wasil, and Harker (1989). Of concern here will be only one example application. It will show some of the basic concepts behind AHP so that its value can be made clear.

AHP is a means of finding defensible relative weights of importance for the various project objectives, beneficial impacts, and the inevitable undesirable impacts. It also is a means of estimating how effectively each project alternative achieves these various objectives and the degree to which it incurs these undesirable impacts. At the same time, AHP is not a formidably complex mathematical computation. Rather, it is an intuitively structured process, meaning people can understand its basics without an advanced education in mathematics. It reflects the real thought process of decision making in a few ways. It divides the analysis into manageable subanalyses. It incorporates learning because the AHP can be repeated after the various evaluators form new opinions or new information comes to light that merits a revision of score(s). It can be restructured to make further decisions after the first decision is made. It can accommodate professional panel judgments, public opinion, and numerical indicators from a variety of sources having different scoring systems and from most any other source appropriate to the particular subanalysis. It is this ability to absorb incommensurable information and unify quantitative and nonquantitative data that makes it a compelling tool.

AHP involves a hierarchy of levels to reflect the structure of the relationships of the needed comparisons. The bottom level will be the various project alternatives that need to be considered before rendering a final decision. In one form, the top of the hierarchy is the ultimate goal(s) of the project. In the form the current example will use, there are two hierarchies: one has the total benefit to be achieved at the top; the other a parallel hierarchy for the total costs. In between the bottom and top levels is the impact level. Each of these impacts would be of a different degree, depending upon the project alternative selected. Thus, the combined set of impacts, some of which would be beneficial and some of which would incur costs would be different for each project alternative. As always, costs need to be balanced against benefits to complete the evaluation.

AHP uses a ratio scaling system from between 1 and 9 proven effective by experience for adequately differentiating between strengths of opinions. A ratio of 1 means both choices are equally important or equally preferred, depending upon the context. A ratio of 3 means "slightly more important," 5 means "strongly more important," 7 means "very strongly more important," and 9 means "extremely strongly more important" (or preferred). The even numbers serve as intermediate gradations. Large ratios between performance indicators or cost values would suggest large ratios for the evaluation scores. Public opinion expressed as preferences between designs might be almost directly transferable if the questions were worded carefully. For some subanalyses, a professional panel might use little more than professional experience to render a judgment. Analysts can convert almost any type of scoring into this ratio scale using some logic and judgment.

The art of using AHP is to create a hierarchy of subanalyses that does not exclude important impacts, but also is not more complicated than it needs to be. Once a project has reached the comparison stage between various alternatives so that officials can make their final selection, the lists of identified beneficial impacts and undesirable impacts should be clear. Thus, the analyst should also have some idea which factors will likely be unimportant to any decision. When in doubt, it is better to initially err on the side of inclusion. If factors are initially excluded, they can never receive a relative weight. On the other hand, if the relative weight of a factor is definitively shown to be very small, the analyst can subsequently delete it and simplify the hierarchy.

An example problem will be used to illustrate the method. The scenario involves an increasingly congested city where public transport runs in mixed traffic and is increasingly slow and costly to operate. The congestion is also interfering with commerce and making the city increasingly dysfunctional and unattractive. The citizens have a high dependence upon personal vehicles and currently face few restrictions on where and when they can drive, but the situation continually deteriorates. The question at hand is whether the entire city needs a major investment in public transportation, and, if so, which type of investment?

Example 12.2

Figure 12.5 shows the benefit hierarchy for a hypothetical large project with citywide impacts. The positive impacts are expressed such that they align closely with key project objectives. Similarly, the negative impacts are expressed such that they align with key project costs. Figure 12.6 shows the corresponding cost hierarchy for the same project.

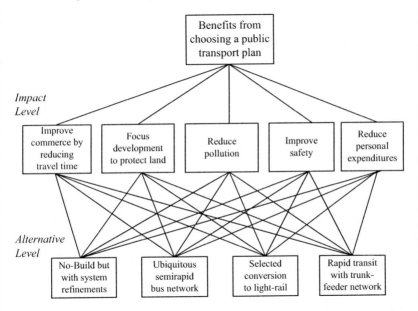

Figure 12.5 Analytic Hierarchy Process (AHP) hierarchy for benefits from citywide transit project.

Once the hierarchy is established, the analyst can estimate the relative weights between the five beneficial impacts and between the four undesirable impacts. The analyst compares each project alternative with the three other alternatives with respect to each impact. Table 12.2 shows the evaluation matrix for both sets of impacts. As an example, the evaluators decided that Improving Commerce is "Very Strongly More Important" than Focusing Development by picking 7. Once this has been established, Focusing Development must have 1/7 the importance of Improving Commerce, and another element in the matrix can be filled. The comparisons continue until all of the matrix elements are filled.

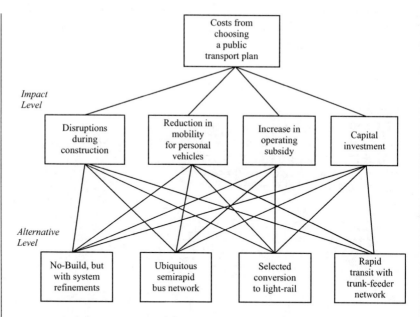

Figure 12.6 Analytic Hierarchy Process (AHP) hierarchy for costs from citywide transit project.

Table 12.2 Comparison of the importance of the impacts

BENEFITS

	Commerce	Development	Pollution	Safety	Expenditures	Weight using column 3 or 4
Commerce	1	7	5	5	3	0.48
Development	1/7	1	1/2	1/2	1/3	0.05
Pollution	1/5	2	1	1	1/3	0.09
Safety	1/5	2	1	1	1/2	0.09
Expenditures	1/3	3	3	3	1	0.29

COSTS

	Disruption	Mobility	Subsidy	Investment	Weight using eigenvector
Disruption	1	1/9	1/3	1/4	0.06
Mobility	9	1	3	2	0.51
Subsidy	3	1/3	1	1/2	0.16
Investment	4	1/2	2	1	0.27

Note: The relative importance results then translate into relative weights by taking the ratio of the value for any one entry in a column to the sum of all entries in the column. These values were computed for the beneficial impact comparison using either the third or fourth column (they are identical) and printed in the rightmost column.

(Continued)

The four project alternatives in this hypothetical example were chosen for the large differences between them that would presumably translate into large differences in evaluation scores. The scores used for this example are plausible ones for such a scenario based on my personal experience. Any similarity to a comparison of real systems is purely coincidental.

When people are asked to make comparisons, one needs to remember that comparisons are not always consistent. Comparing A to B and then A to C on the same ratio scale would algebraically imply a ratio between B and C, but this may not prove to be the same as the value that actually gets picked. Thus, there is some error inherent in the process. This explains why the relative weights do not come out quite the same when different columns are used for the computation. A better estimate of weighting can be found by computing the *eigenvector* for the matrix. It uses the combined information from all of the columns instead of one column. Continuing the computation also gives a measure of error called a *consistency ratio*. If this ratio is reasonably low, the evaluators were reasonable, and the error is of little consequence. See Harker (1989) for details of the computation methodology.

Example 12.2 (continued)

The next step is to do comparisons between each project alternative with respect to each impact. There are five impacts in the benefits matrix and four impacts in the cost matrix, for a total of nine comparisons.

Table 12.3 shows one example—Focusing Development. This specific type of comparison would most likely be done by a professional panel tasked with interpreting and vetting the output from an integrated land use/transportation model loaded with data and calibrated for the purpose of being able to compare these alternatives. Each of the remaining comparisons could be done using different evaluators appropriate to the topic. For example, a comparison with respect to Reduction in Mobility for Personal Vehicles might be done by a professional panel using modeling results but heavily informed by input from public hearings and public comments.

Table 12.3 Comparison of the effectiveness of alternatives with respect to focusing development

	No-Build	Semirapid bus	Light-rail	Rapid transit	Score using eigenvector
No-Build	1	1/3	1/2	1/2	0.06
Semirapid bus	3	1	1/2	1/2	0.12
Light-rail	5	3	1	1/2	0.26
Metro	7	5	3	1	0.56

It is possible to repeat the comparisons using different stakeholders having different interests, levels of expertise, and perspectives, but before assuming that any large differences in results are genuine, it might be advisable to provide additional information to all evaluators because, for example, there may be some misunderstandings due to ambiguities or unfamiliar jargon. As with all other evaluation methods, a genuine large difference of opinion about a particular project factor indicates where more attention needs to be focused. One way AHP can help determine the causes of any differences is to add subcriteria to the primary impact level. These, in turn, also get weighted in a more refined scoring process. See Harker (1989) for more details about subcriteria and for more information in general about the basic AHP process, albeit using a nontransportation example.

Example 12.2 (continued)

Assume that, similar to Table 12.3 for Focusing Development, the analyst has also compared the remaining eight impacts and completed their matrices. The next step is to combine all of the information so that the overall benefits versus overall costs can be compared.

Table 12.4 lists all beneficial impacts and cost impacts in the first column, along with their importance weightings from Table 12.2 in the second column. The next four columns contain the scores for each one of the four project alternatives relative to each impact. For example, the results from Table 12.3 (*shown in italics*) are in the "Focus Development" row. The composite score for each alternative is then computed as follows. For each alternative, first multiply the score for each impact by its importance weighting. Then sum the weighted scores from all impacts. This is repeated separately for both costs and benefits. The final step is to compute the ratio of benefits to costs for each alternative.

The results show that the No-Build course of action is not a wise one. The Benefit-to-Cost Ratio far below 1 shows that investing in only minor refinements to the system will cause continuing costs to be incurred. The high operating subsidy requirement from operating under congested conditions and high personal expenditures far outweigh the investment savings. The other options all have similar benefit/cost ratios greater than 1. The Semirapid Bus alternative has the lowest benefits but also the lowest costs. The Rapid Transit alternative has the highest benefits but also the highest costs.

The results are currently inconclusive between the three types of transit investment projects, but it is also apparent what would swing the decision in various directions. As one example, Focusing Development is seen to be of

(Continued)

little importance with a weight of only 0.05. If it were to take on a high level of importance for one reason or another (say, to make the city more sustainable), the Rapid Transit alternative would excel. It has by far the highest score when it comes to effectiveness at focusing development. For a second example, Capital Investment has a weighting of 0.27 compared to 0.51 for personal mobility. Apparently, evaluators are currently far more concerned about deteriorating traffic conditions than about the higher capital expense of building rail transit. If these priorities were to reverse, the Semirapid Bus network alternative would excel instead.

Table 12.4 Evaluation by combining benefit and cost results

BENEFITS	Weight	No-Build	Semirapid Bus	Light–Rail	Rapid Transit
Improve commerce	0.48	0.10	0.25	0.25	0.40
Focus development	*0.05*	*0.06*	*0.12*	*0.26*	*0.56*
Reduce pollution	0.09	0.10	0.20	0.30	0.40
Improve safety	0.09	0.08	0.22	0.32	0.38
Reduce personal expenditure	0.29	0.04	0.26	0.30	0.40
WEIGHTED SCORE		0.0758	0.239	0.276	0.406
COSTS					
Construction disruption	0.06	0.04	0.15	0.28	0.53
Personal mobility reduction	0.51	0.40	0.20	0.20	0.20
Increase in subsidy	0.16	0.30	0.20	0.20	0.30
Capital investment	0.27	0.06	0.14	0.30	0.50
WEIGHTED SCORE		0.271	0.181	0.232	0.317
Benefit-to-Cost Ratio		0.28	1.32	1.19	1.28

Once the first decision is made, the AHP can be used in *backward-forward* iterations. The backward process takes the project alternative chosen from the forward process and now makes it the goal of AHP, putting it at the top. The levels would descend through problems to be overcome to implement that particular alternative, the actors that might be involved in implementing that alternative, and, at the bottom, the array of possible policies for implementing that alternative (Saaty 1999). The decision then becomes: which of these policies should be selected? This type of iteration could be very useful when analysts have settled on the basic concept or goal but there is more than one policy (or design element or location) that can implement that particular project. Thus, AHP could also be used earlier in a project alternative development process, not just during final project selection.

Example 12.2 also points to a technical issue. Recall that simple benefit/cost ratios are problematic because what is considered a benefit increase versus what is a cost reduction is often arbitrary. Although the analyst can be consistent between alternatives when defining what is a benefit increase or a cost decrease, it still makes a difference in the final computed ratios whether an increase is put in the numerator or a decreased value is put in the denominator. Thus, close overall benefit/cost ratios should be appreciated for the fact that they are close, not for the exact values.

The resulting matrix contains useful incremental benefit versus incremental cost information as well. Other investment questions that can be answered include: 1) which particular project alternative would give the best return on investment for an incremental expansion? and 2) which particular beneficial or undesirable impact increases the most for an incremental expansion of any given project alternative? Such answers would be useful, for example, when there is a likely to be limited amounts of investment capital available periodically instead of guaranteed funding to completion.

This brief treatment hardly does justice to AHP. See the references and bibliography for further information on backward-forward iterations, incremental analysis methods, and other interesting application ideas. For a closely related method also accessible to those without an advanced mathematical background, see Gomes (1989).

Example 12.2 (continued)

Which alternative would give the highest return on further expansion after successful completion of the initial project?

Assuming that the incremental benefits from further investment are the same as the average from previous investment (constant return on investment), this question can be answered by comparing the incremental benefit to incremental cost ratios. The first ratio is determined using the lowest cost alternative in the denominator and the corresponding benefit in the numerator. The second ratio is determined using the differences in costs between the second lowest and lowest alternative in the denominator and the corresponding difference in benefits in the numerator. The third ratio is determined using the differences in benefits and costs between the third lowest and second lowest.

Semi Rapid Bus	Light-Rail	Rapid Transit
$\dfrac{0.239}{0.181} = 1.32$	$\dfrac{0.276 - 0.239}{0.232 - 0.181} = 0.73$	$\dfrac{0.406 - 0.276}{0.317 - 0.232} = 1.53$

With the current weightings, the rapid transit solution would give the most benefit when some capital became available. The ubiquitous bus would be a close second with light-rail showing the least return.

In practice, the assumption of constant return on investment could be suspect. To help test this assumption, estimated benefits from each stage of a project should be compared to costs incurred at this same stage. In the present example, the rapid transit option probably would have minimal returns when there is only one line, much higher benefits when the network becomes large enough to strongly influence travel and development patterns, and diminishing returns once the network becomes ubiquitous.

EcoMobility Modeling Framework

EcoMobility (EM) is a very recent method that benefits from lessons learned using other, slightly older methods that combine the NPV or BCR analysis with multicriteria methods. More specifically, it uses the officially sanctioned Danish Cost Benefit Analysis (CBA-DK) method referenced in Chapter 9 that deals with uncertainty of monetary and monetized estimates with a weighting and effectiveness method that bears some resemblance to the AHP method. The last case study in Chapter 2 used this method. This section provides some of the missing methodological details about the weighting and effectiveness computations.

The establishment of weights is simplified compared to the AHP. It simply used fixed values from a table, using the so-called Rank Order Distribution (ROD) method, which is provided in Table 12.5. It is based on research on different weighting methods and shown to give accurate relative weights in a variety of circumstances (Roberts and Goodwin 2002). Generally, criteria that end up being associated with very small weights can be dropped for consideration as they won't affect the outcome.

The participants in the Decision Conference are asked to consider what the relative rankings of importance are for each of the six criteria. First they do this separately, and then they do this jointly as a group. A log is kept of all of the results for later analysis if there are large differences between private opinions and the joint opinion. The result for this case is shown in Table 12.6. Weights are based on the ROD table, but only two digits are shown to the participants.

The pairwise comparison technique used for judging relative effectiveness is known as REMBRANDT. It bears a resemblance to AHP, as can be seen in Table 12.7, where the first criterion of the six is shown. It uses a scale from 1 to 8 and uses negative numbers instead of inverses. The composite scoring requires some transformations. It is not a weighted sum like AHP but a process requiring the transformation of each score, followed by a geometric mean of each score in

Table 12.5 Rank Order Distribution (ROD) weights

	Criteria								
Rank	2	3	4	5	6	7	8	9	10
1	0.6932	0.5232	0.4180	0.3471	0.2966	0.2590	0.2292	0.2058	0.1867
2	0.3068	0.3240	0.2986	0.2686	0.2410	0.2174	0.1977	0.1808	0.1667
3		0.1528	0.1912	0.1955	0.1884	0.1781	0.1672	0.1565	0.1466
4			0.0922	0.1269	0.1387	0.1406	0.1375	0.1332	0.1271
5				0.0619	0.0908	0.1038	0.1084	0.1095	0.1081
6					0.0445	0.0679	0.0805	0.0867	0.0893
7						0.0334	0.0531	0.0644	0.0709
8							0.0263	0.0425	0.0527
9								0.0211	0.0349
10									0.0173

Source: Roberts and Goodwin 2002.

Table 12.6 The DC participants' joint ranking of the criteria

Criteria	Rank after importance	Weight
Socioeconomic robustness	2	0.24
Improvement for passenger cars and public transport	3	0.19
Positive impact on towns and land use	6	0.04
Positive impact on regional economics	1	0.30
Positive impact on flexibility in logistics	5	0.09
Contribution to the EU green corridors	4	0.14

Source: Jensen et al. 2012.

the row to get the score in the right hand column. For example, the score for the first row of Table 12.5 was computed as follows:

$$Transform\ ij = e^{\ln 2 \times Score ij} \tag{12-1}$$

The resulting transformed values are 1, 0.015625, and 0.0625. Then the totaled score across the column is computed using:

$$Total = \sqrt[3]{Transform\ i1 \times Transform\ i2 \times Transform\ i3} \tag{12-2}$$

Table 12.7 The comparison matrix for the socioeconomic robustness criterion

	Socioeconomic robustness			
	Alt I	Alt2	Alt3	Score
Alt I	0	−6	−4	0.10
Alt2	6	0	3	8.00
Alt3	4	−3	0	1.26

Source: Jensen et al. 2012.

Inserting values:

$$Total\ i = \sqrt[3]{1 \times 0.015625 \times 0.0625} = 0.099 \qquad (12\text{-}3)$$

which is rounded to two decimal places, or 0.10.

The final score for Alternative 1 then involves exponentiating the Total i for each criterion z and multiplying it by all of the other corresponding terms for the other criteria. Introducing the nomenclature $(Total\ i)_z^{weightz}$. the score for the first alternative with 6 criteria is:

$$Composite\ alt\ 1 = (Total\ 1)_1^{\text{weight1}} \times (Total\ 1)_2^{\text{weight2}} \times (Total\ 1)_3^{\text{weight3}} \times (Total\ 1)_4^{\text{weight4}}$$
$$\times (Total\ 1)_5^{\text{weight5}} \times (Total\ 1)_6^{\text{weight6}} \qquad (12\text{-}4)$$

As a last step all of the composite scores can be normalized to sum to one, as is often the convention. Further details of the ranking, weighting and scoring process can be found in Leleur (2012) as well as a more detailed discussion of multicriteria analysis applied to major transport infrastructure projects.

Appendix 12.A briefly describes some additional multicriteria evaluation methods.

Summary

Not everyone will agree which project alternative is "best." Therefore, those charged with making such a decision should have a basis for defending them, but there usually is no process where one just "turns the crank" for a complex project to generate the "right" or "best" answer. There simply is no way to combine monetary and nonmonetary factors, and then evaluate them jointly in a way in which everyone will agree is satisfactory. The incommensurability of factors is something plaguing the decision process.

Comparing the universe of possibilities for every element of the project is impractical. Comparisons should be between a limited number of alternatives. Analysts should consider each promising project alternative's strength in pursuit of some goals and weakness in others, but no candidate should neglect key goals. Once the project alternatives are narrowed down, the next step is to assemble and organize all available information for each. One way to organize results is it to put key goals together with their supporting objectives in a matrix. This should also be done for other relevant information as well. Analysts need to assign scores for each objective when possible. While monetization may sometimes be acceptable when using a weak sustainability approach, strong sustainability would instead set a firm, quantifiable limit for some natural assets. Some factors cannot be portrayed accurately using a scale because of their "nonlinear" nature. Small differences between values from one project alternative to the next could have huge implications.

Another way to organize information is to graphically portray data for two or more indicators simultaneously. One can study how alternatives similar in one respect vary in another respect, or how one individual compares against a group. Another basic type of graphical display is the trend plot, used to reveal whether the indicator is improving or deteriorating over time.

Identifying relevant public policies can provide important information. A project goal may be shown to conflict with other governmental goals or some aspect of one or more of the project alternatives may require public policy changes. A risk element must then be added.

An initial screening can at best identify a clear winner and, at worst, reduce the number of project alternatives left for further consideration. What is needed is a *relative weight of importance* of each scaled result and of the other information. The relative ranking of each remaining alternative will likely change after weights are assigned.

In the conventional economic analysis of investment decisions, one seeks to maximize the net benefits of a project by summing the discounted benefits minus cost for each year, subject to constraints on the quality of the service, on the budget, and so on. If there are no constraint equations, the math program simplifies down to just an NPV equation. In some situations, the maximization of net benefit approach can find the best alternative. If the desired benefits to be achieved are clearly defined, the alternative that achieves them with minimum costs would be the best one. The situation where the cost is fixed instead for all alternatives would be similar. In particular, sets of alternatives where capital expenditure and cash flow constraints are important parts of projects can be investigated as to which already complies and how others might need to be modified in order to comply. Another good use is when several alternatives use similar technologies. These can perhaps be recast into functional relationships instead of specific values and a new alternative that outperforms any of them might be generated.

These simpler approaches are not applicable, however, to project alternatives with longer-term and far-reaching impacts. Each alternative represents a different bundle of both benefits and costs, each with different degrees of incommensurability, different controversies regarding valuation, and different nonlinear information. To accommodate these concerns, the net benefit would then have to be expressed in a range. But this result can be accommodated as one criterion in multicriteria evaluation methods.

The concept of decision making by satisficing means people select the "good enough" solution rather than analyzing until they reach the theoretical optimal solution providing maximum net benefits. If several seem close to each other in overall "goodness," further assessment can still be done. Several assessment methods were described.

Breakeven analysis is based on NPV analysis but modified to incorporate benefits that cannot be readily monetized or whose valuation is controversial. This type of analysis sets a minimum threshold for a benefit in order for the alternative to become feasible. It might well be that the unmonetized benefit for alternative i, UB_i, is large enough that it easily meets the criterion. By adding UB_i to the estimate for net benefits, $(B\text{-}C)_i$, it might also revise the ranking of project alternative i.

Benchmarking is a comparison method based on establishing reference points for performance indicators. It can be useful for situations where each alternative is to be subject to similar performance standards as well as for identifying which project objectives might already be met well and which not so well. Several consortia of similar-sized metro operators and bus fleet operators have obtained useful information for both their individual members and the membership as a whole. While the data and many of the results are not available to nonmembers, analysts can also share in this information occasionally through publications.

A radar plot is a graphical display showing numerous indicators. It compares an individual performance for each indicator to the median of the set and the best of the set. There are three possible levels of comparison. Level 1 is a self-assessment using only internal data. Level 2 can include external peer information. Level 3 is actively working with other organizations. Performance analysis relates to the investment cycle. The benchmarks suggest the goals that should have priority and what types of projects are needed next, in a process of "continuous improvement."

A *professional panel* is a group of experts who do the evaluation. A variation is the Delphi method, where each individual does the evaluation independently. The actual format of the evaluation can vary. It can range from an informal roundtable discussion to a formal matrix completion where the applicable factors are preselected. A formal process has the advantage that analysts evaluate the exact same factors for each project of a similar nature. Sole reliance on such methods may be appropriate where deep technical expertise is required but not where the public implications are huge.

Public participation is the law in the United States and in many other countries because public transportation projects are ultimately supposed to serve the public. Any public outreach must be preceded by research on the most effective ways to contact a cross-section of society. *Charettes* allow the public to visualize and discuss alternatives. Focus groups might be given similar information to discuss but are not self-selected through their own interest. Public hearings are more formal, so there will not be the same degree of interaction. Public comment periods allow people who cannot be physically present to also state their views. As a project moves forward, the same outreach techniques can be used more than once. This information should be fed back into the alternatives development process.

There are also limits to the type of information one can expect from the public. Even the best-intentioned and selfless citizen or elected official will not be able to pick the alternative with the highest net benefit for the community at large, but what they can do is reveal unanticipated flaws, impacts, and needs. Planners play the role of developing alternatives to reconcile the views of different communities. But smaller cities might well be able to develop a community involvement process that generates a transportation investment plan genuinely driven by the public.

A popular vote is a poor basis for final decisions. It can tie the decision to a particular funding formula, rather than to the merits of the project. In the interest of a balanced multimodal transportation system, all types of major investment proposals should be subject to evaluation processes that consider the full range of benefits and costs.

The AHP is a means of finding defensible relative weights of importance for various project objectives as well as for inevitable undesirable impacts. It also is a means of estimating how effectively each alternative achieves these various objectives and the degree to which it incurs these undesirable impacts. AHP is an intuitively structured process that breaks the evaluation into subanalyses. It can accommodate professional panel judgments, public opinion, and numerical indicators from a variety of sources having different scoring systems and most any other source appropriate to the particular subanalysis. The analyst can then compute the overall BCR of all combined impacts.

Once the first decision is made, AHP can be used in backward-forward iterations. The backward process takes the project alternative chosen from the forward process and now makes it the goal of the new AHP. Other investment questions that can be answered include: 1) Which particular project alternative would give the best return on investment for an incremental expansion? and 2) Which particular beneficial or undesirable impact increases the most for an incremental expansion of any given project alternative?

The EcoMobility (EM) method is a more recent development. It combines the NPV value or BCR analysis with a multicriteria analysis. Some of its advantages includes that it deals with the uncertainties involved in monetary and monetized values, it has a simplified weighting system relative to AHP, and it has a software package that allows a facilitator to share the scoring process with participants as a Decision Conference proceeds.

There are numerous other multicriteria methods available to the analyst who is trying to gain additional insights out of the available information. Methods presented in brief in the Appendix include *Data Envelopment Analysis*, *TOPSIS*, and *Modified Concordance Analysis*.

Appendix 12.A

Some Additional Methods of Ranking Alternatives

Some methods for ranking alternatives are unlikely to ever be part of an official process because they suffer from the aforementioned skepticism about "black box" solutions. Elected officials and especially the public are unlikely to understand or accept them, but for the analyst who is trying to gain additional insights from available information, methods that take account of several criteria simultaneously can be useful. They can be used as supplements to benchmarking and other performance comparison techniques. Three other techniques are briefly described here.

Data Envelopment Analysis

The concept of *Data Envelopment Analysis* is to develop sufficiently complex indicators that use the weighted sum of several input resources. These indicators allow comparison between agencies or operators on the basis of several factors instead of only one. The weights x_i for each of these input resources are determined using a math program such that no member of the peer group can have an efficiency greater than 1.

For example, the quantity of service output for an agency k can be measured in annual Revenue-Vehicle-Hours. This is divided by an annual cost for agency k having four input components. The result is a *relative efficiency* indicator:

$$Relative\ Efficiency_k = \frac{(Revenue\ Vehicle-Hours)_k}{x_1(operators + fuel + tires)_k + x_2(vehicle + facilitymaint)_{ki} + x_3(admin + supervision)_{ki} + x_4(other)_k}$$

$$(12-5)$$

This needs to be solved using a math program. One set of constraint equations state that for all peers being compared, no individual peer, j, can have a relative efficiency that exceeds 1.0. A second set of constraints says that the weighting factors x_1, x_2, x_3, x_4 must be greater than zero. The resulting mathematical program for the relative efficiency of agency k is:

Maximize *Relative Efficiency*$_k$
Subject to:

$$\frac{(Revenue\,Vehicle-Hours)_j}{x_1(operator+fuel+tires)_j+x_2(vehicle+facilitymaint)_j+x_3(admin+supervision)_j+x_4(other)_j} \le 1.0$$

for j = 1, 2, 3 . . . . n
$x_1, x_2, x_3, x_4 > 0$ (12-6)

Because the solution for the weighted variables, x_i, are in the denominator of both the objective function and the constraints, this equation appears to be non-linear and difficult to solve. Fortuitously, it can be converted into an equivalent linear program that is easy to solve. This program would have to be solved n times, once for each agency to get the relative efficiency for each.

A similar definition and math program can be created for *relative effectiveness*, in which the output is measured by Annual Passenger Trips. The input resources, however, are not as clear-cut as those for efficiency, which used only cost components. Instead, it must include components that fairly describe all relevant input resources available so peer agencies can be compared on an equal footing. As an example, Chu, Fielding, and Lamar (1992) built a resource input function that included *Revenue Vehicle Hours, Annual Financial Assistance per Passenger, Population Density*, and *Proportion of Households without Automobile*. See Sulek and Lind (2000) for another sample application.

Figure 12.7 shows an example hypothetical peer comparison using this technique. The peer in the top right corner of this relative efficiency versus relative effectiveness plot would be the best in both criteria. One agency would be its

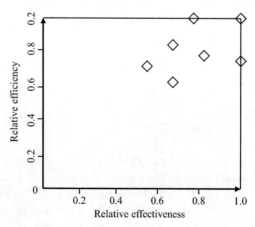

Figure 12.7 Peer comparison using data envelopment analysis.

equal in efficiency, the other its equal in effectiveness. Note the similarity in interpretation to Figure 12.1, in that findings that appear to the right and higher are both better, but instead of using an absolute scale, the DEA notion is that the best performance sets a boundary having a value of 1, making all comparisons relative to the best.

There has been some success using DEA and similar techniques. See Karlaftis (2004) for a study comparing 256 US transit systems. He concluded that efficiency and effectiveness are indeed positively correlated but didn't analyze and individual systems in detail. Hawas et al. (2012) applied DEA to a network and identified a way that routes could be split to reduce operating costs without reducing either efficiency or effectiveness. An analysis by Fu, Yang, and Casello (2007) of demand-responsive systems demonstrated that the method is relatively easy to apply, but was largely inconclusive due to the limited dataset available at the time. See Borger, Kerstans, and Costa (2002) for a survey of historical applications and Cook and Sieford (2009) for a more recent list and an exposition of the variants that have been used. DEA has seen a modest amount of application specifically for transit systems.

When it comes to using this information to evaluate management performance similar issues pertain to encourage efficiency and effectiveness as were discussed in Chapter 11 in the section entitled Issues When Considering Appropriate Organizational Structures and Contract Models. In a nutshell, it can be difficult to really isolate how much of the relative scores stem from factors in management's control versus those that are not. There are sometimes inherent factors in route networks and in agency goals that limit management ability to improve the system.

Nevertheless, as data sets become richer over time because of increasing use of ITS, and as benchmarking efforts evolve with experience, these types of analyses could also evolve. Evermore refined and precise expenditure estimates in the case of efficiency measures and more precise ridership potential and financial support information in effectiveness measures would improve the comparability between agencies. Further research may also find ways to incorporate the effect of route network structure. Perhaps other measures comparing service quality could be developed as well. These would likely involve speed, load factors, and other service-related indicators from the passenger's viewpoint.

Other Multicriteria Evaluation Methods in Brief

The *TOPSIS* method tries to formulate an "ideal solution" and then measure the "separation" of any particular alternative, j, from the ideal. Analysts can use TOPSIS in contexts similar to those in which AHP is suitable. TOPSIS too is designed to deal with several close alternatives, each of which has several impacts. It also converts the various scales for each impact into a normal form. But TOPSIS is more difficult to use and to understand than AHP. Its weighting algorithm is much less intuitive, invoking an entropy method similar to that described for trip distribution in Chapter 7. It determines a weighted impact matrix, again similar to AHP, but then splits the impact matrix into an "ideal solution" matrix for the beneficial impacts and "negative ideal solution" matrix for the cost impacts. The separation of benefits from the ideal for a given alternative, j, is found by taking the square root of the sum of the squares of each difference between the normal weighted impact value with its corresponding element in the ideal solution. The separation of cost impacts from the ideal is similar. See Janic (2001) for an example of the use of TOPSIS in investment decision making for a high-speed rail project.

Modified Concordance Analysis also tries to differentiate alternatives similar to one another with respect to several of the positive and negative impacts. It too requires that a normal matrix be constructed for comparability. But here is where the similarity to all of the previous multicriteria methods ends. Rather than try to determine one set of relative weights like the other methods, Modified Concordance Analysis uses numerous sets of weights on the various terms representing all of these positive and negative impacts. These weights can be changed based on what the analyst knows about the perspectives of various interested parties, or they can be chosen by an experienced analyst, simply based on an expert guess of how various parties are likely to respond. Should any alternative project still be included amongst those with the best scores, no matter which set of weights is chosen, it would be the best compromise. This is because the particular alternative scores well no matter whose perspective is reflected in the relative weightings. Thus every interested party should be satisfied. Note that this is an approach inherently based on the satisficing philosophy.

In practice, there may be a few project alternatives that that score well. That is, the several sets of weights overlap amongst these few alternatives. Such a conclusion is not as good as arriving at a single best compromise project alternative, but it would still be successful in reducing the number of final candidate alternatives, all of which are acceptable to all interested parties. See Giuliano (1985) for an example in multimodal transportation planning where auto as well as transit alternatives are involved.

References

ABBG (American Bus Benchmarking Group). 2011. Press Release (June). http://americanbusbenchmarking.org/press-and-publications/

Bata, Andrew. 1999. "Aiming for Excellence through Benchmarking." Presentation at 1999 American Public Transit Association Rail Conference, Toronto. Based upon W. R. Steinmetz and Robin Hirsch. 1998. *Business Briefing: Global Mass Transit Systems.* London, UK: World Markets Research Centre, 102–11.

Beimborn, Edward, and Robert Puentes. 2003. *Highways and Transit: Leveling the Playing Field in Federal Transportation Policy.* Washington, DC: Center on Urban and Metropolitan Policy; The Brookings Institution.

Boyd, David S., and Amy Gronlund. 1995. "The Ithaca Model: A Practical Experience in Community Based Planning." *Transportation Research Record* 1499: 56–68.

Borger, Bruno De, Kristiaan Kerstens and Alvaro Costa. 2002. "Public Transit Performance: What Does One Learn from Frontier Studies?" *Transport Reviews* 22 (1): 1–38.

Byron, Michael, ed. 2004. *Satisficing and Maximizing: Moral Theorists on Practical Reason*. Cambridge, UK: Cambridge University Press.

Chu, Xuehao, Gordon J. Fielding and Bruce W. Lamar. 1992. "Measuring Transit System Performance Using Data Envelopment Analysis." *Transportation Research A* 26 (3): 223–230.

Cook, Wade D., and Larry M. Seiford. 2009. "Data Envelopment Analysis (DEA)—Thirty Years On." *European Journal of Operational Research* 192: 1–17.

Forst, Wilhelm, and Dieter Hoffmann. 2010. "Optimality Conditions." Chapter 2 in *Optimization—Theory and Practice*. Berlin, Germany: Springer-Verlag.

Friedrich, Rainer, and Peter Bickel. 2001. "Economic Evaluation, Sustainability Indicators, and Alternative Assessment Techniques." Chapter 8 in *Environmental External Costs of Transport*. New York: Springer-Verlag, 83–116.

Fu, Liping, Jingtao Yang and Jeff Casello. 2007. "Quantifying the Technical Efficiency of Paratransit Systems Using the Data Envelopment Analysis Method." *Transportation Research Record* 2034: 115–22.

Golden, Bruce L., Edward A. Wasil and Patrick T. Harker, eds. 1989. *The Analytic Hierarchy Process: Applications and Studies*. Berlin: Springer-Verlag.

Gomes, Luiz F. A. M. 1989. "Multicriteria Ranking of Urban Transportation System Alternatives." *Journal of Advanced Transportation* 23 (1): 43–52.

Giuliano, Genevieve. 1985. "A Multicriteria Method for Transportation Investment Planning." *Transportation Research A* 19 (1): 29–41.

Harker, Patrick T. 1989. "The Art and Science of Decision Making: The Analytic Hierarchy Process." In *The Analytic Hierarchy Process: Applications and Studies*, edited by Bruce L. Golden, Edward A. Wasil and Patrick T. Harker. Berlin: Springer-Verlag.

Hawas, Yaser E., M. Bayzid Khan and Nandita Basu. 2012. "Evaluating and Enhancing the Operational Performance of Public Bus Systems Using GIS-based Data Envelopment Analysis. *Journal of Public Transportation* 15 (2): 19–44.

ISBeRG (International Suburban Rail Benchmarking Group). 2013. Home Page. http://www.isberg-web.org

Janic, Milan. 2001. "Development of High-Speed Systems in Europe: Multicriteria Ranking of Alternatives." Chapter 7 in *New Analytical Advances in Transportation and Spatial Dynamics*, edited by Massimo Gastaldi and Aura Reggiani. Burlington, VT: Ashgate Publishing, 157–87.

Jensen, Anders Vestergaard, Inga Ambrasaite, Kim Bang Salling, Michael Bruhn Barfod and Steen Leleur. 2012. "The EcoMobility Modelling Framework for Sustainable Transport Planning." Chapter 9 in *Rethinking Transport in the Øresund Region: Policies, Strategies and Behaviours*, edited by Carl-Magnus Carlsson, Tareq Emtairah, Britta Gammelgaard, Anders Vestergaard Jensen and Åke Thidell. Lund, Sweden: Lund University, 149–64.

Karlaftis, Matthew G. 2004. "A DEA Approach For Evaluating the Efficiency and Effectiveness of Urban Transit Systems." *European Journal of Operational Research* 152: 354–64.

Kulmala, Risto et al. 2002. *Guidelines for the Evaluation of ITS Projects*. FITS Publication 4/2002, Ministry of Transport and Communications. http://www.vtt.fi/rte/projects/fits/ julkaisut/hanke2/ FITS_4_2002_Guidelines_for_evaluation.pdf

Leleur, Steen. 2012. "SIMDEC." Appendix B in *Complex Strategic Choices: Applying Systemic Planning for Strategic Decision Making*. London, UK: Springer.

Mageen, Jenny, Corrianne Mulley and John Nelson. 2001. *EQUIP: Recommendations and Conclusions*. European Commission, Contract UR-98-RS.3676, 10. http://www.euro projects.ie/equip

Metro (Portland Regional Government). 2009. *2035 Regional High Capacity Transit System Plan: Public Involvement Outreach Summary and Attachments* (May). http://library.oregonmetro.gov/files/hct_pi_outreach_summaryno_attachments.pdf

Mulley, Corianne, Jenny Mageen and John Nelson. 2001. *EQUIP: Final Report*. European Commission, Contract UR-98-RS.3676. http://www.europrojects.ie/equip

Munda, Giuseppe. 2008. "The Use of Weights in a SMCE Framework," Section 4.5 in *Social Multi-Criteria Evaluation for a Sustainable Economy*. London: Springer, 78–84.

Puentes, Robert, and Linda Bailey. 2003. *Improving Metropolitan Decision Making in Transportation: Greater Funding and Devolution for Greater Accountability*. Washington, DC: Center on Urban and Metropolitan Policy; The Brookings Institution.

RGI (Railway Gazette International). 2003. "CoMET and Nova Deliver Tangible Benefits." *Metro Report*, 15–18.

Roberts, R., and P. Goodwin. 2002. "Weight Approximations in Multi-Attribute Decision Models." *Journal of Multi-Criteria Decision Analysis* 11 (6): 291–303.

RTD (Regional Transit District). 2013. 2011 Family of Services Tables and Charts. http://www.rtd-denver.com/PDF_Files/ServiceD/PerfReport_Performance_2011_Complete.pdf

RTSC (Railway and Transport Strategy Center). 2009. *Comet and Nova Newsletter* (April). London, UK: Imperial College. https://workspace.imperial.ac.uk/rtsc/public/CoMET-Nova%20Newletter%20-%20April%202009_Final.pdf

———. 2011. *Comet and Nova Newsletter* (September). London, UK: Imperial College. https://workspace.imperial.ac.uk/rtsc/Public/CoMET%20and%20Nova%20Newsletter%202011.pdf

Saaty, Thomas L. 1999. *Decision Making for Leaders*. Pittsburgh, PA: RWS Publications.

Sulek, Joanne M., and Mary R. Lind. 2000. "A Systems Model for Evaluating Transit Performance." *Journal of Public Transportation* 3 (1): 29–47.

Trompet, M., X. Liu and D. J. Graham. 2011. "Development of a Key Performance Indicator to Compare Regularity of Service between Urban Bus Operators." *Transportation Research Record* 2216: 33–41.

Trompet, M., R. J. Anderson and D. J. Graham. 2009. "Variability in Comparable Performance of Urban Bus Operations." *Transportation Research Record* 2111: 177–84.

Winston, Wayne L. 2003. "Introduction to Linear Programming." Chapter 3 in *Operations Research: Applications and Algorithms*. Pacific Grove, CA: Brooks/Cole.

Further Reading

Banister, David. 2005. *Unsustainable Transport: City Transport in the New Century*. London, UK: Routledge.

ECMT (European Council of Ministers of Transport). 1996. "Sustainable Transport in Central and Eastern European Cities." *Proceedings of the Workshop on Transport and Environment in Central and Eastern European Cities*, 28–30 June 1995, Bucharest, Romania. Paris, France: Organization for Economic Cooperation and Development.

Fielding, Gordon J. 1992. "Transit Performance Evaluation in the U.S.A." *Transportation Research A* 26 (6): 483–91.

Gercek, H., B. Karpak and T. Kilincaslan. 2004. "A Multiple Criteria Approach for the Evaluation of the Rail Transit Networks in Istanbul." *Transportation* 31 (2): 203–28.

Glaister, Stephen. 1994. "Public Transport: The Allocation of Urban Public Transport Subsidy." In *Cost Benefit Analysis*, 2nd ed., edited by Richard Layard and Stephen Glaister. Cambridge, UK: Cambridge University Press, 418–27.

Green, David L., Donald W. Jones and Mark A. Delucchi, eds. 1997. *The Full Costs and Benefits of Transportation; Contributions to Theory, Method and Measurement.* Berlin: Springer-Verlag.

Henning, Theunis, F. P. Sugandree Muruvan, Wanhua A. Feng and Roger C. Dunn. 2011. "The Development of a Benchmarking Tool for Monitoring Progress Towards Sustainable Transportation in New Zealand." *Transport Policy* 18: 480–88.

Leviakangas, Pekka, and Jukka Lahesmaa. 2002. "Profitability Evaluation of Intelligent Transport System Investments." *Journal of Transportation Engineering* 128 (3): 276–86.

Levine, Jonathon, and Steven E. Underwood. 1996. "A Multiattribute Analysis of Goals for Intelligent Transportation System Planning." *Transportation Research C* 4 (2): 97–111.

Lucas, Karen, Greg Marsden, Michael Brooks and Mary Kimble. 2007. "Assessment of Capabilities for Examining Long-Term Social Sustainability of Transport and Land Use Strategies." *Transportation Research Record* 2013: 30–37.

OECD (Organization for Economic Cooperation and Development). 2002. *Impact of Transport Infrastructure on Regional Development.* Washington, DC.

———. 2001. *Assessing the Benefits of Transport.* Washington, DC.

Ryus, Paul et al. 2002. A *Guidebook for Developing a Transit Performance Measurement System.* Report 88. Washington, DC: Transit Cooperative Research Program, National Academy Press. http://www.tcrponline.org

Saaty, Thomas L. 2000. *Fundamentals of Decision Making and Priority Theory.* Vol. 6. AHP Series. Pittsburgh, PA: RWS Publications.

———. 1980. *The AHP: Planning, Priority Setting, Resource Allocation.* New York: McGraw-Hill.

Smith, Brian L., Michael J. Demetsky and Priyad Durvusula. 2003. "A Multiobjective Optimization Model for Flexible Transit Service Design." *Journal of Public Transportation* 6 (1): 81–100.

SUTP (Sustainable Urban Transport Project in Asia). 2003. *Sustainable Transport Sourcebook.* http://www.sutp.org/publications.aspx

Glossary

access time The component of door-to-door travel time spent leaving the point of trip origin to a transit stop

active priority A transit signal priority response based on detection of transit vehicle location and possibly time of detection

annualized operating cost The direct cost of operating and maintaining a transit route or set of routes over a whole year; an average value

annualized total cost The cost of operating and maintaining a transit route or set of routes, including the amortized cost of vehicle ownership, over a whole year; an average value

articulated bus A vehicle with one or more hinges such that it can be much longer than an conventional bus yet still be able to negotiate turns

Automatic Passenger Counter (APC) A subsystem for Computer Aided Dispatching/Automatic Vehicle Location systems that uses sensors mounted in doorways to monitor times of door opening and closing at each stop, as well as number of boarding and alighting passengers

average operating speed A performance indicator computed by dividing the length of a route or line by the travel time required

benchmarking A method of comparing and trending performance measures either internal to a firm/agency or externally with peers, based on establishing reference points

binding (constraint) When a constraint has reached the limit of its inequality relationship and becomes an equality instead

breakeven analysis An evaluation method that finds the minimum additional benefit required to justify an investment; used when imprecise information is available

Build–Operate–Transfer (BOT) A project-implementation method where one single entity is responsible for building transit infrastructure, procuring all needed equipment, and managing the operations for an initial period time before the eventual hand over to public ownership

Bus Rapid Transit (BRT) Service designed to emulate most of the features of Light Rail Transit, including use of right-of-way B, longer station spacings than regular bus services, Transit Signal Priority, and other ITS features and passenger amenities

capacity supply profile   The capacity offered in seats or spaces per hour versus the time of day

classification   Data sets for large numbers of individuals are pooled into range groups, or bins, based on a key characteristic such as annual income to facilitate aggregation into totals

complementary slackness   A mathematical property of costs and passenger or vehicle flows along paths such that flow can only be nonzero if the cost on a candidate path is equal to the lowest cost path

cross-subsidization   The concept of using excess revenues (profits) from one route or line and using them to support another route or line that earns revenues less than its costs

deadhead factor   The ratio of total distance traveled by a vehicle to the distance travel on a route or line with passengers

deadheading   Moving a vehicle to a route or line from a depot or storage location or repositioning a vehicle to another route or line, without passengers

demand-responsive feeder   A method of connecting outlying passengers to a fixed route by using vehicles that only operate when there are specific requests for service

demand-responsive services   Transit services provided only on request, usually requiring advanced reservations

Design–Build model   An approach to major projects making the same firm/consortium responsible for both the design and construction phases

Design–Build–Operate–Maintain model (DBOM)   An approach to major projects making the same firm/consortium responsible for the design, construction, operation, and maintenance phases

diametrical route (or line)   A route or line that begins at an area of lower activity continuing in the direction of increasing activity density but then continues through the center, once again proceeding into areas of lower activity density

direction balance ratio   A performance indicator for efficient use of vehicles, computed by comparing the ratio of passengers boarding in one direction to those boarding in the opposite direction over the same time interval

discounting   The concept of reducing the future value of money to reflect the fact that money is worth more if it is used in the present

duty cycle   The acceleration, braking, cruising speed, and dwell time characteristics of a transit vehicle operating in a repetitive environment typical of route operations

Early Bird discount   Giving a price reduction to parkers who come early and stay in the parking house or parking lot all day, not usually on street parking

ecological economics   A relatively new branch of economics that attempts to monetize the value of nature's services and to identify the opportunity cost of developing or degrading land

economies of density   The concept that higher levels of demand within a given area allow a higher Level-of-Service to be provided with the same budget, or alternatively, equally good service with a lower budget

economies of scale   The unit cost of output decreases with the quantity of output

egress time   The component of door-to-door travel time spent from leaving the vehicle to arrival at final destination

elasticity of demand   The percentage change in ridership over the percentage change in some other quantity

engineering cost model   A cost estimation tool based on the consumption of input resources needed to support a service or investment

environmental justice   The concept that persons or communities that receive project costs without commensurate benefits be compensated

Expected Maximum Utility (EMU)   The combined utility from all choices within a nest that is used for comparison at the next level higher in a nested logit model

fare elasticity of demand   The percentage change in ridership over the percentage change in fare; similar to price elasticity of demand

forecasting   Using a mathematical model to estimate key design values for a chosen year in the future (e.g. values including auto traffic levels and public transport demand levels)

frequency   The rate at which vehicles pass a fixed point, usually expressed per hour; also, the inverse of headway, but usually expressed in that case in minutes

generalized cost   The monetized value-of-time for travel between two points, plus fares, tolls, and other out-of-pocket costs

generalized time   Out-of-pocket costs converted to an equivalent time penalty to add to the travel time between two points

Geographic Information System (GIS)   A computer database that can be systematically overlaid on maps to convey and analyze spatial relationships

Global Positioning System (GPS)   The currently dominant vehicle location system, based on taking position fixes from multiple satellites

gross density   The density computed by dividing an activity level or the number of persons by the size of an area, possibly including water and undevelopable land

headway   The time interval between vehicles passing a fixed point, usually expressed in minutes; also, the inverse of frequency, which is usually expressed as number per hour

headway elasticity of demand   Percentage change in demand over the corresponding percentage change headway of service along a route

hub-and-spoke system   (*See* **Timed Transfer Network**)

hybrid services   Transit service designs that are neither purely fixed route nor purely demand-responsive, but something in between

incremental cost   The additional cost to add another increment of output, usually based on practical considerations of minimum amounts that can added at one time; distinguished from marginal cost, which is for one unit of output

Intelligent Transportation System (ITS)   A package of hardware and software specifically designed for improving transportation operations, information to the public, and/or information for service planning

interlining   The practice of having a vehicle continue onto another route or line rather than reversing at a terminus

joint cost   A cost in which several different services or projects may share, but there is no unambiguous basis for apportioning the costs; an example might be an intermodal terminal where numerous bus and train routes interchange passengers

Land Value Taxation (LVT)   A taxation system first proposed by Henry George (1839–1897) where the primary determinant of property tax is location instead of the value of improvements upon the property

Level-of-Service (LOS)   The combined service characteristics experienced by the user

life-cycle costing   The concept of evaluating an investment on both the initial investment and the annualized operating and maintenance cost, usually only applicable when the benefit is similar for all investment choices

Light-Rail Vehicle (LRV)   A vehicle reminiscent of a streetcar but more complex and powerful in order to operate on right-of-ways A, B and C

line capacity   The maximum throughput of transit units (TUs) or spaces measured at one point on a line on a per-unit time basis; it has numerous variations depending upon safety regime and assumed crowding standards

link   A road or transit right-of-way that connects two nodes in a mathematical model

linked trip   A trip that includes all segments used on public transport vehicles

Locally Preferred Alternative   The project alternative selected locally that is then submitted to the federal government for further review and a funding decision (specific to US)

logit function   A mathematical construct for predicting mode choice that has the requisite probability distribution characteristics (actually, a close approximation of the more theoretically correct probit function, one that is also more intractable computationally)

mainstreaming   Facilitating people with disabilities to use the same facilities as the general public to the maximum extent possible

marginal cost   The cost to carry one more vehicle on a roadway, one more person in a transit vehicle, or, in general, of providing one more unit of service output

Maximum Load Section (MLS)   The segment of a route or line on which the maximum number of passengers is carried; there may sometimes be more than one

Metropolitan Planning Organization (MPO)   A governmental body legally required to do transportation forecasting and to propose a transportation improvement/investment plan for a metropolitan region (specific to US)

Minimum Allowable Rate of Return (MARR)   The lowest discount rate for which the Net Present Value of an investment must be greater than zero, typically set by public policy for public agencies, by minimum profit requirements for private firms

modal energy intensity A coefficient expressing unit energy consumption per unit passenger-distance, incorporating both vehicle technological capability and vehicle occupancy

mode split The fraction of trips by a particular mode along a route or line, between two points, or across an entire region

monetizable An attribute that can be expressed in monetary value by use of proportionality constant or function

monorail A public transport technology that operates exclusively on right-of-way A using tires for both lateral and vertical support on a beam using a special cross-section, typically a proprietary design

National Transit Database (NTD) A source of operating statistics and cost information for each transit agency receiving federal funds that is broken into categories used for cost modeling and estimating (US only)

net contract model A contracting approach for operating transit services in which only enough public subsidy is provided to attract bidders, with the operator retaining all fares collected

net density The density computed by division of activity level or number of persons by developed area, excluding water and other undeveloped/undevelopable land

Net Present Value (NPV) The set of discounted benefits minus discounted costs for an investment or project alternative

no-build scenario A project alternative used to compare what may happen if no action is taken with other alternatives; may sometimes include modest Transportation Systems Management investments

nominal value A monetary value expressed in the current year for which it is expended or received

O-bahn Bus infrastructure that uses vertical beam surfaces that contact small lateral wheels mounted on the bus; used to narrow the right-of-way, to steer buses through tunnels, and to prevent autos from entering the right-of-way

O–D Distribution The second step in the four-step sequential model, it allocates trips generated in the previous phase between spatial zones, most commonly using the principle of entropy maximization

O–D matrix The entire set of volumes between all O–D pairs

opportunity cost The forgone possibilities when resources are committed to a particular project alternative

Origin–Destination pair (O–D pair) The starting point and ending point for a motorized trip, generally spatial zones and not specific addresses in the context of mathematical models

quasiroute A preliminary set of pickup and drop-off points that form the basis for a fuller demand-responsive route that will be filled in later with trips that were requested with shorter notice.

paratransit In the narrow definition, services provided as a public service on a demand-responsive basis; in the broader definition, any for-hire services that are not fixed route (e.g. taxis, jitneys, vanpools, airport shuttles)

passenger count   The difference between cumulative boardings and alightings along a route or line

passive priority   A method of giving transit vehicles priority based on signal timing and street layouts inherently designed to favor transit without active communication

path-link incidence relationship matrix   A condensed form of storing all information about all possible paths between an origin and destination, for all O–D pairs. Its transpose can be used to determine the total flow on a link from all of the paths that use that link

peak-hour factor   A performance indicator describing the degree of demand variability by time of day, computed as the ratio of passengers boarding in the peak hour(s) over the passengers boarding over the entire service day

people mover   The informal name for a guided transit system, usually operated on right-of-way A in either a shuttle or loop configuration, typically serving internal circulation needs of large institutions or downtowns

performance indicator   A statistic used to assess whether a route or line meets acceptable standards and to identify peers for comparison

physical connectivity   The availability and convenience of movement for individuals and their belongings from one mode to the next, or to a mode from trip origin, or from a mode to final trip destination

point load factor   A performance indicator used to measure capacity use, computed by dividing current passengers by total spaces on the vehicle

price elasticity of demand   The percentage change in demand over the corresponding percentage change in price (or fare); includes out-of-pocket expenses such as tolls and parking fees

projection   A method of predicting the future value of a design criterion based simply on extrapolation of present trends

public-private partnership (PPP)   A method of project development in which responsibilities and finances are divided amongst various parties in recognition of the benefits each can receive, hopefully to the mutual benefit of all parties

radial route (or line)   A route or line that begins at a center of activity and continues out in the direction of lower demand density

random utility theory   A mathematical method of comparing performance when several incommensurable random variables are involved

Real-Time Passenger Information (RTPI)   The estimated arrival time for a vehicle at a particular stop based on tracking of actual location versus scheduled location; it can be delivered with signs in the field, over the Internet, over Personal Digital Assistants (PDAs), cell phones, etc.

relative efficiency indicator   An indicator used in comparisons between peers in which the best performing member of the set is set to 1 and all others are set at less than 1

Revealed Preference (RP)   A method of predicting traveler response to a selection of travel choices and their willingness to pay for each based on statistical analysis of previous experience

revenue operating speed   Similar to average operating speed, but could refer to an entire network rather than an individual route or line; does not include time spent deadheading

rickshaw   motorized or nonmotorized three-wheeled public transport vehicle holding two or three passengers; found in South Asia

right-of-way A (ROW A)   A right-of-way with full physical separation from all other paths, providing the highest operating speeds and most reliable travel times

right-of-way B (ROW B)   A right-of-way where transit vehicles have lateral separation from other traffic, but still share intersections with cross traffic

right-of-way C (ROW C)   A right-of-way where transit vehicle operate in mixed traffic, providing the slowest operating speeds and least reliable travel times

sequential four-step model   The most common method for forecasting the automobile and transit demand and facility use over the various major links of a regional network, consisting of 1) trip generation, 2) Origin–Destination Distribution, 3) mode-split computation, and 4) traffic assignment

shadow price   The lowest generalized cost/time of all possible paths between i and j, which also is the marginal change in the value of the total network cost (objective function) with a unit change in flow between i and j

short turning   The creation of a second version of a route or line that reverses before the terminus, used to better match supply to demand and to reduce the Fleet Size requirement

shuttle   A route that consists of only two stops, one at each terminus

simulation model   A computer program that studies the movement and inter-action of individual vehicles in detail, often with the aid of visualization tools

slack   The time added to a schedule to allow for variable travel conditions or to facilitate deviations

space-averaged load factor   A performance indicator used to measure vehicle space consumption efficiency over the length of a route; computed as the ratio of total space-distance consumed over total space-distance offered

spatial zones   A subdivision of a region used for assigning local attributes in a four-step sequential model

Stated Preference (SP)   A method of estimating traveler response to a selection of travel choices and their willingness to pay based upon carefully worded and analyzed sets of questions; needed when there is no previous experience with a proposed project alternative

station capacity   The maximum number of Transit Units per hour as dictated by the need to decelerate, dwell, and accelerate back to cruising speed at stations; usually the station with the longest dwell time sets this limit

summary management reports   Cursory statistics of transit system performance based upon aggregated values (e.g. total Vehicle-Distance or total Vehicle-Hours performed per day, total operator hours paid, total fuel consumption, percent of runs performed on schedule, and so on)

sunk costs   Costs that can no longer be influenced after the initial expenditure and are thus independent of how much or how little this cost-causing item is actually used

sustainable development   The concept that economic development should take place such that nonrenewable resources are not depleted and natural systems of restoration and pollution mitigation are not overloaded

sustainable economics   An economic analysis approach that tries to encourage sustainable development by including the value of services that nature provides, the effect from depletion of renewable resources, and costs and benefits to future generations from decisions made today

system optimum   The resulting traffic or transit assignment across a network that would give lowest total cost; it would result if each individual driver or transit vehicle would do what is best for the system as a whole instead of the individual; it is found by modifying network models using Wardrop's Second Principle, expressed as a mathematical constraint

tangential route (or line)   A route or line that does not enter into a central area but instead connects more peripheral locations, generally having the property of more even loading because demand does not increase continually as with radial routes

Tax-Increment Financing (TIF)   A method of financing a project based on assessing a charge on all properties within a certain distance from transit service in recognition of the fact that property owners benefit from public investment

terminal time   The time used at the end or a route or line, which may include time for final alighting, initial boarding, vehicle repositioning, operator rest, and recovery time in case of late arrival

timed-transfer network (TTN)   A route structure designed such that many vehicles arrive and depart from one point at the same time in order to increase the number of O–D pairs that can be served and the frequency at which they can be served

total operating speed   The average operating speed, computed including not only travel time along routes or lines, but all deadheading movements as well

Transit Oriented Development (TOD)   Community design based on neo-traditional principles of generous walking and bicycling facilities with retail, clinics, recreational and office buildings near a major transit station that forms the nucleus

Transit Signal Priority (TSP)   (*See also* **active priority** and *passive priority*) The control of traffic signal timing, and possibly street layout, in order to favor transit vehicles over private vehicles

Transit Unit (TU)   A group of vehicles connected to one another to increase capacity, called a train for the rail mode, also called a *consist* in the North American professional rail community, and a *rake* in British parlance

TransModel   A source of standardized operating statistics and cost data for transit agencies within the member states of the European Union

transportation system user benefit   A performance measure that includes the benefits from an investment to all transportation system users, not only those using the mode in which the investment takes place (e.g. auto users benefit from time savings if transit diverts previous users from a congested road)

travel time distribution   A statistical description of the variability of travel times due to random events and congestion

trip chaining   The concept that many travelers do not simply make symmetrical outgoing and return trips but meander around to perform a variety of errands

tuk tuk   A three wheeled public transport vehicle holding two to three passengers, found in Southeast Asia

turnkey provider   A single entity entrusted with the entire execution of a project, including supervision and responsibility over all subcontractors

turnover ratio   A performance indicator based on the ratio of fares collected along a route or line to the number of spaces available

ubiquitous network   A public transportation system developed so intensely that it has had links added directly between major O–D pairs rather than according to a geometric pattern

unlinked trip   A trip counted separately, even if it may actually be a transfer between two transit vehicles

user equilibrium   (*See also* **Wardrop's First Principle**) The traffic distribution that results when each traveler makes a decision on his/her best routing (shortest time) independent of the effect on others

utility ratio   (*See* **space-averaged load factor**)

Wardrop's First Principle   The principle used to assign traffic along paths in mathematical models; a constraint states that all paths used between a particular O–D pair will have equal generalized times, which are also the minimum possible; the end result is a network in user equilibrium

Wardrop's Second Principle   The principle that all traffic should be distributed such that all paths have equal *marginal* generalized times; the end result is a network that becomes a system optimum; in practice cannot be enforced with private individual users, but can be partially used for transit portion of the network

way capacity   The maximum number of Transit Units per hour on a line based on the safe stopping distance required to keep the following Transit Unit from colliding with the leading Transit Unit

zone service   A train operating plan in which trains operate express or local along different sections of the route, with connections between zones only at a few stations shared in common

Nomenclature

For all definitions below, the symbol [-] indicates dimensionlessness.

α = peak hour factor [-]

α_{avg} = average vehicle occupancy [persons]

β = deadhead ratio [-], or parameter for generalized cost of traveling between locations i and j [1/time]

γ = schedule efficiency ratio [-]

δ = length of single vehicle [distance]

δ_j = point load factor on segment j [passengers/space]

ε = cost random error term [$] or random error term for utility or disutility function [-]

ϕ_i = calibration factor for Expected Maximum Utility of nest i

η = direction balance ratio [-]

ξ = space-averaged load factor [passenger-distance/space-distance]

τ = turnover ratio [-]

Δbd = difference in bus-distance

Δbh = difference in bus-hours

Δcd = difference in car-distance

Δfs = difference in fleet size

Δtd = difference in train-distance

Δth = difference in train-hours

Δ = difference in

Δ = path-link incidence relationship matrix

λ^{Auto} = mode-split fraction for auto [-]

λ^{Bus} = mode-split fraction for bus [-]

λ^{Rail} = mode-split fraction for rapid transit [-]

a_j = alightings at stop j [passengers]

A = total alightings [passengers]

A_i = calibration factor for distributing trips from origin O_i [-]

A_j = Accumulated alightings after stop j [passengers]

AC_O = Annualized Operating Cost [$/year]

AC_T = Annualized Total Operating Cost [$/year]

b_j = boardings at stop j [passengers]

BH = Bus-Hours (a resource variable)

BD = Bus-Distance (a resource variable)

B = total boardings [passengers]

B_j = accumulated boardings after stop j [passengers], or benefit in year j [$],
  or calibration factor for distributing trips to destination D_j [-]

B_{kj} = benefit from component k in year j [$]

$B_{kj}{}^{\prime}$ = inflated benefit from component k in year j [$]

BPV = Benefit Present Value [$]

C_v = capacity of vehicle [spaces/vehicle]

CD = Car-Distance (a resource variable)

CK = Car-Kilometers (a resource variable)

CM = Car-Miles (a resource variable)

CPV = Cost Present Value [$]

CRF = Capital Recovery Factor [-]

C_a = total expenditure on administration [$]

C_{CD} = component of total cost assumed proportional to Car-Distance [$]

c_{CD} = C_{CD}/CD = attributed cost per unit Car-Distance of service
  [$/car-distance]

C_f = total expenditure on fuel [$]

C_{fm} = total expenditure on facility maintenance [$]

C_j = cost in year j [$]

C_{FS} = component of total cost assumed proportional to peak vehicles in use
  [$]

c_{FS} = C_{FS}/FS = attributed cost per vehicle in peak service [$/vehicle]

C_{kj} = cost of component k in year j [$]

$C_{kj}{}^{\prime}$ = inflated cost for component k in year j [$]

C_o = total expenditure on vehicle operators [$]

C_m = total expenditure on vehicle maintenance [$]

C_s = total expenditure on supervision and control [$]

C_t = total expenditure on tires and other expendables [$]

C_{TH} = component of total cost assumed proportional to Train-Hours [$]

c_{TH} = C_{TH}/TH = attributed cost per Train-Hour of service [$/train-hour]

C_{VH} = component of total cost assumed proportional to Vehicle-Hours [$]

c_{VH} = C_{VH}/VH = attributed cost per Vehicle-Hour of service [$/vehicle-hour]

C_{VD} = component of total cost assumed proportional to Vehicle-Distance [$]

c_{VD} = C_{VD}/VD = attributed cost per unit Vehicle-Distance of service
  [$/vehicle-distance]

d = rate of demand [passengers/time]

e_{kj} = inflation rate for component k in year j [fraction or %]

f = average inflation rate over analysis period [fraction or %] or frequency of service [1/hour]

f_{max} = maximum safe frequency of operation [1/hour], inverse of h_{min}

f^p = volume of people flowing between locations i and j over candidate path p [passengers/time]

f_{ij}^p = volume of people flowing between locations i and j over used path p [passengers/time]

f = unit floor-area consumption factors at radius r from center [distance^2/person]

$\bar{f}(r)$ = average of unit floor-area consumption factors at radius r from center [distance^2/person]

F = future monetary value after compounding [$], or fare [$]

$\boldsymbol{F_a}$ = vector of volume of people flowing over all links a

F_{kj} = fare collected from passenger j on link k [$]

F^p = vector of all volumes of people flowing over all used paths between all location pairs i and j

FS = Fleet Size = peak number of vehicles in service (a resource variable)

$\bar{g}$ = total land used based on average the mix at radius r from the center [distance^2]

g_{ij} = generalized cost of travel between locations i and j [time]

G = generalized cost [$] or Total available area [distance^2]

g^p = generalized cost of a candidate path p between locations i and j

$\boldsymbol{G_{ij}^p}$ = vector of generalized costs for all paths between all ij pairs

G_T = area used for transport purposes [distance^2]

G_{NT} = area used for nontransport purposes [distance^2]

h = headway [minutes or seconds]

h_{min} = minimum safe headway between TUs [minutes or seconds]

i = periodic interest rate [fraction or %], or dummy index when summing boarding or alighting up to stop j, or dummy index for subperiod within a capacity supply profile

I = development intensity of non-transport land area [-]

$\bar{I}(r)$ = optimum development intensity based on mix of non-transport land areas at radius r [-]

I_k = average energy intensity for mode k [kiloJoules/passenger-distance]

I_{kU} = energy intensity for mode k in urban trips [kiloJoules/passenger-distance]

I_{kI} = energy intensity for mode k in intercity/rural trips [kiloJoules/passenger-distance]

IC = Incremental Cost [$/increment]

IVTT = In-Vehicle Travel Time [minutes]

j = index of compounding periods, or index for stops

k = index for mode or cost component [-] or density of vehicles in traffic stream [distance/vehicle]

l_j = length of route segment between stop j and j+1 [distance]
L = route length [distance]
L_n = length of trip on link n [distance]

m = number of vehicles in a Transit Unit or consist size [vehicles]
m_{avg} = average consist size [vehicles]
MARR = Minimum Allowable Rate of Return [fraction or %]
$MARR_c$ = combined MARR including inflation [fraction or %]
MLS = Maximum Load Section

n = number of compounding periods [-], or total number of route segments [-]
N = number of transit units required to operate a schedule [-]
NPV = Net Present Value [$]

OC_i = annual operating cost of subperiod i [$/year]
OC_r = annual cost of operating route r [$/year]
OVTT = Out-of-Vehicle Travel Time [minutes]

P = Present Value after discounting [$], or vehicle purchase price [$], or hourly passenger volume [passengers/hour]
P_j = accumulated passengers on board on route segment j [passengers]
P_{max} = highest hourly ridership over the course of a day [passengers]
P_{total} = sum of all passengers over the course of the day [passengers]
P_x = probability of choosing mode x [-]
$p(r)$ = the number of persons generating activity given the mix of land-uses at radius r [persons]

q = average flow rate of vehicle stream [vehicles/time]

r = radius from center of city [distance]
r = subscript signifying specific to route r
R_j = Revenue in year j [$/year]

S = salvage value [$]

T = cycle time [minutes]
t_a = access time [minutes or seconds]
t_e = egress time [minutes or seconds]
$\overline{TA}$ = average time-area consumption per vehicle [distance^2-second/vehicle]
$\overline{TA}_p$ = average time-area consumption per person [distance^2-second/person]

TD = Train-Distance (a resource variable)

TH = Train-Hours (a resource variable)

TM = Train-Miles (a resource variable)

TK = Train-Kilometers (a resource variable)

tt_j = terminal time at terminal j [minutes or seconds]

tt_{min} = minimum terminal time [minutes or seconds]

T_{ij} = Total trips from Origin i to Destination j [passengers]

T_{ij}^x = Trips from Origin i to Destination j on mode x [passengers]

T_n = travel time on link n [minutes], or travel time corresponding to demand level n [minutes]

T_o = operating time [minutes]

T_{O-D} = Travel time from origin to destination [minutes]

t_{wa} = waiting time between access and vehicle arrival [minutes or seconds]

t_{w12} = waiting time between travel on modes 1 and 2 [minutes or seconds]

U_x = random utility for mode x [-]

UB_i = Unmonetized benefits for alternative i [$]

V = monetized unit value of passenger travel time [$/time]

V_x = explained variable portion of utility for mode x [-]

VH = Vehicle-Hours (a resource variable)

VD = Vehicle-Distance (a resource variable)

VK = Vehicle-Kilometers (a resource variable)

VM = Vehicle-Miles (a resource variable)

v_{max} = cruising speed reached on a route or route segment [distance/hour]

v_0 = average operating speed [distance/hour]

$v_{off-peak}$ = speed during off-peak period [distance/hour]

v_{peak} = speed during off-peak period [distance/hour]

v_{Ravg} = average speed based on Revenue Hours [distance/hour]

v_{Tavg} = average speed based on Total Hours [distance/hour]

x_k = total trips using mode k [trips] or total passenger-kilometers using mode k [passenger-distance]

x_{kU} = total urban trips using mode k [trips] or total urban passenger-kilometers using mode k [passenger-distance]

x_{kI} = total intercity/rural trips using mode k [trips], or total intercity/rural passenger-kilometers using mode k [passenger-distance]

X = cost apportioning factor [-]

Y = cost apportioning factor [-]

Z = cost adjustment factor [-]

Index